WORDS THAT RING THROUGH TIME

▼ ▼ ▼

WORDS
THAT RING
THROUGH
TIME

From Moses and Pericles to Obama
Fifty-One of the Most Important Speeches in
History and How They Changed Our World

▼ ▼ ▼

Terry Golway

Foreword by Lewis Lapham

THE OVERLOOK PRESS
NEW YORK

This edition first published in the United States in 2009 by

The Overlook Press, Peter Mayer Publishers, Inc.
141 Wooster Street
New York, NY 10012
www.overlookpress.com

Cataloging-in-Publication Data is available from the Library of Congress

Book design and type formating by Bernard Schleifer
Printed in the United States of America
FIRST EDITION
1 3 5 7 9 8 6 4 2
ISBN 978-1-59020-231-9

Contents

▼ ▼ ▼

Foreword

▼ ▼ ▼

by Lewis Lapham

SOME YEARS AGO ON ITS EDITORIAL PAGE, *THE NEW YORK TIMES* HANDED down the ruling that "Great publications magnify beyond measure the voice of any single writer." The sentence employed the wrong verb. The instruments of the media amplify a voice, serving the same purpose as a loudspeaker in a ballpark or a prison. What magnifies a voice is the force of mind and the power of expression, which is why Shakespeare's plays still draw a crowd in Central Park, and why the fifty-one voices on the stage of Terry Golway's book speak to us in time present, their common theme announced by Pericles delivering a funeral oration 2400 years ago in Athens. "The whole earth," said Pericles, "is the tomb of famous men . . . make them your examples . . . esteeming courage to be freedom, and freedom to be happiness." So also Golway's dramatis personae, among them Thomas More and Susan B. Anthony, who show themselves to be proofs of the courage risen from the tomb to define the meanings of freedom as an act of conscience or a form of government, as public good and private happiness.

If Golway borrows his theme from Pericles, he is indebted for his purpose to the Roman historian, Livy, who conceived of history as a display window stocked with "fine things to take as models, base things, rotten through and through, to avoid." *Words that Ring Through Time* prefers the fine models to the rotten, and although Golway includes a few texts from the ancient and medieval time zones (Martin Luther refusing to recant his defiance of the Catholic Pope, Elizabeth I rallying her army against the arrival of the Spanish Armada), he locates the majority of his valiant words in the modern era, introducing each of the speeches with a brief setting of the historical context and circumstance. To read the book from front to back is to encounter the defenders of freedom as they have lost or gained ground over the course of the two hundred years subsequent to the 18th century American Revolution—Thomas Jefferson's best hope for the world extended in the United States to black slaves and white women, his affection for liberty declared inoperative in Haile Selassie's Ethiopia, reconfigured by Franklin D. Roosevelt as "an instrument of unimagined power" with which to "wipe out the line that divides the practical from the ideal," extinguished in Adolf Hitler's Nazi Germany, strangled at birth in Ho Chi Minh's Vietnam, restored to the light of day in Nelson Mandela's South Africa.

The voices of time testify to the truth that it is with words that men make and remake the world, bring the mountain to Muhammad, salvage from the decay of the flesh the life of the spirit. Their courage is our inheritance, reminding us that a state of amnesia cannot support either the hope of individual liberty or the practice of democratic self-government, telling us that our history is the weapon with which we defend the future against the past.

Introduction

▼ ▼ ▼

THE SPOKEN WORD HAS NOT LOST ITS POWER TO MOVE, TO INSPIRE, TO ENRAGE, to persuade, and to commemorate. It is hard to imagine that it ever will lose that power, for there is something about language and performance which speaks to us in ways that images, or words on a page, or—heaven forbid— instant messages do not and will never.

Public address is the world's oldest form of mass communication, the method by which prophets, statesmen, dissidents, and demagogues transmitted their ideas, arguments and revelations. Some succeeded better than others—a great speech is more than just words, and a great performance is nothing if it fails to move people and even history itself. Some words sound profound but are judged to be fleeting; some words are carved into granite and celebrated for centuries.

This book chronicles the power of words and performance through centuries of human experience. In doing so, it explores the context and historic circumstances surrounding each speech and each speaker. One can hardly comprehend the power of George Washington's words at Newburgh, N.Y., in 1783, for example, without understanding the peril which confronted the United States even after victory at Yorktown. The power of Red Jacket's lament for Native American culture, of Helen Keller's arguments against war, of Sun Yat-Sen's appeal for pan-Asian solidarity, and of Nelson Mandela's inaugural address as President of South Africa, springs not only from their words and their performance, but from time and circumstance as well.

Of course, we can only imagine most of these performances. Modern technology allows us to judge for ourselves the grave eloquence of Winston Churchill's first speech as British Prime Minister, or passion of John F. Kennedy's fiery oration at the Berlin Wall. More often, we have only context to help us understand why we still revere the words of Pericles and

Cicero, Queen Elizabeth I and Frederick Douglass. We may not hear the pitch of their voices, the ways in which they manipulated tone and tenor, but we know they were effective. If they were not, their words would have slipped into obscurity long ago.

The speeches which follow were selected in part because of their context and circumstances, in part for their use of language, in part for the place they hold in humankind's folk memory. Not all of the speeches are famous, even if the speakers are. Abraham Lincoln's Gettysburg Address and two inaugural addresses are his most-renowned works, but in this collection, we have chosen to highlight his more-obscure speech at the Cooper Union in New York in early 1860. This speech marked him as a candidate and future president; it made the more-familiar addresses possible.

Great speeches often produce historic results, but not always. Winston Churchill rallied Britons in the darkest days of World War II, but Halle Selassie could not move the League of Nations to defend Ethiopia from Benito Mussolini's onslaught. Great speeches can appeal to our best instincts, and our worst. Jesus Christ taught that peacemakers did the work of God. Adolf Hitler asserted that those who sought peace were worthy of contempt. Great speeches stake claims to ideological truths, as a reading of Karl Marx and Margaret Thatcher will show. But they can also seek out common ground, as Barack Obama did in his speech on race in Philadelphia, as Anwar Sadat did when he spoke to the Israeli Knesset.

Great speeches reveal character. Given a death sentence at a young age, Lou Gehrig proclaimed himself to be the luckiest man on the face of the earth. Martin Luther and Thomas More spoke truth to power regardless of consequence. Charles Fox risked his career when he condemned the East India Company. Susan B. Anthony defied those who sought to repress her.

Their personalities and circumstances were vastly different, but they all left behind spoken words to be read and considered, pieces of history to be celebrated or regretted.

What follows is by no means a comprehensive catalog of history's greatest spoken words. Many eloquent speeches have gone unrecorded; one must imagine, for example, the words that inspired enslaved Americans to risk their lives for a chance at freedom, or words that may have been uttered in a classroom, a house of worship, an alley, which inspired one person or dozens or thousands to greatness or even goodness. Those words are recorded only in the human heart and will never be available for study and analysis.

Some speeches are unavailable or difficult to access because of issues of ownership and copyright. For example, the family of Dr. Martin Luther King Jr. retains unprecedented control over the use of his speeches and words. Regrettably, for that reason Dr. King's famous speech at the civil rights march on Washington in 1963 is not included in this volume.

The speeches which follow are testaments to the enduring power of the public spoken word. The collection begins with Moses and ends with Barack Obama, a narrative span linked together through the power of ideas, of voice, and, ultimately, of words.

1: Moses Bids Israel Farewell

MOSES, THE GREAT LIBERATOR OF THE JEWISH PEOPLE, WAS BORN IN EGYPT more than three thousand years ago, during a time of great anxiety on the banks of the Nile River. The Jews, previously welcome in Egypt, found themselves under attack: Under orders from the Pharaoh, Jewish boys were targeted for slaughter in an effort to reduce the growing Jewish population in Egypt. The child Moses was hidden from the soldiers, only to be discovered by the Pharaoh's daughter and reared as Egyptian royalty.

In a story familiar even to those with only a passing knowledge of the Bible, Moses grows to maturity, observes an Egyptian beating a Jew, kills the Egyptian, and flees into the desert. There, God commands him to return to Egypt confront the Pharaoh, and lead the Jews out of slavery and to a new land. When Moses returns to Egypt's court, no longer the adopted royal but a prophet of God, the Pharaoh is amused to hear Moses' demand that he set free the Jews. When he refuses, God brings down plagues and other unpleasantness upon Egypt until finally the Jews are allowed to leave.

Moses led the Jews through the deserts of today's Middle East for forty years, until they were about to cross the River Jordan into the land of Abraham, Isaac and Jacob. But the aging Moses himself would not make the final journey with his people. The great leader and lawgiver, teacher and prophet, would not see the Promised Land. As he prepared for his death, foretold to him by God, Moses gathered the nation of Israel around him for one final oration.

The Book of Deuteronomy consists of the last, long speech of Moses the lawgiver. It is a remembrance of the journey from exile through the desert, a recapitulation of the laws handed down by God, and a harangue against the behavior and practices that got the Israelites in trouble in the past.

After explaining the rewards of keeping the Israelites' covenant with God, and the punishments that surely awaited their failure to do so, Moses prepared to hand over his people to the leadership of his son, Joshua. The final pages of Deuteronomy chronicle Moses' final words before God commanded him to climb Mount Nebo, where he could see the land beyond the Jordan, the land in which he would never live.

The image of Moses glimpsing the promised land just before his death—regardless of the story's veracity—remains one of the most-powerful in Judeo-Christian civilization. Martin Luther King Jr. evoked Mosaic pathos at the conclusion of a speech in Memphis, Tennessee, on April 3, 1968. "I just want to do God's will," King said. "And He's allowed me to go up to the mountain. And I've looked over. And I've seen the promised land. I may not get there with you. But I want you to know tonight, that we, as a people, will get to the promised land." He was murdered the next day.

Before Moses went up to the mountain, before he saw the promised land, he made it clear that he was not altogether confident that his people would manage without him. Today, it might be suggested that the man couldn't let go, and who could blame him? After all, when he disappeared for forty days on Mount Sinai, he returned to find his people worshipping a golden calf. What would they do now that he was leaving them forever?

Other irreplaceable leaders, before and after, no doubt have wondered the same thing. Moses issued a stern warning, leavened by encouragement and the promise of rewards for keeping faith with God.

▼ ▼ ▼

HERE, then, I have today set before you life and prosperity, death and doom.

If you obey the commandments of the Lord, your God, which I enjoin on you today, loving him, and walking in his ways, and keeping his commandments, statutes and decrees, you will live and grow numerous, and the Lord, your God, will bless you in the land you are entering to occupy.

If, however, you turn away your hearts and will not listen, but are led astray and adore and serve other gods, I tell you now that you will certainly perish; you will not have a long life on the land which you are crossing the Jordan to enter and occupy.

I call heaven and earth today to witness against you: I have set before you life and death, the blessing and the curse. Choose life, then, that you and your descendants may live, by loving the Lord, your God, heeding his voice, and holding fast to him. For that will mean life for you, a long life for you to live on the land which the Lord swore he would give to your fathers Abraham, Isaac and Jacob.

I am now one hundred and twenty years old and am no longer able to move about freely; besides, the Lord has told me that I shall not cross this Jordan.

It is the Lord, your God, who will cross before you; he will destroy these nations before you, that you may supplant them. (It is Joshua who will cross before you, as the Lord promised.)

The Lord will deal with them just as he dealt with Sihon and Og, the kings of the Amorites whom he destroyed, and with their country.

When, therefore, the Lord delivers them up to you, you must deal with them exactly as I have ordered you.

Be brave and steadfast; have no fear or dread of them, for it is the Lord, your God, who marches with you; he will never fail you or forsake you.

2: Funeral Oration by Pericles

Athens, 430 BCE

A SOLDIER'S DEATH IS NOT THE SAME AS A CIVILIAN'S DEATH. THE SOLDIER and civilian alike might die young and in tragic circumstances, but the civilian, even in wartime, is rarely seen as a symbol of something larger than self. More often than not, the civilian's death is mourned as a tragedy, or condemned as an outrage, but it does not serve as the inspiration for soaring oratory, the embodiment of a noble cause.

In 433 B.C., the primacy of Athens as a dominant Greek city-state came under challenge from Sparta, and not for the first time. The two rivals had fought once before, from 460 to 446 B.C., but neither side claimed victory nor conceded defeat. Thirty years of peace followed, but as tensions increased again, Pericles prepared Athens for the war he considered inevitable. The two rivals sought to resolve their issues through negotiation, but when Sparta dispatched messengers to Athens with a new list of demands in 431, Pericles broke off talks and the two city-states went to war again.

Sparta took the offensive with a scorched-earth campaign against Attica, a farming community near Athens. Spartan brutality inflamed the Athenians and led Pericles to dispatched a fleet to the Peloponnesian coast, where the soldiers of Athens took out their revenge for the ravaging of Attica.

After a year of fighting, Athens prepared a public funeral to honor the fallen. Pericles, the city-state's famed military commander, political leader, patron of the arts, and chief promoter of democracy, was called upon to deliver the eulogy.

His speech is recorded in Thucydides' classic book, *History of the Peloponnesian War*. Thucydides made a point of telling readers that he reconstructed many of the speeches in his history from memory, so there is no way of knowing whether the words recorded in his book were the actual words Pericles spoke at the funeral.

Nevertheless, historians of the period are confident, based on other studies of Pericles and his times, that the speech genuinely reflected the Athenian's view of democracy and of the city-state's self-image. The speech is not so much about the dead as it is about the cause for which they died— the cause being, in a word, Athens. Pericles believed in an Athenian exceptionalism that will sound familiar to even the most-casual consumer of American oratory in the twenty-first century. Athens, in Pericles' telling, stood for human aspiration, as opposed to Spartan militarism, which sought to crush individual liberty. Substitute the United States for Athens and the Soviet Union for Sparta, and Pericles' oration begins to sound like an artifact from the Cold War.

Garry Wills, H.F. Harding and other writers have observed that Abraham Lincoln's Gettysburg Address, another funeral oration, owes much to Pericles' ability to see in the deaths of soldiers something noble and valuable, something greater than self. Both speeches endow lives cut short with eternal significance, with qualities the listener cannot help but admire.

▼ ▼ ▼

MOST of those who have spoken here before me have commended the lawgiver who added this oration to our other funeral customs. It seemed to them a worthy thing that such an honor should be given at their burial to the dead who have fallen on the field of battle. But I should have preferred that, when men's deeds have been brave, they should be honored in deed only, and with such an honor as this public funeral, which you are now witnessing. Then the reputation of many would not have been imperiled on the eloquence or want of eloquence of one, and their virtues believed or not as he spoke well or ill. For it is difficult to say neither too little nor too much; and even moderation is apt not to give the impression of truthfulness. The friend of the dead who knows the facts is likely to think that the words of the speaker fall short of his knowledge and of his wishes; another who is not so well informed, when he hears of anything which surpasses his own powers, will be envious and will suspect exaggeration. Mankind are tolerant of the praises of others so long as each hearer thinks that he can do as well or nearly as well himself, but, when the speaker rises above him, jealousy is aroused and he begins to be incredulous. However, since our ancestors have set the seal of their approval upon the practice, I must obey, and to the utmost of my power shall endeavor to satisfy the wishes and beliefs of all who hear me.

I will speak first of our ancestors, for it is right and seemly that now, when we are lamenting the dead, a tribute should be paid to their memory. There has never been a time when they did not inhabit this land, which by their valor they will have handed down from generation to generation, and we have received from them a free state. But if they were worthy of praise, still more were our fathers, who added to their inheritance, and after many a struggle transmitted to us their sons this great empire. And we ourselves assembled here today, who are still most of us in the vigor of life, have carried the work of improvement further, and have richly endowed our city with all things, so that she is sufficient for herself both in peace and war. Of the military exploits by which our various possessions were acquired, or of the energy with which we or our fathers drove back the tide of war, Hellenic or Barbarian, I will not speak; for the tale would be long and is familiar to you. But before I praise the dead, I should like to point out by what principles of action we rose to power, and under what institutions and through what manner of life our empire became great. For I conceive that such thoughts are not unsuited to the occasion, and that this numerous assembly of citizens and strangers may profitably listen to them.

Our form of government does not enter into rivalry with the institutions of others. Our government does not copy our neighbors', but is an example to them. It is true that we are called a democracy, for the administration is in the hands of the many and not of the few. But while there exists equal justice to all and alike in their private disputes, the claim of excellence is also recognized; and when a citizen is in any way distinguished, he is preferred to the public service, not as a matter of privilege, but as the reward of merit. Neither is poverty an obstacle, but a man may benefit his country whatever the obscurity of his condition. There is no exclusiveness in our public life, and in our private business we are not suspicious of one another, nor angry with our neighbor if he does what he likes; we do not put on sour looks at him which, though harmless, are not pleasant. While we are thus unconstrained in our private business, a spirit of reverence pervades our public acts; we are prevented from doing wrong by respect for the authorities and for the laws, having a particular regard to those which are ordained for the protection of the injured as well as those unwritten laws which bring upon the transgressor of them the reprobation of the general sentiment.

And we have not forgotten to provide for our weary spirits many relaxations from toil; we have regular games and sacrifices throughout the year; our homes are beautiful and elegant; and the delight which we daily feel in all these things helps to banish sorrow. Because of the greatness of our city the fruits of the whole earth flow in upon us; so that we enjoy the goods of other countries as freely as our own.

Then, again, our military training is in many respects superior to that of our adversaries. Our city is thrown open to the world, though I and we never expel a foreigner and prevent him from seeing or learning anything of which the secret if revealed to an enemy might profit him. We rely not upon management or trickery, but upon our own hearts and hands. And in the matter of education, whereas they from early youth are always undergoing laborious exercises which are to make them brave, we live at ease, and yet are equally ready to face the perils which they face. And here is the proof: The Lacedaemonians come into Athenian territory not by themselves, but with their whole confederacy following; we go alone into a neighbor's country; and although our opponents are fighting for their homes and we on a foreign soil, we have seldom any difficulty in overcoming them. Our enemies have never yet felt our united strength, the care of a navy divides our attention, and on land we are obliged to send our own citizens everywhere. But they, if they meet and defeat a part of our army, are as proud as if they had routed us all, and when defeated they pretend to have been vanquished by us all.

If then we prefer to meet danger with a light heart but without laborious training, and with a courage which is gained by habit and not enforced by law, are we not greatly the better for it? Since we do not anticipate the pain, although, when the hour comes, we can be as Brave as those who never allow themselves to rest; thus our city is equally admirable in peace and in war. For we are lovers of the beautiful in our tastes and our strength lies, in our opinion, not in deliberation and discussion, but that knowledge which is gained by discussion preparatory to action. For we have a peculiar power of thinking before we act, and of acting, too, whereas other men are courageous from ignorance but hesitate upon reflection. And they are surely to be esteemed the Bravest spirits who, having the clearest sense both of the pains and pleasures of life, do not on that account shrink from danger. In doing good, again, we are unlike others; we make our friends by conferring, not by receiving favors. Now he who confers a favor is the firmer friend, because he would rather by kindness keep alive the memory of an obligation; but the recipient is colder in his feelings, because he knows that in requiting another's generosity he will not be winning gratitude but only paying a debt. We alone do good to our neighbors not upon a calculation of interest, but in the confidence of freedom and in a frank and fearless spirit. To sum up: I say that Athens is the school of Hellas, and that the individual Athenian in his own person seems to have the power of adapting himself to the most varied forms of action with the utmost versatility and grace. This is no passing and idle word, but truth and fact; and the assertion is verified by the position to which these qualities have raised the state. For in the hour of trial Athens alone among her contemporaries is superior to the report of her. No enemy who comes against her is indignant at the reverses which he sustains at the hands of such a city; no subject complains that his masters are unworthy of him. And we shall assuredly not be without witnesses; there are mighty monuments of our power which will make us the wonder of this and of succeeding ages; we shall not need the praises of Homer or of any other panegyrist whose poetry may please for the moment, although his representation of the facts will not bear the light of day. For we have compelled every land and every sea to open a path for our valor, and have everywhere planted eternal memorials of our friendship and of our enmity. Such is the city for whose sake these men nobly fought and died; they could not bear the thought that she might be taken from them; and every one of us who survive should gladly toil on her behalf.

I have dwelt upon the greatness of Athens because I want to show you that we are contending for a higher prize than those who enjoy none of these privileges, and to establish by manifest proof the merit of these men whom I am now commemorating. Their loftiest praise has been already spoken. For in magnifying the city I have magnified them, and men like them whose virtues made her glorious. And of how few Hellenes can it be said as of them, that their deeds when weighed in the balance have been found equal to their fame! Methinks that a death such as theirs has been the true measure of a man's worth; it may be the first revelation of his virtues, but is at any rate their final seal. For even those who come short in other ways may justly plead the valor with which they have fought for their country; they have blotted out the evil with the good, and have benefited the state more by their public services than they have injured her by their private actions. None of these men were enervated by wealth or hesitated to resign the pleasures of life; none of them put off the evil day in the hope, natural to poverty, that a man, though poor, may one day become rich. But, deeming that the punishment of their enemies was sweeter than any of these things, and that they could fall in no nobler cause, they determined at the hazard of their lives to be honorably avenged, and to leave the rest. They resigned to hope their unknown chance of happiness; but in the face of death they resolved to rely upon themselves alone. And when the moment came they were minded to resist and suffer, rather than to fly and save their lives; they ran away from the word of dishonor, but on the battle-field their feet stood fast, and in an instant, at the height of their fortune, they passed away from the scene, not of their fear, but of their glory.

Such was the end of these men; they were worthy of Athens, and the living need not desire to have a more heroic spirit, although they may pray for a less fatal issue. The value of such a spirit is not to be expressed in words. Any one can discourse to you for ever about the advantages of a Brave defense, which you know already. But instead of listening to him I would have you day by day fix your eyes upon the greatness of Athens, until you become filled with the love of her; and when you are impressed by the spectacle of her glory, reflect that this empire has been acquired by men who knew their duty and had the courage to do it, who in the hour of conflict had the fear of dishonor always present to them, and who, if ever they failed in an enterprise, would not allow their virtues to be lost to their country, but freely gave their lives to her as the fairest offering which they could present at her feast. The sacrifice which they collectively made was individually repaid to them; for they received again each one for himself a praise which grows not old, and the noblest of all tombs—I speak not of that in which their remains are laid, but of that in which their glory survives, and is proclaimed always and on every fitting occasion both in word and deed. For the whole earth is the tomb of famous men; not only are they commemorated by columns and inscriptions in their own country, but in foreign lands there dwells also an unwritten memorial of them, graven not on stone but in the hearts of men. Make them your examples, and, esteeming courage to be freedom and freedom to be happiness, do not weigh too nicely the perils of war. The unfortunate who has no hope of a change for the better has less reason to throw away his life than the prosperous who, if he survive, is always liable to a change for the worse, and to whom any accidental fall makes the most serious difference. To a man of spirit, cowardice and disaster coming together are far more bitter than death striking him unperceived at a time when he is full of courage and animated by the general hope.

Wherefore I do not now pity the parents of the dead who stand here; I would rather comfort them. You know that your dead have passed away amid manifold vicissitudes; and that they may be deemed fortunate who have gained their utmost honor, whether an honorable death like theirs, or an honorable sorrow like yours, and whose share of happiness has been so ordered that the term of their happiness is likewise the term of their life. I know how hard it is to make you feel this, when the good fortune of others will too often remind you of the gladness which once lightened your hearts. And sorrow is felt at the want of those blessings, not which a man never knew, but which were a part of his life before they were taken from him. Some of you are of an age at which they may hope to have other children, and they ought to bear their sorrow better; not only will the children who may hereafter be born make them forget their own lost ones, but the city will be doubly a gainer. She will not be left desolate, and she will be safer. For a man's counsel cannot have equal weight or worth, when he alone has no children to risk in the general danger. To those of you who have passed their prime, I say: "Congratulate yourselves that you have been happy during the greater part of your days; remember that your life of sorrow will not last long, and be comforted by the glory of those who are gone. For the love of honor alone is ever young, and not riches, as some say, but honor is the delight of men when they are old and useless.

To you who are the sons and brothers of the departed, I see that the struggle to emulate them will be an arduous one. For all men praise the dead, and, however preeminent your virtue may be, I do not say even to approach them, and avoid living their rivals and detractors, but when a man is out of the way, the honor and goodwill which he receives is unalloyed. And, if I am to speak of womanly virtues to those of you who will henceforth be widows, let me sum them up in one short admonition: To a woman not to show more weakness than is natural to her sex is a great glory, and not to be talked about for good or for evil among men.

I have paid the required tribute, in obedience to the law, making use of such fitting words as I had. The tribute of deeds has been paid in part; for the dead have them in deeds, and it remains only that their children should be maintained at the public charge until they are grown up: this is the solid prize with which, as with a garland, Athens crowns her sons living and dead, after a struggle like theirs. For where the rewards of virtue are greatest, there the noblest citizens are enlisted in the service of the state. And now, when you have duly lamented every one his own dead, you may depart.

3: Cicero's First Oration
Against Catiline

Rome, 63 BCE

IMAGINE THIS SETTING: A PERSON WHO HAS SOUGHT NOT ONLY YOUR PROFES-sional downfall but your actual demise unexpectedly shows up to hear what you have to say about the matter. Would the audacity of your enemy leave you speechless? Would you find the words, never mind the courage, to stage a confrontation? Would you have the eloquence to unleash a cannon-ade of invective, opening wounds with the shrapnel of sarcasm and moral righteousness?

Such was the position of Marcus Tellius Cicero in 63 B.C. One of the great orators of the classical world and a consul of the Roman republic, Cicero had made an enemy of a dissolute nobleman named Lucius Catiline, who desperately sought a place in Rome's marbled corridors of power. Among his allies was an up and coming soldier named Julius Caesar, who harbored ambitions for himself and for Rome that no simple republic could meet.

Times were changing in the last century before the Common Era. Rome had amassed power and influence far beyond the Tiber. Though Cicero and his contemporaries did not know it, time was running out on the republic. Rome would soon be an empire, thanks to the ambitions and genius of men like Caesar.

Catiline, who had served the republic in North Africa, challenged Cicero's election as consul in 64 B.C. Bribery won him many votes, but not enough. He lost by a slim margin, prompting Cicero to crack down on cor-ruption and take every opportunity to use his formidable eloquence against him. Catiline tried again to unseat Cicero, and when that failed, he hatched a plot to murder his antagonist and his allies in the Senate while launching a general rebellion against the republic.

Cicero, however, had a political intelligence operation that would have made J. Edgar Hoover proud. From a spurned mistress of one of Catiline's allies, he learned of the plot and brought it to the attention of the Senate, which declared the equivalent of martial law in the city. Cicero obtained evidence of a conspiracy against the government, and asked the Senate to hear the evidence at a special meeting in the temple of Jupiter.

In the audience was Catiline himself, effectively daring Cicero to take him on. Cicero took the bait, but in the end, it was Catiline who was caught. Cicero did not back down. He did not appear to be intimidated. Instead, he launched into an intensely personal attack, naming Catiline immediately. Three more speeches followed, to devastating effect. Catiline was sentenced to death in December, despite Caesar's pleas for life imprisonment. The sentence was delivered, though not in the manner prescribed. Catiline refused to surrender to authorities and fled, only to die in battle with Roman soldiers a year later.

Cicero's first oration against Catiline is considered one of his finest, no small achievement considering his reputation as not simply an orator, but a writer and political philosopher as well.

▼ ▼ ▼

WHEN, O Catiline, do you mean to cease abusing our patience? How long is that madness of yours still to mock us? When is there to be an end of that unbridled audacity of yours, swaggering about as it does now? Do not the nightly guards placed on the Palatine Hill—do not the watches posted throughout the city—does not the alarm of the people, and the union of all good men—does not the precaution taken of assembling the senate in this most defensible place—do not the looks and countenances of this venerable body here present, have any effect upon you? Do you not feel that your plans are detected? Do you not see that your conspiracy is already arrested and rendered powerless by the knowledge which every one here possesses of it? What is there that you did last night, what the night before—where is it that you were—who was there that you summoned to meet you—what design was there which was adopted by you, with which you think that any one of us is unacquainted?

Shame on the age and on its principles! The senate is aware of these things; the consul sees them; and yet this man lives. Lives! aye, he comes even into the senate. He takes a part in the public deliberations; he is watching and marking down and checking off for slaughter every individual among us. And we, gallant men that we are, think that we are doing our duty to the republic if we keep out of the way of his frenzied attacks.

You ought, O Catiline, long ago to have been led to execution by command of the consul. That destruction which you have been long plotting against us ought to have already fallen on your own head.

What? Did not that most illustrious man, Publius Scipio, the Pontifex Maximus, in his capacity of a private citizen, put to death Tiberius Gracchus, though but slightly undermining the constitution? And shall we, who are the consuls, tolerate Catiline, openly desirous to destroy the whole world with fire and slaughter? For I pass over older instances, such as how Caius Servilius Ahala with his own hand slew Spurius Mælius when plotting a revolution in the state. There was—there was once such virtue in this republic that brave men would repress mischievous citizens with severer chastisement than the most bitter enemy. For we have a resolution of the senate, a formidable and authoritative decree against you, O Catiline; the wisdom of the republic is not at fault, nor the dignity of this senatorial body. We, we alone—I say it openly—we, the consuls, are wanting in our duty.

The senate once passed a decree that Lucius Opimius, the consul, should take care that the republic suffered no injury. Not one night elapsed. There was put to death, on some mere suspicion of disaffection, Caius Gracchus, a man whose family had borne the most unblemished reputation for many generations. There was slain Marcus Fulvius, a man of consular rank, and all his children. By a like decree of the senate the safety of the republic was entrusted to Caius Marius and Lucius Valerius, the consuls. Did not the vengeance of the republic, did not execution overtake Lucius Saturninus, a tribune of the people, and Caius Servilius, the pretor, without the delay of one single day? But we, for these twenty days, have been allowing the edge of the senate's authority to grow blunt, as it were. For we are in possession of a similar decree of the senate, but we keep it locked up in its parchment—buried, I may say, in the sheath; and according to this decree you ought, O Catiline, to be put to death this instant. You live—and you live, not to lay aside, but to persist in your audacity.

I wish, O conscript fathers, to be merciful; I wish not to appear negligent amid such danger to the state; but I do now accuse myself of remissness and culpable inactivity. A camp is pitched in Italy, at the entrance of Etruria, in hostility to the republic; the number of the enemy increases every day; and yet the general of that camp, the leader of those enemies, we see within the walls—aye, and even in the senate—planning every day some internal injury to the republic. If, O Catiline, I should now order you to be arrested, to be put to death, I should, I suppose, have to fear lest all good men should say that I had acted tardily, rather than that any one should affirm that I acted cruelly. But yet this, which ought to have been done long since, I have good reason for not doing as yet; I will put you to death, then, when there shall be not one person possible to be found so wicked, so abandoned, so like yourself, as not to allow that it has been rightly done. As long as one person exists who can dare to defend you, you shall live; but you shall live as you do now, surrounded by my many and trusty guards, so that you shall not be able to stir one finger against the republic; many eyes and ears shall still observe and watch you, as they have hitherto done, though you shall not perceive them.

For what is there, O Catiline, that you can still expect, if night is not able to veil your nefarious meetings in darkness, and if private houses cannot conceal the voice of your conspiracy within their walls—if everything is seen and displayed? Change your mind: trust me: forget the slaughter and conflagration you are meditating. You are hemmed in on all sides; all your plans are clearer than the day to us; let me remind you of them. Do you recollect that on the 21st of October I said in the senate that on a certain day, which was to be the 27th of October, C. Manlius, the satellite and servant of your audacity, would be in arms? Was I mistaken, Catiline, not only in so important, so atrocious, so incredible a fact, but, what is much more remarkable, in the very day? I said also in the senate that you had fixed the massacre of the nobles for the 28th of October when many chief men of the senate had left Rome, not so much for the sake of saving themselves as of checking your designs. Can you deny that on that very day you were so hemmed in by my guards and my vigilance that you were unable to stir one finger against the republic; when you said that you would be content with the flight of the rest, and the slaughter of us who remained? What? when you made sure that you would be able to seize Præneste on the 1st of November by a nocturnal attack, did you not find that that colony was fortified by my order, by my garrison, by my watchfulness and care? You do nothing, you plan nothing, you think of nothing which I not only do not hear, but which I do not see and know every particular of.

Listen while I speak of the night before. You shall now see that I watch far more actively for the safety than you do for the destruction of the republic. I say that you came the night before (I will say nothing obscurely) into the Scythedealers' Street, to the house of Marcus Lecca; that many of your accomplices in the same insanity and wickedness came there, too. Do you dare to deny it? Why are you silent? I will prove it if you do deny it; for I see here in the senate some men who were there with you.

O ye immortal gods, where on earth are we? in what city are we living? what constitution is ours? There are here, here in our body, O conscript fathers, in this the most holy and dignified assembly of the whole world, men who meditate my death, and the death of all of us, and the destruction of this city, and of the whole world. I, the consul, see them; I ask them their opinion about the republic, and I do not yet attack, even by words, those who ought to be put to death by the sword. You were, then, O Catiline, at Lecca's that night; you divided Italy into sections; you settled where every-one was to go; you fixed whom you were to leave at Rome, whom you were to take with you; you portioned out the divisions of the city for conflagra-tion; you undertook that you yourself would at once leave the city, and said that there was then only this to delay you—that I was still alive. Two Roman knights were found to deliver you from this anxiety, and to promise that very night, before daybreak, to slay me in my bed. All this I knew almost before your meeting had broken up. I strengthened and fortified my house with a stronger guard; I refused admittance, when they came, to those whom you sent in the morning to salute me, and of whom I had foretold to many eminent men that they would come to me at that time.

As, then, this is the case, O Catiline, continue as you have begun. Leave the city at least; the gates are open; depart. That Manlian camp of yours has been waiting too long for you as its general. And lead forth with you all your friends, or at least as many as you can; purge the city of your presence; you will deliver me from a great fear, when there is a wall between you and me. Among us you can dwell no longer—I will not bear it, I will not permit it, I will not tolerate it. Great thanks are due to the immortal gods, and to this very Jupiter Stator, in whose temple we are, the most ancient protector of this city, that we have already so often escaped so foul, so horrible, and so deadly an enemy to the republic. But the safety of the commonwealth must not be too often allowed to be risked on one man. As long as you, O Catiline, plotted against me while I was the consul-elect, I defended myself, not with a public guard, but by my own private diligence. When, in the next consular comitia, you wished to slay me when I was actually consul, and your competitors also, in the Campus Martius, I checked your nefarious attempt by the assistance and resources of my own friends, without exciting any disturbance publicly. In short, as often as you attacked me, I by myself opposed you, and that, too, though I saw that my ruin was connected with great disaster to the republic. But now you are openly attacking the entire republic.

You are summoning to destruction and devastation the temples of the immortal gods, the houses of the city, the lives of all the citizens—in short, all Italy. Wherefore, since I do not yet venture to do that which is the best thing, and which belongs to my office and to the discipline of our ancestors, I will do that which is more merciful if we regard its rigor, and more expedient for the State. For if I order you to be put to death, the rest of the conspirators will still remain in the republic; if, as I have long been exhorting you, you depart, your companions, those worthless dregs of the republic, will be drawn off from the city, too. What is the matter, Catiline? Do you hesitate to do that when I order you which you were already doing of your own accord? The consul orders an enemy to depart from the city. Do you ask me, Are you to go into banishment? I do not order it; but, if you consult me, I advise it.

For what is there, O Catiline, that can now afford you any pleasure in this city? for there is no one in it, except that band of profligate conspirators of yours, who does not fear you—no one who does not hate you. What brand of domestic baseness is not stamped upon your life? What disgraceful circumstance is wanting to your infamy in your private affairs? From what licentiousness have your eyes, from what atrocity have your hands, from what iniquity has your whole body ever abstained? Is there one youth, when you have once entangled him in the temptations of your corruption, to whom you have not held out a sword for audacious crime, or a torch for licentious wickedness?

What? when lately by the death of your former wife you had made your house empty and ready for a new bridal, did you not even add another incredible wickedness to this wickedness? But I pass that over, and willingly allow it to be buried in silence, that so horrible a crime may not be seen to have existed in this city, and not to have been chastised. I pass over the ruin of your fortune, which you know is hanging over you against the ides of the very next month; I come to those things which relate not to the infamy of your private vices, not to your domestic difficulties and baseness, but to the welfare of the republic and to the lives and safety of us all.

Can the light of this life, O Catiline, can the breath of this atmosphere be pleasant to you, when you know that there is not one man of those here present who is ignorant that you, on the last day of the year, when Lepidus

and Tullus were consuls, stood in the assembly armed; that you had prepared your hand for the slaughter of the consuls and chief men of the state,
and that no reason or fear of yours hindered your crime and madness, but
the fortune of the republic? And I say no more of these things, for they are
not unknown to every one. How often have you endeavored to slay me, both
as consul-elect and as actual consul? How many shots of yours, so aimed
that they seemed impossible to be escaped, have I avoided by some slight
stooping aside, and some dodging, as it were, of my body? You attempt
nothing, you execute nothing, you devise nothing that can be kept hidden
from me at the proper time; and yet you do not cease to attempt and to con-
trive. How often already has that dagger of yours been wrested from your
hands? How often has it slipped through them by some chance, and
dropped down? And yet you cannot any longer do without it; and to what
sacred mysteries it is consecrated and devoted by you I know not, that you
think it necessary to plunge it in the body of the consul.

But now, what is that life of yours that you are leading? For I will
speak to you not so as to seem influenced by the hatred I ought to feel,
but by pity, nothing of which is due to you. You came a little while ago into
the senate; in so numerous an assembly, who of so many friends and connections of yours saluted you? If this in the memory of man never happened to anyone else, are you waiting for insults by word of mouth, when
you are overwhelmed by the most irresistible condemnation of silence? Is
it nothing that at your arrival all those seats were vacated? that all the men
of consular rank, who had often been marked out by you for slaughter, the
very moment you sat down, left that part of the benches bare and vacant?
With what feelings do you think you ought to bear this? On my honor, if
my slaves feared me as all your fellow citizens fear you, I should think I
must leave my house. Do not you think you should leave the city? If I saw
that I was even undeservedly so suspected and hated by my fellow citizens, I would rather flee from their sight than be gazed at by the hostile
eyes of everyone. And do you, who, from the consciousness of your
wickedness, know that the hatred of all men is just and has been long due
to you, hesitate to avoid the sight and presence of those men whose minds
and senses you offend? If your parents feared and hated you, and if you
could by no means pacify them, you would, I think, depart somewhere out
of their sight. Now, your country, which is the common parent of all of us,
hates and fears you, and has no other opinion of you, than that you are
meditating parricide in her case; and will you neither feel awe of her

authority, nor deference for her judgment, nor fear of her power?

And she, O Catiline, thus pleads with you, and after a manner silently speaks to you: There has now for many years been no crime committed but by you; no atrocity has taken place without you; you alone unpunished and unquestioned have murdered the citizens, have harassed and plundered the allies; you alone have had power not only to neglect all laws and investigations, but to overthrow and break through them. Your former actions, though they ought not to have been borne, yet I did bear as well as I could; but now that I should be wholly occupied with fear of you alone, that at every sound I should dread Catiline, that no design should seem possible to be entertained against me which does not proceed from your wickedness, this is no longer endurable. Depart, then, and deliver me from this fear— that, if it be a just one, I may not be destroyed; if an imaginary one, that at least I may at last cease to fear.

If, as I have said, your country were thus to address you, ought she not to obtain her request, even if she were not able to enforce it? What shall I say of your having given yourself into custody? what of your having said, for the sake of avoiding suspicion, that you were willing to dwell in the house of Marcus Lepidus? And when you were not received by him, you dared even to come to me, and begged me to keep you in my house; and when you had received answer from me that I could not possibly be safe in the same house with you, when I considered myself in great danger as long as we were in the same city, you came to Quintus Metellus, the praetor, and being rejected by him, you passed on to your associate, that most excellent man, Marcus Marcellus, who would be, I suppose you thought, most diligent in guarding you, most sagacious in suspecting you, and most bold in punishing you; but how far can we think that man ought to be from bonds and imprisonment who has already judged himself deserving of being given into custody?

Since, then, this is the case, do you hesitate, O Catiline, if you cannot remain here with tranquillity, to depart to some distant land, and to trust your life, saved from just and deserved punishment, to flight and solitude? Make a motion, say you, to the senate (for that is what you demand), and if this body votes that you ought to go into banishment, you say that you will obey. I will not make such a motion—it is contrary to my principles, and yet I will let you see what these men think of you. Be gone from the city, O Catiline; deliver the republic from fear; depart into banishment, if that is the word you are waiting for. What now, O Catiline? Do you not perceive, do you not see the silence of these men; they permit it, they say nothing; why wait you for the authority of their words when you see their wishes in their silence?

But had I said the same to this excellent young man, Publius Sextius, or to that brave man, Marcus Marcellus, before this time the senate would deservedly have laid violent hands on me, consul though I be, in this very temple. But as to you, Catiline, while they are quiet they approve, while they permit me to speak they vote, while they are silent they are loud and eloquent. And not they alone, whose authority forsooth is dear to you, though their lives are unimportant, but the Roman knights, too, those most honorable and excellent men, and the other virtuous citizens who are now surrounding the senate, whose numbers you could see, whose desires you could know, and whose voices you a few minutes ago could hear—aye, whose very hands and weapons I have for some time been scarcely able to keep off from you; but those, too, I will easily bring to attend you to the gates if you leave these places you have been long desiring to lay waste.

And yet, why am I speaking? That anything may change your purpose? that you may ever amend your life? that you may meditate flight or think of voluntary banishment? I wish the gods may give you such a mind; though I see, if alarmed at my words you bring your mind to go into banishment, what a storm of unpopularity hangs over me, if not at present, while the memory of your wickedness is fresh, at all events hereafter. But it is worth while to incur that, as long as that is but a private misfortune of my own, and is unconnected with the dangers of the republic. But we cannot expect that you should be concerned at your own vices, that you should fear the penalties of the laws, or that you should yield to the necessities of the republic, for you are not, O Catiline, one whom either shame can recall from infamy, or fear from danger, or reason from madness.

Wherefore, as I have said before, go forth, and if you wish to make me, your enemy as you call me, unpopular, go straight into banishment. I shall scarcely be able to endure all that will be said if you do so; I shall scarcely be able to support my load of unpopularity if you do go into banishment at the command of the consul; but if you wish to serve my credit and reputation, go forth with your ill-omened band of profligates; betake yourself to Manlius, rouse up the abandoned citizens, separate yourself from the good ones, wage war against your country, exult in your impious banditti, so that you may not seem to have been driven out by me and gone to strangers, but to have gone invited to your own friends.

Though why should I invite you, by whom I know men have been already sent on to wait in arms for you at the forum Aurelium; who I know has fixed and agreed with Manlius upon a settled day; by whom I know that that silver eagle, which I trust will be ruinous and fatal to you and to all your friends, and to which there was set up in your house a shrine as it were of your crimes, has been already sent forward? Need I fear that you can long do without that which you used to worship when going out to murder, and from whose altars you have often transferred your impious hand to the slaughter of citizens?

You will go at last where your unbridled and mad desire has been long hurrying you. And this causes you no grief, but an incredible pleasure. Nature has formed you, desire has trained you, fortune has preserved you for this insanity. Not only did you never desire quiet, but you never even desired any war but a criminal one; you have collected a band of profligates and worthless men, abandoned not only by all fortune but even by hope.

Then what happiness will you enjoy! with what delight will you exult! in what pleasure will you revel! when in so numerous a body of friends, you neither hear nor see one good man. All the toils you have gone through have always pointed to this sort of life; your lying on the ground not merely to lie in wait to gratify your unclean desires, but even to accomplish crimes; your vigilance, not only when plotting against the sleep of husbands, but also against the goods of your murdered victims, have all been preparations for this. Now you have an opportunity of displaying your splendid endurance of hunger, of cold, of want of everything; by which in a short time you will find yourself worn out. All this I effected when I procured your rejection from the consulship, that you should be reduced to make attempts on your country as an exile, instead of being able to distress it as consul, and that that which had been wickedly undertaken by you should be called piracy rather than war.

Now that I may remove and avert, O conscript fathers, any in the least reasonable complaint from myself, listen, I beseech you, carefully to what I say, and lay it up in your inmost hearts and minds. In truth, if my country, which is far dearer to me than my life—if all Italy—if the whole republic were to address me, "Marcus Tullius, what are you doing? will you permit that man to depart whom you have ascertained to be an enemy? whom you see ready to become the general of the war? whom you know to be expected in the camp of the enemy as their chief, the author of all this wickedness, the head of the conspiracy, the instigator of the slaves and abandoned citizens, so that he shall seem not driven out of the city by you, but let loose by you against the city? Will you not order him to be thrown into prison, to be hurried off to execution, to be put to death with the most prompt severity? What hinders you? Is it the customs of our ancestors? But even private men have often in this republic slain mischievous citizens. Is it the laws which have been passed about the punishment of Roman citizens? But in this city those who have rebelled against the republic have never had the rights of citizens. Do you fear odium with posterity? You are showing fine gratitude to the Roman people which has raised you, a man known only by your own actions, of no ancestral renown, through all the degrees of honor at so early an age to the very highest office, if from fear of unpopularity or of any danger you neglect the safety of your fellow citizens. But if you have a fear of unpopularity, is that arising from the imputation of vigor and boldness, or that arising from that of inactivity and indecision most to be feared? When Italy is laid waste by war, when cities are attacked and houses in flames, do you not think that you will be then consumed by a perfect conflagration of hatred?"

To this holy address of the republic, and to the feelings of those men who entertain the same opinion, I will make this short answer: If, O conscript fathers, I thought it best that Catiline should be punished with death, I would not have given the space of one hour to this gladiator to live in. If, forsooth, those excellent men and most illustrious cities not only did not pollute themselves, but even glorified themselves by the blood of Saturninus, and the Gracchi, and Flaccus, and many others of old time, surely I had no cause to fear lest for slaying this parricidal murderer of the citizens any unpopularity should accrue to me with posterity. And if it did threaten me to ever so great a degree, yet I have always been of the disposition to think unpopularity earned by virtue and glory not unpopularity.

Though there are some men in this body who either do not see what threatens, or dissemble what they do see; who have fed the hope of Catiline by mild sentiments, and have strengthened the rising conspiracy by not believing it; influenced by whose authority many, and they not wicked, but only ignorant, if I punished him would say that I had acted cruelly and tyrannically. But I know that if he arrives at the camp of Manlius to which he is going, there will be no one so stupid as not to see that there has been a conspiracy, no one so hardened as not to confess it. But if this man alone were put to death, I know that this disease of the republic would be only checked for a while, not eradicated forever. But if he banishes himself, and takes with him all his friends, and collects at one point all the ruined men from every quarter, then not only will this full-grown plague of the republic be extinguished and eradicated, but also the root and seed of all future evils.

We have now for a long time, O conscript fathers, lived among these dangers and machinations of conspiracy; but somehow or other, the ripeness of all wickedness, and of this long-standing madness and audacity, has come to a head at the time of my consulship. But if this man alone is removed from this piratical crew, we may appear, perhaps, for a short time relieved from fear and anxiety, but the danger will settle down and lie hid in the veins and bowels of the republic. As it often happens that men afflicted with a severe disease, when they are tortured with heat and fever, if they drink cold water, seem at first to be relieved, but afterward suffer more and more severely; so this disease which is in the republic, if relieved by the punishment of this man, will only get worse and worse, as the rest will be still alive.

Wherefore, O conscript fathers, let the worthless be gone—let them separate themselves from the good—let them collect in one place—let them, as I have often said before, be separated from us by a wall; let them cease to plot against the consul in his own house—to surround the tribunal of the city praetor—to besiege the senate-house with swords—to prepare brands and torches to burn the city; let it, in short, be written on the brow of every citizen, what his sentiments are about the republic. I promise you this, O conscript fathers, that there shall be so much diligence in us the consuls, so much authority in you, so much virtue in the Roman knights, so much unanimity in all good men that you shall see everything made plain and manifest by the departure of Catiline—everything checked and punished.

With these omens, O Catiline, be gone to your impious and nefarious war, to the great safety of the republic, to your own misfortune and injury, and to the destruction of those who have joined themselves to you in every wickedness and atrocity. Then do you, O Jupiter, who were consecrated by Romulus with the same auspices as this city, whom we rightly call the stay of this city and empire, repel this man and his companions from your altars and from the other temples—from the houses and walls of the city—from the lives and fortunes of all the citizens; and overwhelm all the enemies of good men, the foes of the republic, the robbers of Italy, men bound together by a treaty and infamous alliance of crimes, dead and alive, with eternal punishments.

4: Jesus and the Blessed

Galilee, circa 30 AD

THE ROMAN REPUBLIC OF CICERO HAD GIVEN WAY TO THE ROMAN EMPIRE OF Tiberius when, in the far-off provinces of Judaea and Galilee, an itinerant preacher named Jesus began attracting crowds of Jews eager to hear his sermons. In a land where prophets were as much a part of the landscape as olive trees, Jesus stood out because of his willingness to condemn religious orthodoxy and corruption. His indignant criticism of those who followed the letter but not the spirit of religious law might win few friends among high priests and Pharisees, but for provincial political figures such as Pontius Pilate, the governor of Judea, such actions were hardly a threat to Roman rule.

If Pilate and the other Roman authorities monitored Jesus as he traveled dusty roads with his platoon of disciples, they would have seen little cause for alarm. Quite the contrary: This self-proclaimed man of God instructed his follows to turn the other cheek, to love those who hated them, to hold in high esteem not military leaders but peacemakers, and to regard material wealth as a sign of not of God's pleasure but of His future condemnation.

All in all, a useful man in his own way, certainly not a political rabble-rouser who would urge rebellion against the empire. Why, he even embraced tax collectors, the most-hated symbol of Roman rule!

Long after the collapse of the Roman empire, long after other empires rose and fell in their place, the sermons of Jesus of Nazareth continue to hold a central place in world history, the inspiration for a worldwide movement known as Christianity. Writers and artists have incorporated Christ's themes of redemption, forgiveness and charity. Indeed, as the critic Robert Hughes observed, it is impossible to think of Western art and culture without Christianity.

Early in his short public career as a preacher, Jesus set forth principles that form the essence of Christianity. If these principles did not seem threatening to the Roman authorities, they were revolutionary all the same—all the more so because generations of men and women who claimed to be Christian have found them impossible to uphold.

In the Christian Bible, two writers, Matthew and Luke, present similar-sounding speeches that encapsulate the Christian message. Matthew's version takes place on a mountainside, and it commonly known as the Sermon on the Mount. Luke places the scene in a plain, after Jesus has gone to pray on a mountain near the Sea of Galilee. While Mathew's version of the Sermon on the Mount—also known as the Beatitudes—is more poetic and literary, Luke's version of Jesus' subsequent remarks are more accessible. Luke himself was a Gentile, and his influential Gospel was designed for non-Jewish audiences.

Luke reports that the Sermon on the Plain attracted crowds from Jerusalem and Judea as well as from the coastal cities of Tyre and Sidon in today's Lebanon. To this diverse audience, Jesus enunciated principles that have survived the centuries and are at the bedrock of Christian belief.

▼ ▼ ▼

B LESSED are you who are poor,
     for yours is the kingdom of God.
Blessed are you who are hungry now,
for you will be filled.
Blessed are you who weep now,
for you will laugh.
Blessed are you when people hate you, and when they exclude you, revile you, and defame you on account of the Son of Man.
Rejoice in that Day and leap for joy, for surely your reward is great in heaven; for that is what their ancestors did to the prophets.
But woe to you who are rich,
for you have received your consolation.
Woe to you who are full now,
for you will be hungry.
Woe to you who are laughing now,
for you will mourn and weep.
Woe to you when all speak well of you, for that is what their ancestors did to the false prophets.

5: Muhammad: Turn Thy Face

Arabian peninsula, circa 620 AD

IN THE SEVENTH CENTURY, A MIDDLE-AGED ARAB TRADER NAMED MUHAMMAD fled from his retreat on Mount Hira on the Arabian peninsula, returned home in an agitated state, and explained to his wife that he had been visited by a messenger from God. That messenger, the Angel Gabriel, was no stranger to those who knew sacred scripture. Noah had received a similar visitation, warning him of the flood to come, and Mary, mother of Jesus, received news of her impending pregnancy from Gabriel.

Gabriel brought Muhammad news that he was to serve as a special messenger from Allah, a destiny which the affluent businessman, husband and father accepted. From roughly 610 to 623 A.D., Gabriel dictated the commands of Allah while Muhammad transcribed. The result was one of the most influential books in history, the Koran, the holy book for the world's one billion Muslims.

Through his preaching, his revealed wisdom and his political skills, Muhammad united the disparate peoples of the Arabian peninsula through Islam. He died in 632, but the faith he founded and nurtured continued to spread. With a century, tribes in North Africa, Asia and today's Middle East adopted Islam and the tenets of the Koran.

The Muslim holy book does not contain Muhammad's words, as the New Testament records the sermons of Jesus, or the Torah chronicles the words of Moses. The Koran is considered the words of Allah, revealed to Muhammad through the medium of Gabriel. Nevertheless, it was Mohammad who brought these influential writings to thousands in his own time, and hundreds of millions in the centuries that followed his death.

This selection, from Book 5 of the Koran, directs the faithful to turn their faces to the Sacred Mosque, which Muslims believe was built in Mecca by angels before humans walked the earth. The current Grand Mosque in Mecca is the largest in the Islamic world.

▼ ▼ ▼

OBSERVE the prayers, and the middle prayer, and stand instant before God. And if ye fear, then afoot or mounted; but when ye are safe remember God, how he taught you what ye did not know.

When the call to prayer soundeth on the Day of Congregation (Friday), then hasten to remember God, and abandon business; that is better for you if ye only knew: and when prayer is done, disperse in the land and seek of the bounty of God.

Turn thy face towards the Sacred Mosque; wherever ye be, turn your faces thitherwards.

Give alms on the path of God, and let not your hands cast you into destruction; but do good, for God loveth those who do good; and accomplish the pilgrimage and the visit to God: but if ye be besieged, then send what is easiest as an offering.

They will ask thee what it is they must give in alms. Say: Let what good ye give be for parents, and kinsfolk, and the orphan, and the needy, and the son of the road; and what good ye do, verily God knoweth it.

They will ask thee what they shall expend in alms; say, The surplus.

If ye give alms openly, it is well; but if ye conceal it, and give it to the poor, it is better for you, and will take away from you some of your sins: and God knoweth what ye do.

O ye who believe, make not your alms of no effects by taunt and vexation, like him who spendeth what he hath to be seen of men, and believeth not in God and the Last Day: for his likeness is as the likeness of a stone with earth upon it, and a heavy rain falleth upon it and leaveth it bare; they accomplish nothing with what they earn, for God guideth not the people that disbelieve. And the likeness of those who expend their wealth for the sake of pleasing God and for the certainty of their souls is as the likeness of a garden on a hill: a heavy rain falleth on it and it bringeth forth its fruit twofold; and if no heavy rain falleth on it, then the dew falleth; and God seeth what ye do.

Kind speech and forgiveness is better than alms which vexation followeth; and God is rich and ruthful.

The hearts of men are at the disposal of God like unto one heart, and He turneth them about in any way that He pleaseth. O Director of hearts, turn our hearts to obey Thee.

The first thing which God created was a pen, and He said to it, "Write." It said, "What shall I write?" And God said, "Write down the quantity of every separate thing to be created." And it wrote all that was and all that will be to eternity.

There is not one among you whose sitting-place is not written by God whether in the fire or in Paradise. The Companions said, "O Prophet! since God hath appointed our place, may we confide in this and abandon our religious and moral duty?" He said, "No, because the happy will do good works, and those who are of the miserable will do bad works."

6: Urban II Declares a Crusade

Clermont, 1095

AT THE TURN OF THE FIRST MILLENNIUM, CHRISTIAN EUROPE WAS SHOWING its age. Youthful Islam had spread from the land of the prophets through North Africa and into Spain, and seemed poised to press forward into southern and central Europe through Asia Minor. Guarding Europe's southern flank was the aging Byzantine empire, the ancient remnant of the eastern Roman empire based in Constantinople. In 1071, a Byzantine army of forty thousand suffered a calamitous defeat at the hands of the Seljuk Turks in Manzikert in today's Turkey. The battle marked the end of the Byzantine Empire's ability to ward off the Islamic forces in the south and east.

In central and western Europe, feuds and wars were common, among the more-dramatic being William of Normandy's conquest of England beginning with the Battle of Hastings in 1066. Without the central administrative power of the Roman empire, Europe was weak and divided, a startling contrast with the aggressive Muslim forces looking for conquest in the heartland of Christianity.

Slightly more than two decades after the Byzantine disaster at Manzikert, Pope Urban II, leader of the Roman Catholic Church, received an urgent appeal from the Byzantine emperor, Alexios I Kommenos, asking for military assistance. The emperor claimed that Muslims who now controlled the land where Jesus lived had shut down access to shrines. It was a credible claim, for in 1009, an Islamic leader burned the Church of the Holy Sepulchre in Jerusalem, enraging Christians who believed the church was built on the site of Jesus' tomb.

Despite a schism over Papal authority between the Roman church and the Eastern church of the Byzantine empire, Urban II not only granted the Emperor's request, but did him one better. At the Council of Clermont, an important Church meeting held in 1095, Urban II delivered a sermon in which he called on Christians throughout Europe to march on the Holy Land to take control back from Muslim rule. The result was the first in several Crusades that changed the history of Christianity and Islam, and the relationship between Europe and the Middle East.

European Christians by the thousands responded to what amounted to a call for holy war. In 1099, the Crusader army captured Jerusalem, but the conflict between Christians and Muslims in the Middle East was just beginning, and, some might argue, it has never ended.

For Europeans, the Crusades were significant not only as a religious mission, but as an intellectual awakening. Mired in the depths of the early Middle Ages, when most adults rarely left the plots of land they worked, the Crusaders saw a new and different world, and were exposed to not only the ferocity of the Islamic troops, but the intellectual and scientific achievements of the Muslim world. The Renaissance cannot be understood without an understanding of what happened when Urban II delivered his sermon in Claremont.

▼ ▼ ▼

ALTHOUGH, O sons of God, you have promised more firmly than ever to keep the peace among yourselves and to preserve the rights of the church, there remains still an important work for you to do. Freshly quickened by the divine correction, you must apply the strength of your righteousness to another matter which concerns you as well as God. For your brethren who live in the east are in urgent need of your help, and you must hasten to give them the aid which has often been promised them. For, as the most of you have heard, the Turks and Arabs have attacked them and have conquered the territory of Romania [the Greek empire] as far west as the shore of the Mediterranean and the Hellespont, which is called the Arm of St. George. They have occupied more and more of the lands of those Christians, and have overcome them in seven battles. They have killed and captured many, and have destroyed the churches and devastated the empire. If you permit them to continue thus for awhile with impunity, the faithful of God will be much more widely attacked by them. On this account I, or rather the Lord, beseech you as Christ's heralds to publish this everywhere and to persuade all people of whatever rank, foot-soldiers and knights, poor and rich, to carry aid promptly to those Christians and to destroy that vile race from the lands of our friends. I say this to those who are present, it is meant also for those who are absent. Moreover, Christ commands it.

All who die by the way, whether by land or by sea, or in battle against the pagans, shall have immediate remission of sins. This I grant them through the power of God with which I am invested. O what a disgrace if such a despised and base race, which worships demons, should conquer a people which has the faith of omnipotent God and is made glorious with the name of Christ! With what reproaches will the Lord overwhelm us if you do not aid those who, with us, profess the Christian religion! Let those who have been accustomed unjustly to wage private warfare against the faithful now go against the infidels and end with victory this war which should have been begun long ago. Let those who for a long time have been robbers, now become knights. Let those who have been fighting against their brothers and relatives now fight in a proper way against the barbarians. Let those who have been serving as mercenaries for small pay now obtain the eternal reward. Let those who have been wearing themselves out in both body and soul now work for a double honor. Behold! on this side will be the sorrowful and poor, on that, the rich; on this side, the enemies of the Lord, on that, his friends. Let those who go not put off the journey, but rent their lands and collect money for their expenses; and as soon as winter is over and spring comes, let them eagerly set out on the way with God as their guide.

7: Martin Luther Refuses to Recant

Diet of Worms, 1521

THE EMERGING NATION-STATES OF RENAISSANCE EUROPE MIGHT WELL HAVE viewed each other with suspicion and envy, but whatever their differences, they shared a common identity as Roman Catholics. The church—there was no need to explain which church—had become synonymous with European culture and civilization. In politics, the power of the papacy extended into the councils of Europe, where it was greeted with varying degrees of welcome but with unanimous realization that the Bishop of Rome was a political, diplomatic and sometimes military force that no king, no prince, could easily dismiss. One Pope, Boniface VIII, insisted in 1302 that those who did not believe in the power of the papacy over all people were doomed to eternal damnation.

With the coming of the Enlightenment and its emphasis on reason and intellect came a new skepticism of traditional authority. Scientists questioned accepted theories about the place of the Earth in the solar system. Philosophers sought new explanations for the mysteries of life. And, eventually, voices within the Roman church raised their voices against what they saw as abuses of clerical and papal power.

As the institutional church embraced secular influence, it became morally indistinguishable from the other monarchies of Europe. For a time in the fourteenth century, dueling Popes claimed the allegiance of Europe's Catholics. It was a tawdry display from an institution that had lost its moral moorings.

Like any other monarch, the Pope required taxation to fund his far-flung empire of influence. Church teaching had it that by good works and prayer, humankind could qualify for indulgences that would partially absolve them of their sins. To help finance the enormous cost of building a magnificent new palace, St. Peter's Basilica, the Church authorized the sale of indulgences to the faithful. During a trip to Rome in the early sixteenth century, a young, earnest German monk heard about these sales and was outraged. His name was Martin Luther.

Luther was nothing if not a serious man of the cloth and student of the

Bible. His trip to Rome and his own observations of the institution of the church led him to conclude that the Catholic Church and the Papacy had lost their way, having succumbed to the corruption of earthly power. His intense reading of the Bible led him to conclude that humans could be saved through faith alone—not by good works, as the church preached.

In 1517, Luther compiled his dissents into a document, known to history at the 95 theses. He nailed a copy to the door of a church in Wittenberg , an act considered to be the beginning of the Protestant Reformation, a religious, political and cultural milestone in European history.

Luther's attack on Church authority spread quickly and achieved enormous attention. The Pope wanted him to withdraw some of his criticisms, but he refused. So, in 1521, Martin Luther was excommunicated from the Catholic Church and ordered to appear at a special proceeding in Worms, Germany, before the secular authorities who ruled the Holy Roman Empire. They, not the Pope, would decide what to do about Martin Luther.

The Holy Roman Emperor, Charles V, was in charge of what was, in essence, a jury. Luther confirmed that he was indeed the author of the 95 theses. He was given an opportunity to recant his criticisms, or face punishment.

His speech in his defense is a masterpiece of polite but firm defiance. It is known best for its summation, which often has been translated as, "Here I stand. I can do no other." It is a dramatic ending, indeed, to a powerful speech, but more authoritative translations render the final paragraph a little less poetically. Still, Luther's speech before the Diet (assembly) of Worms remains a masterpiece of defiance, and courage.

▼ ▼ ▼

I THIS day appear before you in all humility, according to your command, and I implore your majesty and your august highnesses, by the mercies of God, to listen with favor to the defense of a cause which I am well assured is just and right. I ask pardon, if by reason of my ignorance, I am wanting in the manners that befit a court; for I have not been brought up in kings palaces, but in the seclusion of a cloister.

Two questions were yesterday put to me by his imperial majesty; the first, whether I was the author of the books whose titles were read; the second, whether I wished to revoke or defend the doctrine I have taught. I answered the first, and I adhere to that answer.

As to the second, I have composed writings on very different subjects.

In some I have discussed Faith and Good Works, in a spirit at once so pure, clear, and Christian, that even my adversaries themselves, far from finding anything to censure, confess that these writings are profitable, and deserve to be perused by devout persons. The pope's bull, violent as it is, acknowledges this. What, then, should I be doing if I were now to retract these writings? Wretched man! I alone, of all men living, should be abandoning truths approved by the unanimous voice of friends and enemies, and opposing doctrines that the whole world glories in confessing!

I have composed, secondly, certain works against popery, wherein I have attacked such as by false doctrines, irregular lives, and scandalous examples, afflict the Christian world, and ruin the bodies and souls of men. And is not this confirmed by the grief of all who fear God? Is it not manifest that the laws and human doctrines of the popes entangle, vex, and distress the consciences of the faithful, while the crying and endless extortions of Rome engulf the property and wealth of Christendom, and more particularly of this illustrious nation?

If I were to revoke what I have written on that subject, what should I do… but strengthen this tyranny, and open a wider door to so many and flagrant impieties? Bearing down all resistance with fresh fury, we should behold these proud men swell, foam, and rage more than ever! And not merely would the yoke which now weighs down Christians be made more grinding by my retractation—it would thereby become, so to speak, lawful—for, by my retractation, it would receive confirmation from your most serene majesty, and all the States of the Empire. Great God! I should thus be like to an infamous cloak, used to hide and cover over every kind of malice and tyranny.

In the third and last place, I have written some books against private individuals, who had undertaken to defend the tyranny of Rome by destroying the faith. I freely confess that I may have attacked such persons with more violence than was consistent with my profession as an ecclesiastic: I do not think of myself as a saint; but neither can I retract these books because I should, by so doing, sanction the impieties of my opponents, and they would thence take occasion to crush God's people with still more cruelty.

Yet, as I am a mere man, and not God, I will defend myself after the example of Jesus Christ, who said: "If I have spoken evil, bear witness against me." How much more should I, who am but dust and ashes, and so prone to error, desire that everyone should bring forward what he can against my doctrine.

Therefore, most serene emperor, and you illustrious princes, and all, whether high or low, who hear me, I implore you by the mercies of God to prove to me by the writings of the prophets and apostles that I am in error. As soon as I shall be convinced, I will instantly retract all my errors, and will myself be the first to seize my writings, and commit them to the flames.

What I have just said I think will clearly show that I have well considered and weighed the dangers to which I am exposing myself; but far from being dismayed by them, I rejoice exceedingly to see the Gospel this day, as of old, a cause of disturbance and disagreement. It is the character and destiny of God's word. "I came not to send peace unto the earth, but a sword," said Jesus Christ. God is wonderful and awful in His counsels. Let us have a care, lest in our endeavors to arrest discords, we be bound to fight against the holy word of God and bring down upon our heads a frightful deluge of inextricable dangers, present disaster, and everlasting desolations. . . . Let us have a care lest the reign of the young and noble prince, the Emperor Charles, on whom, next to God, we build so many hopes, should not only commence, but continue and terminate its course under the most fatal auspices. I might cite examples drawn from the oracles of God. I might speak of Pharaohs, of kings of Babylon, or of Israel, who were never more contributing to their own ruin than when, by measures in appearances most prudent, they thought to establish their authority! "God removeth the mountains and they know not."

In speaking thus, I do not suppose that such noble princes have need of my poor judgment; but I wish to acquit myself of a duty that Germany has a right to expect from her children. And so commending myself to your august majesty, and your most serene highnesses, I beseech you in all humility, not to permit the hatred of my enemies to rain upon me an indignation I have not deserved.

Since your most serene majesty and your high mightinesses require of me a simple, clear and direct answer, I will give one, and it is this: I cannot submit my faith either to the pope or to the council, because it is as clear as noonday that they have fallen into error and even into glaring inconsistency with themselves. If, then, I am not convinced by proof from Holy Scripture, or by cogent reasons, if I am not satisfied by the very text I have cited, and if my judgment is not in this way brought into subjection to God's word, I neither can nor will retract anything; for it cannot be right for a Christian to speak against his country. I stand here and can say no more. God help me. Amen.

8: Thomas More Confronts His Accuser

London, July 7, 1535

EUROPE'S RELIGIOUS CONVULSIONS INEVITABLY AFFECTED THE CONTINENT'S power arrangements, added zeal to diplomatic and economic feuds, and tested the courage and principles of those who dissented from the prevailing views of their lords and fellow subjects. Not surprisingly, the conflict among Christians produced martyrs, perhaps the most famous being Sir Thomas More.

Thomas More was one of Renaissance England's most brilliant minds, a lawyer trained in the classics, a philosopher whose political treatise, *Utopia*, remains a classic work from the period, a practicing politician with a sharp sense of irony, and a servant of the Crown who believed that Parliament, not the monarch, held ultimate power in England.

He was brought into Henry's inner councils in 1518 and rose quickly to become one of the king's most trusted aides. The two men collaborated on a book entitled *Defense of the Seven Sacraments*, which assailed Martin Luther's criticism of the Roman Catholic Church.

More continued in the king's good graces even after he opposed Henry's decision to seek a divorce from Catherine of Aragon in 1527. Two years later, Henry appointed More as Lord Chancellor, the kingdom's most powerful office short of the throne itself. But the two men soon were at odds over Henry's insistence on dissolving his marriage. More refused to play the role of deferential courtier, declining to join other prominent Englishmen who signed a petition urging the Pope to annul Henry's marriage to Catherine and opposing the King's decision to declare himself head of the church in England, negating the Pope's authority. More resigned as Lord Chancellor in 1532, but did not go quietly. He continued to oppose the King's position, defending the authority of the Pope and the Catholic Church.

When Henry VIII disposed of Catherine, married Anne Boleyn and

had her crowned as Queen in 1533, Thomas More was conspicuous by his
absence at the coronation. It was a deliberate snub, a public show of the former Lord Chancellor's disapproval. It was too much for the King, weary of
More's defiance. When More refused to accept Parliament's Act of
Succession, which declared Anne to be Queen also denied the Pope's
authority over matters of religion in England, Henry ordered him to the
Tower of London to reflect on his views.

More was arraigned on charges of treason for his criticism of the Act of
Succession. But while his views about Papal authority were well known, he
had never publicly challenged the King's claim to be head of the church in
England. However, when he was brought to trial in July, 1535, the government's Solicitor General, Lord Rich, swore that More had explicitly denied
the king's right to declare himself head of the Church of England in a private conversation. The price for such an opinion, in Henry's England, was
death.

On July 7, More rose to speak in his own defense before a panel that
included relatives of the new Queen. He was in poor health after months
spent in the Tower of London. His memory and his understanding, he said,
"are both impaired, together with my bodily health." The judges allowed
him to be seated while he addressed the charges against him. After attacking the specifics of the indictment, he addressed the most damaging evidence against him, Lord Rich's claim that he denied the King's authority.
More accused Rich of lying under oath, a grave charge.

In this excerpt from his speech, recorded by his son-in-law, More dis-
plays his contempt for Rich while continuing to uphold the authority of
Rome on religious matters. Towards the end of the statement, More learns
that he has been found guilty and has been sentenced to death. He remains
defiant, even in the face of interruptions by his successor as Lord
Chancellor and by another member of the Court, Lord Norfolk.

After finishing, Thomas More was led from the court and beheaded.
He has lived on as a symbol of conscience and intellectual freedom.

▼ ▼ ▼

IN good faith, Mr. Rich, I am more concerned for your perjury,
than my own danger; and I must tell you, that neither myself nor
anybody else to my knowledge, ever took you to be a man of such reputation, that I or any other would have anything to do with you in a mat-

ter of importance. You know that I have been acquainted with your manner of life and conversation long time, even from your youth to the present juncture, for we lived in the same parish; and you very well know, I am sorry I am forced to speak it, you always lay under the odium of a very lying tongue, of a great gamester, and of no good name and character either there or in the Temple, where you was educated. Can it therefore seem likely to your Lordships, that I should in so weighty an affair as this, act so unadvisedly, as to trust Mr. Rich, a man I had always so mean an opinion of, in reference to his truth and honesty, so very much before my Sovereign Lord the King, to whom I am so deeply indebted for his manifold favors, or any of his noble and grave counselors, that I should only impart to Mr. Rich the secrets of my conscience in respect to the King's supremacy, the particular secrets, and only point about which I have been so long pressed to explain myself? which I never did, nor never would reveal; when the act was once made, either to the King himself, or any of his privy-counselors, as is well known to your honors, who have been sent upon no other account at several times by his Majesty to me in the Tower. I refer it to your judgments, my lords, whether this can seem credible to any of your lordships.

But supposing what Mr. Rich has swore should be true, seeing the words were spoke in familiar and private conversation, and that there was nothing at all asserted, but only cases put without any offensive circumstances; it cannot in justice be said, that they were spoke maliciously, and where there is no malice, there is no offence . . .

For as much as, my lords, this indictment is grounded upon an act of Parliament, directly repugnant to the laws of God and his Holy Church, the Supreme Government of which, or of any part thereof, no temporal person may by any law presume to take upon him, being what right belongs to the see of Rome, which by special prerogative was granted by the mouth of our Savior Christ himself to St. Peter, and the Bishops of *Rome* his successors only, whilst he lived, and was personally present here on Earth: it is therefore, amongst Catholic Christians, insufficient in law, to charge any Christian to obey it . . .

Well, seeing I am condemned, God knows how justly, I will freely speak for the disburdening my conscience, what I think of this law. When I perceived it was the King's pleasure to sift out from whence the Pope's authority was derived; I confess I studied seven years together to find out the truth of it, and I could not meet with the works of any one doctor, approved by the Church, that avouch a layman was, or ever could be the Head of the Church.

Chancellor. Would you be esteemed wiser, or to have a sincerer conscience than all the bishops, learned doctors, nobility and commons of this realm?

More. I am able to produce against one bishop which you can produce on your side, a hundred holy and Catholic bishops for my opinion; and against one realm, the consent of Christendom for a thousand years.

Norfolk: Sir Thomas, you shew your obstinate and malicious mind.

More. Noble sir, it's no malice or obstinacy that makes me say this, but the just necessity of the cause obliges me to it for the discharge of my conscience; and call God to witness, that nothing but this has excited me to it.

As the blessed Apostle St. Paul, as we read in the Acts of the Apostles, was present, and consenting to the death of Protomartyr Stephen, keeping their clothes that stoned him to death, and yet they are both now holy saints in heaven, and there shall continue friends to eternity; so I verily trust, and shall therefore heartily pray, that albeit your lordships have been on earth my judges to condemnation, yet that we may hereafter meet joyfully together in Heaven to our everlasting salvation: and God preserve you, especially my Sovereign Lord the King, and grant him faithful counselors.

9: Elizabeth I Faces the Armada
"I Myself Will Be Your General"
Tilbury, 1588

THE RENAISSANCE IN EUROPE GAVE BIRTH NOT ONLY TO NEW LEARNING AND discovery, but new rivalries among the continent's growing nation-states. Spain, having forced its Islamic conquerors to retreat back to North Africa, emerged as the most powerful and richest of the rising empires of Europe, thanks to its fortuitous sponsorship of Christopher Columbus's journeys across the Atlantic Ocean.

The Spanish were Catholics, at a time when divisions between Protestant and Catholic monarchs were bitter and seemingly irreconcilable. Nevertheless, relations between Catholic Spain and Protestant England were rather cozy indeed when Elizabeth I took the throne in 1558. The Spanish king, Philip II, while devoted to the Catholic Church, also happened to be Elizabeth's brother-in-law. When Philip's wife, Mary, died in 1558, the king proposed marriage to Elizabeth, but she refused the offer. As the saying goes, they remained good friends. Until, that is, they became enemies.

As Philip was a staunch Catholic, Elizabeth became a staunch Protestant. She also entertained serious ambitions for her fractious and divided nation. Spain, however, presented an obstacle to English ambitions in the increasingly powerful Atlantic world. Philip's navy was the best in the world. England was no match for it, at least not in a conventional sense.

Determined to weaken her brother-in-law, Elizabeth gave her tacit permission to private captains eager to harass Spanish shipping in the Atlantic. The riches of the New World were the source of Philip's strength not only at home, but abroad, where his army sought to overturn Protestant rule in the Netherlands. Privateers such as Francis Drake enjoyed tremendous success in making off with treasures bound for Spain.

Philip's ties to his sister-in-law were frayed beyond repair. He conspired to have Elizabeth killed and her cousin, the Catholic Mary Queen of Scots, put on the throne in her place. Elizabeth got wind of the conspiracy, and, in 1587, ordered Mary's execution.

Philip decided it was time to stop fighting around the edges. He ordered construction of a huge fleet, an Armada, to bring the fight to Elizabeth. In May, 1588, the fleet of more than one hundred ships set sail bound for the English Channel. Such a fleet could hardly leave unnoticed; word soon made its way to London that a huge Spanish fleet was on its way.

It was not a David and Goliath battle by any stretch of the imagination. Spain certainly was the greater power, but England had a larger fleet, with nearly two hundred ships, which was faster and more maneuverable. Still, the occasion was grave, enough so that the Queen herself visited her troops in Tilbury, a strategic town on the River Thames, as they prepared for the Spanish onslaught.

Her speech is notable for its defiance, for its courage, and for its appeal to duty. More than anything else, though, the speech is remarkable because of the speaker—a woman, a Queen, successor to the hyper-masculine Henry VIII. She felt obliged to refer to her gender and to deprecate it, but her words tell more about her character.

The winds, and skill, were with the English. The Spanish suffered heavy losses in combat and in bad weather. The threat passed, and soon England would take command of the Atlantic seas.

▼ ▼ ▼

MY loving people, we have been persuaded by some, that are careful of our safety, to take heed how we commit ourselves to armed multitudes, for fear of treachery; but I assure you, I do not desire to live to distrust my faithful and loving people. Let tyrants fear; I have always so behaved myself that, under God, I have placed my chiefest strength and safeguard in the loyal hearts and good will of my subjects. And therefore I am come amongst you at this time, not as for my recreation or sport, but being resolved, in the midst and heat of the battle, to live or die amongst you all; to lay down, for my God, and for my kingdom, and for my people, my honor and my blood, even the dust. I know I have but the body of a weak and feeble woman; but I have the heart of a king, and of a king of England, too; and think foul scorn that Parma or Spain, or any prince of Europe, should dare to invade the borders of my realms: to which, rather than any dishonor should grow by me, I myself will take up arms; I myself will be your general, judge, and rewarder of every one of your virtues in the field. I know already, by your forwardness, that you have deserved rewards and crowns; and we do assure you, on the word of a prince, they shall be duly paid you. In the mean my lieutenant general shall be in my stead, than whom never prince commanded a more noble and worthy subject; not doubting by your obedience to my general, by your concord in the camp, and by your valor in the field, we shall shortly have a famous victory over the enemies of my God, of my kingdom, and of my people.

10: John Winthrop's "City Upon a Hill"

June, 1630

With a single phrase in a sermon about Christian charity, John Winthrop inspired an image of the United States that most twenty-first century Americans would immediately recognize.

Winthrop was a Puritan, a member of a Protestant sect that believed the Reformation did not go far enough in purging the English church of Catholic symbols, rituals, and ceremonies. The sect appealed to what would be, in today's language, the middle classes—artisans, shopkeepers, and farmers. During the first quarter of the seventeenth century, the Puritans, inspired by the words and theology of John Calvin, developed a broad critique not only of the Church of England, but of English society and politics as well. They saw themselves as righteous, and the world around them as corrupt.

The Puritans believed they had an ally in King James I, a fellow Calvinist who succeeded to the English throne after the death of Queen Elizabeth I in 1603. Elizabeth was hostile to the Puritans, but James, who was raised in Scotland as a Presbyterian, seemed to share the Puritan critique of the established Church of England. But James disappointed many Puritans at a conference called shortly after his coronation, when some Puritans were dissatisfied with his lack of commitment to rid religious ceremonies of traces of Catholic ritual. It was during this conference, held at Hampton Court, that the King suggested that all Protestant sects ought to agree on a common translation of the Bible. That led to publication of a translation known as the King James version of the Bible.

James and the Puritans co-existed for more than two decades, but relations deteriorated when he died and his son, Charles I, took the throne. Charles was married to a Catholic woman and was considered to be a closet Catholic himself, or close to it. He promoted the career of William Laud, a Church of England clergyman who enjoyed the pomp and ceremony of religious ritual, marking him as far too sympathetic to Catholicism. Laud, named a bishop in 1628, became a polarizing figure in English society as he sought to crack down on the growing power of the Puritan movement.

The King himself joined in the crackdown in 1629 by dismissing Parliament, a seat of Puritan power. Convinced that the English church and larger society were irredeemably corrupt, some Puritans decided to create a new society far from the influence of James and Bishop Laud.

There already was precedent for such a journey. Ten years earlier, in 1620, a group of about a hundred Puritans left England for the New World in a ship called the *Mayflower*. These emigrants gave up on England and its church well before others—in fact, they were separatists who no longer considered themselves part of the official Church of England. Unlike other Puritans, who simply wished to purify the church, the passengers on the *Mayflower*, known to history at the Pilgrims, left the church along with their native land.

A decade after the Pilgrims founded the Plymouth Bay colony, John Winthrop joined another group that looked westward for salvation from corruption and sin. He and like-minded believers set sail in a ship called the *Arbella* in April, 1630. A prosperous lawyer, Winthrop was elected as head of the group, and it fell to him to him to give meaning to the Puritans' drastic decision to abandon all that they knew for a world they could hardly imagine.

The result was a speech that has been quoted by John F. Kennedy, Ronald Reagan and many others since, for it is seen as a founding document of American exceptionalism—that is, the belief that the United States is exempt from the fatal flaws of the Old World, and has been endowed with a special mission to spread its virtue to all humankind. This strain of civic evangelism is rooted in the notion that America ought to serve as an example for nations and peoples everywhere.

Winthrop exhorted his fellow Puritans that they must be "as a city upon a hill," cautioning them that the "eyes of all people are upon us." Kennedy, in his farewell speech to the Massachusetts legislatures before becoming President, and Reagan, in his farewell speech as president, both cited Winthrop's speech as an inspiration for America's role in the modern world.

But Winthrop, of course, was hardly seeking to define the American experience, since, in 1630, there was not much of one to define. He was hardly a democrat, and as history would prove, he was intolerant of the only sort of dissent that mattered to him—challenges to his vision of piety.

In fact, Winthrop's exhortation, which may have been given aboard the *Arabella* or before it set sail, was meant to inspire the Puritans to be pious. And in its entirety, the speech attempts to articulate a common cause for the Puritan settlers. This strong-willed group, which dared to challenge the status quo in England, would not survive without cooperation and common purpose.

Winthrop and his followers thought they would land in Virginia. Instead, they landed farther north, in today's Massachusetts. Winthrop became the first governor of the Massachusetts Bay Colony. In that position, he had much to say, but nothing he said surpassed his founding statement of purpose. It remains a vital testament to America's evangelical self-image.

N OW the only way to avoid this shipwreck and to provide for our posterity is to follow the counsel of Micah, to do justly, to love mercy, to walk humbly with our God, for this end, we must be knit together in this work as one man, we must entertain each other in brotherly affection, we must be willing to abridge ourselves of our superfluities, for the supply of other's necessities, we must uphold a familiar commerce together in all meekness, gentleness, patience and liberallity, we must delight in each other, make other's conditions our own, rejoice together, mourn together, labor, and suffer together, always having before our eyes our Commission and Community in the work, our Community as members of the same body, so shall we keep the unity of the spirit in the bond of peace, the Lord will be our God and delight to dwell among us, as his own people, and will command a blessing upon us in all our ways, so that we shall see much more of his wisdom, power, goodness and truth than formerly we have been acquainted with, we shall find that the God of Israel is among us, when ten of us shall be able to resist a thousand of our enemies, when he shall make us a praise and glory, that men shall say of succeeding plantations: the Lord make it like that of New England: for we must consider that we shall be as a City upon a Hill, the eyes of all people are upon us; so that if we shall deal falsely with our god in this work we have undertaken and so cause him to withdraw his present help from us, we shall be made a story and a byword through the world, we shall open the mouths of enemies to speak evil of the ways of god and all professors for God's sake; we shall shame the faces of many of God's worthy servants, and cause their prayers to be turned into curses upon us till we be consumed out of the good land whither we are going: And to shut up this discourse with that exhortation of Moses that faithful servant of the Lord in his last farewell to Israel (Deut. 30). Beloved there is now set before us life, and good, death and evil in that we are commanded this day to love the Lord our God, and to love one another, to walk in his ways and to keep his commandments and his ordinance, and his laws, and the Articles of our Covenant with him that we may live and be multiplied, and that the Lord our God may bless us in the land whither we go to possess it: But if our hearts shall turn away so that we will not obey, but shall be seduced and worship other Gods our pleasures, and profits, and serve them, it is propounded unto us this day, we shall surely perish out of the good land whither we pass over this vast sea to possess it;

Therefore let us choose life,
that we, and our Seed,
may live; by obeying his
voice, and cleaving to him,
for he is our life, and
our prosperity.

11: Oliver Cromwell
Dismisses Parliament
"In the Name of God, Go!"
London, April 20, 1653

THE PURITANS WHO CROSSED THE ATLANTIC OCEAN TO FOUND A NEW SOCIETY in a new England believed they would create a society that would serve as an example for all God-fearing peoples. But the vast majority of English Puritans believed that they need not cross an ocean in order to carry out God's work. They sought to create their own city upon a hill in the land of their birth.

Through the 1730's, their critique of the established Church of England called into question not just religious dogma and ritual, but the foundation of the English state, the monarchy and the institutions that supported them. King Charles I, who succeeded to the throne in 1625, summed up the place of religion in early modern England: "People are governed by the pulpit more than the sword in times of peace. Religion it is that keeps the subject in obedience."[1]

The Puritans developed an egalitarian attitude that made them increasingly skeptical of authority vested in bishops and other instruments of church and state privilege. The Puritan dissents were rooted in interpretations of faith and salvation, but religion and power were so intertwined in early modern England that disagreement over matters of faith was inevitably a political act.

Tensions began to gather through the reign of Charles, whose toleration of Roman Catholics—his wife was Catholic, as were some of his close aides—repulsed the Puritans. In Scotland, another hotbed of religious dissent, a rebel army waged war against Charles in 1639. Strapped for funds to fight the war, the King had to turn to Parliament, another important base of Puritan support. The House of Commons understood that a change in power relations was in the offing: It impeached several of the King's aides, and one of them, Earl of Strafford, was executed. The following year, 1641, a rebellion broke out in Ireland. The old order was breaking down.

Outright civil war between Parliament and the King broke out not long after the Irish rebelled. A minority within the Parliamentary movement gathered together to form an armed force called the New Model Army, a professional army which represented some of the most ideological forces in England. After sporadic negotiations and fighting, the army came under the control of a strange, intemperate, righteous man named Oliver Cromwell.

The conflict between crown and Parliament reached a bloody conclusion on January 30, 1649, when King Charles I, defeated, humiliated and imprisoned, was executed as a traitor. The Parliamentarians, free now to put into place the ideology they preached, abolished the monarchy and other remnants of royal privilege, including the House of Lords.

After Charles' execution, Parliament reigned supreme. With the king in his grave and royal patronage banished, England began an experiment in republican government, known as the Commonwealth period. Some members of the House of Commons became increasingly skeptical of the role Cromwell's New Model Army wished to play in affairs of state. Cromwell, for his part, was impatient with the pace of reform and was less than pleased by what he believed to be the ungodly conduct of many of Parliament's members. So, on April 20, 1653, he decided to force the issue.

He entered the House of Commons with an escort of musketeers. The troops remained outside the chamber, for the moment anyway. The House was debating a bill about procedures for an election later in the year, a measure Cromwell viewed—or at least he claimed to view—as little more than an exercise in protecting the status quo. Summoning his vast reserve of anger and righteousness, Cromwell rose to speak. He condemned the men in the room as unworthy and impious. He ranted, he stamped his feet on the floor, and he let forth a barrage of outrage whose power was only enhanced when he called on his musketeers to enter the room. Suitably reinforced, he condemned the parliamentarians as drunkards and worse.

His speech is a classic piece of invective, the work of a man versed in Scripture and the classics, convinced of his own righteousness and the corruption of those who disagreed with him. He presumed that he spoke for the nation as he denounced the members of Parliament as layabouts and frauds.

Finally, wielding his power as Commander in Chief of the New Model Army, this champion of Parliament forced members to leave and disband, or suffer the consequences. The members, taking the hint, left the room, and England's short experiment in republican rule came to an end. After this speech, Cromwell assumed more power than the king he had helped murder. He would rule as Lord Protector of the English Commonwealth until his death in 1658. His son succeeded him, mocking the very notion of republican rule. In 1660, the monarchy was restored. Cromwell's body was dug up and abused, although Britons today seem to have forgiven him his excesses.

▼ ▼ ▼

IT is high time for me to put an end to your sitting in this place, which you have dishonored by your contempt of all virtue, and defiled by your practice of every vice; ye are a factious crew, and enemies to all good government; ye are a pack of mercenary wretches, and would like Esau sell your country for a mess of pottage, and like Judas betray your God for a few pieces of money.

Is there a single virtue now remaining amongst you? Is there one vice you do not possess? Ye have no more religion than my horse; gold is your God; which of you have not barter'd your conscience for bribes? Is there a man amongst you that has the least care for the good of the Commonwealth?

Ye sordid prostitutes, have you not defil'd this sacred place, and turn'd the Lord's temple into a den of thieves, by your immoral principles and wicked practices? Ye are grown intolerably odious to the whole nation; you were deputed here by the people to get grievances redress'd, are yourselves gone! So! Take away that shining bauble there, and lock up the doors.

In the name of God, go!

12. Patrick Henry Makes the Case for Liberty, or Death

Virginia, March 25, 1775

ALL EYES WERE INDEED ON MASSACHUSETTS IN THE MID-1770's. THE SPIRIT of dissent which led John Winthrop and his fellow Puritans to cross the Atlantic Ocean remained part of the colony's collective culture. Religious purity was less important in the mid-eighteenth century that it was in Winthrop's time. By the 1770's, Enlightenment ideas about liberty, freedom and the sources of power and authority had begun to transform the attitudes of literate men and women, even in backwater colonies far from European centers of learning.

In the province of Massachusetts, colonists began to question the relationship between themselves and the institutions in London which purported to govern them. They were not alone, but by 1775, they were collectively the most outspoken critics of British policy in North America. After years of tension, which saw troops open fire on civilians, and rebels dressed as Indians committing an egregious act of vandalism in Boston Harbor, the Crown and Parliament responded with the bluntest instruments in their arsenal. The province was declared to be in a state of rebellion, military rule replaced civilian government, and the port of Boston was ordered closed. If the other American colonies regarded Massachusetts as a city upon a hill, they would do well to consider the consequences of following its example.

Even after a continental congress met in the fall of 1774 to consider a common response to English policies in America, it was far from certain that other colonial leaders would see the struggle in Massachusetts as their own. Upset though they were over taxation and other policies, political leaders in America still regarded themselves as good and loyal subjects of the King. Parliament might well be in the hands of fools, despots and other villains, but the king still was the king. Many believed America ought to tread carefully in these dangerous waters of quasi-rebellion.

In Virginia, a lawyer and rising member of the House of Burgesses named Patrick Henry was convinced that a separation between the New World and the Old was inevitable. He was not alone, nor was he the first to reach such a conclusion. But Patrick Henry had a gift for oratory, and on March 23, 1775, he summoned that gift into battle.

He proposed that the colony of Virginia, the largest among the thirteen, begin preparing for war. The resolution was not so explicit; it simply called on the colony to take defensive measures and to starting arming its citizens. But there was no doubt that war was on Henry's mind.

When Massachusetts took a similar step, Parliament declared the colony to be in open rebellion, justifying a more intense military crackdown. Now the young hothead Henry was proposing similar trouble in Virginia.

Virginia was several hundred miles from Massachusetts. Many Virginians had never met a person from Massachusetts, and vice versa. Boston might well have been London, save that many Virginians felt a connection to the English capital. They felt little, or none, to Boston.

Henry, however, saw in the plight of Massachusetts a larger struggle not simply between colonies and mother country, but between conflicting ideas and ideals. After proposing this dangerous escalation in tensions, Henry addressed his colleagues in the House of Burgesses. He knew many were reluctant to make a bad situation worse. He knew, too, that not everybody in the House saw themselves in a common struggle with the men and women of Boston.

In his speech, he acknowledged these objections and then demolished them. He spoke without notes—leading some scholars to wonder if he really uttered some of the most remarkable sentences in the history of American rhetoric. The speech itself was not published until 1816.

Regardless, the record shows that his resolutions narrowly passed. Skeptical and perhaps even frightened men in the House of Burgesses agreed to prepare for war against a mighty empire. Whatever Patrick Henry said, it must have been good.

▼ ▼ ▼

NO man thinks more highly than I do of the patriotism, as well as abilities, of the very worthy gentlemen who have just addressed the House. But different men often see the same subject in different lights; and, therefore, I hope it will not be thought disrespectful to those gentlemen if, entertaining as I do opinions of a character very opposite to theirs,

I shall speak forth my sentiments freely and without reserve. This is no time for ceremony. The question before the House is one of awful moment to this country. For my own part, I consider it as nothing less than a question of freedom or slavery; and in proportion to the magnitude of the subject ought to be the freedom of the debate. It is only in this way that we can hope to arrive at truth, and fulfill the great responsibility which we hold to God and our country. Should I keep back my opinions at such a time, through fear of giving offense, I should consider myself as guilty of treason towards my country, and of an act of disloyalty toward the Majesty of Heaven, which I revere above all earthly kings.

Mr. President, it is natural to man to indulge in the illusions of hope. We are apt to shut our eyes against a painful truth, and listen to the song of that siren till she transforms us into beasts. Is this the part of wise men, engaged in a great and arduous struggle for liberty? Are we disposed to be of the number of those who, having eyes, see not, and, having ears, hear not, the things which so nearly concern their temporal salvation? For my part, whatever anguish of spirit it may cost, I am willing to know the whole truth; to know the worst, and to provide for it.

I have but one lamp by which my feet are guided, and that is the lamp of experience. I know of no way of judging of the future but by the past. And judging by the past, I wish to know what there has been in the conduct of the British ministry for the last ten years to justify those hopes with which gentlemen have been pleased to solace themselves and the House. Is it that insidious smile with which our petition has been lately received? Trust it not, sir; it will prove a snare to your feet. Suffer not yourselves to be betrayed with a kiss. Ask yourselves how this gracious reception of our petition comports with those warlike preparations which cover our waters and darken our land. Are fleets and armies necessary to a work of love and reconciliation? Have we shown ourselves so unwilling to be reconciled that force must be called in to win back our love? Let us not deceive ourselves, sir. These are the implements of war and subjugation; the last arguments to which kings resort. I ask gentlemen, sir, what means this martial array, if its purpose be not to force us to submission? Can gentlemen assign any other possible motive for it? Has Great Britain any enemy, in this quarter of the world, to call for all this accumulation of navies and armies? No, sir, she has none. They are meant for us: they can be meant for no other. They are sent over to bind and rivet upon us those chains which the British ministry have been so long forging. And what have we to oppose to them? Shall we try argument? Sir, we have been trying that for the last ten years. Have we anything new to offer upon the subject? Nothing. We have held the subject up in every light of which it is capable; but it has been all in vain. Shall we resort to entreaty and humble supplication? What terms shall we find which have not been already exhausted? Let us not, I beseech you, sir, deceive ourselves. Sir, we have done everything that could be done to avert the storm which is now coming on. We have petitioned; we have remonstrated; we have supplicated; we have prostrated ourselves before the throne, and have implored its interposition to arrest the tyrannical hands of the ministry and Parliament. Our petitions have been slighted; our remonstrances have produced additional violence and insult; our supplications have been disregarded; and we have been spurned, with contempt, from the foot of the throne! In vain, after these things, may we indulge the fond hope of peace and reconciliation. There is no longer any room for hope. If we wish to be free— if we mean to preserve inviolate those inestimable privileges for which we have been so long contending—if we mean not basely to abandon the noble struggle in which we have been so long engaged, and which we have pledged ourselves never to abandon until the glorious object of our contest shall be obtained—we must fight! I repeat it, sir, we must fight! An appeal to arms and to the God of hosts is all that is left us!

They tell us, sir, that we are weak; unable to cope with so formidable an adversary. But when shall we be stronger? Will it be the next week, or the next year? Will it be when we are totally disarmed, and when a British guard shall be stationed in every house? Shall we gather strength by irresolution and inaction? Shall we acquire the means of effectual resistance by lying supinely on our backs and hugging the delusive phantom of hope, until our enemies shall have bound us hand and foot? Sir, we are not weak if we make a proper use of those means which the God of nature hath placed in our power. The millions of people, armed in the holy cause of liberty, and in such a country as that which we possess, are invincible by any force which our enemy can send against us. Besides, sir, we shall not fight our battles alone. There is a just God who presides over the destinies of nations, and who will raise up friends to fight our battles for us. The battle, sir, is not to the strong alone; it is to the vigilant, the active, the brave. Besides, sir, we have no election. If we were base enough to desire it, it is now too late to retire from the contest. There is no retreat but in submission and slavery! Our chains are forged! Their clanking may be heard on the plains of Boston! The war is inevitable—and let it come! I repeat it, sir, let it come.

It is in vain, sir, to extenuate the matter. Gentlemen may cry, Peace, Peace— but there is no peace. The war is actually begun! The next gale that sweeps from the north will bring to our ears the clash of resounding arms! Our brethren are already in the field! Why stand we here idle? What is it that gentlemen wish? What would they have? Is life so dear, or peace so sweet, as to be purchased at the price of chains and slavery? Forbid it, Almighty God! I know not what course others may take; but as for me, give me liberty or give me death!

13: Washington Addresses Dissidents in the Army

Newburgh, March 15, 1783

THE TURNING POINT OF THE AMERICAN REVOLUTION MAY WELL HAVE BEEN the battles near Saratoga, New York, after which the duly impressed French dispatched aid and comfort to the enemies of their enemies. But there were several times after Saratoga when the war might very well have tipped in Britain's favor, never more so that in the winter of 1780-81, when Lord Cornwallis seemed on the verge of re-conquering the South for the Crown.

The British, however, were not the only challenge to the Revolution and the republican virtues that inspired the founders. American troops, the armed wing of the revolution, themselves posed a threat to the founders' ideals of democracy, liberty and control of the military.

The troops who endured long years of war during the Revolution could sometimes be a grouchy lot, and with reason. Pay was sporadic at best, the continental currency was laughable at times, and there were moments when it surely seemed as though the people in whose name they were fighting—Americans—seemed more sympathetic to the British, or were otherwise utterly apathetic.

With the great victory over Cornwallis at Yorktown in 1781, all these issues seemed to be resolved. While battles continued in fits and starts after Yorktown, the war was over, and all of the principals knew it.

But the war was one issue. The Revolution was quite another matter. Dr. Benjamin Rush, a signer of the Declaration of Independence, understood the difference. "The American war is over," he wrote after Cornwallis surrendered. "But that is far from being the case with the American Revolution. On the contrary, nothing but the first act of the great drama is closed."[1]

Rush was right about the drama to come. The curtain came up on another act in Newburgh, New York, in mid-March, 1783. Washington had marched his army to the Hudson Valley after Yorktown, and there his main Continental force awaited the outcome of peace talks. In the interim, these victorious soldiers grew increasingly dissatisfied with the political wing of the Revolution. Many officers had not been paid in years, and the promise of pensions suddenly seemed impossible to fulfill. Individual states were unwilling to pay, but were also unwilling to cede to Congress the authority to raise revenue to pay the troops.

Unrest among the troops began to spread like camp fever in the winter of 1783. Washington received word from his aide, Alexander Hamilton, that Congress would be unable to make good on the money owed to the unlikely victors in Washington's camp. The troops were hearing similar talk. The discontent received a jolt of possibility in an anonymous letter circulated in camp in mid-March, probably written by an aide to General Horatio Gates, a Washington rival. The letter played on the justified resentments of men who had sacrificed immensely in service to a nation which now seemed unwilling to reward them for their service. The document mocked Washington without naming him, encouraging the troops to "suspect the man who would advise to more moderation and longer forebearance."[2]

The anonymous correspondent urged other officers to meet the following day, March 11, to discuss what the army might do to get the attention of Congress. Washington obtained a copy of the circular, and immediately appreciated the gravity of the challenge. The officers behind the challenge were threatening mutiny—even graver, the very idea of civilian control over the military. Advocates of the challenge wanted the troops to use their influence, based on their arms, to force state governments to pay what the federal government couldn't.

Washington banned the planned meeting and scheduled his own. On March 15, 1783, a Saturday, the disgruntled officers met in a building in Newburgh called the Temple. Several generals took their places at a dais in front of the room. The most prominent soldier in the room was General Horatio Gates, the British-born Continental commander who was whispered about as a possible replacement for Washington during the dark days of late 1777 and early 1778.

It appeared that Gates would lead a full-throated venting session of the discontented until Washington himself entered the room. His presence was not expected, which made his entrance all the more dramatic. Facing a group inclined to think of him as an apologist for congressional disrespect, Washington delivered a harangue against the anonymous author and chief troublemaker. Amid Washington's characteristically baroque sentences, it is not hard to pick out notes of pure contempt for those who sought to stir up distrust and discontent.

The speech did not appear to change the looks of skepticism and even disgust on the faces of his listeners. Washington appeared to finish, but then pulled out a document from his pocket, a letter from a friendly member of Congress. The letter contained a stark explanation of the nation's perilous finances.

Washington stared at the letter. The room was silent. Finally, the commander in chief reached into a pocket again, searching for his spectacles. Nobody in the room had ever seen their seemingly invulnerable commander wearing glasses.

"Gentlemen," he said, "you will permit me to put on my spectacles, for I have not only grown gray but almost blind in the service of my country."[3]

The mood changed in an instant. Whatever their complaints, whatever their legitimate suffering, the officers knew that none of their number had risked as much, suffered as much, and had been maligned as much as the tall Virginian before them. Hardened officers wept.

Washington read the letter and left the stage. The officers decided to send a far less threatening message to Congress—after they voted to thank Washington for his advice.

▼ ▼ ▼

GENTLEMEN: By an anonymous summons, an attempt has been made to convene you together; how inconsistent with the rules of propriety! how unmilitary! and how subversive of all order and discipline, let the good sense of the Army decide.

In the moment of this summons, another anonymous production was sent into circulation, addressed more to the feelings and passions, than to the reason and judgment of the Army. The author of the piece is entitled to much credit for the goodness of his pen and I could wish he had as much credit for the rectitude of his heart, for, as men see through different optics, and are induced by the reflecting faculties of the mind, to use different means to attain the same end, the author of the address should have had more charity than to mark for suspicion the man who should recommend moderation and longer forbearance, or, in other words, who should not think as he thinks, and act as he advises. But he had another plan in view, in which candor and liberality of sentiment, regard to justice, and love of country, have no part; and he was right, to insinuate the darkest suspicion, to effect the blackest designs.

That the address is drawn with great art, and is designed to answer the most insidious purposes. That it is calculated to impress the mind with an idea of premeditated injustice in the Sovereign power of the United States, and rouse all those resentments which must unavoidably flow from such a belief. That the secret mover of this scheme (whoever he may be) intended to take advantage of the passions, while they were warmed by the recollection of past distresses, without giving time for cool, deliberative thinking, and that composure of mind which is so necessary to give dignity and stability to measures is rendered too obvious, by the mode of conducting the business, to need other proof than a reference to the proceeding.

Thus much, gentlemen, I have thought it incumbent on me to observe to you, to shew upon what principles I opposed the irregular and hasty meeting which was proposed to have been held on Tuesday last: and not because I wanted a disposition to give you every opportunity consistent with your own honor, and the dignity of the army, to make known your grievances. If my conduct heretofore has not evinced to you that I have been a faithful friend to the Army, my declaration of it at this moment would be equally unavailing and improper. But as I was among the first who embarked in the cause of our common country. As I have never left your side one moment, but when called from you on public duty. As I have been the constant companion and witness of your distresses, and not among the last to feel and acknowledge your merits. As I have ever considered my own military reputation as inseperably connected with that of the Army. As my heart has ever expanded with joy, when I have heard its praises, and my indignation has arisen, when the mouth of detraction has been opened against it, it can scarcely be supposed, at this late stage of the war, that I am indifferent to its interests. But, who are they to be promoted? The way is plain, says the anonymous addresser. If war continues, remove into the unsettled country; there establish yourselves, and leave an ungrateful country to defend itself. But how are they to defend our wives, our children, our farms, and other property which we leave behind us? Or, in this state of hostile separation, are we to take the two first (the latter cannot be removed), to perish in a wilderness, with hunger, cold and nakedness? If peace takes place, never sheath your swords says he until you have obtained full and ample justice; this dreadful alternative, of either deserting our country in the extremest hour of her distress, or turning our arms against it (which is the apparent object, unless Congress can be compelled into instant compliance), has something so shocking in it, that humanity revolts at the idea. My God! What can this writer have in view, by recommending such measures? Can he be a friend to the Army? Can he be a friend to this country? Rather, is he not an insidious foe? Some emissary, perhaps from New York, plotting the ruin of both, by sowing the seeds of discord and seperation between the civil and military powers of the continent? And what a compliment does he pay to our understandings, when he recommends measures in either alternative, impracticable in their nature?

But here, gentlemen, I will drop the curtain, because it would be as imprudent in me to assign my reasons for this opinion, as it would be insulting to your conception, to suppose you stood in need of them. A moment's reflection will convince every dispassionate mind of the physical impossibility of carrying either proposal into execution.

There might, gentlemen, be an impropriety in my taking notice, in this address to you, of an anonymous production, but the manner in which that performance has been introduced to the army, the effect it was intended to have, together with some other circumstances, will amply justify my observations on the tendency of that writing. With respect to the advice given by the author, to suspect the man who shall recommend moderate measures and longer forbearance, I spurn it, as every man who regards liberty, and reveres that justice for which we contend, undoubtedly must; for if men are to be precluded from offering their sentiments on a matter which may involve the most serious and alarming consequences that can invite the consideration of Mankind, reason is of no use to us; the freedom of speech may be taken away, and dumb and silent we may be led, like sheep, to the slaughter.

I cannot, in justice to my own belief, and what I have great reason to conceive is the intention of Congress, conclude this address, without giving it as my decided opinion, that that honorable body entertains exalted sentiments of the services of the Army; and, from a full conviction of its merits and sufferings, will do it complete justice. That their endeavors, to discover and establish funds for this purpose, have been unwearied, and will not cease till they have succeed, I have not a doubt. But, like all other large bodies, where there is a variety of different interests to reconcile, their deliberations are slow. Why then should we distrust them? and, in consequence of that distrust, adopt measures which may cast a shade over that glory which has been so justly acquired; and tarnish the reputation of an Army which is celebrated through all Europe, for its fortitude and patriotism? and for what is this done? to bring the object we seek nearer? No! most certainly, in my opinion, it will cast it at a greater distance.

For myself (and I take no merit in giving the assurance, being induced to it from principles of gratitude, veracity and justice), a grateful sense of the confidence you have ever placed in me, a recollection of the cheerful assistance, and prompt obedience I have experienced from you, under every vicissitude of fortune, and the sincere affection I feel for an Army I have so long had the honor to command, will oblige me to declare, in this public and solemn manner, that, in the attainment of complete justice for all your toils and dangers, and in the gratification of every wish, so far as may be done consistently with the great duty I owe my country, and those powers we are bound to respect, you may freely command my services to the utmost of my abilities.

While I give you these assurances, and pledge myself in the most unequivocal manner to exert whatever ability I am possessed of in your favor, let me entreat you, gentlemen, on your part, not to take any measures which, viewed in the calm light of reason, will lessen the dignity, and sully the glory, you have hitherto maintained; let me request you to rely on the plighted faith of your country, and place a full confidence in the purity of the intentions of Congress; that, previous to your dissolution as an Army they will cause all your accounts to be fairly liquidated, as directed in their resolutions, which were published to you two days ago, and that they will adopt the most effectual measures in their power to render ample justice to you, for your faithful and meritorious services. And let me conjure you, in the name of our common country, as you value your own sacred honor, as you respect the rights of humanity, and as you regard the military and national character of America, to express your utmost horror and detestation of the man who wishes, under any specious pretences, to overturn the liberties of our country, and who wickedly attempts to open the flood gates of civil discord, and deluge our rising empire in blood. By thus determining, and thus acting, you will pursue the plain and direct road to the attainment of your wishes. You will defeat the insidious designs of our enemies, who are compelled to resort from open force to secret artifice. You will give one more distinguished proof of unexampled patriotism and patient virtue, rising superior to the pressure of the most complicated sufferings; and you will, by the dignity of your conduct, afford occasion of posterity to say, when speaking of the glorious example you have exhibited to mankind, "had this day been wanting, the world had never seen the last stage of perfection to which human nature is capable of attaining."

14: Charles Fox Assails the East India Company

London, December 1, 1783

GREAT BRITAIN STILL WAS IN SHOCK OVER THE LOSS OF ITS COLONIES IN North America when Foreign Secretary Charles Fox introduced a radical and possibly revolutionary bill in the House of Commons. Fox, one of the finest speakers in an age of great English orators, sought to strip the scandal-plagued East India Company of its power, vesting authority over the company in commissioners appointed by Parliament and the Crown. The East India Company had become a symbol of imperial arrogance and incompetence, points not lost on Fox, a persistent critic of British policy in America in the 1770s. Fox moved from critic to policymaker in April 1783, as Britain conceded independence to the new United States. He and Lord North, once enemies, put together a group of Tories and Whigs to form a coalition government that ousted the Earl of Shelburne. King George III was horrified, for he had come to despise Fox, but he was powerless to prevent Fox and North from taking office.

Fox, in his role as Foreign Secretary and critic of the status quo, almost immediately assailed the center of British administration in India, the East India Company. He believed that royal patronage and sheer incompetence made the company a symbol of an old social and political order he wished to replace. In a speech on the House of Commons floor on December 1, 1783, he outlined the case against the company.

Fox's speech is very much a product of the revolutionary late eighteenth century. Government, he said, exists to enhance individual freedom. "What is the end of all government?" he asked. "Certainly the happiness of the governed." This extraordinary assertion is a variation on themes sounded in America in the 1770's, when revolutionary thinkers argued that government must have the consent of the governed, and that there existed a right a pursue happiness.

While not an anti-colonial, anti-imperial document, Fox's speech must be seen as a critique of Britain's management of its burgeoning overseas empire. Leaving imperial policy in the hands of merchants, he argued, had led to "mismanagement" and "imbecility."

It is a measure of the radical notions put forward in this speech that King George III himself announced that anybody who supported Fox's bill was an enemy of the Crown. Fox was unshaken. He took the House floor again to condemn the King's influence.

The bill passed the Commons, but was defeated in the Lords. Fox was dismissed from power, but remained a powerful, critical force in British politics into the early nineteenth century. His statement on the East India Company is an example of the ways in which radical new ideas were shaping political debate as a new century dawned.

T HE HONORABLE gentleman charges me with abandoning that cause, which, he says, in terms of flattery, I had once so successfully asserted. I tell him in reply, that if he were to search the history of my life, he would find that the period of it in which I struggled most for the real, substantial cause of liberty is this very moment I am addressing you. Freedom, according to my conception of it, consists in the safe and sacred possession of a man's property, governed by laws defined and certain; with many personal privileges, natural, civil, and religious, which he cannot surrender without ruin to himself, and of which to be deprived by any other power is despotism. This bill, instead of subverting, is destined to give stability to these principles; instead of narrowing the basis of freedom, it tends to enlarge it; instead of suppressing, its object is to infuse and circulate the spirit of liberty.

What is the most odious species of tyranny? Precisely that which this bill is meant to annihilate: that a handful of men, free themselves, should execute the most base and abominable despotism over millions of their fellow creatures; that innocence should be the victim of oppression; that industry should toil for rapine; that the harmless laborer should sweat, not for his own benefit, but for the luxury and rapacity of tyrannic depredation; in a word that thirty millions of men, gifted by Providence with the ordinary endowments of humanity, should groan under a system of despotism unmatched in all the histories of the world.

What is the end of all government? Certainly the happiness of the governed. Others may hold other opinions, but this is mine, and I proclaim it. What are we to think of a government whose good fortune is supposed to spring from the calamities of its subjects, whose aggrandizement grows out of the miseries of mankind? This is the kind of government exercised under the East India Company upon the natives of Hindustan; and the subversion of that infamous government is the main object of the bill in question. But in the progress of accomplishing this end, it is objected that the charter of the company should not be violated; and upon this point, sir, I shall deliver my opinion without disguise. A charter is a trust to one or more persons for some given benefit. If this trust be abused, if the benefit be not obtained, and its failure arise from palpable guilt, or (what in this case is fully as bad) from palpable ignorance or mismanagement, will any man gravely say that that trust should not be resumed and delivered to other hands; more especially in the case of the East India Company, whose manner of executing this trust, whose laxity and languor have produced, and tend to produce consequences diametrically opposite to the ends of confiding that trust, and of the institution for which it was granted?

I beg of gentlemen to beware of the lengths to which their arguments upon the intangibility of this charter may be carried. Every syllable virtually impeaches the establishment by which we sit in the House, in the enjoyment of this freedom and of every other blessing of our government. These kinds of arguments are batteries against the main pillar of the British Constitution. Some men are consistent of their own private opinions, and discover the inheritance of family maxims, when they question the principles of the Revolution; but I have no scruple in subscribing to the articles of that creed which produced it. Sovereigns are sacred, and reverence is due to every king; yet, with all my attachments to the person of a first magistrate, had I lived in the reign of James II, I should most certainly have contributed my efforts, and borne part in those illustrious struggles which vindicated an empire from hereditary servitude, and recorded this valuable doctrine, "that trust abused is revocable."

15: Robespierre Justifies Terror

Paris, Feb. 5, 1794

LESS THAN A DECADE AFTER ENGLISH COLONISTS IN NORTH AMERICA, ACTING in the name of republicanism and liberty, won their independence from the British crown, ordinary citizens took to the streets of Paris to demand equality, justice and an end to royal prerogative. Long-simmering divisions and tensions in France exploded in July, 1789, as mobs assailed the Bastille, a brooding fortress that came to represent the most repressive aspects of France's absolute monarchy. The Bastille fell on July 14. King Louis XVI, who, ironically enough, had supported the American rebellion against King George III, found himself at war with his subjects, who demanded the very kinds of rights the Americans had won.

Hampered by debt and a sluggish economy, the inheritor of a baroque system of privilege and patronage, Louis XVI and his queen, Marie Antoinette, became symbols of an old age that was passing, an age of deference, of absolute authority, of monarchs who claimed to rule in the name of God. Even before the fall of the Bastille, popular dissatisfaction with the King and all he symbolized inspired a confrontation in France's legislature, the Estates General. Members of the Third Estate, which represented the vast majority of the nation, demanded greater power and recognition, leading to the creation of a new legislative body, which became known as the National Constituent Assembly. Louis resisted the Assembly at first, but soon conceded its existence in an effort to staunch the spread of revolution.

When the Bastille fell, however, the spirit of rebellion spread from Paris to the countryside. The Assembly moved quickly to dismantle the prerogatives of those who benefited from the Crown's patronage and power: the Catholic Church, the nobles, and the aristocrats who aided and abetted a feudal regime. The Assembly drafted and published a document entitled the Declaration of the Rights of Man, which asserted that people, by virtue of their humanity, were entitled to rights that no government could take away. The dictates of natural law, not the whims of government, were the source of equality among men.

Power passed from the once all-powerful King to the Assembly. As the new regime progressed, with Louis still recognized as the head of state but stripped of his claim to absolute power, members of the Assembly fought over the meaning and extent of the revolution. Some supported the notion of an emasculated monarch sitting above the political fray but serving as a symbol of the nation. More radical members, however, sought the outright abolition of the crown and the establishment of a republic. Among those radicals was an eloquent attorney named Maximilian Robespierre.

Robespierre was a true believer in the virtue and purity of republicanism, the dangerous ideology which questioned the very foundations of monarchy and privilege, and which had spread from England's former colonies in America to the cafes of Paris during the last decade of the flickering eighteenth century. Like the republican Puritans of Oliver Cromwell's era, Robespierre was confident in his own righteousness and virtue. Such an attitude did not necessarily win him friends at a time when the revolution in France still was being contested in the Assembly. But what he lacked in friends he made up for in passion.

Ruthless and eloquent, he was convinced that half a revolution simply wasn't good enough. The sweeping political changes that took place after the storming of the Bastille simply weren't enough. He despised the monarchy and the privilege and entitlement it represented.

The Assembly continued to dismantle the privileges of the old regime while it wrote a new constitution. Small groups of royalists, seeing their power dwindle, agitated for a return to the old order, with the support, they hoped, of Europe's other crowned heads. Louis himself was placed under arrest along with his family in the spring of 1791 in order to prevent him from launching a counter-revolution.

Later that year, the Assembly passed a new constitution which allowed Louis to continue in office as head of state with highly limited powers. The king accepted the new order in a speech to the Assembly. But the crisis was not over. The Assembly remained badly divided, the nation's treasury was threadbare, and, in the spring of 1792, France went to war with Austria and Prussia in an Old World conflict over power and influence on the Continent. The war led to further popular discontent as France's enemies crossed the frontier and prepared to engage the revolution's army on French soil.

As the threat from abroad mounted, radicals in Paris staged a rebellion in August, 1792, and seized Louis and his wife. The famed Paris Commune took control of the capital and forced a change of government. The Assembly melted away in the face of the commune's power and determination. On September 21, 1792, a new legislative body, the Convention, formally ended the monarchy and so completed the work of the radicals. France was now a republic. Meanwhile, France's citizen army turned back the Prussian threat, preventing an expected assault on Paris.

What to do with the king now that he no longer had a role in guiding the nation? France's enemies demanded that Louis be returned to his throne. If that was the result they desired, their demands were ill-considered. France's new government came to see Louis as an enemy of the revolution and of the republic. He was executed on January 21, 1793. His wife went to the guillotine in October.

The bloodshed did not stop there. After the king and queen were executed, a Committee of Public Safety assumed supreme power in France. Robespierre was elected to the Committee and played an important role in the bloody purges and mass murders which the Committee ordered in the name of the people. The mass killings of suspected enemies of the revolution—The Reign of Terror—did not cause Robespierre a moment of regret, as he explained in the following speech from February 5, 1794. Terror, he said, is "nothing else than swift, severe, indomitable justice." In the end, terror had its origins in virtue, he said. And virtue justified any act carried out in its name.

Robespierre's cold-blooded justification for terror and violence is as chilling today, perhaps even more so, as it was when it was delivered. It is the voice of a fanatical believer in a cause, a voice not unfamiliar to twenty-first century listeners.

▼ ▼ ▼

CITIZEN-representatives of the people.
   Some time ago we set forth the principles of our foreign policy; today we come to expound the principles of our internal policy.

After having proceeded haphazardly for a long time, swept along by the movement of opposing factions, the representatives of the French people have finally demonstrated a character and a government. A sudden change in the nation's fortune announced to Europe the regeneration that had been effected in the national representation. But up to the very moment when I am speaking, it must be agreed that we have been guided, amid such stormy circumstances, by the love of good and by the awareness of our country's needs rather than by an exact theory and by precise rules of conduct, which we did not have even leisure enough to lay out.

It is time to mark clearly the goal of the revolution, and the end we want to reach; it is time for us to take account both of the obstacles that still keep us from it, and of the means we ought to adopt to attain it: a simple and important idea which seems never to have been noticed. . . .

For ourselves, we come today to make the world privy to your political secrets, so that all our country's friends can rally to the voice of reason and the public interest; so that the French nation and its representatives will be respected in all the countries of the world where the knowledge of their real principles can penetrate; so that the intriguers who seek always to replace other intriguers will be judged by sure and easy rules.

We must take far-sighted precautions to return the destiny of liberty into the hands of the truth, which is eternal, rather than into those of men, who are transitory, so that if the government forgets the interests of the people, or if it lapses into the hands of the corrupt individuals, according to the natural course of things, the light of recognized principles will illuminate their treachery, and so that every new faction will discover death in the mere thought of crime. . . .

What is the goal toward which we are heading? The peaceful enjoyment of liberty and equality; the reign of that eternal justice whose laws have been inscribed, not in marble and stone, but in the hearts of all men, even in that of the slave who forgets them and in that of the tyrant who denies them.

We seek an order of things in which all the base and cruel passions are enchained, all the beneficent and generous passions are awakened by the laws; where ambition becomes the desire to merit glory and to serve our country; where distinctions are born only of equality itself; where the citizen is subject to the magistrate, the magistrate to the people, and the people to justice; where our country assures the well-being of each individual, and where each individual proudly enjoys our country's prosperity and glory; where every soul grows greater through the continual flow of republican sentiments, and by the need of deserving the esteem of a great people; where the arts are the adornments of the liberty which ennobles them and commerce the source of public wealth rather than solely the monstrous opulence of a few families.

In our land we want to substitute morality for egotism, integrity for formal codes of honor, principles for customs, a sense of duty for one of mere propriety, the rule of reason for the tyranny of fashion, scorn of vice for scorn of the unlucky, self-respect for insolence, grandeur of soul over vanity, love of glory for the love of money, good people in place of good society. We wish to substitute merit for intrigue, genius for wit, truth for glamour, the charm of happiness for sensuous boredom, the greatness of man for the pettiness of the great, a people who are magnanimous, powerful, and happy, in place of a kindly, frivolous, and miserable people—which is to say all the virtues and all the miracles of the republic in place of all the vices and all the absurdities of the monarchy.

We want, in a word, to fulfill nature's desires, accomplish the destiny of humanity, keep the promises of philosophy, absolve providence from the long reign of crime and tyranny. Let France, formerly illustrious among the enslaved lands, eclipsing the glory of all the free peoples who have existed, become the model for the nations, the terror of oppressors, the consolation of the oppressed, the ornament of the world—and let us, in sealing our work with our blood, see at last the early dawn of the universal bliss -that is our ambition, that is our goal.

What kind of government can realize these wonders? Only a democratic or republican government—these two words are synonyms, despite the abuses in common speech, because an aristocracy is no closer than a monarchy to being a republic. . . .

Democracy is a state in which the sovereign people, guided by laws which are of their own making, do for themselves all that they can do well, and by their delegates do all that they cannot do for themselves. . . .

Now, what is the fundamental principle of popular or democratic government, that is to say, the essential mainspring which sustains it and makes it move? It is virtue. I speak of the public virtue which worked so many wonders in Greece and Rome and which ought to produce even more astonishing things in republican France—that virtue which is nothing other than the love of the nation and its law.

But as the essence of the republic or of democracy is equality, it follows that love of country necessarily embraces the love of equality. . . .

But the French are the first people of the world who have established real democracy, by calling all men to equality and full rights of citizenship; and there, in my judgment, is the true reason why all the tyrants in league against the Republic will be vanquished.

There are important consequences to be drawn immediately from the principles we have just explained.

Since the soul of the Republic is virtue, equality, and since your goal is to found, to consolidate the Republic, it follows that the first rule of your political conduct ought to be to relate all your efforts to maintaining equality and developing virtue; because the first care of the legislator ought to be to fortify the principle of the government. Thus everything that tends to excite love of country, to purify morals, to elevate souls, to direct the passions of the human heart toward the public interest, ought to be adopted or established by you. Everything which tends to concentrate them in the abjection of selfishness, to awaken enjoyment for petty things and scorn for great ones, ought to be rejected or curbed by you. Within the scheme of the French revolution, that which is immoral is impolitic, that which is corrupting is counter-revolutionary. Weakness, vice, and prejudices are the road to royalty. . . .

We deduce from all this a great truth—that the characteristic of popular government is to be trustful towards the people and severe towards itself.

Here the development of our theory would reach its limit, if you had only to steer the ship of the Republic through calm waters. But the tempest rages, and the state of the revolution in which you find yourselves imposes upon you another task. . . .

We must smother the internal and external enemies of the Republic or perish with them. Now, in this situation, the first maxim of your policy ought to be to lead the people by reason and the people's enemies by terror.

If the mainspring of popular government in peacetime is virtue, amid revolution it is at the same time [both] virtue and terror: virtue, without which terror is fatal; terror, without which virtue is impotent. Terror is nothing but prompt, severe, inflexible justice; it is therefore an emanation of virtue. It is less a special principle than a consequence of the general principle of democracy applied to our country's most pressing needs.

It has been said that terror was the mainspring of despotic government. Does your government, then, resemble a despotism? Yes, as the sword which glitters in the hands of liberty's heroes resembles the one with which tyranny's lackeys are armed. Let the despot govern his brutalized subjects by terror; he is right to do this, as a despot. Subdue liberty's enemies by terror, and you will be right, as founders of the Republic. The government of the revolution is the despotism of liberty against tyranny. Is force made only to protect crime? And is it not to strike the heads of the proud that lightning is destined? . . .

To punish the oppressors of humanity is clemency; to pardon them is barbarity. The rigor of tyrants has only rigor for a principle; the rigor of the republican government comes from charity.

Therefore, woe to those who would dare to turn against the people the terror which ought to be felt only by its enemies! Woe to those who, confusing the inevitable errors of civic conduct with the calculated errors of perfidy, or with conspirators' criminal attempts, leave the dangerous schemer to pursue the peaceful citizen! Perish the scoundrel who ventures to abuse the sacred name of liberty, or the redoubtable arms which liberty has entrusted to him, in order to bring mourning or death into patriots' hearts! This abuse has existed, one cannot doubt it. It has been exaggerated, no doubt, by the aristocracy. But if in all the Republic there existed only one virtuous man persecuted by the enemies of liberty, the government's duty would be to seek him out vigorously and give him a dazzling revenge. . . .

How frivolous it would be to regard a few victories achieved by patriotism as the end of all our dangers. Glance over our true situation. You will become aware that vigilance and energy are more necessary for you than ever. An unresponding ill-will everywhere opposes the operations of the government. The inevitable influence of foreign courts is no less active for being more hidden, and no less baneful. One senses that crime, frightened, has only covered its tracks with greater skill. . . .

You could never have imagined some of the excesses committed by hypocritical counter-revolutionaries in order to blight the cause of the revolution. Would you believe that in the regions where superstition has held the greatest sway, the counter-revolutionaries are not content with burdening religious observances under all the forms that could render them odious, but have spread terror among the people by sowing the rumor that all children under ten and all old men over seventy are going to be killed? This rumor was spread particularly through the former province of Brittany and in the departments of the Rhine and the Moselle. It is one of the crimes imputed to [Schneider,] the former public prosecutor of the criminal court of Strasbourg. That man's tyrannical follies make everything that has been said of Caligula and Heliogabalus [cruel Roman emperors] credible; one can scarcely believe it, despite the evidence. He pushed his delirium to the point of commandeering women for his own use—we are told that he even employed that method in selecting a wife. Whence came this sudden swarm of foreigners, priests, nobles, intriguers of all kinds, which at the same instant spread over the length and breadth of the Republic, seeking to execute, in the name of philosophy, a plan of counter-revolution which has only been stopped by the force of public reason? Execrable conception, worthy of the genius of foreign courts leagued against liberty, and of the corruption of all the internal enemies of the Republic! . . .

In deceitful hands all the remedies for our ills turn into poisons. Everything you can do, everything you can say, they will turn against you, even the truths which we come here to present this very day. . . .

Such an internal situation ought to seem to you worthy of all your attention, above all if you reflect that at the same time you have the tyrants of Europe to combat, a million and two hundred thousand men under arms to maintain, and that the government is obliged continually to repair, with energy and vigilance, all the injuries which the innumerable multitude of our enemies has prepared for us during the course of five years.

What is the remedy for all these evils? We know no other than the development of that general motive force of the Republic—virtue.

Democracy perishes by two kinds of excess: either the aristocracy of those who govern, or else the popular scorn for the authorities whom the people themselves have established, scorn which makes each clique, each individual take unto himself the public power and bring the people through excessive disorders, to annihilation or to the power of one man.

The double task of the moderates and the false revolutionaries is to toss us back and forth perpetually between these two perils.

But the people's representatives can avoid them both, because government is always the master at being just and wise; and, when it has that character, it is sure of the confidence of the people.

It is indeed true that the goal of all our enemies is to dissolve the Convention. It is true that the tyrant of Great Britain and his allies promise their parliament and subjects that they will deprive you of your energy and of the public confidence which you have merited; that is the first instruction for all their agents. . . .

We are beginning a solemn debate upon all the objects of its [the Convention's] anxiety, and everything that can influence the progress of the revolution. We adjure it not to permit any particular hidden interest to usurp ascendancy here over the general will of the assembly and the indestructible power of reason.

16: Georges Danton: We Must Dare, Dare Again, Always Dare

Paris, September 2, 1792

GEORGES DANTON WAS A LAWYER AND ORATOR WHO EAGERLY SIDED WITH the radicals who marched against privilege and the monarchy in France beginning in 1789. He was elected to the Paris Commune in late 1791 as the revolution took an increasingly violent turn, leading to the imprisonment of King Louis XVI. Other European nations feared that the chaos in Paris would spread, leading to mass marches in the streets of other capitals. Austria and Prussia formed an alliance to oppose the revolution, and in late summer, 1792, the two nations sent their armies eastward towards Paris even as a mass uprising finally overthrew the monarchy on August 10.

The French revolutionaries faced the possibility of war with outside powers even as they confronted counter-revolutionary forces within the nation itself. A combination of counter-revolutionary insurgency and the power of Austria and Prussia might well doom the revolution. So, when word reached Paris in late August, 1792, that the Austrians and Prussians were moving east and were besieging Verdun, some members of the Commune argued that the government ought to flee the capital.

Danton, the Minister for Justice, already had achieved fame as one of the Revolution's great spokesmen when he rose in the Assembly on September 2 to bolster the nation's morale. Unlike many of the Revolution's orators, Danton spoke extemporaneously, and what his speeches may have lacked in structure, they made up for in passion.

His goal on the morning of September 2 was to demolish the arguments of defeatists. His short speech directed his audience's attention to the siege of Verdun, which he interpreted as a test of the Revolution's zeal and determination. His tribute to the garrison at Verdun was a shot across the bow of his more nervous colleagues: "You know the garrison swears to immolate the first who breathes a proposition of surrender." So much for those who believed the government should flee Paris.

Danton's speech is a stirring call to arms to defend France's revolution from outsiders. It was a short speech, and there was no quibbling over what he might mean. "We ask that anyone refusing to give personal service or to furnish arms shall be punished with death," he said. Not much room for interpretation there.

His final, ringing sentence is engraved on his tomb, and ranks as one of the great revolutionary sound bites in Western history. Those words are engraved on his tombstone. He was put in a grave in 1794, convicted as an enemy of the very revolution he helped to save two years earlier.

▼ ▼ ▼

IT is gratifying to the ministers of a free people to have to announce to them that their country will be saved. All are stirred, all are excited, all burn to fight. You know that Verdun is not yet in the power of our enemies. You know that its garrison swears to immolate the first who breathes a proposition of surrender.

One portion of our people will proceed to the frontiers, another will throw up intrenchments, and the third with pikes will defend the hearts of our cities. Paris will second these great efforts. The commissioners of the Commune will solemnly proclaim to the citizens the invitation to arm and march to the defense of the country. At such a moment you can proclaim that the capital deserves well of all France.

At such a moment this National Assembly becomes a veritable committee of war. We ask that you concur with us in directing this sublime movement of the people, by naming commissioners who will second us in these great measures. We ask that anyone refusing to give personal service or to furnish arms shall be punished with death. We ask that a set of instructions be drawn up for the citizens to direct their movements. We ask that couriers be sent to all the departments to notify them of the decrees that you proclaim here. The tocsin we are about to ring is not an alarm signal; it sounds the charge on the enemies of our country. To conquer them we must dare, dare again, always dare, and France is saved!

17: Thomas Jefferson and the World's Best Hope

Washington, DC, March 4, 1801

THERE'S NOTHING QUITE LIKE AN OLD-FASHIONED POWER STRUGGLE TO make enemies of one-time friends, allies and comrades. In the American presidential election of 1800, John Adams against Thomas Jefferson, two men who established the intellectual framework of the American Revolution fought a bitter campaign that become a milestone in the young Republic's political maturity.

History has come to view Adams, the New England lawyer from a modest background, and Jefferson, the wealthy intellectual from Virginia, as the yin and yang of the Revolution. The short, stout Adams seemed to represent a conservative elite, while the tall, lean Jefferson emerged as champion of an egalitarian republic. Never mind that Adams's Massachusetts was a hotbed of radicalism during the 1770's, or that Jefferson's Virginia was the slave-holding capital of the Republic. The two men, collaborators in establishing the intellectual framework of the Revolution, were destined to represent the left and right of the Revolution. And their respective supporters coalesced to become the first political parties in U.S. history: the Federalists, who supported Adams, and the Republicans, who rallied behind Jefferson.

The tensions between the two men and their backers surfaced during the Presidential election of 1796, when Adams defeated Jefferson in the race to succeed George Washington. Four years later, these two iconic founders of the Republic re-engaged each other in one of the nastiest presidential campaigns in U.S. history.

Jefferson's supporters charged that the sixty-five-year-old Adams was old and senile, and that he preferred British-style monarchy and aristocratic rule. Adams's allies played the French card, associating Jefferson and his supporters with the violence and anarchy in revolutionary France. There was talk, not necessarily in whispers, that Jefferson had taken up with his female slaves.

In the early republican period, only members of the Electoral College cast ballots for president. In fact, they actually voted for two people—the candidate with the most votes became president, and the runner-up became vice-president. The election of 1800 ended in a tie, but not between Jefferson and Adams, but between Jefferson and Aaron Burr, a New York politician and onetime officer in the Continental Army. The two men had seventy-three votes. Adams finished third.

As good fortune would have it, the still-new Constitution had a formula for breaking ties. The election was thrown into the hands of the House of Representatives, where Burr's power base, a new entity known as Tammany Hall, tried to win over Federalists who despised Jefferson. But the Federalists were also bargaining with Jefferson's supporters in hopes of holding onto their jobs in a new administration. After thirty-six votes, Jefferson at last prevailed, while second-place finisher Burr became vice president.

For the first time in U.S. history, then, a sitting president was ousted from office. For the first time in U.S. history, a party in power had to surrender office to its political enemies.

The ceremonial handover from Adams to Jefferson, Federalists to Democrat-Republicans, took place on March 4, 1801. Adams chose to leave Washington, D.C., before Jefferson took office, a churlish gesture but an indication of how nasty the election had been, and how bitter the break between the two men. As he delivered his inaugural address—a custom established by Washington in 1793—Jefferson was well aware of the divisions he was inheriting.

His speech is remembered for the grace he displayed at an historic moment in U.S. history. As the first president to lead a peaceful transition of power from one faction to another, Jefferson felt obliged to remind his listeners that even if they differed on issues, in the end they were comrades, not enemies.

"We are all Republicans, we are all Federalists," he said. In an eight-word sentence, Jefferson established an essential theme of the typical inaugural address. Unity of purpose, Jefferson said, was more important than division by party. More than a century and a half later, John Kennedy said essentially the same thing when he described his inauguration as "not a triumph of party, but a celebration of freedom."

But Jefferson's speech was more than a backward-looking attempt to heal the election's wounds. It also was, in the words of historian Stephen Howard Browne, a "call for nationhood." He described the United States as "the world's best hope"—a theme that would be repeated by dozens of his successors—and expounded on America's mission to serve as a "bulwark against antirepublicanism." At stake, in Jefferson's words, was not merely the survival of a nation, but the triumph of an idea. Republican government, he said, was the "strongest Government on earth," the only one "where every man, at the call of the law, would fly to the standard . . . and would meet invasions of the public order as his own personal concern."

Jefferson's speech, then, did more than establish the unifying theme that has become part of every subsequent inaugural address. It established the United States as a defender of a new form of government.

▼ ▼ ▼

CALLED upon to undertake the duties of the first executive office of our country, I avail myself of the presence of that portion of my fellow-citizens which is here assembled to express my grateful thanks for the favor with which they have been pleased to look toward me, to declare a sincere consciousness that the task is above my talents, and that I approach it with those anxious and awful presentiments which the greatness of the charge and the weakness of my powers so justly inspire. A rising nation, spread over a wide and fruitful land, traversing all the seas with the rich productions of their industry, engaged in commerce with nations who feel power and forget right, advancing rapidly to destinies beyond the reach of mortal eye—when I contemplate these transcendent objects, and see the honor, the happiness, and the hopes of this beloved country committed to the issue and the auspices of this day, I shrink from the contemplation, and humble myself before the magnitude of the undertaking. Utterly, indeed, should I despair did not the presence of many whom I here see remind me that in the other high authorities provided by our Constitution I shall find resources of wisdom, of virtue, and of zeal on which to rely under all difficulties. To you, then, gentlemen, who are charged with the sovereign functions of legislation, and to those associated with you, I look with encouragement for that guidance and support which may enable us to steer with safety the vessel in which we are all embarked amidst the conflicting elements of a troubled world.

During the contest of opinion through which we have passed the animation of discussions and of exertions has sometimes worn an aspect which might impose on strangers unused to think freely and to speak and to write what they think; but this being now decided by the voice of the nation, announced according to the rules of the Constitution, all will, of course, arrange themselves under the will of the law, and unite in common efforts for the common good. All, too, will bear in mind this sacred principle, that though the will of the majority is in all cases to prevail, that will to be rightful must be reasonable; that the minority possess their equal rights, which equal law must protect, and to violate would be oppression. Let us, then, fellow-citizens, unite with one heart and one mind. Let us restore to social intercourse that harmony and affection without which liberty and even life itself are but dreary things. And let us reflect that, having banished from our land that religious intolerance under which mankind so long bled and suffered, we have yet gained little if we countenance a political intolerance as despotic, as wicked, and capable of as bitter and bloody persecutions. During the throes and convulsions of the ancient world, during the agonizing spasms of infuriated man, seeking through blood and slaughter his long-lost liberty, it was not wonderful that the agitation of the billows should reach even this distant and peaceful shore; that this should be more felt and feared by some and less by others, and should divide opinions as to measures of safety. But every difference of opinion is not a difference of principle. We have called by different names brethren of the same principle. We are all Republicans, we are all Federalists. If there be any among us who would wish to dissolve this Union or to change its republican form, let them stand undisturbed as monuments of the safety with which error of opinion may be tolerated where reason is left free to combat it. I know, indeed, that some honest men fear that a republican government cannot be strong, that this Government is not strong enough; but would the honest patriot, in the full tide of successful experiment, abandon a government which has so far kept us free and firm on the theoretic and visionary fear that this Government, the world's best hope, may by possibility want energy to preserve itself? I trust not. I believe this, on the contrary, the strongest Government on earth. I believe it the only one where every man, at the call of the law, would fly to the standard of the law, and would meet invasions of the public order as his own personal concern. Sometimes it is said that man cannot be trusted with the government of himself. Can he, then, be trusted with the government of others? Or have we found angels in the forms of kings to govern him? Let history answer this question.

Let us, then, with courage and confidence pursue our own Federal and Republican principles, our attachment to union and representative government. Kindly separated by nature and a wide ocean from the exterminating havoc of one quarter of the globe; too high-minded to endure the degradations of the others; possessing a chosen country, with room enough for our descendants to the thousandth and thousandth generation; entertaining a due sense of our equal right to the use of our own faculties, to the acquisitions of our own industry, to honor and confidence from our fellow-citizens, resulting not from birth, but from our actions and their sense of them; enlightened by a benign religion, professed, indeed, and practiced in various forms, yet all of them inculcating honesty, truth, temperance, gratitude, and the love of man; acknowledging and adoring an overruling Providence, which by all its dispensations proves that it delights in the happiness of man here and his greater happiness hereafter—with all these blessings, what more is necessary to make us a happy and a prosperous people? Still one thing more, fellow-citizens—a wise and frugal Government, which shall restrain men from injuring one another, shall leave them otherwise free to regulate their own pursuits of industry and improvement, and shall not take from the mouth of labor the bread it has earned. This is the sum of good government, and this is necessary to close the circle of our felicities.

About to enter, fellow-citizens, on the exercise of duties which comprehend everything dear and valuable to you, it is proper you should understand what I deem the essential principles of our Government, and consequently those which ought to shape its Administration. I will compress them within the narrowest compass they will bear, stating the general principle, but not all its limitations. Equal and exact justice to all men, of whatever state or persuasion, religious or political; peace, commerce, and honest friendship with all nations, entangling alliances with none; the support of the State governments in all their rights, as the most competent administrations for our domestic concerns and the surest bulwarks against antirepublican tendencies; the preservation of the General Government in its whole constitutional vigor, as the sheet anchor of our peace at home and safety abroad; a jealous care of the right of election by the people—a mild and safe corrective of abuses which are lopped by the sword of revolution where peaceable remedies are unprovided; absolute acquiescence in the decisions of the majority, the vital principle of republics, from which is no appeal but to force, the vital principle and immediate parent of despotism; a well-disciplined militia, our best reliance in peace and for the first moments of war till regulars may relieve them; the supremacy of the civil over the military authority; economy in the public expense, that labor may be lightly burdened; the honest payment of our debts and sacred preservation of the public faith; encouragement of agriculture, and of commerce as its hand-maid; the diffusion of information and arraignment of all abuses at the bar of the public reason; freedom of religion; freedom of the press, and free-dom of person under the protection of the habeas corpus, and trial by juries impartially selected. These principles form the bright constellation which has gone before us and guided our steps through an age of revolution and reformation. The wisdom of our sages and blood of our heroes have been devoted to their attainment. They should be the creed of our political faith, the text of civic instruction, the touchstone by which to try the services of those we trust; and should we wander from them in moments of error or of alarm, let us hasten to retrace our steps and to regain the road which alone leads to peace, liberty, and safety.

I repair, then, fellow-citizens, to the post you have assigned me. With experience enough in subordinate offices to have seen the difficulties of this the greatest of all, I have learnt to expect that it will rarely fall to the lot of imperfect man to retire from this station with the reputation and the favor which bring him into it. Without pretensions to that high confidence you reposed in our first and greatest revolutionary character, whose pre-eminent services had entitled him to the first place in his country's love and destined for him the fairest page in the volume of faithful history, I ask so much confidence only as may give firmness and effect to the legal admin-istration of your affairs. I shall often go wrong through defect of judgment. When right, I shall often be thought wrong by those whose positions will not command a view of the whole ground. I ask your indulgence for my own errors, which will never be intentional, and your support against the errors of others, who may condemn what they would not if seen in all its parts. The approbation implied by your suffrage is a great consolation to me for the past, and my future solicitude will be to retain the good opin-ion of those who have bestowed it in advance, to conciliate that of others by doing them all the good in my power, and to be instrumental to the hap-piness and freedom of all.

Relying, then, on the patronage of your good will, I advance with obe-dience to the work, ready to retire from it whenever you become sensible how much better choice it is in your power to make. And may that Infinite Power which rules the destinies of the universe lead our councils to what is best, and give them a favorable issue for your peace and prosperity.

18: Red Jacket Defends Native American Religions

Central New York: 1805

ALTHOUGH HE IS NOT FORGOTTEN IN WESTERN NEW YORK, WHERE SCHOOLS and a peninsula are named in his honor, a Seneca Indian named Red Jacket surely is one of the more-overlooked orators of the early nineteenth century.

Red Jacket's Seneca name was Segoyewatha. He was given the name "Red Jacket" because of the coat he wore—a gift from the British military for his services as an ally during the American Revolution. He was born around 1750 in the Finger Lakes region of New York, near today's small city of Geneva. The area was home to the Iroquois Confederacy, which included Red Jacket's Senecas, and was the middle ground between British-controlled Canada and the new American republic after 1783.

After the war, the Iroquois attempted to negotiate a middle ground between the Americans and British in an attempt to preserve their nations and their way of life. They produced skilled diplomats and political leaders, but none as noteworthy as Red Jacket. In 1792, Red Jacket and other Iroquois representatives met with President George Washington to discuss continued pressure on the tribes from white settlers. Washington presented Red Jacket with a medal, which he wore while sitting for a portrait several years later.

While he clearly enjoyed favorable relations with the ever-expanding American nation, Red Jacket was hardly an apologist for the encroaching white settlers. He particularly resented white efforts to convert the Iroquois to Christianity. Evangelical Baptists established a noticeable presence in central New York at the turn of the nineteenth century, a development Red Jacket denounced as little more than conquest with a gentler face.

In 1805, a missionary from Boston asked the chief's permission to evangelize among his tribe. Ever the diplomat, Red Jacket allowed the missionary to speak to a group of Senecas. After hearing him out, Red Jacket rose to reply. The skills that had made him the Cicero of the Iroquois were evident in a speech that was in turns defiant, sarcastic, lawyerly, bitter, and majestic. He spoke directly to the missionary, referring to him as "brother" and building up to a full-scale assault on the clergyman and Christianity itself.

"Brother: you say there is but one way to worship and serve the Great Spirit. If there is but one religion, why do you white people differ so much about it? Why not all agreed, as you can all read the book?"

When Red Jacket finished, the target of his eloquence stormed away, refusing to shake the chief's hand. He was not the last white man to feel the sting of Red Jacket's words. In later years, as white settlement overtook old Iroquois lands, Red Jacket delivered several other speeches in defense of native culture. The speeches were transcribed by other Senecas, and recently were collected and published in English.

Red Jacket died in 1836, an alcoholic who buried several of his children and who saw the way of life he defended slipping away.

▼ ▼ ▼

FRIEND and brother; it was the will of the Great Spirit that we should meet together this day. He orders all things, and he has given us a fine day for our council. He has taken his garment from before the sun, and caused it to shine with brightness upon us; our eyes are opened, that we see clearly; our ears are unstopped, that we have been able to hear distinctly the words that you have spoken; for all these favors we thank the Great Spirit, and him only.

Brother, this council fire was kindled by you; it was at your request that we came together at this time; we have listened with attention to what you have said. You requested us to speak our minds freely; this gives us great joy, for we now consider that we stand upright before you, and can speak what we think; all have heard your voice, and all speak to you as one man; our minds are agreed.

Brother, you say you want an answer to your talk before you leave this place. It is right you should have one, as you are a great distance from home, and we do not wish to detain you; but we will first look back a little, and tell you what our fathers have told us, and what we have heard from the white people.

Brother, listen to what we say. There was a time when our forefathers owned this great island. Their seats extended from the rising to the setting sun. The Great Spirit had made it for the use of Indians. He had created the buffalo, the deer, and other animals for food. He made the bear and the beaver, and their skins served us for clothing. He had scattered them over the country, and taught us how to take them. He had caused the earth to produce corn for bread. All this he had done for his red children because he loved them. If we had any disputes about hunting grounds, they were generally settled without the shedding of much blood. But an evil day came upon us; your forefathers crossed the great waters, and landed on this island. Their numbers were small; they found friends, and not enemies; they told us they had fled from their own country for fear of wicked men, and come here to enjoy their religion. They asked for a small seat; we took pity on them, granted their request, and they sat down amongst us; we gave them corn and meat; they gave us poison in return. The white people had now found our country; tidings were carried back, and more came amongst us; yet we did not fear them, we took them to be friends; they called us brothers; we believed them, and gave them a larger seat. At length, their numbers had greatly increased; they wanted more land; they wanted our country. Our eyes were opened, and our minds became uneasy. Wars took place; Indians were hired to fight against Indians, and many of our people were destroyed. They also brought strong liquor among us; it was strong and powerful, and has slain thousands.

Brother, our seats were once large, and yours were very small; you have now become a great people, and we have scarcely a place left to spread our blankets; you have got our country, but are not satisfied; you want to force your religion upon us.

Brother, continue to listen. You say you are sent to instruct us how to worship the Great Spirit agreeably to his mind, and if we do not take hold of the religion which you white people teach, we shall be unhappy hereafter. You say that you are right, and we are lost; how do we know this to be true? We understand that your religion is written in a book; if it was intended for us as well as you, why has not the Great Spirit given it to us, and not only to us, but why did he not give to our forefathers the knowledge of that book, with the means of understanding it rightly? We only know what you tell us about it. How shall we know when to believe, being so often deceived by the white people?

Brother, you say there is but one way to worship and serve the Great Spirit; if there is but one religion, why do you white people differ so much about it? Why not all agree, as you can all read the book?

Brother, we do not understand these things. We are told that your religion was given to your forefathers, and has been handed down from father to son. We also have a religion which was given to our forefathers, and has been handed down to us their children. We worship that way. It teacheth us to be thankful for all the favors we receive; to love each other, and to be united. We never quarrel about religion.

Brother, the Great Spirit has made us all; but he has made a great difference between his white and red children; he has given us a different complexion, and different customs; to you he has given the arts; to these he has not opened our eyes; we know these things to be true. Since he has made so great a difference between us in other things, why may we not conclude that he has given us a different religion according to our understanding. The Great Spirit does right; he knows what is best for his children; we are satisfied.

Brother, we do not wish to destroy your religion, or take it from you; we only want to enjoy our own.

Brother, you say you have not come to get our land or our money, but to enlighten our minds. I will now tell you that I have been at your meetings, and saw you collecting money from the meeting. I cannot tell what this money was intended for, but suppose it was for your minister; and if we should conform to your way of thinking, perhaps you may want some from us.

Brother, we are told that you have been preaching to the white people in this place. These people are our neighbors; we are acquainted with them; we will wait a little while and see what effect your preaching has upon them. If we find it does them good, makes them honest and less disposed to cheat Indians, we will then consider again what you have said.

Brother, you have now heard our answer to your talk, and this is all we have to say at present. As we are going to part, we will come and take you by the hand, and hope the Great Spirit will protect you on your journey, and return you safe to your friends.

19: Napoleon Bids Farewell to the Old Guard

April 20, 1814

FROM THE CHAOS OF THE FRENCH REVOLUTION ROSE AN AMBITIOUS YOUNG army officer named Napoleon Bonaparte. He seized power in 1799 in the aftermath of the Revolution's terror and counter-terror, inheriting a state that had been irrevocably changed and which heralded the beginning of a more democratic and egalitarian social order in Europe.

Napoleon is remembered today as one of the great military figures of all time, even though, like Robert E. Lee and Erwin Rommel, he lost everything in the end. But unlike Lee and Rommel, who kept themselves apart from politics, Adolf Hitler, Napoleon was a deeply political figure who believed in the ideals of French republicanism. He fought not just for the sake of conquest and empire, although he surely wished for both, but to overturn the old social order of privilege and repression.

The Old Order, of course, was not about to roll over for the radical republicans in France. A European coalition invaded France after the frightening execution of King Louis XVI , hoping to eliminate the revolutionary government and restore the monarchy in Paris. The French resisted, and in 1797, they sought to seize the offensive against their British and Austrian enemies. Napoleon Bonaparte, true believer and budding military genius, was dispatched to northern Italy to take on the mighty Austrians. His victory at the Battle of Rivoli established Napoleon as a military genius.

Europe would be in an almost constant state of war for nearly two decades. In the middle of it all was Napoleon. He raised an army, the Grande Armee, of a half-million men led by officers who represented the new French ideal of meritocratic republicanism. Gone were the officers who attained their rank through family connections or royal patronage. In their place were veterans of past campaigns who earned their promotions on the battlefield.

His army traveled with little baggage, and they carried the burden of their cause with ease. By 1805, Napoleon was master of the Continent, his eyes fixed on his enemies across the English Channel. He did not make the crossing, choosing instead to invade Russia in 1812. Tens of thousands of Russian and French soldiers paid dearly for that decision. With winter on their side, the Russians resisted Napoleon's advance, forcing him to withdraw west from Moscow, through the sites of past glories, all the way to Paris. Some 20,000 of his army of a half-million remained.

He rebuilt the army, regrouped, and set out again on campaigns, but in 1813, he lost a major battle against an alliance of Prussians, Austrians, Russians and Swedes. His enemies could not be stopped, and they captured Paris in March, 1814. Napoleon abdicated as emperor on April 6, 1814.

He was to be exiled to the island of Elba off the coast of Italy. But before he left, he met with hardened veterans of his years of campaigning, the surviving members of the officer corps that had thrilled to his early victories and shared the bitterness of his defeats. He called them the "soldiers of the Old Guard." They, like the rank and file French troops, swore by their commander, who seemed to understand the life of the common soldier but who also instilled a sense of discipline and purpose among his men.

With his officers listening with weary hearts, Napoleon delivered what he believed to be, or at least what sounded like, his farewell speech. It is a masterful small piece of self-pity ("I have sacrificed all of my interests to those of the country"), self-deprecation ("Do not regret my fate") and genuine emotion (Would I could press you all to my heart.") Precisely why they had fought for so long, Napoleon did not say, although he assured them that they surely would have won if the war had continued.

This was not, in the end, Napoleon's farewell. He would return to power ten months later. The Old Guard would be summoned to action again, Europe would again be in flames, until a final defeat at Waterloo in 1815.

▼ ▼ ▼

SOLDIERS of my Old Guard: I bid you farewell. For twenty years I have constantly accompanied you on the road to honor and glory. In these latter times, as in the days of our prosperity, you have invariably been models of courage and fidelity. With men such as you our cause could not be lost; but the war would have been interminable; it would have been civil war, and that would have entailed deeper misfortunes on France.

I have sacrificed all of my interests to those of the country.

I go, but you, my friends, will continue to serve France. Her happiness was my only thought. It will still be the object of my wishes. Do not regret my fate; if I have consented to survive, it is to serve your glory. I intend to write the history of the great achievements we have performed together. Adieu, my friends. Would I could press you all to my heart.

20: Simón Bolivar Rallies South America

Angostura, September 15, 1819

SIMÓN BOLIVAR WAS BORN IN 1783, THE YEAR WHEN REVOLUTION IN NORTH America ended with the defeat of the British empire. By the time he died in 1830, Bolivar had succeeded in bringing republican revolution to South America, overthrowing Spanish rule along the way.

Bolivar dominated South American history in the early nineteenth century just as surely as Napoleon Bonaparte dominated Europe before 1815. Like the Frenchman, Bolivar was a skilled military leader, an advocate for an idiosyncratic brand of republicanism, and a figure of historic proportions who was widely despised at the time of his death in 1830.

Ironically, Napoleon's intrigues helped fuel Bolivar's determination to rid South America, particularly his native Venezuela, of Spanish colonial rule. When Napoleon installed his brother on the throne of Spain in 1808, Bolivar joined a movement to resist and overthrow Spanish influence in the Americas. Venezuela, the land of Bolivar's birth, declared its independence from Spain in 1811CK, and Bolivar, the son of a wealthy family in Caracas, was dispatched to London as a diplomat for the rebels, hoping to achieve for Venezuela what Benjamin Franklin had won for the United States during his ministry in Paris during the American Revolution.

Diplomacy, however, was not Bolivar's forte. He turned to Venezuela within months, delivered an impassioned speech in favor of independence, and then joined the rebel army. During the ebb and flow of fighting in South America between 1811 and 1819, Bolivar fought Spanish and royalist forces throughout northern South America, earning him the nickname of "El Libertador." But Bolivar's vision for South America went beyond military victory. He saw the fight for independence as a regional and not just a national struggle. In early 1819, Bolivar, now a continental hero thanks to his military exploits, convened a congress of South American nationalists in the city of Angostura. His goal was to create a super-state consisting of today's Venezuela, Colombia, Ecuador, and Panama, to be called Gran Colombia.

On February 15, 1819, South America's most famous military commander addressed the opening of congress in Angostura. The speech outlined El Libertador's political views, which were grounded in republicanism but also reflected a healthy skepticism of the popular will. The speech also was an exploration of what it meant to be a Spanish-American. "We are not Europeans; we are not Indians; we are but a mixed species of aborigines and Spaniards," he said. That duality had consequences beyond mere personal identity. "Americans by birth and Europeans by law, we find ourselves in a dual conflict: we are disputing with the natives for titles of ownership, and at the same time we are struggling to maintain ourselves in the country that gave us birth against the opposition of the invaders." Bolivar's exposition offered a fascinating look at South American identity and its implicit contrast with North Americans. In the United States and Canada, European conquest was so complete that no leader of Bolivar's stature would have reason to refer to himself, or the nation, as a "mixed species" of aborigines and Englishmen.

Bolivar was a republican who believed his fellow South Americans would do better to imitate a British-style parliamentary system rather than the federal system of the great republic to his north. What's more, in a counter-intuitive piece of logic, he argued that a Senate based on heredity, like the British House of Lords, would be "the very soul of our republic" because it would "always oppose any attempt on the part of the people to infringe upon the jurisdiction and authority of their magistrates." In his view, the republican ideal ought "not be left to chance and the outcome of elections," a view that was not unique to Bolivar. The U.S. Constitution's provision for an Electoral College was just one example of similar skepticism of the people's will among revolutionary republicans of the late eighteenth and early nineteenth centuries.

Bolivar's speech created a sensation because of its practical ideas and theoretical framework. Months later, the Congress approved his vision for the creation of a sprawling new republic, and appointed him as its President. Gran Colombia won its independence from Spain in 1821CK, but it soon proved unwieldy and short-lived, and the man who envisioned it would be condemned as a would-be dictator before his death in 1830.

Time, however, has been kind to Bolivar. Today, he is recognized as a man whose military and political skills helped create five independent

South American nations—Bolivia, Venezuela, Colombia, Peru and Ecuador.

▼ ▼ ▼

WE are not Europeans; we are not Indians; we are but a mixed species of aborigines and Spaniards. Americans by birth and Europeans by law, we find ourselves engaged in a dual conflict: we are disputing with the natives for titles of ownership, and at the same time we are struggling to maintain ourselves in the country that gave us birth against the opposition of the invaders. Thus our position is most extraordinary and complicated. But there is more. As our role has always been strictly passive and political existence nil, we find that our quest for liberty is now even more difficult of accomplishment; for we, having been placed in a state lower than slavery, had been robbed not only of our freedom but also of the right to exercise an active domestic tyranny. . .We have been ruled more by deceit than by force, and we have been degraded more by vice than by superstition. Slavery is the daughter of darkness: an ignorant people is a blind instrument of its own destruction. Ambition and intrigue abuses the credulity and experience of men lacking all political, economic, and civic knowledge; they adopt pure illusion as reality; they take license for liberty, treachery for patriotism, and vengeance for justice. If a people, perverted by their training, succeed in achieving their liberty, they will soon lose it, for it would be of no avail to endeavor to explain to them that happiness consists in the practice of virtue; that the rule of law is more powerful than the rule of tyrants, because, as the laws are more inflexible, every one should submit to their beneficent austerity; that proper morals, and not force, are the bases of law; and that to practice justice is to practice liberty.

Although those people [North Americans], so lacking in many respects, are unique in the history of mankind, it is a marvel, I repeat, that so weak and complicated a government as the federal system has managed to govern them in the difficult and trying circumstances of their past. But, regardless of the effectiveness of this form of government with respect to North America, I must say that it has never for a moment entered my mind to compare the position and character of two states as dissimilar as the English-American and the Spanish-American. Would it not be most difficult to apply to Spain the English system of political, civil, and religious liberty? Hence, it would be even more difficult to adapt to Venezuela the laws of North America.

Nothing in our fundamental laws would have to be altered were we to adopt a legislative power similar to that held by the British Parliament. Like the North Americans, we have divided national representation into two chambers: that of Representatives and the Senate. The first is very wisely constituted. It enjoys all its proper functions, and it requires no essential revision, because the Constitution, in creating it, gave it the form and powers which the people deemed necessary in order that they might be legally and properly represented.

If the Senate were hereditary rather than elective, it would, in my opinion, be the basis, the tie, the very soul of our republic. In political storms this body would arrest the thunderbolts of the government and would repel any violent popular reaction. Devoted to the government because of a natural interest in its own preservation, a hereditary senate would always oppose any attempt on the part of the people to infringe upon the jurisdiction and authority of their magistrates. . . The creation of a hereditary senate would in no way be a violation of political equality. I do not solicit the establishment of a nobility, for as a celebrated republican has said, that would simultaneously destroy equality and liberty. What I propose is an office for which the candidates must prepare themselves, an office that demands great knowledge and the ability to acquire such knowledge. All should not be left to chance and the outcome of elections. The people are more easily deceived than is Nature perfected by art; and although these senators, it is true, would not be bred in an environment that is all virtue, it is equally true that they would be raised in an atmosphere of enlightened education. The hereditary senate will also serve as a counterweight to both government and people; and as a neutral power it will weaken the mutual attacks of these two eternally rival powers.

The British executive power possesses all the authority properly appertaining to a sovereign, but he is surrounded by a triple line of dams, barriers, and stockades. He is the head of government, but his ministers and subordinates rely more upon law than upon his authority, as they are personally responsible; and not even decrees of royal authority can exempt them from this responsibility. The executive is commander-in-chief of the army and navy; he makes peace and declares war; but Parliament annually determines what sums are to be paid to these military forces. While the courts and judges are dependent on the executive power, the laws originate in and are made by Parliament. Give Venezuela such an executive power in the person of a president chosen by the people or their representatives, and you will have taken a great step toward national happiness. No matter what citizen occupies this office, he will be aided by the Constitution, and therein being authorized to do good, he can do no harm, because his ministers will cooperate with him only insofar as he abides by the law. If he attempts to infringe upon the law, his own ministers will desert him, thereby isolating him from the Republic, and they will even bring charges against him in the Senate. The ministers, being responsible for any transgressions committed, will actually govern, since they must account for their actions.

A republican magistrate is an individual set apart from society, charged with checking the impulse of the people toward license and the propensity of judges and administrators toward abuse of the laws. He is directly subject to the legislative body, the senate, and the people: he is the one man who resists the combined pressure of the opinions, interests, and passions of the social state and who, as Carnot states, does little more than struggle constantly with the urge to dominate and the desire to escape domination. This weakness can only be corrected by a strongly rooted force. It should be strongly proportioned to meet the resistance which the executive must expect from the legislature, from the judiciary, and from the people of a republic. Unless the executive has easy access to all the administrative resources, fixed by a just distribution of powers, he inevitably becomes a nonentity or abuses his authority. By this I mean that the result will be the death of the government, whose heirs are anarchy, usurpation, and tyranny. . .

Therefore, let the entire system of government be strengthened, and let the balance of power be drawn up in such a manner that it will be permanent and incapable of decay because of its own tenuity. Precisely because no form of government is so weak as the democratic, its framework must be firmer, and its institutions must be studied to determine their degree of stability...unless this is done, we will have to reckon with an ungovernable, tumultuous, and anarchic society, not with a social order where happiness, peace, and justice prevail.

21: The Cause of Old Ireland
Daniel O'Connell's Last Monster Meeting
October 1, 1843

DANIEL O'CONNELL WAS THE FIRST ROMAN CATHOLIC ELECTED TO THE British House of Commons since the Reformation. A brilliant lawyer from County Clare, Ireland, O'Connell led a successful mass movement in the 1820s to abolish laws that kept Catholics out of public life in the United Kingdom. Until O'Connell's election, Catholics were effectively barred from the Commons, and from other civil offices, because they were required to take an oath renouncing their faith. O'Connell launched a peaceful mass movement in Ireland to demand a measure of rights for Catholics, regarded as potential traitors by Britain's Protestant ruling class. When he was elected in 1828, Britain's Prime Minister, Lord Wellington, and the King, George IV, reluctantly dropped the oath, fearing civil war if they held fast to the status quo.

O'Connell became a hero in Catholic Ireland, where he was proclaimed "the Liberator," and a villain in London, at least among the capital's bitterly anti-Catholic editors and politicians. O'Connell's eloquent denunciations of British policy in Ireland earned him the undying enmity of Britain's Tories, especially the once and future Prime Minister, Robert Peel. But O'Connell was more than an orator, fluent in both English and Irish. He was a shrewd political tactician who formed alliances with British Whigs and liberals who pledged their support for reform in Ireland in return for the support of O'Connell and other Irish-Catholic MPs who followed in his wake.

After winning a series of reforms in Ireland during the 1830s but not achieving sweeping change for Ireland's Catholics, O'Connell returned to a cause he adopted early in his tenure in the Commons but then dropped for pragmatic reasons—repeal of union between Ireland and Great Britain. Until 1801, Ireland had its own, all-Protestant Parliament in Dublin which allowed the Irish a limited form of self-government, although London exercised ultimate authority. But under the Act of Union of 1800, the Irish parliament was abolished, and Ireland was absorbed into the greater United Kingdom.

O'Connell was no republican revolutionary: he did not advocate complete independence from London. Repeal of the Union, in his view, would simply restore a measure of self-government to Ireland under the British crown. In early 1840, O'Connell announced the formation of a new mass political organization, the Repeal Association. Like O'Connell's campaign for Catholic emancipation in the 1820s, the Repeal Association mobilized the Irish masses and the power of public opinion. Almost anyone could afford to join the Association—dues were as inexpensive as a shilling a year—and hundreds of thousands did. The Repeal Association was, in some ways, a precursor to the great American political machine that was, after all, perfected by Irish-Americans. Repeal wardens organized rural villages and city neighborhoods, and headquarters churned out propaganda. Above all, there was the boss: Daniel O'Connell, the barrel-chested, golden-voiced Liberator himself.

He was elected Lord Mayor of Dublin in late 1841, the first Catholic to hold that office in a century and a half. For O'Connell, the victory foreshadowed an even greater triumph. As he took office, he told his followers, "Let them tell you, if they dare, that I won't carry the Repeal of the Union."[1] Seemingly at the height of his powers as he neared the age of seventy, O'Connell's agitation inspired several young, college-educated men and women, most of them Protestant. They called themselves Young Ireland, and they founded a newspaper called *The Nation*, which further served to arouse Ireland against the Union.

With a disciplined political organization, effective propaganda outlets and a considerable treasury, O'Connell confronted the British government with an astonishing display of mass politics. He began holding huge, open-air meetings to build support for Repeal, just as he successfully waged a peaceful revolution for Catholic Emancipation in the 1820s. The Repeal Association's ward bosses turned out Irishmen and women from the villages and parishes; Young Ireland publicized the cause among urban, middle-class readers, and together they convened for what O'Connell called with great delight, "monster meetings." And monstrous they were, attracting crowds measured in the hundreds of thousands. In the spring of 1843, London began building up troop strength in Ireland, anticipating a military confrontation with O'Connell's legions despite his insistence on non-violence. O'Connell held thirty-five meetings that attracted at least a hundred thousand people in the summer of 1843. In August, a million people—in a country of about eight million—gathered to hear (as if they all could) O'Connell speak at a meeting on the ancient Hill of Tara in County Meath, where the ancient high kings of Ireland were crowned many centuries earlier.

About two months after the meeting at Tara, with Britain poised for war, O'Connell called another mass rally, this one at Mullaghmast in County Kildare on October 1, 1843. Four hundred thousand Irish people heeded the call. O'Connell, dressed in the robes of state that accompanied his office as Lord Mayor of Dublin, delivered yet another stirring speech that recalled outrages against Ireland's Catholics without calling for violent reprisals. It was a speech filled with sentiment and emotion, hardly a lawyerly brief documenting Ireland's grievances. It was corny—"Among the nations of the earth, Ireland stands number one in the strength of her sons and in the beauty and purity of her daughters"—and sentimental, and it revealed O'Connell's style of leadership. He concluded by saying, "be obedient to me, and Ireland will be free."

His listeners, enraptured, were more than happy to obey. Ireland had not seen the likes of Daniel O'Connell in many a day.

The British government had heard enough. O'Connell scheduled another monster meeting the following week at Clontarf in County Dublin. This one, he vowed, would be the largest of all. The day before the meeting, on October 7, British Prime Minister Robert Peel banned it, declaring the proposed gathering to be an illegal assembly.

O'Connell had a choice: Call off the meeting and avoid a confrontation, or go ahead with the plan and damn the consequences. He backed down. The meeting was called off. O'Connell wanted no part of a potentially explosive and deadly confrontation.

The Repeal movement was never the same. O'Connell disappointed his young supporters, and they began to draw up plans for the sort of insurrection the Liberator wished to avoid. Soon enough, however, very little of this mattered. In 1845, a fungus developed in the potato fields of Ireland. The potato was the main food source for millions of poor Irish farmers and laborers. The crop failed, and failed again and again. When O'Connell died in 1847, tens of thousands of Irish people were starving to death, and even more were boarding ships bound for North America. The Great Famine would kill about a million people by 1852 and would send another two million people into exile.

▼ ▼ ▼

I ACCEPT with the greatest alacrity the high honor you have done me in calling me to the chair of this majestic meeting. I feel more honored than I ever did in my life, with one single exception, and that related to, if possible, an equally majestic meeting at Tara. But I must say that if a comparison were instituted between them, it would take a more discriminating eye than mine to discover any difference between them. There are the same incalculable numbers; there is the same firmness; there is the same determination; there is the same exhibition of love to old Ireland; there is the same resolution not to violate the peace; not to be guilty of the slightest outrage; not to give the enemy power by committing a crime, but peacefully and manfully to stand together in the open day, to protest before man and in the presence of God against the iniquity of continuing the Union.

At Tara I protested against the Union—I repeat the protest at Mullaghmast. I declare solemnly my thorough conviction as a constitutional lawyer, that the Union is totally void in point of principle and of constitutional force. I tell you that no portion of the empire had the power to traffic on the rights and liberties of the Irish people. The Irish people nominated them to make laws, and not legislatures. They were appointed to act under the Constitution, and not annihilate it. Their delegation from the people was confined within the limits of the Constitution, and the moment the Irish Parliament went beyond those limits and destroyed the Constitution, that moment it annihilated its own power, but could not annihilate the immortal spirit of liberty which belongs, as a rightful inheritance, to the people of Ireland. Take it, then, from me that the Union is void.

I admit there is the force of a law, because it has been supported by the policeman's truncheon, by the soldier's bayonet, and by the horseman's sword; because it is supported by the courts of law and those who have power to adjudicate in them; but I say solemnly, it is not supported by constitutional right. The Union, therefore, in my thorough conviction, is totally void, and I avail myself of this opportunity to announce to several hundreds of thousands of my fellow subjects that the Union is an unconstitutional law and that it is not fated to last long—its hour is approaching.

America offered us her sympathy and support. We refused the support, but we accepted the sympathy; and while we accepted the sympathy of the Americans, we stood upon the firm ground of the right of every human being to liberty; and I, in the name of the Irish nation, declare that no support obtained from America should be purchased by the price of abandoning principle for one moment, and that principle is that every human being is entitled to freedom.

My friends, I want nothing for the Irish but their country, and I think the Irish are competent to obtain their own country for themselves. I like to have the sympathy of every good man everywhere, but I want not armed support or physical strength from any country. The Republican party in France offered me assistance. I thanked them for their sympathy, but I distinctly refused to accept any support from them. I want support from neither France nor America, and if that usurper, Louis Philippe, who trampled on the liberties of his own gallant nation, thought fit to assail me in his newspaper, I returned the taunt with double vigor, and I denounce him to Europe and the world as a treacherous tyrant, who has violated the compact with his own country, and therefore is not fit to assist the liberties of any other country.

I want not the support of France; I want not the support of America; I have physical support enough about me to achieve any change; but you know well that it is not my plan—I will not risk the safety of one of you. I could not afford the loss of one of you—I will protect you all, and it is better for you all to be merry and alive, to enjoy the repeal of the Union; but there is not a man of you there that would not, if we were attacked unjustly and illegally, be ready to stand in the open field by my side. Let every man that concurs in that sentiment lift up his hand.

The assertion of that sentiment is our sure protection; for no person will attack us, and we will attack nobody. Indeed, it would be the height of absurdity for us to think of making any attack; for there is not one man in his senses, in Europe or America, that does not admit that the repeal of the Union is now inevitable. The English papers taunted us, and their writers laughed us to scorn; but now they admit that it is impossible to resist the application for repeal. More power to you. But that even shows we have power enough to know how to use it. Why, it is only this week that one of the leading London newspapers, called the *Morning Herald*, which had a reporter at the Lismore meeting, published an account of that great and mighty meeting, and in that account the writer expressly says that it will be impossible to refuse so peaceable, so determined, so unanimous a people as the people of Ireland the restoration of their domestic legislature.

For my own part, I would have thought it wholly unnecessary to call together so large a meeting as this, but for the trick played by Wellington, and Peel, and Graham, and Stanley, and the rest of the paltry administration, by whose government this country is disgraced. I do not suppose so worthless an administration ever before got together. Lord Stanley is a renegade from Whiggism, and Sir James Graham is worse. Sir Robert Peel has five hundred colors on his bad standard, and not one of them is permanent. Today it is orange, tomorrow it will be green, the day after neither one nor the other, but we shall take care that it shall never be dyed in blood.

Then there is the poor old Duke of Wellington, and nothing was ever so absurd as their deification of him in England. The English historian—rather the Scotch one—Alison, an arrant Tory, admits that the Duke of Wellington was surprised at Waterloo, and if he got victoriously out of that battle, it was owing to the valor of the British troops and their unconquerable determination to die, but not to yield. No man is ever a good soldier but the man who goes into the battle determined to conquer or not come back from the battle-field. No other principle makes a good soldier; conquer or die is the battle-cry for the good soldier; conquer or die is his only security. The Duke of Wellington had troops at Waterloo that had learned that word, and there were Irish troops among them. You all remember the verses made by poor Shan Van Vocht:

> "At famed Waterloo
> Duke Wellington would look blue
> If Paddy was not there too,
> Says the Shan Van Vocht."

Yes, the glory he got there was bought by the blood of the English, Irish, and Scotch soldiers—the glory was yours. He is nominally a member of the administration, but yet they would not intrust him with any kind of office. He has no duty at all to perform, but as a sort of Irish antirepeal warden. I thought I never would be obliged to the ministry, but I am obliged to them. They put a speech abusing the Irish into the queen's mouth. They accused us of disaffection, but they lied; it is their speech; there is no disaffection in Ireland. We were loyal to the sovereigns of Great Britain, even when they were our enemies; we were loyal to George III, even when he betrayed us; we were loyal to George IV when he blubbered and cried when we forced him to emancipate us; we were loyal to old Billy, though his minister put into his mouth a base, bloody, and intolerant speech against Ireland; and we are loyal to the queen, no matter what our enemies may say to the contrary. It is not the queen's speech, and I pronounce it to be a lie.

There is no dissatisfaction in Ireland, but there is this—a full determination to obtain justice and liberty. I am much obliged to the ministry for that speech, for it gives me, among other things, an opportunity of addressing such meetings as this. I had held the monster meetings. I had fully demonstrated the opinion of Ireland. I was convinced their unanimous determination to obtain liberty was sufficiently signified by the many meetings already held; but when the minister's speech came out, it was necessary to do something more. Accordingly, I called a monster meeting at Loughrea. I called another meeting in Cliffden. I had another monster meeting in Lismore, and here now we are assembled on the Rath of Mullaghmast.

O my friends, I will keep you clear of all treachery—there shall be no bargain, no compromise with England—we shall take nothing but repeal, and a Parliament in College Green. You will never, by my advice, confide in any false hopes they hold out to you; never confide in anything coming from them, or cease from your struggle, no matter what promise may be held to you, until you hear me say I am satisfied; and I will tell you where I will say that—near the statue of King William, in College Green. No; we came here to express our determination to die to a man, if necessary, in the cause of old Ireland. We came to take advice of each other, and, above all, I believe you came here to take my advice. I can tell you, I have the game in my hand—I have the triumph secure—I have the repeal certain, if you but obey my advice.

I will go slow—you must allow me to do so—but you will go sure. No man shall find himself imprisoned or persecuted who follows my advice. I have led you thus far in safety; I have swelled the multitude of repealers until they are identified with the entire population, or nearly the entire population, of the land, for seven-eighths of the Irish people are now enrolling themselves repealers. I do not want more power; I have power enough; and all I ask of you is to allow me to use it. I will go on quietly and slowly, but I will go on firmly, and with a certainty of success. I am now arranging a plan for the formation of the Irish House of Commons.

It is a theory, but it is a theory that may be realized in three weeks. The repeal arbitrators are beginning to act; the people are submitting their differences to men chosen by themselves. You will see by the newspapers that Doctor Gray and my son, and other gentlemen, have already held a petty session of their own, where justice will be administered free of all expense to the people. The people shall have chosen magistrates of their own in the room of the magistrates who have been removed. The people shall submit their differences to them, and shall have strict justice administered to them that shall not cost them a single farthing. I shall go on with that plan until we have all the disputes settled and decided by justices appointed by the people themselves.

I wish to live long enough to have perfect justice administered to Ireland, and liberty proclaimed throughout the land. It will take me some time to prepare my plan for the formation of the new Irish House of Commons—that plan which we will yet submit to her majesty for her approval when she gets rid of her present paltry administration and has one that I can support. But I must finish that job before I go forth, and one of my reasons for calling you together is to state my intentions to you. Before I arrange my plan, the Conciliation Hall will be finished, and it will be worth any man's while to go from Mullaghmast to Dublin to see it.

When we have it arranged I will call together three hundred, as the *Times* called them, "bogtrotters," but better men never stepped on pavement. But I will have the three hundred, and no thanks to them. Wales is up at present, almost in a state of insurrection. The people there have found that the landlords' power is too great, and has been used tyrannically, and I believe you agree with them tolerably well in that. They insist on the sacredness of the right of the tenants to security of possession, and with the equity of tenure which I would establish we will do the landlords full justice, but we will do the people justice also. We will recollect that the land is the landlord's, and let him have the benefit of it, but we will also recollect that the labor belongs to the tenant, and the tenant must have the value of his labor, not transitory and by the day, but permanently and by the year.

Yes, my friends, for this purpose I must get some time. I worked the present repeal year tolerably well. I believe no one in January last would believe that we could have such a meeting within the year as the Tara demonstration. You may be sure of this—and I say it in the presence of Him who will judge me—that I never will wilfully deceive you. I have but one wish under heaven, and that is for the liberty and prosperity of Ireland. I am for leaving England to the English, Scotland to the Scotch; but we must have Ireland for the Irish. I will not be content until I see not a single man in any office, from the lowest constable to the lord chancellor, but Irishmen. This is our land, and we must have it. We will be obedient to the queen, joined to England by the golden link of the Crown, but we must have our own Parliament, our own bench, our own magistrates, and we will give some of the shoneens who now occupy the bench leave to retire, such as those lately appointed by Sugden. He is a pretty boy, sent here from England; but I ask: Did you ever hear such a name as he has got? I remember, in Wexford, a man told me he had a pig at home which he was so fond of that he would call it Sugden. No; we shall get judicial independence for Ireland. It is for this purpose we are assembled here today, as every countenance I see around me testifies. If there is anyone here who is for the Union, let him say so. Is there anybody here for the repeal? [Cries of "All, all!"]

Yes, my friends, the Union was begot in iniquity—it was perpetuated in fraud and cruelty. It was no compact, no bargain, but it was an act of the most decided tyranny and corruption that was ever yet perpetrated. Trial by jury was suspended—the right of personal protection was at an end—courts-martial sat throughout the land—and the County of Kildare, among others, flowed with blood. We shall stand peaceably side by side in the face of every enemy. Oh, how delighted was I in the scenes which I witnessed as I came along here today! How my heart throbbed, how my spirit was elevated, how my bosom swelled with delight at the multitude which I beheld, and which I shall behold, of the stalwart and strong men of Kildare! I was delighted at the activity and force that I saw around me, and my old heart grew warm again in admiring the beauty of the dark-eyed maids and matrons of Kildare. Oh, there is a starlight sparkling from the eye of a Kildare beauty that is scarcely equaled, and could not be excelled, all over the world. And remember that you are the sons, the fathers, the brothers, and the husbands of such women, and a traitor or a coward could never be connected with any of them. Yes, I am in a county, remarkable in the history of Ireland for its bravery and its misfortune, for its credulity in the faith of others, for its people judged of the Saxon by the honesty and honor of their own natures. I am in a county celebrated for the sacredness of shrines and fanes. I am in a county where the lamp of Kildare's holy shrine burned with its sacred fire, through ages of darkness and storm—that fire which for six centuries burned before the high altar without being extinguished, being fed continuously, without the slightest interruption, and it seemed to me to have been not an inapt representation of the continuous fidelity and religious love of country of the men of Kildare.

Yes, you have those high qualities—religious fidelity, continuous love of country. Even your enemies admit that the world has never produced any people that exceeded the Irish in activity and strength. The Scottish philosopher has declared, and the French philosopher has confirmed it, that number one in the human race is, blessed be Heaven, the Irishman. In moral virtue, in religion, in perseverance, and in glorious temperance, you excel. Have I any teetotalers here? Yes, it is teetotalism that is repealing the Union. I could not afford to bring you together, I would not dare to bring you together, but that I had the teetotalers for my police.

Yes, among the nations of the earth, Ireland stands number one in the physical strength of her sons and in the beauty and purity of her daughters. Ireland, land of my forefathers, how my mind expands, and my spirit walks abroad in something of majesty, when I contemplate the high qualities, inestimable virtues, and true purity and piety and religious fidelity of the inhabitants of your green fields and productive mountains. Oh, what a scene surrounds us! It is not only the countless thousands of brave and active and peaceable and religious men that are here assembled, but Nature herself has written her character with the finest beauty in the verdant plains that surround us.

Let any man run around the horizon with his eye, and tell me if created nature ever produced anything so green and so lovely, so undulating, so teeming with production. The richest harvests that any land can produce are those reaped in Ireland; and then here are the sweetest meadows, the greenest fields, the loftiest mountains, the purest streams, the noblest rivers, the most capacious harbors—and her water power is equal to turn the machinery of the whole world. O my friends, it is a country worth fighting for—it is a country worth dying for; but, above all, it is a country worth being tranquil, determined, submissive, and docile for; disciplined as you are in obedience to those who are breaking the way, and trampling down the barriers between you and your constitutional liberty, I will see every man of you having a vote, and every man protected by the ballot from the agent or landlord. I will see labor protected, and every title to possession recognized, when you are industrious and honest. I will see prosperity again throughout your land—the busy hum of the shuttle and the tinkling of the smithy shall be heard again. We shall see the nailer employed even until the middle of the night, and the carpenter covering himself with his chips. I will see prosperity in all its gradations spreading through a happy, contented, religious land. I will hear the hymn of a happy people go forth at sunrise to God in praise of His mercies—and I will see the evening sun set down among the uplifted hands of a religious and free population. Every blessing that man can bestow and religion can confer upon the faithful heart shall spread throughout the land. Stand by me—join with me—I will say be obedient to me, and Ireland shall be free.

22: Karl Marx on Free Trade

Brussels, January 9, 1848

REVOLUTIONS ENGULFED EUROPE AND THE EUROPEAN PSYCHE IN 1848. Italy, France, Poland, Hungary, the German states, and Ireland saw uprisings against established orders, and while the results were mixed, the challenge to the continent's ruling elites was unmistakable.

Not coincidentally, the year also saw publication of Karl Marx's and Engels' book, *The Communist Manifesto*, published in German in February. Marx's ideology of class conflict provided an ideological context for the popular rebellions against Europe's economic and political hierarchies.

Just weeks before the *Manifesto* appeared, Marx, twenty-eight years old at the time and already known for his radicalism and brilliance, was scheduled to speak in Brussels to a group of advocates for free trade. Dominated by English industrialists, the Free Trade Congress opposed Europe's dogmatic embrace of protective tariffs which, they argued, protected the interests of landed aristocrats at the expense of the growing legions of workers in Europe's cities.

The free trade movement won an unexpected victory two years earlier, when Britain repealed protective legislation known as the Corn Laws, which levied high taxes on imported corn and grain. The measures ensured that Britain's wealthy landlords could command artificially high prices for their grain without fear of being undercut by foreign competition. Agitation against the Corn Laws began in the late 1830s and won the support of the opposition Whig Party in Parliament. The Conservatives, with their core constituency of landlords and their rural power base, resisted the movement, charging that industrialists wanted cheaper food so they could pay their workers less. Ironically, the radical Chartist movement agreed with the Conservative analysis.

The conflict reached a climax in late 1845, when a potato blight in Ireland threatened the island with mass starvation. Conservative Prime Minister Robert Peel announced for repeal, shocking his party and setting in motion a political cataclysm. The government fell, but when the opposition Whigs could not put together a government, Peel returned to office and rammed through a bill abolishing the Corn Laws. It was a bitter victory, however. Peel resigned shortly after the bill passed in May, 1846.

The collapse of the Corn Laws in Britain was an important moment not only in Britain itself, where abolition created a first-rate political crisis, but in Europe as well. Britain's subsequent prosperity was attributed to its free-trade policies, although other European nations were reluctant to import Britain's new ideas.

A group of British Members of Parliament, economists, and journalists traveled to Brussels in late 1847 to join Continental converts to free trade to agitate for the removal of protective tariffs. Among those observing the proceedings was a German journalist named Frederick Engels, who was less than entertained as the various luminaries made the case for free trade. "I can assure you," he wrote, "never did I hear such dull, tedious, trivial stuff," he wrote. He was more impressed when one speaker, Georg Weerth of Prussia, noted that while free traders insisted that their policies would benefit working people, no workers were present to offer such testimony. Engels agreed with the speaker's contention that while free trade was better than protection, it only led to more competition, which would "never change" the "miserable condition" of workers.[1]

Weerth's speech met with something less than universal enthusiasm. The enthusiasts decided that their spirits would not be improved if they allowed another invited speaker, Karl Marx, to weigh in on the subject. Advocates spoke at length until the meeting adjourned without hearing from Marx.

Frustrated but determined, Marx persuaded a Belgian newspaper to publish his speech, which complemented Weerth's critique of free trade, except that Marx saw free trade as a step towards "the emancipation of the proletariat."[2] Free trade, he believed, would break up nationalities and increase class tensions, leading inevitably to the liberation of the world's workers. Publication of the speech prompted an invitation from the Democratic Association, a radical association in which Marx was active. He finally delivered the speech on January 9, 1848, in Brussels. It was, in a sense, the inaugural address of the Year of Revolution. A month later, *The Communist Manifesto* appeared on bookshelves in Europe.

▼ ▼ ▼

GENTLEMEN,

The Repeal of the Corn Laws in England is the greatest triumph of free trade in the nineteenth century. In every country where manufacturers talk of free trade, they have in mind chiefly free trade in corn and raw materials in general. To impose protective duties on foreign corn is infamous, it is to speculate on the famine of peoples.

Cheap food, high wages, this is the sole aim for which English free-traders have spent millions, and their enthusiasm has already spread to their brethren on the Continent. Generally speaking, those who wish for free trade desire it in order to alleviate the condition of the working class.

But, strange to say, the people for whom cheap food is to be procured at all costs are very ungrateful. Cheap food is as ill-esteemed in England as cheap government is in France. The people see in these self-sacrificing gentlemen, in Bowring, Bright and Co., their worst enemies and the most shameless hypocrites.

Everyone knows that in England the struggle between Liberals and Democrats takes the name of the struggle between Free-Traders and Chartists.

Let us now see how the English free-traders have proved to the people the good intentions that animate them.

This is what they said to the factory workers:

"The duty levied on corn is a tax upon wages; this tax you pay to the landlords, those medieval aristocrats; if your position is wretched one, it is on account of the dearness of the immediate necessities of life."

The workers in turn asked the manufacturers:

"How is it that in the course of the last thirty years, while our industry has undergone the greatest development, our wages have fallen far more rapidly, in proportion, than the price of corn has gone up?

"The tax which you say we pay the landlords is about 3 pence a week per worker. And yet the wages of the hand-loom weaver fell, between 1815 and 1843, from 28s. per week to 5s., and the wages of the power-loom weavers, between 1823 and 1843, from 20s. per week to 8s.

"And during the whole of this period that portion of the tax which we paid to the landlord has never exceeded 3 pence. And then in the year 1834, when bread was very cheap and business going on very well, what did you tell us? You said, 'If you are unfortunate, it is because you have too many children, and your marriages are more productive than your labor!'

"These are the very words you spoke to us, and you set about making new Poor Laws, and building work-houses, the Bastilles of the proletariat."

To this the manufacturer replied:

"You are right, worthy laborers; it is not the price of corn alone, but competition of the hands among themselves as well, which determined wages.

"But ponder well one thing, namely, that our soil consists only of rocks and sandbanks. You surely do not imagine that corn can be grown in flowerpots. So if, instead of lavishing our capital and our labor upon a thoroughly sterile soil, we were to give up agriculture, and devote ourselves exclusively to industry, all Europe would abandon its factories, and England would form one huge factory town, with the whole of the rest of Europe for its countryside."

While thus haranguing his own workingmen, the manufacturer is interrogated by the small trader, who says to him:

"If we repeal the Corn Laws, we shall indeed ruin agriculture; but for all that, we shall not compel other nations to give up their own factories and buy from ours.

"What will the consequence be? I shall lose the customers that I have at present in the country, and the home trade will lose its market."

The manufacturer, turning his back upon the workers, replies to the shopkeeper:

"As to that, you leave it to us! Once rid of the duty on corn, we shall import cheaper corn from abroad. Then we shall reduce wages at the very time when they rise in the countries where we get out corn.

"Thus in addition to the advantages which we already enjoy we shall also have that of lower wages and, with all these advantage, we shall easily force the Continent to buy from us."

But now the farmers and agricultural laborers join in the discussion.

"And what, pray, is to become of us?

"Are we going to pass a sentence of death upon agriculture, from which we get our living? Are we to allow the soil to be torn from beneath our feet?"

As its whole answer, the Anti-Corn Law League has contented itself with offering prizes for the three best essays upon the wholesome influence of the repeal of the Corn Laws on English agriculture.

These prizes were carried off by Messrs. Hope, Morse, and Greg, whose essays were distributed in thousands of copies throughout the countryside.

The first of the prize-winners devotes himself to proving that neither the tenant farmer nor the agricultural laborer will lose by the free importation of foreign corn, but only the landlord.

"The English tenant farmer," he exclaims, "need not fear the repeal of the Corn Laws, because no other country can produce such good corn so cheaply as England.

"Thus, even if the price of corn fell, it would not hurt you, because this fall would only affect rent, which would go down, and not at all industrial profit and wages, which would remain stationary."

The second prize-winner, Mr. Morse, maintains, on the contrary, that the price of corn will rise in consequence of repeal. He takes infinite pains to prove that protective duties have never been able to secure a remunerative price for corn.

In support for his assertion, he cites the fact that, whenever foreign corn has been imported, the price of corn in England has gone up considerably, and then when little corn has been imported, the price has fallen extremely. This prize-winner forgets that the importation was not the cause of the high price, but that the high price was the cause of the importation.

And in direct contradiction to his co-prize-winner, he asserts that every rise in the price of corn is profitable to both the tenant farmer and the laborer, but not to the landlord.

The third prize-winner, Mr. Greg, who is a big manufacturer and whose work is addressed to the large tenant farmers, could not hold with such stupidities. His language is more scientific.

He admits that the Corn Laws can raise rent only by raising the price of corn, and that they can raise the price of corn only by compelling capital to apply itself to land of inferior quality, and this is explained quite simply.

In proportion as population increases, if foreign corn cannot be imported, less fertile soil has to be used, the cultivation of which involves more expense and the product of this soil is consequently dearer.

There being a forced sale for corn, the price will of necessity be determined by the price of the product of the most costly soil. The difference between this price and the cost of production upon soil of better quality constitutes the rent.

If, therefore, as a result of the repeal of the Corn Laws, the price of corn, and consequently the rent, falls, it is because inferior soil will no longer be cultivated. Thus, the reduction of rent must inevitably ruin a part of the tenant farmers.

These remarks were necessary in order to make Mr. Greg's language comprehensible.

"The small farmers," he says, "who cannot support themselves by agriculture will find a resource in industry. As to the large tenant farmers, they cannot fail to profit. Either the landlords will be obliged to sell them land very cheap, or leases will be made out for very long periods. This will enable tenant farmers to apply large sums of capital to the land, to use agricultural machinery on a larger scale, and to save manual labor, which will, moreover, be cheaper, on account of the general fall in wages, the immediate consequences of the repeal of the Corn Laws."

Dr. Browning conferred upon all these arguments the consecration of religion, by exclaiming at a public meeting,

"Jesus Christ is Free Trade, and Free Trade is Jesus Christ."

One can understand that all this hypocrisy was not calculated to make cheap bread attractive to the workers.

Besides, how could the workingman understand the sudden philanthropy of the manufacturers, the very men still busy fighting against the Ten Hours' Bill, which was to reduce the working day of the mill hands from 12 hours to 10?

To give you an idea of the philanthropy of these manufacturers I would remind you, gentlemen, of the factory regulations in force in all the mills.

Every manufacturer has for his own private use a regular penal code in which fines are laid down for every voluntary or involuntary offence. For instance, the worker pays so much if he has the misfortune to sit down on a chair; if he whispers, or speaks, or laughs; if he arrives a few moments too late; if any part of the machine breaks, or he does not turn out work of the quality desired, etc., etc. The fines are always greater than the damage really done by the worker. And to give the worker every opportunity for incurring fines, the factory clock is set forward, and he is given bad raw material to make into good pieces of stuff. An overseer not sufficiently skillful in multiplying cases of infractions or rules is discharged.

You see, gentlemen, this private legislation is enacted for the especial purpose of creating such infractions, and infractions are manufactured for the purpose of making money. Thus the manufacturer uses every means of reducing the nominal wage, and of profiting even by accidents over which the worker has no control.

These manufacturers are the same philanthropists who have tried to make the workers believe that they were capable of going to immense expense for the sole purpose of ameliorating their lot. Thus, on the one hand, they nibble at the wages of the worker in the pettiest way, by means of factory regulations, and, on the other, they are undertaking the greatest sacrifices to raise those wages again by means of the Anti-Corn Law League.

They build great palaces at immense expense, in which the League takes up, in some respects, its official residence; they send an army of missionaries to all corners of England to preach the gospel of free trade; they have printed and distributed gratis thousands of pamphlets to enlighten the worker upon his own interests, they spend enormous sums to make the press favorable to their cause; they organize a vast administrative system for the conduct of the free trade movement, and they display all their wealth of eloquence at public meetings. It was at one of these meetings that a worker cried out:

"If the landlords were to sell our bones, you manufacturers would be the first to buy them in order to put them through a steam-mill and make flour of them."

The English workers have very well understood the significance of the struggle between the landlords and the industrial capitalists. They know very well that the price of bread was to be reduced in order to reduce wages, and that industrial profit would rise by as much as rent fell.

Ricardo, the apostle of the English free-traders, the most eminent economist of our century, entirely agrees with the workers upon this point. In his celebrated work on political economy, he says:

"If instead of growing our own corn... we discover a new market from which we can supply ourselves... at a cheaper price, wages will fall and profits rise. The fall in the price of agricultural produce reduces the wages, not only of the laborer employed in cultivating the soil, but also of all those employed in commerce or manufacture."

And do not believe, gentlemen, that it is a matter of indifference to the worker whether he receives only four francs on account of corn being cheaper, when he had been receiving five francs before.

Have not his wages always fallen in comparison with profit, and is it not clear that his social position has grown worse as compared with that of the capitalist? Besides which he loses more as a matter of fact.

So long as the price of corn was higher and wages were also higher, a small saving in the consumption of bread sufficed to procure him other enjoyments. But as soon as bread is very cheap, and wages are therefore very cheap, he can save almost nothing on bread for the purchase of other articles.

The English workers have made the English free-traders realize that they are not the dupes of their illusions or of their lies; and if, in spite of this, the workers made common cause with them against the landlords, it was for the purpose of destroying the last remnants of feudalism and in order to have only one enemy left to deal with. The workers have not miscalculated, for the landlords, in order to revenge themselves upon the manufacturers, made common cause with the workers to carry the Ten Hours' Bill, which the latter had been vainly demanding for thirty years, and which was passed immediately after the repeal of the Corn Laws.

When Dr. Bowring, at the Congress of Economists, drew from his pocket a long list to show how many head of cattle, how much ham, bacon, poultry, etc., was imported into England, to be consumed, as he asserted, by the workers, he unfortunately forgot to tell you that all the time the workers of Manchester and other factory towns were finding themselves thrown into the streets by the crisis which was beginning.

As a matter of principle in political economy, the figures of a single year must never be taken as the basis for formulating general laws. One must always take the average period of from six to seven years—a period of time during which modern industry passes through the various phases of prosperity, overproduction, stagnation, crisis, and completes its inevitable cycle.

Doubtless, if the price of all commodities falls—and this is the necessary consequence of free trade—I can buy far more for a franc than before. And the worker's france is as good as any other man's. Therefore, free trade will be very advantageous to the worker. There is only one little difficulty in this, namely, that the worker, before he exchanges his franc for other commodities, has first exchanged his labor with the capitalist. If in this exchange he always received the said franc for the same labor and the price of all other commodities fell, he would always be the gainer by such a bargain. The difficult point does not lie in proving that, if the price of all commodities falls, I will get more commodities for the same money.

Economists always take the price of labor at the moment of its exchange with other commodities. But they altogether ignore the moment at which labor accomplishes its own exchange with capital.

When less expense is required to set in motion the machine which produces commodities, the things necessary for the maintenance of this machine, called a worker, will also cost less. If all commodities are cheaper, labor, which is a commodity too, will also fall in price, and, as we shall see later, this commodity, labor, will fall far lower in proportion than the other commodities. If the worker still pins his faith to the arguments of the economists, he will find that the franc has melted away in his pocket, and that he has only 5 sous left.

Thereupon the economists will tell you:

"Well, we admit that competition among the workers, which will certainly not have diminished under free trade, will very soon bring wages into harm, only with the low price of commodities. But, on the other hand, the low price of commodities will increase consumption, the larger consumption will require increased production, which will be followed by a larger demand for hands, and this larger demand for hands will be followed by a rise in wages."

The whole line of argument amounts to this: Free trade increases productive forces. If industry keeps growing, if wealth, if the productive power, if, in a word, productive capital increases, the demand for labor, the price of labor, and consequently the rate of wages, rise also.

The most favorable condition for the worker is the growth of capital. This must be admitted. If capital remains stationary, industry will not merely remain stationary but will decline, and in this case the worker will be the first victim. He goes to the wall before the capitalist. And in the case where capital keeps growing, in the circumstances which we have said are the best for the worker, what will be his lot? He will go to the wall just the same. The growth of productive capital implies the accumulation and the concentration of capital. The centralization of capital involves a greater division of labor and a greater use of machinery. The greater division of labor destroys the especial skill of the laborer; and by putting in the place of this skilled work labor which anybody can perform, it increase competition among the workers.

This competition becomes fiercer as the division of labor enables a single worker to do the work of three. Machinery accomplishes the same result on a much larger scale. The growth of productive capital, which forces the industrial capitalists to work with constantly increasing means, ruins the small industrialists and throws them into the proletariat. Then, the rate of interest falling in proportion as capital accumulates, the small rentiers, who can no longer live on their dividends, are forced to go into industry and thus swell the number of proletarians.

Finally, the more productive capital increases, the more it is compelled to produce for a market whose requirements it does not know, the more production precedes consumption, the more supply tries to force demand, and consumption crises increase in frequency and in intensity. But every crisis in turn hastens the centralization of capital and adds to the proletariat.

Thus, as productive capital grows, competition among the workers grows in a far greater proportion. The reward of labor diminishes for all, and the burden of labor increases for some.

In 1829, there were in Manchester 1,088 cotton spinners employed in 36 factories. In 1841, there were no more than 448, and they tended 53,353 more spindles than the 1,088 spinners did in 1829. If manual labor had increased in the same proportion as the productive power, the number of spinners ought to have reached the figure of 1,848; improved machinery had, therefore, deprived 1,400 workers of employment.

We know beforehand the reply of the economists. The men thus deprived of work, they say, will find other kinds of employment. Dr. Bowring did not fail to reproduce this argument at the Congress of Economists, but neither did he fail to supply his own refutation.

In 1835, Dr. Bowring made a speech in the House of Commons upon the 50,000 hand-loom weavers of London who for a very long time had been starving without being able to find that new kind of employment which the free-traders hold out to them in the distance.

We will give the most striking passages of this speech of Dr. Bowring:

"This distress of the weavers... is an incredible condition of a species of labor easily learned—and constantly intruded on and superseded by cheaper means of production. A very short cessation of demand, where the competition for work is so great . . . produces a crisis. The hand-loom weavers are on the verge of that state beyond which human existence can hardly be sustained, and a very trifling check hurls them into the regions of starvation. . . . The improvements of machinery . . . by superseding manual labor more and more, infallibly bring with them in the transition much of temporary suffering. . . . The national good cannot be purchased but at the expense of some individual evil. No advance was ever made in manufactures but at some cost to those who are in the rear; and of all discoveries, the power-loom is that which most directly bears on the condition of the hand-loom weaver. He is already beaten out of the field in many articles; he will infallibly be compelled to surrender many more."

Further on he says:

"I hold in my hand the correspondence which has taken place between the Governor-General of India and the East India Company, on the subject of the Dacca hand-loom weavers. . . . Some years ago the East India Company annually received of the produce of the looms of India to the amount of from 6,000,000 to 8,000,000 of pieces of cotton goods. The demand gradually fell to somewhat more than 1,000,000, and has now nearly ceased altogether. In 1800, the United States took from India nearly 800,000 pieces of cotton; in 1830, not 4,000. In 1800, 1,000,000 pieces were shipped to Portugal; in 1830, only 20,000. Terrible were the accounts of the wretchedness of the poor Indian weavers, reduced to absolute starvation. And what was the sole cause? The presence of the cheaper English manufacture. . . . Numbers of them died of hunger, the remainder were, for the most part, transferred to other occupations, principally agricultural. Not to have changed their trade was inevitable starvation. And at this moment that Dacca district is supplied with yarn and cotton cloth from the power-looms of England. . . . The Dacca muslins, celebrated over the whole world for their beauty and fineness, are also annihilated from the same cause. And the present suffering, to numerous classes in India, is scarcely to be paralleled in the history of commerce."[3]

Dr. Bowring's speech is the more remarkable because the facts quoted by him are exact, and the phrases with which he seeks to palliate them are wholly characterized by the hypocrisy common to all free trade sermons. He represents the workers as means of production which must be superseded by less expensive means of production. He pretends to see in the labor of which he speaks a wholly exceptional kind of labor, and in the machine which has crushed out the weavers an equally exceptional machine. He forgets that there is no kind of manual labor which may not any day be subjected to the fate of the hand-loom weavers.

"It is, in fact, the constant aim and tendency of every improvement in machine to supersede human labor altogether, or to diminish its cost by substituting the industry of women and children for that of men; or that of ordinary laborers for trained artisans. In most of the water-twist, or throstle cotton-mills, the spinning is entirely managed by females of sixteen years and upwards. The effect of substituting the self-acting mule for the common mule, is to discharge the greater part of the men spinners, and to retain adolescents and children."[4]

These words of the most enthusiastic free-trader, Dr. Ure, serve to complement the confessions of Dr. Bowring. Dr. Bowring speaks of certain individual evils, and, at the same time, says that these individual evils destroy whole classes; he speaks of the temporary sufferings during the transition period, and at the very time of speaking of them, he does not deny that these temporary evils have implied for the majority the transition from life to death, and for the rest a transition from a better to a worse condition. If he asserts, farther on, that the sufferings of these workers are inseparable from the progress of industry, and are necessary to the prosperity of the nation, he simply says that the prosperity of the bourgeois class presupposes as necessary the suffering of the laboring class.

All the consolation which Dr. Bowring offers the workers who perish, and, indeed, the whole doctrine of compensation which the free-traders propound, amounts to this:

You thousands of workers who are perishing, do not despair! You can die with an easy conscience. Your class will not perish. It will always be numerous enough for the capitalist class to decimate it without fear of annihilating it. Besides, how could capital be usefully applied if it did not take care always to keep up its exploitable material, i.e., the workers, to exploit them over and over again?

But, besides, why propound as a problem still to be solved the question: What influence will the adoption of free trade have upon the condition of the working class? All the laws formulated by the political economists from Quesnay to Ricardo have been based upon the hypothesis that the trammels which still interfere with commercial freedom have disappeared. These laws are confirmed in proportion as free trade is adopted. The first of these laws is that competition reduces the price of every commodity to the minimum cost of production. Thus the minimum of wages is the natural price of labor. And what is the minimum of wages? Just so much as is required for production of the articles indispensable for the maintenance of the worker, for putting him in a position to sustain himself, however badly, and to propagate his race, however slightly.

But do not imagine that the worker receives only this minimum wage, and still less that he always receives it.

No, according to this law, the working class will sometimes be more fortunate. It will sometimes receive something above the minimum, but this surplus will merely make up for the deficit which it will have received below the minimum in times of industrial stagnation. That is to say that, within a given time which recurs periodically, in the cycle which industry passes through while undergoing the vicissitudes of prosperity, overproduction, stagnation and crisis, when reckoning all that the working class will have had above and below necessaries, we shall see that, in all, it will have received neither more nor less than the minimum; i.e., the working class will have maintained itself as a class after enduring any amount of misery and misfortune, and after leaving many corpses upon the industrial battlefield. But what of that? The class will still exist; nay, more, it will have increased.

But this is not all. The progress of industry creates less expensive means of subsistence. Thus spirits have taken the place of beer, cotton that of wool and linen, and potatoes that of bread.

Thus, as means are constantly being found for the maintenance of labor on cheaper and more wretched food, the minimum of wages is constantly sinking. If these wages began by making the man work to live, they end by making him live the life of a machine. His existence has not other value than that of a simple productive force, and the capitalist treats him accordingly.

This law of commodity labor, of the minimum of wages, will be confirmed in proportion as the supposition of the economists, free trade, becomes an actual fact. Thus, of two things one: either we must reject all political economy based on the assumption of free trade, or we must admit that under this free trade the whole severity of the economic laws will fall upon the workers.

To sum up, what is free trade, what is free trade under the present condition of society? It is freedom of capital. When you have overthrown the few national barriers which still restrict the progress of capital, you will merely have given it complete freedom of action. So long as you let the relation of wage labor to capital exist, it does not matter how favorable the conditions under which the exchange of commodities takes place, there will always be a class which will exploit and a class which will be exploited. It is really difficult to understand the claim of the free-traders who imagine that the more advantageous application of capital will abolish the antagonism between industrial capitalists and wage workers. On the contrary, the only result will be that the antagonism of these two classes will stand out still more clearly.

Let us assume for a moment that there are no more Corn Laws or national or local custom duties; in fact that all the accidental circumstances which today the worker may take to be the cause of his miserable condition have entirely vanished, and you will have removed so many curtains that hide from his eyes his true enemy.

He will see that capital become free will make him no less a slave than capital trammeled by customs duties.

Gentlemen! Do not allow yourselves to be deluded by the abstract word freedom. Whose freedom? It is not the freedom of one individual in relation to another, but the freedom of capital to crush the worker.

Why should you desire to go on sanctioning free competition with this idea of freedom, when this freedom is only the product of a state of things based upon free competition?

We have shown what sort of brotherhood free trade begets between the different classes of one and the same nation. The brotherhood which free trade would establish between the nations of the Earth would hardly be more fraternal. To call cosmopolitan exploitation universal brotherhood is an idea that could only be engendered in the brain of the bourgeoisie. All the destructive phenomena which unlimited competition gives rise to within one country are reproduced in more gigantic proportions on the world market. We need not dwell any longer upon free trade sophisms on this subject, which are worth just as much as the arguments of our prize-winners Messrs. Hope, Morse, and Greg.

For instance, we are told that free trade would create an international division of labor, and thereby give to each country the production which is most in harmony with its natural advantage.

You believe, perhaps, gentlemen, that the production of coffee and sugar is the natural destiny of the West Indies.

Two centuries ago, nature, which does not trouble herself about commerce, had planted neither sugar-cane nor coffee trees there.

And it may be that in less than half a century you will find there neither coffee nor sugar, for the East Indies, by means of cheaper production, have already successfully combatted this alleged natural destiny of the West Indies. And the West Indies, with their natural wealth, are already as heavy a burden for England as the weavers of Dacca, who also were destined from the beginning of time to weave by hand.

One other thing must never be forgotten, namely, that, just as everything has become a monopoly, there are also nowadays some branches of industry which dominate all others, and secure to the nations which most largely cultivate them the command of the world market. Thus in international commerce cotton alone has much greater commercial than all the other raw materials used in the manufacture of clothing put together. It is truly ridiculous to see the free-traders stress the few specialities in each branch of industry, throwing them into the balance against the products used in everyday consumption and produced most cheaply in those countries in which manufacture is most highly developed.

If the free-traders cannot understand how one nation can grow rich at the expense of another, we need not wonder, since these same gentlemen also refuse to understand how within one country one class can enrich itself at the expense of another.

Do not imagine, gentlemen, that in criticizing freedom of trade we have the least intention of defending the system of protection.

One may declare oneself an enemy of the constitutional regime without declaring oneself a friend of the ancient regime.

Moreover, the protectionist system is nothing but a means of establishing large-scale industry in any given country, that is to say, of making it dependent upon the world market, and from the moment that dependence upon the world market is established, there is already more or less dependence upon free trade. Besides this, the protective system helps to develop free trade competition within a country. Hence we see that in countries where the bourgeoisie is beginning to make itself felt as a class, in Germany for example, it makes great efforts to obtain protective duties. They serve the bourgeoisie as weapons against feudalism and absolute government, as a means for the concentration of its own powers and for the realization of free trade within the same country.

But, in general, the protective system of our day is conservative, while the free trade system is destructive. It breaks up old nationalities and pushes the antagonism of the proletariat and the bourgeoisie to the extreme point. In a word, the free trade system hastens the social revolution. It is in this revolutionary sense alone, gentlemen, that I vote in favor of free trade.

23: Frederick Douglass's Fourth of July Speech

Rochester, New York, 1852

FOR A BRIEF AND ULTIMATELY DELUSIONAL MOMENT IN 1850, MANY CITIZENS of the United States believed that they had been spared a catastrophic showdown over the spread of slavery. As the nation's debate over enslavement became more vitriolic, as tensions between the industrial North and the slave-market South frayed to the breaking point, politicians in Washington jerry-rigged a complicated series of bills designed to appease majorities in both sections.

The Compromise of 1850 allowed the admission of California as a free state, a victory for the anti-slave North which opposed extension of slavery into new states. But the new territories of the Southwest were to be organized without any restrictions on slavery; the decision whether to be free or slave would be up to residents when they applied for statehood. Reliance on popular sovereignty mollified the South's 14 slave states. Two more carefully balanced bills were added to the package. The slave trade—the practice of selling and buying the bodies of black people—was banned from the nation's seat of government, the District of Columbia. But slaveowners received their pound of flesh when Congress passed a new law governing the capture of fugitive slaves. The law bound Americans North and South to assist slaveholders seeking the return of escaped slaves.

The Fugitive Slave Law received little attention during the long debates over the Compromise of 1850. But it proved to be the most controversial and most contentious piece of the package. It proved difficult and even impossible to enforce in some Northern states, enraging white Southerners. But blacks in the North feared that they might get caught up in the slave catcher's net, leading thousands to flee to Canada.

One escaped slave who had no need to fear the government's new powers was a thirty-four-year-old native of Maryland named Frederick Douglass. Born into slavery in 1817, Douglass taught himself to read and write. As a teenager, he studied a collection of famous speeches entitled *The Columbian Orator*, which included selections from Greek and Roman orations as well as more contemporary speeches by George Washington and the British statesman William Pitt. "The reading of these speeches enabled me to give tongue to many interesting thoughts," Douglas later wrote.[1]

He fled his enslavers in 1838 and joined the abolitionist movement in New England. Literate and eloquent, he quickly became one of the movement's most-charismatic leaders. But his public prominence did not shield him from the era's fears and hatreds. He was barred from a church in New Bedford, Mass., from the cabin of a steamship sailing from New York to Boston, and from an omnibus in Boston. Each time, he later wrote, he was told: "We don't allow niggers here."[2]

After a brief exile in Great Britain in the mid-1840s, Douglass settled in Rochester, N.Y. and founded an abolitionist newspaper he called *The North Star*, although the name was changed to *Frederick Douglass' Paper* to avoid confusion with other journals with similar titles. Already an ally of William Lloyd Garrison, the era's most prominent white abolitionist, Douglass attracted the attention of others, including educator Horace Mann, Representative Charles Sumner and Senator William Seward. Through the newspaper and Douglass' presence in the city, Rochester became a hub of abolitionist activity. He delivered an anti-slavery lecture every Sunday in the city's Corinthian Hall, and traveled frequently to other cities in western and central New York to preach the abolitionist gospel. Less prominent, but equally effective, was Douglass' self-described role as a "station master and conductor" on the Underground Railroad.[3] Living near the Canadian border, Douglass was well-positioned to help escapees made the final leg of their journey and so foil the slave catchers.

As the Compromise of 1850 began to unravel because of the North's opposition to the Fugitive Slave Law and the South's insistence that the law was part of the bargain it struck, the abolitionists of Rochester asked their most famous citizen, Frederick Douglass, to deliver an oration to commemorate Independence Day on July 4, 1852. The venue was familiar—Corinthian Hall, site of Douglass' weekly lectures. But if the city's abolitionists were expecting a message of self-congratulation mixed in with a denunciation of Southern slaveholders, they were very much mistaken. The Fourth of July might be a day of joy and celebration for his audience, but not for him, nor for the four million human beings whose enslavement mocked the very notion of independence.

Douglass told the crowd that he would speak of slavery from the point of view of the enslaved, not from the more abstract perspective of a Northern abolitionist. Such a perspective was bound to make his audience squirm in its seats, and that was precisely Douglass' intention. He anticipated the reaction of his listeners, saying that he could imagine them thinking he ought to argue more and "denounce less," persuade, not rebuke. But he shrewdly built an argument against more argument, asserting that at least in Corinthian Hall, there was agreement on the evils of enslavement, on the right of a slave to ownership of his or her own body.

It was, he said, a waste of his time to argue against a system that was so evidently evil. Denunciation, in the manner of an Old Testament prophet, was the only proper course. In this speech, Douglass invited his audience of abolitionists to consider what the Fourth of July meant to the enslaved. It is a powerful recitation of the nation's hypocrisy and a vigorous denunciation of his own listeners who preferred to reason with the unreasonable.

▼ ▼ ▼

FELLOW Citizens, I am not wanting in respect for the fathers of this republic. The signers of the Declaration of Independence were brave men. They were great men, too great enough to give frame to a great age. It does not often happen to a nation to raise, at one time, such a number of truly great men. The point from which I am compelled to view them is not, certainly, the most favorable; and yet I cannot contemplate their great deeds with less than admiration. They were statesmen, patriots and heroes, and for the good they did, and the principles they contended for, I will unite with you to honor their memory . . . .

. . . Fellow citizens, pardon me, allow me to ask, why am I called upon to speak here today? What have I, or those I represent, to do with your national independence? Are the great principles of political freedom and of natural justice, embodied in that Declaration of Independence, extended to us? and am I, therefore, called upon to bring our humble offering to the national altar, and to confess the benefits and express devout gratitude for the blessings resulting from your independence to us?

Would to God, both for your sakes and ours, that an affirmative answer could be truthfully returned to these questions! Then would my task be light, and my burden easy and delightful. For who is there so cold, that a nation's sympathy could not warm him? Who so obdurate and dead to the claims of gratitude, that would not thankfully acknowledge such priceless benefits? Who so stolid and selfish, that would not give his voice to swell the hallelujahs of a nation's jubilee, when the chains of servitude had been torn from his limbs? I am not that man. In a case like that, the dumb might eloquently speak, and the "lame man leap as an hart."

But such is not the state of the case. I say it with a sad sense of the disparity between us. I am not included within the pale of this glorious anniversary! Your high independence only reveals the immeasurable distance between us. The blessings in which you, this day, rejoice, are not enjoyed in common. The rich inheritance of justice, liberty, prosperity and independence, bequeathed by your fathers, is shared by you, not by me. The sunlight that brought light and healing to you, has brought stripes and death to me. This Fourth July is yours, not mine. You may rejoice, I must mourn. To drag a man in fetters into the grand illuminated temple of liberty, and call upon him to join you in joyous anthems, were inhuman mockery and sacrilegious irony. Do you mean, citizens, to mock me, by asking me to speak today? If so, there is a parallel to your conduct. And let me warn you that it is dangerous to copy the example of a nation whose crimes, towering up to heaven, were thrown down by the breath of the Almighty, burying that nation in irrevocable ruin! I can today take up the plaintive lament of a peeled and woe-smitten people!

"By the rivers of Babylon, there we sat down. Yea! we wept when we remembered Zion. We hanged our harps upon the willows in the midst thereof. For there, they that carried us away captive, required of us a song; and they who wasted us required of us mirth, saying, Sing us one of the songs of Zion. How can we sing the Lord's song in a strange land? If I forget thee, O Jerusalem, let my right hand forget her cunning. If I do not remember thee, let my tongue cleave to the roof of my mouth."

Fellow citizens, above your national, tumultuous joy, I hear the mournful wail of millions! whose chains, heavy and grievous yesterday, are, today, rendered more intolerable by the jubilee shouts that reach them. If I do forget, if I do not faithfully remember those bleeding children of sorrow this day, "may my right hand forget her cunning, and may my tongue cleave to the roof of my mouth!" To forget them, to pass lightly over their wrongs, and to chime in with the popular theme, would be treason most scandalous and shocking, and would make me a reproach before God and the world. My subject, then, fellow citizens, is American slavery. I shall see this day and its popular characteristics from the slave's point of view. Standing there

identified with the American bondman, making his wrongs mine, I do not
hesitate to declare, with all my soul, that the character and conduct of this
nation never looked blacker to me than on this Fourth of July! Whether we
turn to the declarations of the past, or to the professions of the present, the
conduct of the nation seems equally hideous and revolting. America is false
to the past, false to the present, and solemnly binds herself to be false to the
future. Standing with God and the crushed and bleeding slave on this occasion, I will, in the name of humanity which is outraged, in the name of liberty which is fettered, in the name of the constitution and the Bible which
are disregarded and trampled upon, dare to call in question and to
denounce, with all the emphasis I can command, everything that serves to
perpetuate slavery—the great sin and shame of America! "I will not equiv-
ocate; I will not excuse" I will use the severest language I can command;
and yet not one word shall escape me that any man, whose judgment is not
blinded by prejudice, or who is not at heart a slaveholder, shall not confess
to be right and just.

But I fancy I hear some one of my audience say, "It is just in this circumstance that you and your brother abolitionists fail to make a favorable
impression on the public mind. Would you argue more, an denounce less;
would you persuade more, and rebuke less; your cause would be much
more likely to succeed." But, I submit, where all is plain there is nothing to
be argued. What point in the anti-slavery creed would you have me argue?
On what branch of the subject do the people of this country need light?
Must I undertake to prove that the slave is a man? That point is conceded
already. Nobody doubts it. The slaveholders themselves acknowledge it in
the enactment of laws for their government. They acknowledge it when
they punish disobedience on the part of the slave. There are seventy-two
crimes in the State of Virginia which, if committed by a black man (no matter how ignorant he be), subject him to the punishment of death; while only
two of the same crimes will subject a white man to the like punishment.
What is this but the acknowledgment that the slave is a moral, intellectual,
and responsible being? The manhood of the slave is conceded. It is admitted in the fact that Southern statute books are covered with enactments forbidding, under severe fines and penalties, the teaching of the slave to read
or to write. When you can point to any such laws in reference to the beasts
of the field, then I may consent to argue the manhood of the slave. When
the dogs in your streets, when the fowls of the air, when the cattle on your
hills, when the fish of the sea, and the reptiles that crawl, shall be unable to

distinguish the slave from a brute, then will I argue with you that the slave is a man!

For the present, it is enough to affirm the equal manhood of the Negro race. Is it not astonishing that, while we are ploughing, planting, and reaping, using all kinds of mechanical tools, erecting houses, constructing bridges, building ships, working in metals of brass, iron, copper, silver and gold; that, while we are reading, writing and ciphering, acting as clerks, merchants and secretaries, having among us lawyers, doctors, ministers, poets, authors, editors, orators and teachers; that, while we are engaged in all manner of enterprises common to other men, digging gold in California, capturing the whale in the Pacific, feeding sheep and cattle on the hill-side, living, moving, acting, thinking, planning, living in families as husbands, wives and children, and, above all, confessing and worshipping the Christian's God, and looking hopefully for life and immortality beyond the grave, we are called upon to prove that we are men!

Would you have me argue that man is entitled to liberty? that he is the rightful owner of his own body? You have already declared it. Must I argue the wrongfulness of slavery? Is that a question for Republicans? Is it to be settled by the rules of logic and argumentation, as a matter beset with great difficulty, involving a doubtful application of the principle of justice, hard to be understood? How should I look today, in the presence of Amercans, dividing, and subdividing a discourse, to show that men have a natural right to freedom? speaking of it relatively and positively, negatively and affirmatively. To do so, would be to make myself ridiculous, and to offer an insult to your understanding. There is not a man beneath the canopy of heaven that does not know that slavery is wrong for him.

What, am I to argue that it is wrong to make men brutes, to rob them of their liberty, to work them without wages, to keep them ignorant of their relations to their fellow men, to beat them with sticks, to flay their flesh with the lash, to load their limbs with irons, to hunt them with dogs, to sell them at auction, to sunder their families, to knock out their teeth, to burn their flesh, to starve them into obedience and submission to their masters? Must I argue that a system thus marked with blood, and stained with pollution, is wrong? No! I will not. I have better employment for my time and strength than such arguments would imply.

What, then, remains to be argued? Is it that slavery is not divine; that God did not establish it; that our doctors of divinity are mistaken? There is blasphemy in the thought. That which is inhuman, cannot be divine! Who can reason on such a proposition? They that can, may; I cannot. The time for such argument is passed.

At a time like this, scorching irony, not convincing argument, is needed. O! had I the ability, and could reach the nation's ear, I would, today, pour out a fiery stream of biting ridicule, blasting reproach, withering sarcasm, and stern rebuke. For it is not light that is needed, but fire; it is not the gentle shower, but thunder. We need the storm, the whirlwind, and the earthquake. The feeling of the nation must be quickened; the conscience of the nation must be roused; the propriety of the nation must be startled; the hypocrisy of the nation must be exposed; and its crimes against God and man must be proclaimed and denounced.

What, to the American slave, is your Fourth of July? I answer; a day that reveals to him, more than all other days in the year, the gross injustice and cruelty to which he is the constant victim. To him, your celebration is a sham; your boasted liberty, an unholy license; your national greatness, swelling vanity; your sounds of rejoicing are empty and heartless; your denunciation of tyrants, brass fronted impudence; your shouts of liberty and equality, hollow mockery; your prayers and hymns, your sermons and thanksgivings, with all your religious parade and solemnity, are, to him, mere bombast, fraud, deception, impiety, and hypocrisy—a thin veil to cover up crimes which would disgrace a nation of savages. There is not a nation on the earth guilty of practices more shocking and bloody than are the people of the United States, at this very hour.

Go where you may, search where you will, roam through all the monarchies and despotisms of the Old World, travel through South America, search out every abuse, and when you have found the last, lay your facts by the side of the everyday practices of this nation, and you will say with me, that, for revolting barbarity and shameless hypocrisy, America reigns without a rival. . . .

. . . Allow me to say, in conclusion, notwithstanding the dark picture I have this day presented, of the state of the nation, I do not despair of this country. There are forces in operation which must inevitably work the downfall of slavery. "The arm of the Lord is not shortened," and the doom of slavery is certain. I, therefore, leave off where I began, with hope. While drawing encouragement from "the Declaration of Independence," the great principles it contains, and the genius of American Institutions, my spirit is also cheered by the obvious tendencies of the age. Nations do not now stand in the same relation to each other that they did ages ago. No nation can now shut itself up from the surrounding world and trot round in the same old path of its fathers without interference. The time was when such could be done. Long established customs of hurtful character could formerly fence themselves in, and do their evil work with social impunity. Knowledge was then confined and enjoyed by the privileged few, and the multitude walked on in mental darkness. But a change has now come over the affairs of mankind. Walled cities and empires have become unfashionable. The arm of commerce has borne away the gates of the strong city. Intelligence is penetrating the darkest corners of the globe. It makes its pathway over and under the sea, as well as on the earth. Wind, steam, and lightning are its chartered agents. Oceans no longer divide, but link nations together. From Boston to London is now a holiday excursion. Space is comparatively annihilated. Thoughts expressed on one side of the Atlantic are distinctly heard on the other.

The far off and almost fabulous Pacific rolls in grandeur at our feet. The Celestial Empire, the mystery of ages, is being solved. The fiat of the Almighty, "Let there be Light," has not yet spent its force. No abuse, no outrage whether in taste, sport or avarice, can now hide itself from the all-pervading light. The iron shoe, and crippled foot of China must be seen in contrast with nature. Africa must rise and put on her yet unwoven garment. 'Ethiopia, shall, stretch. out her hand unto God." In the fervent aspirations of William Lloyd Garrison, I say, and let every heart join in saying it:

> God speed the year of jubilee
> The wide world o'er!
> When from their galling chains set free,
> Th' oppress'd shall vilely bend the knee,
> And wear the yoke of tyranny
> Like brutes no more.
> That year will come, and freedom's reign,
> To man his plundered rights again
> Restore.
> God speed the day when human blood
> Shall cease to flow!
> In every clime be understood,
> The claims of human brotherhood,
> And each return for evil, good,
> Not blow for blow;

That day will come all feuds to end,
And change into a faithful friend
Each foe.
God speed the hour, the glorious hour,
When none on earth
Shall exercise a lordly power,
Nor in a tyrant's presence cower;
But to all manhood's stature tower,
By equal birth!
That hour will come, to each, to all,
And from his Prison-house, to thrall
Go forth.
Until that year, day, hour, arrive,
With head, and heart, and hand I'll strive,
To break the rod, and rend the gyve,
The spoiler of his prey deprive—
So witness Heaven!
And never from my chosen post,
Whate'er the peril or the cost,
Be driven.

24: Abraham Lincoln's Address
at Cooper Institute
New York, February 27, 1860

ABRAHAM LINCOLN DELIVERED TWO OF THE GREATEST SPEECHES EVER GIVEN by a President of the United States. The words of the Gettysburg Address and his second inaugural address contain soaring flights of oratory, and were given under extraordinary circumstances. Both were works of literary art as well as political documents. But neither speech might have been given were it not for a lesser-known address, daunting in length, given in New York on an unseasonably warm February evening in 1860. On that night in New York, Abraham Lincoln emerged as a leading candidate for the Republican Party's presidential nomination.

Lincoln's performance in Cooper Union served as his introduction to the Republican Party's eastern establishment. He was hardly an unknown to men like Horace Greeley, editor of the *New York Tribune*, and other Republicans in the region. Lincoln made a name for himself with his tireless efforts on behalf of the party's candidate for President in 1856, John C. Fremont. And, of course, his debates with Stephen A. Douglas during the race for U.S. Senate in Illinois in 1858 made him a legend among some Republicans.

For all the notoriety he achieved in the late '50s, however, Lincoln was a stranger in the east, the intellectual center of the abolitionist and anti-slavery movement. Only four years removed from running its first candidate for President, the Republican Party was searching for the man who would carry its banner in the fall campaign of 1860. Fremont had run well in the northeast in 1856, and if the new nominee could expand the party's reach into the west, it stood a chance of capturing the White House despite ceding the entire South.

Lincoln, of course, was a westerner, a native of Kentucky and a longtime resident of Illinois. His anti-slavery credentials were impeccable; indeed, it was he who, during his debates with Douglas, revitalized the party's anti-slavery core, arguing that slavery was, at its heart, a moral issue. But Lincoln was no abolitionist; while he abhorred enslavement, he was not prepared to argue that it must be abolished where it existed. Rather, he sought to halt its spread to new territories in the west.

He was, then, a moderate at a time when moderation seemed in short supply. As Lincoln made the long train ride from Springfield to New York in late winter, 1860, the country still was in shock over John Brown's failed attempt to ignite a slave rebellion with his raid on Harper's Ferry in 1859. Even conventional politics had taken a violent turn: One of the Republican Party's most radical anti-slave men, Senator Charles Sumner of Massachusetts, was nearly beaten to death on the Senate floor in 1854.

One of the most mentioned candidates for the 1860 Republican presidential nomination was William Seward, the brilliant abolitionist Senator from New York. In accepting an invitation to speak in Seward's home state, Lincoln was making an important political gesture, and one that did not go unnoticed by Seward's opponents. Chief among them was Horace Greeley, whose *New York Tribune* was a powerful, national voice of the party. Greeley and the *Tribune* were eager to hear what the lawyer from Illinois had to say, and how he said it.

Lincoln worked hard on his speech, harder, he later said, than on any other speech in his career thus far. He knew the stakes involved; he knew the speech would be scrutinized—he knew he would be scrutinized, by power Republicans who shaped public opinion. And Lincoln had great respect for the power of those who molded public sentiment.

Lincoln had been arguing with his fellow Illinois resident, Douglas, for years about the extension of slavery into territories formed from the Louisiana Purchase and from land in the southwest won from Mexico in 1849CK. Douglas, poised to run for president in 1860 on the Democratic line, built his career on his advocacy of popular sovereignty, that is, allowing the people of the territories to decide for themselves whether to be free or slave. Douglas was unconcerned about the result of that decision; what mattered to him was who made the choice. He believed the ballot made its own morality.

Lincoln disagreed profoundly, as a matter of morality and as a matter of law. He argued that the Constitution itself was an anti-slavery document, countering Douglas' more conventional assertion that the Constitution protected slavery. The founders, Douglas said, knew what they were doing.

Lincoln was determined to prove Douglas wrong. He spent hours going through records of old debates about the writing and adoption of the Constitution to construct a well-reasoned argument designed to show that many of the men who signed the document expected slavery to wither away. Name by name, he identified the signers who supported legislation keeping slavery out of the northwest territories in the Republic's earliest years.

Conventional wisdom had it that the Declaration of Independence, with its assertion that all men were created equal, contained the ideals of the abolitionist and anti-slavery movement, while the Constitution embodied the protections which Southern slaveholders insisted upon. Lincoln hoped to show his New York audience that the two documents had the same roots in opposition to slavery.

He left Springfield on Feburary 23, bound not only for New York, but also for New Hampshire, where his son, Robert, attended Philips Exeter Academy, and for a speaking tour of New England. Even as his train chugged through the plains of Illinois and Ohio, into the mountains and valleys of Pennsylvania, and through New Jersey from Camden to Jersey City, excitement in New York was mounting. the *Tribune* and Republican Party publicists turned the speech into a full-fledged media event, with Lincoln, the western orator who went toe to toe and word for word with Stephen A. Douglas, as the star.

Lincoln was originally scheduled to speak in Brooklyn in the church of abolitionist Henry Ward Beecher. When he arrived in New York on Saturday, February 25, he was told of a change in venue. The lecture's new sponsors, the Young Men's Central Republican Union, booked him in the Great Hall at the Cooper Union Institute in downtown Manhattan. Some fifteen hundred people were expected.

He skipped a dinner engagement on Sunday night to go over last-minute revisions to his speech. At some point the following day, hours before he was due on stage at Cooper Union, Lincoln visited the studio of photographer Mathew Brady and posed for a picture. The resulting image shows a beardless Lincoln, standing tall in dark clothing, stiff and formal as most images from that age tend to be. The image was circulated throughout the northeast.

According to legend, it began to snow later in the afternoon, accounting for the scattering of empty seats that greeted Lincoln when he appeared on stage. But Lincoln scholar Harold Holzer has shown, using newly discovered weather data, that temperatures were unseasonably warm that night. The empty seats, Holzer argued, might simply have been a reflection of

Lincoln's competition that night. There were other lectures in the city on February 27, not to mention a performance by the great diva of the age, Jenny Lind.[1]

Dressed in black, Lincoln took the stage and confronted his New York audience with a long, well-seasoned brief that re-interpreted the Constitution's position on slavery. In his thin, high and clear voice, Lincoln argued for a return to the Constitution's original intent—to keep slavery where it existed, and prevent it from spreading elsewhere. In the second half of the speech, he addressed himself to the South as the self-conscious representative of an anti-slave party. "You charge that we stir up insurrection among your slaves. We deny it; and what is your proof? Harper's Ferry! John Brown! John Brown was no Republican, and you have failed to implicate a single Republican in his Harper's Ferry enterprise." In the speech's last section, he spoke to fellow Republicans and all Americans of good will. "Let us have faith that right makes might, and in that faith, let us, to the end, dare to do our duty as we understand it."

The New Yorkers in the hall greeted Lincoln's speech with sustained applause. Newspapers carried the speech in its entirety the following day. Other papers around the country recognized its importance and reprinted it as well.

The speech transformed Lincoln into a national figure. He was nominated for President at the Republican convention less than three months later.

▼ ▼ ▼

MR. PRESIDENT and fellow citizens of New York:
        The facts with which I shall deal this evening are mainly old and familiar; nor is there anything new in the general use I shall make of them. If there shall be any novelty, it will be in the mode of presenting the facts, and the inferences and observations following that presentation.

In his speech last autumn, at Columbus, Ohio, as reported in *The New-York Times*," Senator Douglas said:

"Our fathers, when they framed the Government under which we live, understood this question just as well, and even better, than we do now."

I fully endorse this, and I adopt it as a text for this discourse. I so adopt it because it furnishes a precise and an agreed starting point for a discussion between Republicans and that wing of the Democracy headed by Senator

Douglas. It simply leaves the inquiry: "What was the understanding those fathers had of the question mentioned?"

What is the frame of government under which we live?

The answer must be: "The Constitution of the United States." That Constitution consists of the original, framed in 1787 (and under which the present government first went into operation) and twelve subsequently framed amendments, the first ten of which were framed in 1789.

Who were our fathers that framed the Constitution? I suppose the "thirty-nine" who signed the original instrument may be fairly called our fathers who framed that part of the present Government. It is almost exactly true to say they framed it, and it is altogether true to say they fairly represented the opinion and sentiment of the whole nation at that time. Their names, being familiar to nearly all, and accessible to quite all, need not now be repeated.

I take these "thirty-nine," for the present, as being "our fathers who framed the Government under which we live."

What is the question which, according to the text, those fathers understood "just as well, and even better than we do now?"

It is this: Does the proper division of local from federal authority, or anything in the Constitution, forbid our Federal Government to control as to slavery in our Federal Territories?

Upon this, Senator Douglas holds the affirmative, and Republicans the negative. This affirmation and denial form an issue; and this issue—this question—is precisely what the text declares our fathers understood "better than we."

Let us now inquire whether the "thirty-nine," or any of them, ever acted upon this question; and if they did, how they acted upon it—how they expressed that better understanding?

In 1784, three years before the Constitution—the United States then owning the Northwestern Territory, and no other, the Congress of the Confederation had before them the question of prohibiting slavery in that Territory; and four of the "thirty-nine" who afterward framed the Constitution, were in that Congress, and voted on that question. Of these, Roger Sherman, Thomas Mifflin, and Hugh Williamson voted for the prohibition, thus showing that, in their understanding, no line dividing local from federal authority, nor anything else, properly forbade the Federal Government to control as to slavery in federal territory. The other of the four—James M'Henry—voted against the prohibition, showing that, for some cause, he thought it improper to vote for it.

In 1787, still before the Constitution, but while the Convention was in session framing it, and while the Northwestern Territory still was the only territory owned by the United States, the same question of prohibiting slavery in the territory again came before the Congress of the Confederation; and two more of the "thirty-nine" who afterward signed the Constitution, were in that Congress, and voted on the question. They were William Blount and William Few; and they both voted for the prohibition—thus showing that, in their understanding, no line dividing local from federal authority, nor anything else, properly forbids the Federal Government to control as to slavery in Federal territory. This time the prohibition became a law, being part of what is now well known as the Ordinance of '87.

The question of federal control of slavery in the territories, seems not to have been directly before the Convention which framed the original Constitution; and hence it is not recorded that the "thirty-nine," or any of them, while engaged on that instrument, expressed any opinion on that precise question.

In 1789, by the first Congress which sat under the Constitution, an act was passed to enforce the Ordinance of '87, including the prohibition of slavery in the Northwestern Territory. The bill for this act was reported by one of the "thirty-nine," Thomas Fitzsimmons, then a member of the House of Representatives from Pennsylvania. It went through all its stages without a word of opposition, and finally passed both branches without yeas and nays, which is equivalent to a unanimous passage. In this Congress there were sixteen of the thirty-nine fathers who framed the original Constitution. They were John Langdon, Nicholas Gilman, William. S. Johnson, Roger Sherman, Robert Morris, Thomas Fitzsimmons, William Few, Abraham Baldwin, Rufus King, William Paterson, George Clymer, Richard Bassett, George Read, Pierce Butler, Daniel Carroll, James Madison.

This shows that, in their understanding, no line dividing local from federal authority, nor anything in the Constitution, properly forbade Congress to prohibit slavery in the federal territory; else both their fidelity to correct principle, and their oath to support the Constitution, would have constrained them to oppose the prohibition.

Again, George Washington, another of the "thirty-nine," was then President of the United States, and as such approved and signed the bill; thus completing its validity as a law, and thus showing that, in his understanding, no line dividing local from federal authority, nor anything in the

Constitution, forbade the Federal Government to control as to slavery in federal territory.

No great while after the adoption of the original Constitution, North Carolina ceded to the Federal Government the country now constituting the State of Tennessee; and a few years later Georgia ceded that which now constitutes the States of Mississippi and Alabama. In both deeds of cession it was made a condition by the ceding States that the Federal Government should not prohibit slavery in the ceded territory. Besides this, slavery was then actually in the ceded country. Under these circumstances, Congress, on taking charge of these countries, did not absolutely prohibit slavery within them. But they did interfere with it—take control of it—even there, to a certain extent. In 1798, Congress organized the Territory of Mississippi. In the act of organization, they prohibited the bringing of slaves into the Territory, from any place without the United States, by fine, and giving freedom to slaves so bought. This act passed both branches of Congress without yeas and nays. In that Congress were three of the "thirty-nine" who framed the original Constitution. They were John Langdon, George Read and Abraham Baldwin. They all, probably, voted for it. Certainly they would have placed their opposition to it upon record, if, in their understanding, any line dividing local from federal authority, or anything in the Constitution, properly forbade the Federal Government to control as to slavery in federal territory.

In 1803, the Federal Government purchased the Louisiana country. Our former territorial acquisitions came from certain of our own States; but this Louisiana country was acquired from a foreign nation. In 1804, Congress gave a territorial organization to that part of it which now constitutes the State of Louisiana. New Orleans, lying within that part, was an old and comparatively large city. There were other considerable towns and settlements, and slavery was extensively and thoroughly intermingled with the people. Congress did not, in the Territorial Act, prohibit slavery; but they did interfere with it—take control of it—in a more marked and extensive way than they did in the case of Mississippi. The substance of the provision therein made, in relation to slaves, was:

First. That no slave should be imported into the territory from foreign parts.

Second. That no slave should be carried into it who had been imported into the United States since the first day of May, 1798.

Third. That no slave should be carried into it, except by the owner, and for his own use as a settler; the penalty in all the cases being a fine upon the violator of the law, and freedom to the slave.

This act also was passed without yeas and nays. In the Congress which passed it, there were two of the "thirty-nine." They were Abraham Baldwin and Jonathan Dayton. As stated in the case of Mississippi, it is probable they both voted for it. They would not have allowed it to pass without recording their opposition to it, if, in their understanding, it violated either the line properly dividing local from federal authority, or any provision of the Constitution.

In 1819-20, came and passed the Missouri question. Many votes were taken, by yeas and nays, in both branches of Congress, upon the various phases of the general question. Two of the "thirty-nine"—Rufus King and Charles Pinckney—were members of that Congress. Mr. King steadily voted for slavery prohibition and against all compromises, while Mr. Pinckney as steadily voted against slavery prohibition and against all com-promises. By this, Mr. King showed that, in his understanding, no line divid-ing local from federal authority, nor anything in the Constitution, was vio-lated by Congress prohibiting slavery in federal territory; while Mr. Pinckney, by his votes, showed that, in his understanding, there was some sufficient reason for opposing such prohibition in that case.

The cases I have mentioned are the only acts of the "thirty-nine," or of any of them, upon the direct issue, which I have been able to discover.

To enumerate the persons who thus acted, as being four in 1784, two in 1787, seventeen in 1789, three in 1798, two in 1804, and two in 1819-20—there would be thirty of them. But this would be counting John Langdon, Roger Sherman, William Few, Rufus King, and George Read each twice, and Abraham Baldwin, three times. The true number of those of the "thirty-nine" whom I have shown to have acted upon the question, which, by the text, they understood better than we, is twenty-three, leaving sixteen not shown to have acted upon it in any way.

Here, then, we have twenty-three out of our thirty-nine fathers "who framed the government under which we live," who have, upon their official responsibility and their corporal oaths, acted upon the very question which the text affirms they "understood just as well, and even better than we do now;" and twenty-one of them—a clear majority of the whole "thirty-nine"—so acting upon it as to make them guilty of gross political impropri-ety and willful perjury, if, in their understanding, any proper division between local and federal authority, or anything in the Constitution they had made themselves, and sworn to support, forbade the Federal Government to control as to slavery in the federal territories. Thus the twenty-one acted; and, as actions speak louder than words, so actions, under such responsibility, speak still louder.

Two of the twenty-three voted against Congressional prohibition of slavery in the federal territories, in the instances in which they acted upon the question. But for what reasons they so voted is not known. They may have done so because they thought a proper division of local from federal authority, or some provision or principle of the Constitution, stood in the way; or they may, without any such question, have voted against the prohibition, on what appeared to them to be sufficient grounds of expediency. No one who has sworn to support the Constitution can conscientiously vote for what he understands to be an unconstitutional measure, however expedient he may think it; but one may and ought to vote against a measure which he deems constitutional, if, at the same time, he deems it inexpedient. It, therefore, would be unsafe to set down even the two who voted against the prohibition, as having done so because, in their understanding, any proper division of local from federal authority, or anything in the Constitution, forbade the Federal Government to control as to slavery in federal territory.

The remaining sixteen of the "thirty-nine," so far as I have discovered, have left no record of their understanding upon the direct question of federal control of slavery in the federal territories. But there is much reason to believe that their understanding upon that question would not have appeared different from that of their twenty-three compeers, had it been manifested at all.

For the purpose of adhering rigidly to the text, I have purposely omitted whatever understanding may have been manifested by any person, however distinguished, other than the thirty-nine fathers who framed the original Constitution; and, for the same reason, I have also omitted whatever understanding may have been manifested by any of the "thirty-nine" even, on any other phase of the general question of slavery. If we should look into their acts and declarations on those other phases, as the foreign slave trade, and the morality and policy of slavery generally, it would appear to us that on the direct question of federal control of slavery in federal territories, the sixteen, if they had acted at all, would probably have acted just as the twenty-three did. Among that sixteen were several of the most noted antislavery men of those times—as Dr. Franklin, Alexander Hamilton and

Gouverneur Morris—while there was not one now known to have been otherwise, unless it may be John Rutledge, of South Carolina.

The sum of the whole is that of our thirty-nine fathers who framed the original Constitution, twenty-one—a clear majority of the whole—certainly understood that no proper division of local from federal authority, nor any part of the Constitution, forbade the Federal Government to control slavery in the federal territories; while all the rest probably had the same understanding. Such, unquestionably, was the understanding of our fathers who framed the original Constitution; and the text affirms that they understood the question "better than we."

But, so far, I have been considering the understanding of the question manifested by the framers of the original Constitution. In and by the original instrument, a mode was provided for amending it; and, as I have already stated, the present frame of "the Government under which we live" consists of that original, and twelve amendatory articles framed and adopted since. Those who now insist that federal control of slavery in federal territories violates the Constitution, point us to the provisions which they suppose it thus violates; and, as I understand, that all fix upon provisions in these amendatory articles, and not in the original instrument. The Supreme Court, in the Dred Scott case, plant themselves upon the fifth amendment, which provides that no person shall be deprived of "life, liberty or property without due process of law;" while Senator Douglas and his peculiar adherents plant themselves upon the tenth amendment, providing that "the powers not delegated to the United States by the Constitution" "are reserved to the States respectively, or to the people."

Now, it so happens that these amendments were framed by the first Congress which sat under the Constitution—the identical Congress which passed the act already mentioned, enforcing the prohibition of slavery in the Northwestern Territory. Not only was it the same Congress, but they were the identical, same individual men who, at the same session, and at the same time within the session, had under consideration, and in progress toward maturity, these Constitutional amendments, and this act prohibiting slavery in all the territory the nation then owned. The Constitutional amendments were introduced before, and passed after the act enforcing the Ordinance of '87; so that, during the whole pendency of the act to enforce the Ordinance, the Constitutional amendments were also pending.

The seventy-six members of that Congress, including sixteen of the framers of the original Constitution, as before stated, were preeminently our fathers who framed that part of "the Government under which we live," which is now claimed as forbidding the Federal Government to control slavery in the federal territories.

Is it not a little presumptuous in any one at this day to affirm that the two things which that Congress deliberately framed, and carried to maturity at the same time, are absolutely inconsistent with each other? And does not such affirmation become impudently absurd when coupled with the other affirmation from the same mouth, that those who did the two things, alleged to be inconsistent, understood whether they really were inconsistent better than we—better than he who affirms that they are inconsistent?

It is surely safe to assume that the thirty-nine framers of the original Constitution, and the seventy-six members of the Congress which framed the amendments thereto, taken together, do certainly include those who may be fairly called "our fathers who framed the Government under which we live." And so assuming, I defy any man to show that anyone of them ever, in his whole life, declared that, in his understanding, any proper division of local from federal authority, or any part of the Constitution, forbade the Federal Government to control as to slavery in the federal territories. I go a step further. I defy any one to show that any living man in the whole world ever did, prior to the beginning of the present century (and I might almost say prior to the beginning of the last half of the present century) declare that, in his understanding, any proper division of local from federal authority, or any part of the Constitution, forbade the Federal Government to control as to slavery in the federal territories. To those who now so declare, I give, not only "our fathers who framed the Government under which we live," but with them all other living men within the century in which it was framed, among whom to search, and they shall not be able to find the evidence of a single man agreeing with them.

Now, and here, let me guard a little against being misunderstood. I do not mean to say we are bound to follow implicitly in whatever our fathers did. To do so, would be to discard all the lights of current experience—to reject all progress—all improvement. What I do say is that if we would supplant the opinions and policy of our fathers in any case, we should do so upon evidence so conclusive, and argument so clear, that even their great authority, fairly considered and weighed, cannot stand; and most surely not in a case whereof we ourselves declare they understood the question better than we.

If any man at this day sincerely believes that a proper division of local from federal authority, or any part of the Constitution, forbids the Federal Government to control as to slavery in the federal territories, he is right to say so, and to enforce his position by all truthful evidence and fair argument which he can. But he has no right to mislead others, who have less access to history, and less leisure to study it, into the false belief that "our fathers who framed the Government under which we live" were of the same opinion—thus substituting falsehood and deception for truthful evidence and fair argument. If any man at this day sincerely believes "our fathers who framed the Government under which we live" used and applied principles, in other cases, which ought to have led them to understand that a proper division of local from federal authority or some part of the Constitution, forbids the Federal Government to control as to slavery in the federal territories, he is right to say so. But he should, at the same time, brave the responsibility of declaring that, in his opinion, he understands their principles better than they did themselves; and especially should he not shirk that responsibility by asserting that they "understood the question just as well, and even better, than we do now."

But enough! Let all who believe that "our fathers, who framed the Government under which we live, understood this question just as well, and even better, than we do now," speak as they spoke, and act as they acted upon it. This is all Republicans ask—all Republicans desire—in relation to slavery. As those fathers marked it, so let it be again marked, as an evil not to be extended, but to be tolerated and protected only because of and so far as its actual presence among us makes that toleration and protection a necessity. Let all the guarantees those fathers gave it, be, not grudgingly, but fully and fairly, maintained. For this Republicans contend, and with this, so far as I know or believe, they will be content.

And now, if they would listen—as I suppose they will not—I would address a few words to the Southern people.

I would say to them: You consider yourselves a reasonable and a just people; and I consider that in the general qualities of reason and justice you are not inferior to any other people. Still, when you speak of us Republicans, you do so only to denounce us as reptiles, or, at the best, as no better than outlaws. You will grant a hearing to pirates or murderers, but nothing like it to "Black Republicans." In all your contentions with one another, each of you deems an unconditional condemnation of "Black Republicanism" as the first thing to be attended to. Indeed, such condemnation of us seems to be an indispensable prerequisite—license, so to speak—among you to be admitted or permitted to speak at all. Now, can you, or not, be prevailed upon to pause and to consider whether this is quite just to us, or even to yourselves? Bring forward your charges and specifications, and then be patient long enough to hear us deny or justify.

You say we are sectional. We deny it. That makes an issue; and the burden of proof is upon you. You produce your proof; and what is it? Why, that our party has no existence in your section—gets no votes in your section. The fact is substantially true; but does it prove the issue? If it does, then in case we should, without change of principle, begin to get votes in your section, we should thereby cease to be sectional. You cannot escape this conclusion; and yet, are you willing to abide by it? If you are, you will probably soon find that we have ceased to be sectional, for we shall get votes in your section this very year. You will then begin to discover, as the truth plainly is, that your proof does not touch the issue. The fact that we get no votes in your section, is a fact of your making, and not of ours. And if there be fault in that fact, that fault is primarily yours, and remains until you show that we repel you by some wrong principle or practice. If we do repel you by any wrong principle or practice, the fault is ours; but this brings you to where you ought to have started—to a discussion of the right or wrong of our principle. If our principle, put in practice, would wrong your section for the benefit of ours, or for any other object, then our principle, and we with it, are sectional, and are justly opposed and denounced as such. Meet us, then, on the question of whether our principle, put in practice, would wrong your section; and so meet it as if it were possible that something may be said on our side. Do you accept the challenge? No! Then you really believe that the principle which "our fathers who framed the Government under which we live" thought so clearly right as to adopt it, and endorse it again and again, upon their official oaths, is in fact so clearly wrong as to demand your condemnation without a moment's consideration.

Some of you delight to flaunt in our faces the warning against sectional parties given by Washington in his Farewell Address. Less than eight years before Washington gave that warning, he had, as President of the United States, approved and signed an act of Congress, enforcing the prohibition of slavery in the Northwestern Territory, which act embodied the policy of the Government upon that subject up to and at the very moment he penned that warning; and about one year after he penned it, he wrote LaFayette that he considered that prohibition a wise measure, expressing in the same connection his hope that we should at some time have a confederacy of free States.

Bearing this in mind, and seeing that sectionalism has since arisen upon this same subject, is that warning a weapon in your hands against us, or in our hands against you? Could Washington himself speak, would he cast the blame of that sectionalism upon us, who sustain his policy, or upon you who repudiate it? We respect that warning of Washington, and we commend it to you, together with his example pointing to the right application of it.

But you say you are conservative—eminently conservative—while we are revolutionary, destructive, or something of the sort. What is conservatism? Is it not adherence to the old and tried, against the new and untried? We stick to, contend for, the identical old policy on the point in controversy which was adopted by "our fathers who framed the Government under which we live;" while you with one accord reject, and scout, and spit upon that old policy, and insist upon substituting something new. True, you disagree among yourselves as to what that substitute shall be. You are divided on new propositions and plans, but you are unanimous in rejecting and denouncing the old policy of the fathers. Some of you are for reviving the foreign slave trade; some for a Congressional Slave-Code for the Territories; some for Congress forbidding the Territories to prohibit Slavery within their limits; some for maintaining Slavery in the Territories through the judiciary; some for the "gur-reat pur-rinciple" that "if one man would enslave another, no third man should object," fantastically called "Popular Sovereignty;" but never a man among you is in favor of federal prohibition of slavery in federal territories, according to the practice of "our fathers who framed the Government under which we live." Not one of all your various plans can show a precedent or an advocate in the century within which our Government originated. Consider, then, whether your claim of conservatism for yourselves, and your charge of destructiveness against us, are based on the most clear and stable foundations.

Again, you say we have made the slavery question more prominent than it formerly was. We deny it. We admit that it is more prominent, but we deny that we made it so. It was not we, but you, who discarded the old policy of the fathers. We resisted, and still resist, your innovation; and thence comes the greater prominence of the question. Would you have that question reduced to its former proportions? Go back to that old policy. What has been will be again, under the same conditions. If you would have the peace of the old times, readopt the precepts and policy of the old times.

You charge that we stir up insurrections among your slaves. We deny it; and what is your proof? Harper's Ferry! John Brown!! John Brown was no

Republican; and you have failed to implicate a single Republican in his Harper's Ferry enterprise. If any member of our party is guilty in that matter, you know it or you do not know it. If you do know it, you are inexcusable for not designating the man and proving the fact. If you do not know it, you are inexcusable for asserting it, and especially for persisting in the assertion after you have tried and failed to make the proof. You need to be told that persisting in a charge which one does not know to be true is simply malicious slander.

Some of you admit that no Republican designedly aided or encouraged the Harper's Ferry affair, but still insist that our doctrines and declarations necessarily lead to such results. We do not believe it. We know we hold to no doctrine, and make no declaration, which were not held to and made by "our fathers who framed the Government under which we live." You never dealt fairly by us in relation to this affair. When it occurred, some important State elections were near at hand, and you were in evident glee with the belief that, by charging the blame upon us, you could get an advantage of us in those elections. The elections came, and your expectations were not quite fulfilled. Every Republican man knew that, as to himself at least, your charge was a slander, and he was not much inclined by it to cast his vote in your favor. Republican doctrines and declarations are accompanied with a continual protest against any interference whatever with your slaves, or with you about your slaves. Surely, this does not encourage them to revolt. True, we do, in common with "our fathers, who framed the Government under which we live," declare our belief that slavery is wrong; but the slaves do not hear us declare even this. For anything we say or do, the slaves would scarcely know there is a Republican party. I believe they would not, in fact, generally know it but for your misrepresentations of us, in their hearing. In your political contests among yourselves, each faction charges the other with sympathy with Black Republicanism; and then, to give point to the charge, defines Black Republicanism to simply be insurrection, blood and thunder among the slaves.

Slave insurrections are no more common now than they were before the Republican party was organized. What induced the Southampton insurrection, twenty-eight years ago, in which at least three times as many lives were lost as at Harper's Ferry? You can scarcely stretch your very elastic fancy to the conclusion that Southampton was "got up by Black Republicanism." In the present state of things in the United States, I do not think a general, or even a very extensive slave insurrection is possible. The indispensable concert of action cannot be attained. The slaves have no means of rapid communication; nor can incendiary freemen, black or white, supply it. The explosive materials are everywhere in parcels; but there neither are, nor can be supplied, the indispensable connecting trains.

Much is said by Southern people about the affection of slaves for their masters and mistresses; and a part of it, at least, is true. A plot for an uprising could scarcely be devised and communicated to twenty individuals before some one of them, to save the life of a favorite master or mistress, would divulge it. This is the rule; and the slave revolution in Haiti was not an exception to it, but a case occurring under peculiar circumstances. The gunpowder plot of British history, though not connected with slaves, was more in point. In that case, only about twenty were admitted to the secret; and yet one of them, in his anxiety to save a friend, betrayed the plot to that friend, and, by consequence, averted the calamity. Occasional poisonings from the kitchen, and open or stealthy assassinations in the field, and local revolts extending to a score or so, will continue to occur as the natural results of slavery; but no general insurrection of slaves, as I think, can happen in this country for a long time. Whoever much fears, or much hopes for such an event, will be alike disappointed.

In the language of Mr. Jefferson, uttered many years ago, "It is still in our power to direct the process of emancipation, and deportation, peaceably, and in such slow degrees, as that the evil will wear off insensibly; and their places be, *pari passu*, filled up by free white laborers. If, on the contrary, it is left to force itself on, human nature must shudder at the prospect held up."

Mr. Jefferson did not mean to say, nor do I, that the power of emancipation is in the Federal Government. He spoke of Virginia; and, as to the power of emancipation, I speak of the slaveholding States only. The Federal Government, however, as we insist, has the power of restraining the extension of the institution—the power to insure that a slave insurrection shall never occur on any American soil which is now free from slavery.

John Brown's effort was peculiar. It was not a slave insurrection. It was an attempt by white men to get up a revolt among slaves, in which the slaves refused to participate. In fact, it was so absurd that the slaves, with all their ignorance, saw plainly enough it could not succeed. That affair, in its philosophy, corresponds with the many attempts, related in history, at the assassination of kings and emperors. An enthusiast broods over the oppression of a people till he fancies himself commissioned by Heaven to liberate

them. He ventures the attempt, which ends in little else than his own execution. Orsini's attempt on Louis Napoleon, and John Brown's attempt at
Harper's Ferry were, in their philosophy, precisely the same. The eagerness
to cast blame on old England in the one case, and on New England in the
other, does not disprove the sameness of the two things.

And how much would it avail you, if you could, by the use of John
Brown, Helper's Book, and the like, break up the Republican organization?
Human action can be modified to some extent, but human nature cannot
be changed. There is a judgment and a feeling against slavery in this nation,
which cast at least a million and a half of votes. You cannot destroy that
judgment and feeling—that sentiment—by breaking up the political organization which rallies around it. You can scarcely scatter and disperse an
army which has been formed into order in the face of your heaviest fire; but
if you could, how much would you gain by forcing the sentiment which created it out of the peaceful channel of the ballot-box, into some other channel? What would that other channel probably be? Would the number of
John Browns be lessened or enlarged by the operation?

But you will break up the Union rather than submit to a denial of your
Constitutional rights.

That has a somewhat reckless sound; but it would be palliated, if not
fully justified, were we proposing, by the mere force of numbers, to deprive
you of some right, plainly written down in the Constitution. But we are proposing no such thing.

When you make these declarations, you have a specific and well-under-
stood allusion to an assumed Constitutional right of yours, to take slaves
into the federal territories, and to hold them there as property. But no such
right is specifically written in the Constitution. That instrument is literally
silent about any such right. We, on the contrary, deny that such a right has
any existence in the Constitution, even by implication.

Your purpose, then, plainly stated, is that you will destroy the Government, unless you be allowed to construe and enforce the Constitution as
you please, on all points in dispute between you and us. You will rule or ruin
in all events.

This, plainly stated, is your language. Perhaps you will say the Supreme
Court has decided the disputed Constitutional question in your favor. Not
quite so. But waiving the lawyer's distinction between dictum and decision,
the Court have decided the question for you in a sort of way. The Court
have substantially said, it is your Constitutional right to take slaves into the

federal territories, and to hold them there as property. When I say the decision was made in a sort of way, I mean it was made in a divided Court, by a bare majority of the Judges, and they not quite agreeing with one another in the reasons for making it; that it is so made as that its avowed supporters disagree with one another about its meaning, and that it was mainly based upon a mistaken statement of fact—the statement in the opinion that "the right of property in a slave is distinctly and expressly affirmed in the Constitution."

An inspection of the Constitution will show that the right of property in a slave is not "distinctly and expressly affirmed" in it. Bear in mind, the Judges do not pledge their judicial opinion that such right is impliedly affirmed in the Constitution; but they pledge their veracity that it is "distinctly and expressly" affirmed there—"distinctly," that is, not mingled with anything else—"expressly," that is, in words meaning just that, without the aid of any inference, and susceptible of no other meaning.

If they had only pledged their judicial opinion that such right is affirmed in the instrument by implication, it would be open to others to show that neither the word "slave" nor "slavery" is to be found in the Constitution, nor the word "property" even, in any connection with language alluding to the things slave, or slavery; and that wherever in that instrument the slave is alluded to, he is called a "person;"—and wherever his master's legal right in relation to him is alluded to, it is spoken of as "service or labor which may be due"—as a debt payable in service or labor. Also, it would be open to show, by contemporaneous history, that this mode of alluding to slaves and slavery, instead of speaking of them, was employed on purpose to exclude from the Constitution the idea that there could be property in man.

To show all this, is easy and certain.

When this obvious mistake of the Judges shall be brought to their notice, is it not reasonable to expect that they will withdraw the mistaken statement, and reconsider the conclusion based upon it?

And then it is to be remembered that "our fathers, who framed the Government under which we live"—the men who made the Constitution—decided this same Constitutional question in our favor, long ago—decided it without division among themselves, when making the decision; without division among themselves about the meaning of it after it was made, and, so far as any evidence is left, without basing it upon any mistaken statement of facts.

Under all these circumstances, do you really feel yourselves justified to break up this Government unless such a court decision as yours is, shall be at once submitted to as a conclusive and final rule of political action? But you will not abide the election of a Republican president! In that supposed event, you say, you will destroy the Union; and then, you say, the great crime of having destroyed it will be upon us! That is cool. A highwayman holds a pistol to my ear, and mutters through his teeth, "Stand and deliver, or I shall kill you, and then you will be a murderer!"

To be sure, what the robber demanded of me—my money—was my own; and I had a clear right to keep it; but it was no more my own than my vote is my own; and the threat of death to me, to extort my money, and the threat of destruction to the Union, to extort my vote, can scarcely be distinguished in principle.

A few words now to Republicans. It is exceedingly desirable that all parts of this great Confederacy shall be at peace, and in harmony, one with another. Let us Republicans do our part to have it so. Even though much provoked, let us do nothing through passion and ill temper. Even though the Southern people will not so much as listen to us, let us calmly consider their demands, and yield to them if, in our deliberate view of our duty, we possibly can. Judging by all they say and do, and by the subject and nature of their controversy with us, let us determine, if we can, what will satisfy them.

Will they be satisfied if the Territories be unconditionally surrendered to them? We know they will not. In all their present complaints against us, the Territories are scarcely mentioned. Invasions and insurrections are the rage now. Will it satisfy them, if, in the future, we have nothing to do with invasions and insurrections? We know it will not. We so know, because we know we never had anything to do with invasions and insurrections; and yet this total abstaining does not exempt us from the charge and the denunciation.

The question recurs, what will satisfy them? Simply this: We must not only let them alone, but we must somehow convince them that we do let them alone. This, we know by experience, is no easy task. We have been so trying to convince them from the very beginning of our organization, but with no success. In all our platforms and speeches we have constantly protested our purpose to let them alone; but this has had no tendency to convince them. Alike unavailing to convince them, is the fact that they have never detected a man of us in any attempt to disturb them.

These natural and apparently adequate means all failing, what will convince them? This, and this only: cease to call slavery wrong, and join them in calling it right. And this must be done thoroughly—done in acts as well as in words. Silence will not be tolerated—we must place ourselves avowedly with them. Senator Douglas' new sedition law must be enacted and enforced, suppressing all declarations that slavery is wrong, whether made in politics, in presses, in pulpits, or in private. We must arrest and return their fugitive slaves with greedy pleasure. We must pull down our Free State constitutions. The whole atmosphere must be disinfected from all taint of opposition to slavery, before they will cease to believe that all their troubles proceed from us.

I am quite aware they do not state their case precisely in this way. Most of them would probably say to us, "Let us alone, do nothing to us, and say what you please about slavery." But we do let them alone—have never disturbed them—so that, after all, it is what we say which dissatisfies them. They will continue to accuse us of doing, until we cease saying.

I am also aware they have not, as yet, in terms, demanded the overthrow of our Free State Constitutions. Yet those Constitutions declare the wrong of slavery, with more solemn emphasis, than do all other sayings against it; and when all these other sayings shall have been silenced, the overthrow of these Constitutions will be demanded, and nothing be left to resist the demand. It is nothing to the contrary, that they do not demand the whole of this just now. Demanding what they do, and for the reason they do, they can voluntarily stop nowhere short of this consummation. Holding, as they do, that slavery is morally right, and socially elevating, they cannot cease to demand a full national recognition of it, as a legal right, and a social blessing.

Nor can we justifiably withhold this, on any ground save our conviction that slavery is wrong. If slavery is right, all words, acts, laws, and constitutions against it, are themselves wrong, and should be silenced, and swept away. If it is right, we cannot justly object to its nationality—its universality; if it is wrong, they cannot justly insist upon its extension—its enlargement. All they ask, we could readily grant, if we thought slavery right; all we ask, they could as readily grant, if they thought it wrong. Their thinking it right, and our thinking it wrong, is the precise fact upon which depends the whole controversy. Thinking it right, as they do, they are not to blame for desiring its full recognition, as being right; but, thinking it wrong, as we do, can we yield to them? Can we cast our votes with their view, and against our own? In view of our moral, social, and political responsibilities, can we do this?

Wrong as we think slavery is, we can yet afford to let it alone where it is, because that much is due to the necessity arising from its actual presence in the nation; but can we, while our votes will prevent it, allow it to spread into the National Territories, and to overrun us here in these Free States? If our sense of duty forbids this, then let us stand by our duty, fearlessly and effectively. Let us be diverted by none of those sophistical contrivances wherewith we are so industriously plied and belabored—contrivances such as groping for some middle ground between the right and the wrong, vain as the search for a man who should be neither a living man nor a dead man—such as a policy of "don't care" on a question about which all true men do care—such as Union appeals beseeching true Union men to yield to Disunionists, reversing the divine rule, and calling, not the sinners, but the righteous to repentance—such as invocations to Washington, imploring men to unsay what Washington said, and undo what Washington did.

Neither let us be slandered from our duty by false accusations against us, nor frightened from it by menaces of destruction to the Government nor of dungeons to ourselves. Let us have faith that right makes might, and in that faith, let us, to the end, dare to do our duty as we understand it.

25: Garibaldi Addresses His Troops
"To Arms, Then, All of You!"

Naples, September, 1860

ON THE MOONLIT NIGHT OF MAY 5, 1860, IN THE PORT TOWN OF QUARTO ON the east coast of the Italian peninsula, fifty-three-year-old Giuseppe Garibaldi assembled a thousand men armed with aging muskets, ordered them to board a pair of hijacked steamers, and set out into the Tyrrhenian Sea. They sailed south, towards Sicily, a thousand eager young men dressed in civilian clothes and inspired to create a modern nation-state on the Italian peninsula, even at the cost of their lives.

Garibaldi acted on his own accord. The small force he headed was a private army sailing on behalf of an idea, not a government. The idea, the dream, was Italian unification, a merger of the peninsula's various kingdoms, duchies and papal states under a single government that spoke for all of Italy.

The goal was within sight. The dominant northern Italian kingdom of Piedmont extended its influence to the south and east in the aftermath of a war against Austria in 1859. Fighting with allies from France, the Piedmont Italians wrested control of Lombardy, with its important city of Milan, from Austria, but France called a halt to the brief war before the Italians achieved any further gains, including the capture of Austrian-held Venice.

Count Camillo Cavour, head of the Piedmont government, believed French assistance would be critical if the northern kingdom wished to extend its control further down the Italian boot. To ensure that support, Cavour agreed in early 1860 to give the French the northwest province of Savoy and the city of Nice, in the southwest corner of the kingdom.

Giuseppe Garibaldi was a native of Nice and an ardent Italian nationalist. He denounced Cavour and the deal with France, saying it made him a "foreigner in his own country."[1] His criticisms carried weight, for he had fought in the campaign against Austria in 1859. He had served as a general in 1848 when northern Italians first attempted to throw off Austrian domination. He was a protégé of sorts of the great patriot Guiseppe Mazzini, although Garibaldi was a monarchist and Mazzini a stalwart republican. Brave, impetuous and plain-spoken, Garibaldi was a hero for many Italians, a man any government would be loath to alienate.

After Cavour surrendered Savoy and Nice, Garbaldi decided to take matters into his own hands. Sicilians had shown signs of rebellion against the independent kingdom of Naples. With some prodding from Garibaldi and his men, perhaps Sicily might rise and touch off a revolution in the south. With his small private army, the Thousand, as they became known, he sailed from Quarto and invaded the Sicilian town of Marsala on May 11. Upon landing, Garibaldi claimed the island for King Victor Emanuel, ruler of Piedmont, and proclaimed himself Sicily's temporary dictator. His loyalty to Victor Emanuel was a sore point with some of his troops, who shared Mazzini's idea that a unified Italy ought to be a republic. But most fought anyway, for their love of the bearded, charismatic Garibaldi outweighed their doubts about his political judgment.

If they had doubts about his military expertise as well, they were soon put to rest. Although outnumbered and desperately short of weapons and ammunition, Garibaldi ordered his troops to assail a government strong point near the Sicilian town of Calatafimi. "Here we either make Italy or die," he told his troops.[2] Outmanned three to one, Garibaldi's men took the town, and within a month, they were masters of the island. The government of Count Cavour was aghast—historians disagree on whether Cavour actively sought to block Garibaldi's success, or whether he simply looked the other way and hoped it would fail. Cavour had reasons to oppose Garibaldi: His bitter criticism of the government after the Savoy-Nice deal won him no friends in government. What's more, Garibaldi's freelance insurrection in Sicily inspired a nationalist rebellion on the mainland that threatened the independent Papal states and Rome, where France— Cavour's most important ally—had troops on the ground. Garibaldi's adventure threatened to involved French troops, which surely would have played havoc with Cavour's carefully planned alliance.

Nevertheless, Cavour gladly accepted Garibaldi's gift. He sent administrators to complete the takeover of Sicily—making sure that those selected were hostile to Garibaldi and whatever ambitions he might harbor for the south. When Garibaldi's new ally on the mainland, Agostino Bertani, prepared to invade the Papal states with his private army, the Cavour government stepped in and order Bertani to proceed to Sicily instead.

Garibaldi and his troops crossed the Strait of Messina in August and brought revolution to the Italian mainland. He landed in Calabria and began marching north towards Naples with more than ten thousand soldiers. Word reached him that the Cavour government was preparing a force of its own to take Naples and deny Garibaldi a glorious victory. But Garibaldi moved too quickly, and by now was far too popular even among some enemy soldiers, who offered little or no resistance. He entered Naples on September 7, 1860, not as a foreign conqueror but as a hero, and appointed himself ruler of the city, one of the largest in Europe at the time. During his tenure, Garibaldi introduced free public education, required toleration of Protestant denominations, and chipped away at the secular powers of the Catholic Church.

The conquest of the south was not yet complete, for a Neapolitan army of forty thousand had gathered north of the city, between Garibaldi and Rome. Meanwhile, the Cavour government hastily moved to co-opt the revolution Garibaldi started. Government troops invaded the Papal states, although they avoided Rome and a potentially disastrous confrontation with French troops protecting the Papacy. After seizing control of the Pope's secular power base, they continued to move south, toward Garibaldi's army. Cavour, worried about Garibaldi's intentions and desperate to prevent revolution from spinning out of control, conceded that the government had been powerless to prevent the fall of Naples, but now, he said, "we must stop him elsewhere." The emperor of France, Louis Napoleon, was similarly concerned about Garibaldi's revolution and the possibility that he might march on Rome.[3]

At this critical moment in September, 1860, Garibaldi returned to Sicily to settle a bitter political dispute over how and when the island would be formally annexed into the greater Piedmont kingdom. Before leaving, however, he delivered the following speech to his troops, now more than thirty thousand strong. In it, he reaffirmed his loyalty to the king and urged that his followers do likewise. If he was indeed an enemy of Cavour's government, nobody could accuse him of treason.

Garibaldi's speech, which makes up for its clumsy start with clear, ringing language, was a call to arms to Italians accustomed to thinking of themselves as anything but—their associations were provincial, not national. But in the person of Victor Emanuel, he argued, Italians could put aside their regional differences to rally around a representative of themselves and their ambitions.

Despite the speech's passion, Garbaldi's army faltered during his short absence, but upon his return, his army won a tremendous victory over the Neapolitans in the Volturno Valley in October. That victory, combined with the government's triumph in the Papal states, secured the virtual unification of the peninsula save for Rome and Venice. Garibaldi, Cavour, and Mazzini all are remembered today as founders of the modern Italian nation-state, but it was Garibaldi's daring and bravery that inspired Italians by the tens of thousands to fight for something called Italy.

▼ ▼ ▼

WE must now consider the period which is just drawing to a close as almost the last stage of our national resurrection, and prepare ourselves to finish worthily the marvelous design of the elect of twenty generations, the completion of which Providence has reserved for this fortunate age.

Yes, young men, Italy owes to you an undertaking which has merited the applause of the universe. You have conquered and you will conquer still, because you are prepared for the tactics that decide the fate of battles. You are not unworthy of the men who entered the ranks of a Macedonian phalanx, and who contended not in vain with the proud conquerors of Asia. To this wonderful page in our country's history another more glorious still will be added, and the slave shall show at last to his free brothers a sharpened sword forged from the links of his fetters.

To arms, then, all of you! all of you! And the oppressors and the mighty shall disappear like dust. You, too, women, cast away all the cowards from your embraces; they will give you only cowards for children, and you who are the daughters of the land of beauty must bear children who are noble and brave. Let timid doctrinaires depart from among us to carry their servility and their miserable fears elsewhere. This people is its own master. It wishes to be the brother of other peoples, but to look on the insolent with a proud glance, not to grovel before them imploring its own freedom. It will no longer follow in the trail of men whose hearts are foul. No! No! No!

Providence has presented Italy with Victor Emmanuel. Every Italian should rally round him. By the side of Victor Emmanuel every quarrel should be forgotten, all rancor depart. Once more I repeat my battle-cry: "To arms, all—all of you!" If March, 1861, does not find one million of Italians in arms, then alas for liberty, alas for the life of Italy. Ah, no, far be from me a thought which I loathe like poison. March of 1861, or if need be February, will find us all at our post—Italians of Calatafimi, Palermo, Ancona, the Volturno, Castelfidardo, and Isernia, and with us every man of this land who is not a coward or a slave. Let all of us rally round the glorious hero of Palestro and give the last blow to the crumbling edifice of tyranny. Receive, then, my gallant young volunteers, at the honored conclusion of ten battles, one word of farewell from me.

I utter this word with deepest affection and from the very bottom of my heart. Today I am obliged to retire, but for a few days only. The hour of battle will find me with you again, by the side of the champions of Italian liberty. Let those only return to their homes who are called by the imperative duties which they owe to their families, and those who by their glorious wounds have deserved the credit of their country. These, indeed, will serve Italy in their homes by their counsel, by the very aspect of the scars which adorn their youthful brows. Apart from these, let all others remain to guard our glorious banners. We shall meet again before long to march together to the redemption of our brothers who are still slaves of the stranger. We shall meet again before long to march to new triumphs.

26: Susan B. Anthony
A Woman's Right to Suffrage
"Are Women Persons?"

Monroe County, 1873

SUSAN B. ANTHONY ROSE EARLY ON THE MORNING OF NOVEMBER 5, 1872, FOR a most unusual appointment. She and fourteen other women walked through the quiet streets of Rochester, NY, to a polling place, where they cast their votes in the presidential race between incumbent Ulysses S. Grant and Horace Greeley. The women were brand new to the voting process, having registered just four days earlier.

Local election officials carefully orchestrated the process that morning. They arranged for the women to vote as early as possible to avoid any public spectacle. The women, after all, were not eligible to vote.

Susan B. Anthony and her allies were not the first women to defy laws restricting the franchise to men. In the years following the Civil War, dozens of women attempted to vote or at least to register as voters, inspired by the burgeoning suffrage movement that was allied with the temperance and abolitionist movements in the mid-nineteenth century. After the Civil War, women argued that the Fourteenth Amendment, passed after the Civil War, implicitly recognized their right to vote because it guaranteed equal protection of the law for all persons. When black males were given the vote with passage of the Fifteenth Amendment, some women demanded a Sixteenth Amendment, one that would widen the franchise to the other half of the nation's adult population. The suffrage advocates were having an impact—the territories of Wyoming and Utah gave women the vote in 1869 and 1870, respectively.

Susan B. Anthony, reared in an egalitarian Quaker family in Rochester, emerged as one of the movement's most effective leaders in the 1850s. She was passionate and tireless, traits that more than made up for a somewhat staid and stern persona. In her formative years as a public speaker and advocate, she worked with some of the great abolitionist leaders in the North, in part through her father's active role in the anti-slavery cause. The crusade to free the enslaved and the campaign to win equality for women were, for Anthony and many others, part of the same struggle.

Anthony and Elizabeth Cady Stanton formed the National Woman Suffrage Association after the war to agitate for Constitutional recognition of a woman's right to vote. Anthony took matters into her own hands on Election Day, 1872, by turning the ritual of voting into an act of civil disobedience. While other women joined her, newspaper coverage focused on the "apostle of woman's rights," as newspapers dubbed Anthony.

Three weeks after the election, which Grant won, an embarrassed United States marshal arrested Anthony in her home for the crime of casting an ineligible vote in a federal election. Her compatriots were arrested, too, but Anthony garnered the most attention. She was formally indicted in late January, and while awaiting trial, she went to the polling place again, this time to vote in a local election in early March. This time, however, no other women joined her. She noted in her diary that "the rest of the women [were] all frightened . . ."[1]

As her trial approached, Anthony went on a speaking tour throughout Monroe County in upstate New York. She addressed her audiences as "fellow citizens," making her point in the first three seconds of her speech: Although a woman, she, too, was a citizen and was entitled to the rights accorded citizens. The rhetoric of the abolitionist movement and the results of the Civil War provide context for her argument. Discrimination against women, she said, ought to be as "null and void" as discrimination against blacks. Citing court decision, she noted that a citizen was defined as "a person in the United States, entitled to vote and hold office."

"Are women persons?" she asked, uttering the line by which the speech is best known.

Monroe County officials ruled that her tour prejudiced potential jurors, so the trial was moved to nearby Ontario County. Undaunted, Anthony embarked on a tour of that county as well. Despite these efforts and the force of her stump speech, she was found guilty on June 17, 1873, after the presiding judge ordered the jurors to return a guilty verdict and then dismissed them when Anthony's lawyer protested. Susan B. Anthony was fined a hundred dollars. Not surprisingly, she never paid it.

The Nineteenth Amendment, granting suffrage to women, was passed in 1920.

▼ ▼ ▼

FRIENDS and fellow citizens: I stand before you tonight under indictment for the alleged crime of having voted at the last presidential election, without having a lawful right to vote. It shall be my work this evening to prove to you that in thus voting, I not only committed no crime, but, instead, simply exercised my citizen's rights, guaranteed to me and all United States citizens by the National Constitution, beyond the power of any state to deny.

The preamble of the Federal Constitution says:

"We, the people of the United States, in order to form a more perfect union, establish justice, insure domestic tranquillity, provide for the common defense, promote the general welfare, and secure the blessings of liberty to ourselves and our posterity, do ordain and establish this Constitution for the United States of America."

It was we, the people; not we, the white male citizens; nor yet we, the male citizens; but we, the whole people, who formed the Union. And we formed it, not to give the blessings of liberty, but to secure them; not to the half of ourselves and the half of our posterity, but to the whole people— women as well as men. And it is a downright mockery to talk to women of their enjoyment of the blessings of liberty while they are denied the use of the only means of securing them provided by this democratic-republican government—the ballot.

For any state to make sex a qualification that must ever result in the disfranchisement of one entire half of the people, is to pass a bill of attainder, or, an ex post facto law, and is therefore a violation of the supreme law of the land. By it the blessings of liberty are forever withheld from women and their female posterity.

To them this government has no just powers derived from the consent of the governed. To them this government is not a democracy. It is not a republic. It is an odious aristocracy; a hateful oligarchy of sex; the most hateful aristocracy ever established on the face of the globe; an oligarchy of wealth, where the rich govern the poor, an oligarchy of learning, where the educated govern the ignorant, or even an oligarchy of race, where the Saxon rules the African, might be endured; but this oligarchy of sex, which makes father, brothers, husband, sons, the oligarchs over the mother and sisters, the wife and daughters, of every household—which ordains all men sovereigns, all women subjects, carries dissension, discord, and rebellion into every home of the nation.

Webster, Worcester, and Bouvier all define a citizen to be a person in the United States, entitled to vote and hold office.

The only question left to be settled now is: Are women persons? And I hardly believe any of our opponents will have the hardihood to say they are not. Being persons, then, women are citizens; and no state has a right to make any law, or to enforce any old law, that shall abridge their privileges or immunities. Hence, every discrimination against women in the constitutions and laws of the several states is today null and void, precisely as is every one against Negroes.

27: William Jennings Bryan and the Cross of Gold

Chicago, July 9, 1896

THE U.S. ECONOMY COLLAPSED IN 1893, BRINGING AN END TO AN ERA KNOWN as the Gilded Age, a time during which a few entrepreneurs, monopolists, and bankers made vast fortunes while laborers, factory workers, farmers, immigrants, and former slaves struggled to find a place in the nation's industrial economy. The struggle between rich and poor in the late nineteenth century was constant and, on occasion, violent. A labor dispute in Chicago in 1886 turned deadly when a bomb went off during a demonstration in Haymarket Square. Seven police officers and an unknown number of civilians died. More than a dozen workers died in 1894 when federal troops broke up a strike against the Pullman Palace Car Company in Chicago.

The severe economic downturn beginning in 1893 added to the nation's growing anxiety over the gap between rich and poor. Factory workers in the cities of the northeast and Midwest demanded higher wages and better working conditions. Farmers in the Great Plains sought relief from crushing debt. Both sought change through collective action, workers through labor unions, farmers through a cooperative movement known as the Grange.

From the West came calls for a dramatic change in U.S. currency policy. Farmers and their advocates argued in favor of free coinage of silver, rather than strict adherence to the gold standard. Coinage of silver appealed to struggling farmers because it would led to inflation, making it easier to pay off their debts. But Democratic President Grover Cleveland, a conservative, pro-business politician from the Northeast, resisted calls to increase the nation's money supply. Voters handed Cleveland's party a spectacular defeat in the congressional elections of 1894—the Democrats lost an astounding 113 seats in the House of Representatives.

As the presidential election year of 1896 unfolded, many Democrats repudiated Cleveland's unpopular policies and began to look elsewhere for a nominee. But as they gathered at their convention in Chicago, so recently the site of violent clashes between workers and the state, they were leaderless. No consensus had formed around potential candidate who could build a new coalition of the disaffected in place of the old, Cleveland coalition of northeastern businessmen, prosperous farmers, free-traders, and political reformers.

William Jennings Bryan, a 36-year-old lawyer and former Congressman from Nebraska, was one of several speakers chosen to deliver speeches about the gold and silver controversy at the convention. Bryan was an accomplished orator and a deeply religious man who wrote many of his speeches in collaboration with his wife, Mary Baird, who also was a lawyer. A devout advocate for free silver, Bryan prepared a speech designed to challenge fellow Democrats who wished to continue Cleveland's hard-money, gold-standard policies even in the face of a severe depression.

As delegates wondered who might emerge from the convention with the party's nomination, young Bryan took the stage to take part in the debate over bimetallism, that is, the dispute over gold and silver. In a speech filled with religious allusions and populist outrage, Bryan assailed the eastern-based Cleveland wing of the party for supporting policies that hurt farmers and working people. He addressed himself directly to the party's gold supporters, saying, "When you come before us and tell us that we are about to disturb your business interests, we reply that you have disturbed our business interests by your course."

It was a breathtaking challenge, delivered with righteous indignation and overt sectional appeals the likes of which had not been seen since the Civil War. "It is the issue of 1776 all over again," he said, but in his formulation, the British were the "inhabitants" of Massachusetts and New York.

In concluding this rousing speech, Bryan said he spoke for the nation's "producing masses," and vowed that, "you shall not press down upon the brow of labor this crown of thorns; you shall not crucify mankind upon a cross of gold."

Like no other convention speech before or since, Bryan's Cross of Gold speech touched off a wild demonstration. It was more than a speech; it was a political milestone, signaling an end of the old Democratic Party of Grover Cleveland and a new party made up of the economically disenfranchised. The convention now had its champion. Bryan became the youngest presidential nominee in the nation's history. He went on to campaign vigorously in an age when candidates still believed it was unseemly to stump for votes. Despite those efforts, he lost the general election to William McKinley. He would lose two other bids for the White House in the years to come.

The Cross of Gold speech, however, continues to hold a place in American rhetoric and in American political science. It is among the greatest speeches ever given at an American political convention, and it reconfigured the Democratic Party on the eve of the twentieth century.

▼ ▼ ▼

IT would be presumptuous, indeed, to present myself against the distinguished gentlemen to whom you have listened if this were but a measuring of ability; but this is not a contest among persons. The humblest citizen in all the land when clad in the armor of a righteous cause is stronger than all the whole hosts of error that they can bring. I come to speak to you in defense of a cause as holy as the cause of liberty—the cause of humanity. When this debate is concluded, a motion will be made to lay upon the table the resolution offered in commendation of the administration and also the resolution in condemnation of the administration. I shall object to bringing this question down to a level of persons. The individual is but an atom; he is born, he acts, he dies; but principles are eternal; and this has been a contest of principle.

Never before in the history of this country has there been witnessed such a contest as that through which we have passed. Never before in the history of American politics has a great issue been fought out as this issue has been by the voters themselves.

On the 4th of March, 1895, a few Democrats, most of them members of Congress, issued an address to the Democrats of the nation asserting that the money question was the paramount issue of the hour; asserting also the right of a majority of the Democratic Party to control the position of the party on this paramount issue; concluding with the request that all believers in free coinage of silver in the Democratic Party should organize and take charge of and control the policy of the Democratic Party. Three months later, at Memphis, an organization was perfected, and the silver Democrats went forth openly and boldly and courageously proclaiming their belief and declaring that if successful they would crystallize in a platform the declaration which they had made; and then began the conflict with a zeal approaching the zeal which inspired the crusaders who followed Peter the Hermit. Our silver Democrats went forth from victory unto victory, until they are assembled now, not to discuss, not to debate, but to enter up the judgment rendered by the plain people of this country.

But in this contest, brother has been arrayed against brother, and father against son. The warmest ties of love and acquaintance and association have been disregarded. Old leaders have been cast aside when they refused to give expression to the sentiments of those whom they would lead, and new leaders have sprung up to give direction to this cause of freedom. Thus has the contest been waged, and we have assembled here under as binding and solemn instructions as were ever fastened upon the representatives of a people.

We do not come as individuals. Why, as individuals we might have been glad to compliment the gentleman from New York [Senator Hill], but we knew that the people for whom we speak would never be willing to put him in a position where he could thwart the will of the Democratic Party. I say it was not a question of persons; it was a question of principle; and it is not with gladness, my friends, that we find ourselves brought into conflict with those who are now arrayed on the other side. The gentleman who just preceded me [Governor Russell] spoke of the old state of Massachusetts. Let me assure him that not one person in all this convention entertains the least hostility to the people of the state of Massachusetts.

But we stand here representing people who are the equals before the law of the largest cities in the state of Massachusetts. When you come before us and tell us that we shall disturb your business interests, we reply that you have disturbed our business interests by your action. We say to you that you have made too limited in its application the definition of a businessman. The man who is employed for wages is as much a businessman as his employer. The attorney in a country town is as much a businessman as the corporation counsel in a great metropolis. The merchant at the crossroads store is as much a businessman as the merchant of New York. The farmer who goes forth in the morning and toils all day, begins in the spring and toils all summer, and by the application of brain and muscle to the natural resources of this country creates wealth, is as much a businessman as the man who goes upon the Board of Trade and bets upon the price of grain. The miners who go 1,000 feet into the earth or climb 2,000 feet upon the cliffs and bring forth from their hiding places the precious metals to be poured in the channels of trade are as much businessmen as the few financial magnates who in a backroom corner the money of the world.

We come to speak for this broader class of businessmen. Ah my friends, we say not one word against those who live upon the Atlantic Coast; but those hardy pioneers who braved all the dangers of the wilderness, who have made the desert to blossom as the rose—those pioneers away out there, rearing their children near to nature's heart, where they can mingle their voices with the voices of the birds—out there where they have erected schoolhouses for the education of their children and churches where they praise their Creator, and the cemeteries where sleep the ashes of their dead—are as deserving of the consideration of this party as any people in this country.

It is for these that we speak. We do not come as aggressors. Our war is not a war of conquest. We are fighting in the defense of our homes, our families, and posterity. We have petitioned, and our petitions have been scorned. We have entreated, and our entreaties have been disregarded. We have begged, and they have mocked when our calamity came.

We beg no longer; we entreat no more; we petition no more. We defy them!

The gentleman from Wisconsin has said he fears a Robespierre. My friend, in this land of the free you need fear no tyrant who will spring up from among the people. What we need is an Andrew Jackson to stand as Jackson stood, against the encroachments of aggregated wealth.

They tell us that this platform was made to catch votes. We reply to them that changing conditions make new issues; that the principles upon which rest Democracy are as everlasting as the hills; but that they must be applied to new conditions as they arise. Conditions have arisen and we are attempting to meet those conditions. They tell us that the income tax ought not to be brought in here; that is not a new idea. They criticize us for our criticism of the Supreme Court of the United States. My friends, we have made no criticism. We have simply called attention to what you know. If you want criticisms, read the dissenting opinions of the Court. That will give you criticisms.

They say we passed an unconstitutional law. I deny it. The income tax was not unconstitutional when it was passed. It was not unconstitutional when it went before the Supreme Court for the first time. It did not become unconstitutional until one judge changed his mind; and we cannot be expected to know when a judge will change his mind.

The income tax is a just law. It simply intends to put the burdens of government justly upon the backs of the people. I am in favor of an income tax. When I find a man who is not willing to pay his share of the burden of the government which protects him, I find a man who is unworthy to enjoy the blessings of a government like ours.

He says that we are opposing the national bank currency. It is true. If you will read what Thomas Benton said, you will find that he said that in searching history he could find but one parallel to Andrew Jackson. That was Cicero, who destroyed the conspiracies of Cataline and saved Rome. He did for Rome what Jackson did when he destroyed the bank conspiracy and saved America.

We say in our platform that we believe that the right to coin money and issue money is a function of government. We believe it. We believe it is a part of sovereignty and can no more with safety be delegated to private individuals than can the power to make penal statutes or levy laws for taxation.

Mr. Jefferson, who was once regarded as good Democratic authority, seems to have a different opinion from the gentleman who has addressed us on the part of the minority. Those who are opposed to this proposition tell us that the issue of paper money is a function of the bank and that the government ought to go out of the banking business. I stand with Jefferson rather than with them, and tell them, as he did, that the issue of money is a function of the government and that the banks should go out of the governing business.

They complain about the plank which declares against the life tenure in office. They have tried to strain it to mean that which it does not mean. What we oppose in that plank is the life tenure that is being built up in Washington which establishes an office-holding class and excludes from participation in the benefits the humbler members of our society. . . .

Let me call attention to two or three great things. The gentleman from New York says that he will propose an amendment providing that this change in our law shall not affect contracts which, according to the present laws, are made payable in gold. But if he means to say that we cannot change our monetary system without protecting those who have loaned money before the change was made, I want to ask him where, in law or in morals, he can find authority for not protecting the debtors when the act of 1873 was passed when he now insists that we must protect the creditor. He says he also wants to amend this platform so as to provide that if we fail to maintain the parity within a year that we will then suspend the coinage of silver. We reply that when we advocate a thing which we believe will be successful we are not compelled to raise a doubt as to our own sincerity by trying to show what we will do if we are wrong.

I ask him, if he will apply his logic to us, why he does not apply it to himself. He says that he wants this country to try to secure an international agreement. Why doesn't he tell us what he is going to do if they fail to secure an international agreement. There is more reason for him to do that than for us to expect to fail to maintain the parity. They have tried for thirty years—thirty years—to secure an international agreement, and those are waiting for it most patiently who don't want it at all.

Now, my friends, let me come to the great paramount issue. If they ask us here why it is we say more on the money question than we say upon the tariff question, I reply that if protection has slain its thousands the gold standard has slain its tens of thousands. If they ask us why we did not embody all these things in our platform which we believe, we reply to them that when we have restored the money of the Constitution, all other necessary reforms will be possible, and that until that is done there is no reform that can be accomplished.

Why is it that within three months such a change has come over the sentiments of the country? Three months ago, when it was confidently asserted that those who believed in the gold standard would frame our platforms and nominate our candidates, even the advocates of the gold standard did not think that we could elect a President; but they had good reasons for the suspicion, because there is scarcely a state here today asking for the gold standard that is not within the absolute control of the Republican Party.

But note the change. Mr. McKinley was nominated at St. Louis upon a platform that declared for the maintenance of the gold standard until it should be changed into bimetallism by an international agreement. Mr. McKinley was the most popular man among the Republicans; and everybody three months ago in the Republican Party prophesied his election. How is it today? Why, that man who used to boast that he looked like Napoleon, that man shudders today when he thinks that he was nominated on the anniversary of the Battle of Waterloo. Not only that, but as he listens he can hear with ever increasing distinctness the sound of the waves as they beat upon the lonely shores of St. Helena.

Why this change? Ah, my friends is not the change evident to anyone who will look at the matter? It is because no private character, however pure, no personal popularity, however great, can protect from the avenging wrath of an indignant people the man who will either declare that he is in favor of fastening the gold standard upon this people, or who is willing to surrender the right of self-government and place legislative control in the hands of foreign potentates and powers. . . .

We go forth confident that we shall win. Why? Because upon the paramount issue in this campaign there is not a spot of ground upon which the enemy will dare to challenge battle. Why, if they tell us that the gold standard is a good thing, we point to their platform and tell them that their platform pledges the party to get rid of a gold standard and substitute bimetallism. If the gold standard is a good thing, why try to get rid of it? If the gold standard, and I might call your attention to the fact that some of the very people who are in this convention today and who tell you that we ought to declare in favor of international bimetallism and thereby declare that the gold standard is wrong and that the principles of bimetallism are better— these very people four months ago were open and avowed advocates of the gold standard and telling us that we could not legislate two metals together even with all the world.

I want to suggest this truth, that if the gold standard is a good thing we ought to declare in favor of its retention and not in favor of abandoning it; and if the gold standard is a bad thing, why should we wait until some other nations are willing to help us to let it go?

Here is the line of battle. We care not upon which issue they force the fight. We are prepared to meet them on either issue or on both. If they tell us that the gold standard is the standard of civilization, we reply to them that this, the most enlightened of all nations of the earth, has never declared for a gold standard, and both the parties this year are declaring against it. If the gold standard is the standard of civilization, why, my friends, should we not have it? So if they come to meet us on that, we can present the history of our nation. More than that, we can tell them this, that they will search the pages of history in vain to find a single instance in which the common people of any land ever declared themselves in favor of a gold standard. They can find where the holders of fixed investments have.

Mr. Carlisle said in 1878 that this was a struggle between the idle holders of idle capital and the struggling masses who produce the wealth and pay the taxes of the country; and my friends, it is simply a question that we shall decide upon which side shall the Democratic Party fight. Upon the side of the idle holders of idle capital, or upon the side of the struggling masses? That is the question that the party must answer first; and then it must be answered by each individual hereafter. The sympathies of the Democratic Party, as described by the platform, are on the side of the struggling masses, who have ever been the foundation of the Democratic Party.

There are two ideas of government. There are those who believe that if you just legislate to make the well-to-do prosperous, that their prosperity will leak through on those below. The Democratic idea has been that if you legislate to make the masses prosperous their prosperity will find its way up and through every class that rests upon it.

You come to us and tell us that the great cities are in favor of the gold standard. I tell you that the great cities rest upon these broad and fertile prairies. Burn down your cities and leave our farms, and your cities will spring up again as if by magic. But destroy our farms and the grass will grow in the streets of every city in the country.

My friends, we shall declare that this nation is able to legislate for its own people on every question without waiting for the aid or consent of any other nation on earth, and upon that issue we expect to carry every single state in the Union.

I shall not slander the fair state of Massachusetts nor the state of New York by saying that when citizens are confronted with the proposition, "Is this nation able to attend to its own business?"—I will not slander either one by saying that the people of those states will declare our helpless impotency as a nation to attend to our own business. It is the issue of 1776 over again. Our ancestors, when but three million, had the courage to declare their political independence of every other nation upon earth. Shall we, their descendants, when we have grown to seventy million, declare that we are less independent than our forefathers? No, my friends, it will never be the judgment of this people. Therefore, we care not upon what lines the battle is fought. If they say bimetallism is good but we cannot have it till some nation helps us, we reply that, instead of having a gold standard because England has, we shall restore bimetallism, and then let England have bimetallism because the United States have.

If they dare to come out in the open field and defend the gold standard as a good thing, we shall fight them to the uttermost, having behind us the producing masses of the nation and the world. Having behind us the commercial interests and the laboring interests and all the toiling masses, we shall answer their demands for a gold standard by saying to them, you shall not press down upon the brow of labor this crown of thorns. You shall not crucify mankind upon a cross of gold.

28: King Albert of Belgium Defies the Kaiser's Army

Brussels, August 4, 1914

THE ARMIES OF EUROPE WERE IN MOTION ON THE EVENING OF AUGUST 2, 1914, when the German ambassador to Belgium, Otto von Below, removed a note from his safe and delivered it to the office of the Belgian Foreign Minister, Julien Davignon. Von Below left the office quickly, drawing nervously on a cigarette. Davignon read the note and handed it to aides, muttering, "bad news, bad news."[1]

The note, composed in Berlin several days earlier and transmitted to von Below in Brussels, informed the Belgian government that German armies would soon cross into the country from the east because, the note asserted, falsely, the French were about to invade Belgium from the west as part of a plan to march to Berlin. Belgium had nothing to fear from Germany, the note read, but if the Belgians resisted the invasion, they would be treated as enemies and would be punished accordingly. Berlin demanded a response within twelve hours.

Belgium, a small country of fewer than 10 million people, wanted nothing to do with the rush to arms among Europe's great powers in the late summer of 1914. Long treated as a parade grounds for armies moving east and west along the continent's northern tier, Belgium had enjoyed neutrality, peace and independence since the mid-1800s. As great power after great power mobilized its armies and gathered its allies after the assassination of Austrian Archduke Franz Ferdinand in Serbia in late June, Belgium watched with a mixture of apprehension and reassurance. They were squeezed between France and Germany, members of rival alliances, but all sides understood that Belgium was neutral, like Switzerland. Surely nobody would be rash enough to violate that neutrality and so invite the world's scorn and contempt.

Now, however, the time had come to account for rash behavior. Belgium's King Albert and his government were forced to consider the unthinkable: The certainty of invasion, the violation of their country's treasured neutrality. Some government officials sought to take comfort in Germany's assurances that Belgians had nothing to fear. The King, however, had no illusions about German designs. He told his ministers that Belgium must resist the invaders, despite the country's small military (seven divisions, compared with the planned German assault of thirty four divisions).

The great capitals of Europe focused their attention on Brussels during the twelve hours that Germany allotted Belgium to make up its mind. Just as Berlin's deadline ran out, the Belgians delivered their reply to the German legation. "The Belgian Government, if they were to accept the proposals submitted to them, would sacrifice the honor of the nation and betray their duty toward Europe . . . [The] Belgian Government are firmly resolved to repel, by all means in their power, every attack upon their rights."[2]

The following day, August 4, German troops crossed into Belgium. King Albert I summoned the nation's Parliament for an extraordinary session at eleven o'clock that morning. Albert was not a man born to rule. He was, in fact, a monarch by accident, succeeding King Leopold II in 1909 only because the dead king's only son had died, and so had the dead king's oldest nephew, Albert's older brother Baudouin. Despite his lack of preparation, or perhaps because of it, Albert proved to be a popular king, disdaining the imperial pomposities of Europe's other royal courts for a more informal life. He was extremely well-read and he loved the outdoors life.

Unprepared as Belgium was, fearful as the onslaught would be, Albert had to find the words to stir his country's pride and inspire its courage. Belgium, unlike Germany, had no great sense of destiny or purpose. It was a small nation of sometimes intense divisions over language, ethnicity and religion. With the world watching, Albert delivered a ringing call to arms to a nation that disdained the martial spirit, and appealed to a common identity for a nation given to factional and parochial disputes.

His courage in the face of aggression was as admirable as the words he used to summon Belgians to the defense of their nation.

▼ ▼ ▼

IN the name of the nation, I give it a brotherly greeting. Everywhere in Flanders and Wallonia, in the towns and in the countryside, one single feeling binds all hearts together: the sense of patriotism. One single vision fills all minds: that of our independence endangered. One single duty imposes itself upon our wills: the duty of stubborn resistance.

In these solemn circumstances two virtues are indispensable: a calm but unshaken courage, and the close union of all Belgians.

Both virtues have already asserted themselves, in a brilliant fashion, before the eyes of a nation full of enthusiasm.

The irreproachable mobilization of our army, the multitude of voluntary enlistments, the devotion of the civil population, the abnegation of our soldiers' families, have revealed in an unquestionable manner the reassuring courage which inspires the Belgian people.

It is the moment for action.

I have called you together, gentlemen, in order to enable the Legislative Chambers to associate themselves with the impulse of the people in one and the same sentiment of sacrifice.

You will understand, gentlemen, how to take all those immediate measures which the situation requires, in respect both of the war and of public order.

No one in this country will fail in his duty.

If the foreigner, in defiance of that neutrality whose demands we have always scrupulously observed, violates our territory, he will find all the Belgians gathered about their sovereign, who will never betray his constitutional oath, and their Government, invested with the absolute confidence of the entire nation.

I have faith in our destinies; a country which is defending itself conquers the respect of all; such a country does not perish!

29: Padriag Pearse: Ireland Unfree Will Never be at Peace

Dublin, August 1, 1915

IN THE LATE SUMMER OF 1915, AS THE GREAT POWERS OF EUROPE BLED EACH other dry on the fields of Flanders and the steppes of eastern Europe, an end to Britain's eternal Irish problem seemed at hand. Parliament passed legislation a year earlier granting Ireland a form of self-government known as home rule. Ireland would have its own parliament, but it would remain under the British crown and subject to British foreign policy.

Home rule was a compromise designed to grant the rebellious Irish a measure of independence while, at the same time, keeping them tied to Mother England. Moderate nationalists in Ireland welcomed the compromise, even though home rule was promptly postponed until after the war, and pledged Irish support for Britain's conflict with the Kaiser and his allies. But radicals in Ireland and in the United States bitterly opposed home rule and the very notion of loyalty to Britain. With His Majesty's armies digging trenches on the western front, they believed the time was ripe to strike for Ireland's complete independence.

Padraig Pearse, a poet and schoolmaster, was among the leaders of a secret organization called the Irish Republican Brotherhood which was determined to bring about an independent republic in Ireland shorn of all ties to the crown. The IRB had a counterpart among Erin's exiles in America called Clan na Gael, or family of the Irish. Its leader was a New York journalist named John Devoy.

On June 29, 1915, a venerable Irish agitator named Jeremiah O'Donovan Rossa died in his adopted home of Staten Island, New York. Rossa was a legend among Irish radicals for his uncompromising, fiery denunciations of British rule in Ireland. Rossa, like Devoy, was a veteran of a movement called the Fenians which tried in vain to launch a rebellion in Ireland in the 1860s. A new generation of Irish radicals, represented by

Pearse, saw the aging Fenians as heroes despite their failures.

Rossa was a symbol of uncompromising resistance to Britain's presence in Ireland. And as a symbol, he might be more effective in death than he was in life. Devoy arranged for his body to be shipped to Ireland, where the IRB made arrangements for a political protest disguised as a funeral. The IRB chose Pearse, with his poet's gift for language, to deliver a graveside oration.

Pearse and his fellow conspirators knew that this was to be no ordinary funeral. The IRB was arming itself, thanks to funds from America, and was reaching out to Germany, through Devoy in New York, for military assistance. But as he prepared his tribute to Rossa, Pearse wondered how far his rhetoric should go. Was this the moment to link the struggles of the past to that of the future? How far did he dare go? He consulted with another IRB leader, Tom Clarke, who told him: "Make it as hot as hell. Throw discretion to the wind."[1]

On August 1, 1915, the conspirators escorted the body of Jeremiah O'Donovan Rossa through the streets of Dublin to the city's massive Glasnevin Cemetery. It was a rainy, gloomy day in Dublin. As mourners gathered around Rossa's gravesite, Pearse, wearing the uniform of a militia group called the Irish Volunteers, stepped forward to deliver the words that would connect the life of the dead Fenian to the lives of those at his grave.

The oration acknowledged what so many in Ireland believed—that the issue of Irish freedom was settled. The prospect of home rule after the war had, at last, pacified the island. But Pearse knew that his audience believed otherwise.

With his repetitious description of Ireland's enemies—not the British, but "the fools, the fools, the fools"—Pearse argued that the cause of Ireland was not settled, that compromise and intimidation would not bring peace.

Less than a year later, Pearse, Clarke and about a thousand Irish men and women launched a futile rebellion in Dublin on Easter Monday. The rebellion lasted less than a week. The rebellion's leaders, including Pearse and Clarke, were brought before a firing squad and executed.

Even then, the cause continued. Inspired in part by the Easter rebels, the Irish rose again in 1920, winning independence for twenty-six of the island's thirty-two counties in 1921.

▼ ▼ ▼

IT has been thought right, before we turn away from this place in which we have laid the mortal remains of O'Donovan Rossa that one among us should, in the name of all, speak the praise of that valiant man, and endeavor to formulate the thought and the hope that are in us as we stand around his grave. And if there is anything that makes it fitting that I rather than another, I rather than one of the grayhaired men who were young with him and shared in his labor and in his suffering, should speak here, it is perhaps that I may be taken as speaking on behalf of a new generation that has been re-baptised in the Fenian faith and that has accepted the responsibility of carrying out the Fenian program.

I propose to you then that, here by the grave of this unrepentant Fenian, we renew our baptismal vows; that, here by the grave of this unconquered and unconquerable man, we ask of God, each one for himself, such unshakable purpose, such high and gallant courage, such unbreakable strength of soul as belonged to O'Donovan Rossa. Deliberately here we avow ourselves, as he avowed himself in the dock, Irishmen of one allegiance only. We of the Irish volunteers and you others who are associated with us in today's task and duty are bound together and must stand together henceforth in brotherly union for the achievement of the freedom of Ireland. And we know only one definition of freedom: it is Tone's definition, it is Mitchel's definition, it is Rossa's definition. Let no man blaspheme the cause that the dead generations of Ireland served by giving it any other name or definition than their name and their definition.

We stand at Rossa's grave not in sadness but rather in exaltation of spirit that it has been given to us to come thus into so close a communion with that brave and splendid Gael. Splendid and holy causes are served by men who are themselves splendid and holy. O'Donovan Rossa was splendid in the proud manhood of him, splendid in the heroic grace of him, splendid in the Gaelic strength and clarity and truth of him. All that splendor and pride and strength was compatible with a humility and a simplicity of devotion to Ireland, to all that was olden and beautiful and Gaelic in Ireland, the holiness and simplicity of patriotism of a Michael O'Cleary or of an Eoghan O'Growney. The clear true eyes of this man almost alone in his day visioned Ireland as we of today would surely have her: not free merely, but Gaelic as well; not Gaelic merely, but free and noble as well.

In a closer spiritual communion with him now than ever before or perhaps ever again, in spiritual communion with those of his day, living and dead, who suffered with him in English prisons, in communion of spirit too with our own dear comrades who suffer in English prisons today, and speaking on their behalf as well as on our own we pledge to Ireland our love, and we pledge to English rule in Ireland our hate. This is a place of peace, sacred to the dead, where men should speak with all charity and with all restraint but I hold it a Christian thing, as O'Donovan Rossa held it, to hate evil, to hate untruth, to hate oppression; and, hating them, to strive to overthrow them. Our foes are strong and wise and wary; but, strong and wise and wary as they are, they cannot undo the miracles of God who ripens in the hearts of young men the seeds sown by the young men of a former generation. And the seed sown by the young men of '65 and '67 are coming to their miraculous ripening today.

Rulers and Defenders of Realms had need to be wary if they would guard against such processes. Life springs from death and from the graves of patriot men and women spring living nations. The Defenders of this Realm have worked well in secret and in the open. They think that they have purchased half of us and intimidated the other half. They think that they have foreseen everything, think that they have provided against everything; but the fools, the fools, the fools!—they have left us our Fenian dead, and, while Ireland holds these graves, Ireland unfree shall never be at peace.

30: Helen Keller,
Strike Against War

New York, January 5, 1916

THE FIRST FULL YEAR OF WORLD WAR I PRODUCED LITTLE IN TERMS OF decisive results and much in terms of slaughter and destruction. The guns of August, 1914, gave way to stalemates on the western and eastern fronts by December, 1915. Never had so many died for so little strategic gain—in late 1915 in Loos, France, members of the British Expeditionary Force attacked a German line fortified by machine gunners who could hardly believe that enemy officers would send troops into the open against such fortified positions. The gunners took aim and fired, and men fell by the thousands. When the British finally retreated, they left behind eight thousand of the fifteen thousand who made the assault. The Germans were so appalled that they held their fire as the surviving enemy retreated.[1]

Even as Europe became an abattoir, the war spread to other parts of the world. Colonial possessions in Africa came under attack, and war broke out in Asia when Japan seized the Marianas, Caroline and Marshall islands. Sultan Mehmed V of the Ottoman Empire called on the world's Muslims to launch a holy war against Britain, France and Russia. A British attempt to invade Turkey, seat of the Ottoman Empire, ended in disaster on the shores of Gallipoli.

None of the major combatants was victorious, and none was defeated. The new year of 1916 promised renewed offensives on three continents and at sea, and more death and destruction.

The United States remained neutral, alone among the world's great powers in resisting the global call to arms. American neutrality, however, did not mean American passivity. In late 1915, President Woodrow Wilson's administration authorized an expansion of U.S. armed services amid growing tensions between Washington and Berlin following the sinking of the passenger ship *Lusitania* off the Irish coast in May, 1915. One hundred and twenty-four Americans were among the eleven hundred who died in the attack.

As Washington seemed to be drifting towards war with Germany, as American banks loaned billions of dollars to the Western Allies and American factories supplied the Allies with munitions and other goods, pro-neutrality argued against intervention. One of the most eloquent speakers on behalf not simply of American neutrality but of active opposition to the war was a woman who could not hear herself talk, who could not see her audience. Her name was Helen Keller.

Today Helen Keller is remembered as an inspirational figure who over-came childhood deafness and blindness to become a writer, lecturer and advocate for the handicapped. She lost the ability to see and hear nineteen months after her birth, in 1880. Soon afterwards, she became mute as well. At age seven, Keller was introduced to an extraordinary teacher named Anne Sullivan. Under Sullivan's guidance, young Helen explored the sym-bols and usage of language. When she was ten, Keller decided she would learn, somehow, to speak. She did so by touching the face of her teachers, feeling for the ways in which they manipulated their tongue, mouth and jaws to produce sounds.

Her ability to enunciate was limited, and, without the ability to hear, she could not know how to manipulate her voice as orators do for dramatic effect. She was difficult to understand, but she became a popular lecturer in the early years of the twentieth century.

She was more than an inspirational speaker, and her interests were not limited to improving the lives of other deaf and blind people. Helen Keller was a political activist, an avowed leftist who regularly condemned the depredations of big business, not an unheard-of position during the Progressive Era.

When war broke out in Europe in 1914, Helen Keller became a fierce critic of militarism and of the connections between private industry and the war machines of the great powers. In late 1915, as the Wilson Administration launched a campaign of what it called limited preparedness for war, she lashed out at big business, which she blamed for the nation's apparent drift towards war.

On January 5, 1916, Keller spoke at an anti-war rally in New York City as prominent voices, including former President Theodore Roosevelt and leading businessmen, increased their demands that the U.S. take more aggressive steps to prepare for war. With President Wilson up for re-election later in the year, pro-war and anti-war camps hoped to influence debate over U.S. policy during the campaign.

Keller's audience would have had difficulty understanding her, but there was no mistaking the themes she emphasized. She demanded, first, that nobody pity her. She had voluntarily and actively chosen to engage in public debate, so she expected only a "fair field" from her critics. She then went on with an appeal to American workers to use the power of their labor as a force for peace. Without the American worker, she said, there would be no war machine. Without the American worker, there would be no war.

Her speech was passionate and self-righteous, a polemic designed not so much to change minds as to inspire others to follow her pacifist lead. It argued that war invariably was the product of disputes between capitalists, and that American workers once again were on the verge of becoming victims of a pointless slaughter. Her scorn was not limited to capital; she argued that workers were "childish and silly," and their leaders were eager to exploit these flaws.

Her presence, her courage, gave power to her words, even if they were difficult to understand. Few could argue that Helen Keller spoke without thinking, or that she represented interests other than her own conscience. She could not hear her words; she could not see her listeners. She once was mute, but she had found her voice. Few other advocates of any cause had more moral authority than Helen Keller.

▼ ▼ ▼

TO begin with, I have a word to say to my good friends, the editors, and others who are moved to pity me. Some people are grieved because they imagine I am in the hands of unscrupulous persons who lead me astray and persuade me to espouse unpopular causes and make me the mouthpiece of their propaganda. Now, let it be understood once and for all that I do not want their pity; I would not change places with one of them. I know what I am talking about. My sources of information are as good and reliable as anybody else's. I have papers and magazines from England, France, Germany and Austria that I can read myself. Not all the editors I have met can do that. Quite a number of them have to take their French and German second hand. No, I will not disparage the editors. They are an overworked, misunderstood class. Let them remember, though, that if I cannot see the fire at the end of their cigarettes, neither can they thread a needle in the dark. All I ask, gentlemen, is a fair field and no favor. I have entered the fight against preparedness and against the economic system under which we live. It is to be a fight to the finish, and I ask no quarter.

The future of the world rests in the hands of America. The future of America rests on the backs of 80,000,000 working men and women and their children. We are facing a grave crisis in our national life. The few who profit from the labor of the masses want to organize the workers into an army which will protect the interests of the capitalists. You are urged to add to the heavy burdens you already bear the burden of a larger army and many additional warships. It is in your power to refuse to carry the artillery and the dread-noughts and to shake off some of the burdens, too, such as limousines, steam yachts and country estates. You do not need to make a great noise about it. With the silence and dignity of creators you can end wars and the system of selfishness and exploitation that causes wars. All you need to do to bring about this stupendous revolution is to straighten up and fold your arms.

We are not preparing to defend our country. Even if we were as helpless as Congressman Gardner says we are, we have no enemies foolhardy enough to attempt to invade the United States. The talk about attack from Germany and Japan is absurd. Germany has its hands full and will be busy with its own affairs for some generations after the European war is over.

With full control of the Atlantic Ocean and the Mediterranean Sea, the allies failed to land enough men to defeat the Turks at Gallipoli; and then they failed again to land an army at Salonica in time to check the Bulgarian invasion of Serbia. The conquest of America by water is a nightmare confined exclusively to ignorant persons and members of the Navy League.

Yet, everywhere, we hear fear advanced as argument for armament. It reminds me of a fable I read. A certain man found a horseshoe. His neighbor began to weep and wail because, as he justly pointed out, the man who found the horseshoe might someday find a horse. Having found the shoe, he might shoe him. The neighbor's child might someday go so near the horse's heels as to be kicked, and die. Undoubtedly the two families would quarrel and fight, and several valuable lives would be lost through the finding of the horseshoe. You know the last war we had we quite accidentally picked up some islands in the Pacific Ocean which may some day be the cause of a quarrel between ourselves and Japan. I'd rather drop those islands right now and foret about them than go to war to keep them. Wouldn't you?

Congress is not preparing to defend the people of the United States. It is planning to protect the capital of American speculators and investors in Mexico, South America, China, and the Philippine Islands. Incidentally this preparation will benefit the manufacturers of munitions and war machines.

Until recently there were uses in the United States for the money taken from the workers. But American labor is exploited almost to the limit now, and our national resources have all been appropriated. Still the profits keep piling up new capital. Our flourishing industry in implements of murder is filling the vaults of New York's banks with gold. And a dollar that is not being used to make a slave of some human being is not fulfilling its purpose in the capitalistic scheme. That dollar must be invested in South America, Mexico, China, or the Philippines.

It was no accident that the Navy League came into prominence at the same time that the National City Bank of New York established a branch in Buenos Aires. It is not a mere coincidence that six business associates of J.P. Morgan are officials of defense leagues. And chance did not dictate that Mayor Mitchel should appoint to his Committee of Safety a thousand men that represent a fifth of the wealth of the United States. These men want their foreign investments protected.

Every modern war has had its root in exploitation. The Civil War was fought to decide whether the slaveholders of the South or the capitalists of the North should exploit the West. The Spanish-American War decided that the United States should exploit Cuba and the Philippines. The South African War decided that the British should exploit the diamond mines. The Russo-Japanese War decided that Japan should exploit Korea. The present war is to decide who shall exploit the Balkans, Turkey, Persia, Egypt, India, China, Africa. And we are whetting our sword to scare the victors into sharing the spoils with us. Now, the workers are not interested in the spoils; they will not get any of them anyway.

The preparedness propagandists have still another object, and a very important one. They want to give the people something to think about besides their own unhappy condition. They know the cost of living is high, wages are low, employment is uncertain and will be much more so when the European call for munitions stops. No matter how hard and incessantly the people work, they often cannot afford the comforts of life; many cannot obtain the necessities.

Every few days we are given a new war scare to lend realism to their propaganda. They have had us on the verge of war over the *Lusitania*, the

Gulflight, the *Ancona*, and now they want the workingmen to become excited over the sinking of the *Persia*. The workingman has no interest in any of
these ships. The Germans might sink every vessel on the Atlantic Ocean
and the Mediterranean Sea, and kill Americans with every one—the
American workingman would still have no reason to go to war.

All the machinery of the system has been set in motion. Above the
complaint and din of the protest from the workers is heard the voice of
authority.

"Friends," it says, "fellow workmen, patriots; your country is in danger!
There are foes on all sides of us. There is nothing between us and our enemies except the Pacific Ocean and the Atlantic Ocean. Look at what has
happened to Belgium. Consider the fate of Serbia. Will you murmur about
low wages when your country, your very liberties, are in jeopardy? What are
the miseries you endure compared to the humiliation of having a victorious
German army sail up the East River? Quit your whining, get busy and prepare to defend your firesides and your flag. Get an army, get a navy; be
ready to meet the invaders like the loyal-hearted freemen you are."

Will the workers walk into this trap? Will they be fooled again? I am
afraid so. The people have always been amenable to oratory of this sort. The
workers know they have no enemies except their masters. They know that
their citizenship papers are no warrant for the safety of themselves or their
wives and children. They know that honest sweat, persistent toil and years
of struggle bring them nothing worth holding on to, worth fighting for. Yet,
deep down in their foolish hearts they believe they have a country. Oh blind
vanity of slaves!

The clever ones, up in the high places, know how childish and silly the
workers are. They know that if the government dresses them up in khaki
and gives them a rifle and starts them off with a brass band and waving banners, they will go forth to fight valiantly for their own enemies. They are
taught that brave men die for their country's honor. What a price to pay for
an abstraction—the lives of millions of young men; other millions crippled
and blinded for life; existence made hideous for still more millions of
human being; the achievement and inheritance of generations swept away
in a moment—and nobody better off for all the misery! This terrible sacrifice would be comprehensible if the thing you die for and call country fed,
clothed, housed and warmed you, educated and cherished your children. I
think the workers are the most unselfish of the children of men; they toil
and live and die for other people's country, other people's sentiments, other

people's liberties and other people's happiness! The workers have no liberties of their own; they are not free when they are compelled to work twelve or ten or eight hours a day. They are not free when they are ill paid for their exhausting toil. They are not free when their children must labor in mines, mills and factories or starve, and when their women may be driven by poverty to lives of shame. They are not free when they are clubbed and imprisoned because they go on strike for a raise of wages and for the elemental justice that is their right as human beings.

We are not free unless the men who frame and execute the laws represent the interests of the lives of the people and no other interest. The ballot does not make a free man out of a wage slave. There has never existed a truly free and democratic nation in the world. From time immemorial men have followed with blind loyalty the strong men who had the power of money and of armies. Even while battlefields were piled high with their own dead they have tilled the lands of the rulers and have been robbed of the fruits of their labor. They have built palaces and pyramids, temples and cathedrals that held no real shrine of liberty.

As civilization has grown more complex the workers have become more and more enslaved, until today they are little more than parts of the machines they operate. Daily they face the dangers of railroad, bridge, skyscraper, freight train, stokehold, stockyard, lumber raft and mine. Panting and straining at the docks, on the railroads and underground and on the seas, they move the traffic and pass from land to land the precious commodities that make it possible for us to live. And what is their reward? A scanty wage, often poverty, rents, taxes, tributes and war indemnities.

The kind of preparedness the workers want is reorganization and reconstruction of their whole life, such as has never been attempted by statesmen or governments. The Germans found out years ago that they could not raise good soldiers in the slums so they abolished the slums. They saw to it that all the people had at least a few of the essentials of civilization—decent lodging, clean streets, wholesome if scanty food, proper medical care and proper safeguards for the workers in their ocupations. That is only a small part of what should be done, but what wonders that one step toward the right sort of preparedness has wrought for Germany! For eighteen months it has kept itself free from invasion while carrying on an extended war of conquest, and its armies are still pressing on with unabated vigor. It is your business to force these reforms on the Administration. Let there be no more talk about what a government can or cannot do. All these things have been done by all the belligerent nations in the hurly-burly of war. Every fundamental industry has been managed better by the governments than by private corporations.

It is your duty to insist upon still more radical measure. It is your business to see that no child is employed in an industrial establishment or mine or store, and that no worker is needlessly exposed to accident or disease. It is your business to make them give you clean cities, free from smoke, dirt and congestion. It is your business to make them pay you a living wage. It is your business to see that this kind of preparedness is carried into every department on the nation, until everyone has a chance to be well born, well nourished, rightly educated, intelligent and serviceable to the country at all times.

Strike against all ordinances and laws and institutions that continue the slaughter of peace and the butcheries of war. Srike against war, for without you no battles can be fought. Strike against manufacturing scrapnel and gas bombs and all other tools of murder. Strike against preparedness that means death and misery to millions of human being. Be not dumb, obedient slaves in an army of destruction. Be heroes in an army of construction.

31: Woodrow Wilson's Fourteen Points

Washington, January 8, 1918

WHY WERE THE YOUNG MEN OF BRITAIN, FRANCE, GERMANY, AUSTRIA, AND Russia dying by the millions? Surely it was not to advance a few hundred yards here and there. Surely it was not, as the Allies contended early in the war, so that Belgium and other small nations might be free. The Allies, after all, were imperial powers, as were the Central Powers. Their commitment to self-determination and independence could hardly be taken seriously.

Why was the United States of America engaged in this conflict far from home, siding with one set of colonial powers against another? Why, after standing aloof from the war for three years and winning re-election in 1916 because of his determined neutrality, did Woodrow Wilson lead his country into the murderous conflict in April, 1917?

In Soviet Russia, Leon Trotsky believed he knew the answer to some of those questions. He told his fellow Bolsheviks that the United States entered the war to further the ambitions of American capitalists who wished to make a fortune from selling war material.[1]

As 1918 opened, the governments of Britain and France had good reason to fear not only defeat on the battlefield, for Germany had regained momentum in the war, but revolution at home. The Bolshevik victory in Russia gave new urgency to talk of a negotiated peace before other governments went the way of the Czar and Alexander Kerensky. The prospect of growing public outrage over the war's carnage, combined with Trotsky's challenge to the Allies to join the Soviets and Germans in peace talks, prompted the French, British and Americans to explain not only why they were fighting, but on what terms they would stop.

In New York, a group of academics, diplomats and politicians gathered under the auspices of Colonel Edward House, Wilson's chief advisor, had been preparing a sweeping declaration of principles even before Trotsky's challenge. House delivered a long memorandum from the group to Wilson in early January, 1918. Wilson, who had stood apart from the war for so long, was determined in this desperate hour, after so many millions of deaths, to give meaning to the conflict, and to ensure that it would never be repeated. Wilson believed he and the nation he led had the moral authority, despite its involvement in the war, to advocate for universal principles of freedom, liberty and self-determination, to speak not as an Old World militarist, but as a New World idealist.

Wilson and House began crafting a bold, sweeping speech from the New York group's memorandum. As they did so, they learned that British Prime Minister David Lloyd George, worried about growing demands in Britain for an immediate end to the war, intended to deliver a major restatement of his nation's war aims. Lloyd George did so on January 5, 1918, to an audience of trade unionists who were among the most outspoken critics of the war. The speech was no rousing call for more sacrifice, for no responsible leader could make such an appeal after more than three years of carnage. Instead, he presented a vision of a post-war Europe led not by autocrats and dictators, but by democrats who ruled with the consent of the governed.

In its idealism and language, Lloyd George's speech was strikingly similar to the address Wilson was preparing. The President nearly abandoned his own speech, but House persuaded him to continue. Over the next few days, Wilson continued to gather his thoughts and give voice to the principles he believed would lead not simply to a cessation of arms, important though that was, but to justice. He worked on his own, consulting House but nobody else, although he allowed Secretary of State Robert Lansing to see the speech's final draft. When Congress was summoned to hear the speech on Tuesday, January 8, none of them knew what the President would say.

As biographer August Heckscher noted, Wilson's audience on January 8 was not limited to Congress. The President quite consciously spoke to the world, and he began not by speaking of war but by emphasizing the "processes of peace." The speech outlined a vision for a world freed from the grasp of death and destruction, of a world "made fit and safe to live in," a world in which "every peace-loving nation" was able to "determine its own institutions."

The speech outlined, one by one, fourteen principles upon which a post-war world might be founded. Those points included, famously, the notion of "open covenants . . . openly arrived at" and the "removal, so far as possible, of all economic barriers" among nation-states. In addition to those broad aims, Wilson outlined specific goals—the evacuation of foreign armies from both Russia and Belgium, the adjustment of Italy's frontiers, an independent Polish state, and "a general association of nations" to nourish peace and ensure justice.

Quite deliberately, Wilson said that the United States had "no jealousy of German greatness . . . We do not wish to injure her or to block in any way her legitimate influence or power." He assured Russia's new Soviet government of a "sincere welcome into the society of free nations under institutions of her own choosing" and asserted that the "treatment accorded Russia by her sister nations in the months to come will be the acid test of their good will." With the Russians prepared to act on their threat to make peace with Germany, as they did, Wilson's olive branch contained more than a little calculation.

The speech established a framework for the coming of peace and the settlement of a post-war world. In the end, of course, Wilson's vision was not implemented. His own country rejected the notion of a "general association of nations." Nevertheless, as a document, Wilson's Fourteen Points speech remains a classic expression of great-power idealism, delivered at a time when idealism had died of exhaustion in the trenches of the Western Front.

▼ ▼ ▼

GENTLEMEN of the Congress:
Once more, as repeatedly before, the spokesmen of the Central Empires have indicated their desire to discuss the objects of the war and the possible basis of a general peace. Parleys have been in progress at Brest-Litovsk between Russian representatives and representatives of the Central Powers to which the attention of all the belligerents have been invited for the purpose of ascertaining whether it may be possible to extend these parleys into a general conference with regard to terms of peace and settlement.

The Russian representatives presented not only a perfectly definite statement of the principles upon which they would be willing to conclude peace but also an equally definite program of the concrete application of those principles. The representatives of the Central Powers, on their part, presented an outline of settlement which, if much less definite, seemed susceptible of liberal interpretation until their specific program of practical terms was added. That program proposed no concessions at all either to the sovereignty of Russia or to the preferences of the populations with whose fortunes it dealt, but meant, in a word, that the Central Empires were to keep every foot of territory their armed forces had occupied—every province, every city, every point of vantage—as a permanent addition to their territories and their power.

It is a reasonable conjecture that the general principles of settlement which they at first suggested originated with the more liberal statesmen of Germany and Austria, the men who have begun to feel the force of their own people's thought and purpose, while the concrete terms of actual settlement came from the military leaders who have no thought but to keep what they have got. The negotiations have been broken off. The Russian representatives were sincere and in earnest. They cannot entertain such proposals of conquest and domination.

The whole incident is full of significances. It is also full of perplexity. With whom are the Russian representatives dealing? For whom are the representatives of the Central Empires speaking? Are they speaking for the majorities of their respective parliaments or for the minority parties, that military and imperialistic minority which has so far dominated their whole policy and controlled the affairs of Turkey and of the Balkan states which have felt obliged to become their associates in this war?

The Russian representatives have insisted, very justly, very wisely, and in the true spirit of modern democracy, that the conferences they have been holding with the Teutonic and Turkish statesmen should be held within open, not closed, doors, and all the world has been audience, as was desired. To whom have we been listening, then? To those who speak the spirit and intention of the resolutions of the German Reichstag of the 9th of July last, the spirit and intention of the Liberal leaders and parties of Germany, or to those who resist and defy that spirit and intention and insist upon conquest and subjugation? Or are we listening, in fact, to both, unreconciled and in open and hopeless contradiction? These are very serious and pregnant questions. Upon the answer to them depends the peace of the world.

But, whatever the results of the parleys at Brest-Litovsk, whatever the confusions of counsel and of purpose in the utterances of the spokesmen of the Central Empires, they have again attempted to acquaint the world with their objects in the war and have again challenged their adversaries to say what their objects are and what sort of settlement they would deem just and satisfactory. There is no good reason why that challenge should not be responded to, and responded to with the utmost candor. We did not wait for it. Not once, but again and again, we have laid our whole thought and purpose before the world, not in general terms only, but each time with sufficient definition to make it clear what sort of definite terms of settlement must necessarily spring out of them. Within the last week Mr. Lloyd George has spoken with admirable candor and in admirable spirit for the people and Government of Great Britain.

There is no confusion of counsel among the adversaries of the Central Powers, no uncertainty of principle, no vagueness of detail. The only secrecy of counsel, the only lack of fearless frankness, the only failure to make definite statement of the objects of the war, lies with Germany and her allies. The issues of life and death hang upon these definitions. No statesman who has the least conception of his responsibility ought for a moment to permit himself to continue this tragical and appalling outpouring of blood and treasure unless he is sure beyond a peradventure that the objects of the vital sacrifice are part and parcel of the very life of Society and that the people for whom he speaks think them right and imperative as he does.

There is, moreover, a voice calling for these definitions of principle and of purpose which is, it seems to me, more thrilling and more compelling than any of the many moving voices with which the troubled air of the world is filled. It is the voice of the Russian people. They are prostrate and all but hopeless, it would seem, before the grim power of Germany, which has hitherto known no relenting and no pity. Their power, apparently, is shattered. And yet their soul is not subservient. They will not yield either in principle or in action. Their conception of what is right, of what is humane and honorable for them to accept, has been stated with a frankness, a largeness of view, a generosity of spirit, and a universal human sympathy which must challenge the admiration of every friend of mankind; and they have refused to compound their ideals or desert others that they themselves may be safe.

They call to us to say what it is that we desire, in what, if in anything, our purpose and our spirit differ from theirs; and I believe that the people of the United States would wish me to respond, with utter simplicity and frankness. Whether their present leaders believe it or not, it is our heartfelt desire and hope that some way may be opened whereby we may be privileged to assist the people of Russia to attain their utmost hope of liberty and ordered peace.

It will be our wish and purpose that the processes of peace, when they are begun, shall be absolutely open and that they shall involve and permit henceforth no secret understandings of any kind. The day of conquest and aggrandizement is gone by; so is also the day of secret covenants entered into in the interest of particular governments and likely at some unlooked-for moment to upset the peace of the world. It is this happy fact, now clear to the view of every public man whose thoughts do not still linger in an age that is dead and gone, which makes it possible for every nation whose purposes are consistent with justice and the peace of the world to avow now or at any other time the objects it has in view.

We entered this war because violations of right had occurred which touched us to the quick and made the life of our own people impossible unless they were corrected and the world secure once for all against their recurrence. What we demand in this war, therefore, is nothing peculiar to ourselves. It is that the world be made fit and safe to live in; and particularly that it be made safe for every peace-loving nation which, like our own, wishes to live its own life, determine its own institutions, be assured of justice and fair dealing by the other peoples of the world as against force and selfish aggression. All the peoples of the world are in effect partners in this interest, and for our own part we see very clearly that unless justice be done to others it will not be done to us. The program of the world's peace, therefore, is our program; and that program, the only possible program, as we see it, is this:

I. Open covenants of peace, openly arrived at, after which there shall be no private international understandings of any kind but diplomacy shall proceed always frankly and in the public view.

II. Absolute freedom of navigation upon the seas, outside territorial waters, alike in peace and in war, except as the seas may be closed in whole or in part by international action for the enforcement of international covenants.

III. The removal, so far as possible, of all economic barriers and the establishment of an equality of trade conditions among all the nations consenting to the peace and associating themselves for its maintenance.

IV. Adequate guarantees given and taken that national armaments will be reduced to the lowest point consistent with domestic safety.

V. A free, open-minded, and absolutely impartial adjustment of all colonial claims, based upon a strict observance of the principle that in determining all such questions of sovereignty the interests of the populations concerned must have equal weight with the equitable claims of the government whose title is to be determined.

VI. The evacuation of all Russian territory and such a settlement of all questions affecting Russia as will secure the best and freest cooperation of the other nations of the world in obtaining for her an unhampered and unembarrassed opportunity for the independent determination of her own political development and national policy and assure her of a sincere welcome into the society of free nations under institutions of her own choosing; and, more than a welcome, assistance also of every kind that she may need and may herself desire. The treatment accorded Russia by her sister nations in the months to come will be the acid test of their good will, of their comprehension of her needs as distinguished from their own interests, and of their intelligent and unselfish sympathy.

VII. Belgium, the whole world will agree, must be evacuated and restored, without any attempt to limit the sovereignty which she enjoys in common with all other free nations. No other single act will serve as this will serve to restore confidence among the nations in the laws which they have themselves set and determined for the government of their relations with one another. Without this healing act the whole structure and validity of international law is forever impaired.

VIII. All French territory should be freed and the invaded portions restored, and the wrong done to France by Prussia in 1871 in the matter of Alsace-Lorraine, which has unsettled the peace of the world for nearly fifty years, should be righted, in order that peace may once more be made secure in the interest of all.

IX. A readjustment of the frontiers of Italy should be effected along clearly recognizable lines of nationality.

X. The peoples of Austria-Hungary, whose place among the nations we wish to see safeguarded and assured, should be accorded the freest opportunity to autonomous development.

XI. Rumania, Serbia, and Montenegro should be evacuated; occupied territories restored; Serbia accorded free and secure access to the sea; and the relations of the several Balkan states to one another determined by friendly counsel along historically established lines of allegiance and nationality; and international guarantees of the political and economic independence and territorial integrity of the several Balkan states should be entered into.

XII. The Turkish portion of the present Ottoman Empire should be assured a secure sovereignty, but the other nationalities which are now under Turkish rule should be assured an undoubted security of life and an absolutely unmolested opportunity of autonomous development, and the Dardanelles should be permanently opened as a free passage to the ships and commerce of all nations under international guarantees.

XIII. An independent Polish state should be erected which should include the territories inhabited by indisputably Polish populations, which should be assured a free and secure access to the sea, and whose political and economic independence and territorial integrity should be guaranteed by international covenant.

XIV. A general association of nations must be formed under specific covenants for the purpose of affording mutual guarantees of political independence and territorial integrity to great and small states alike.

In regard to these essential rectifications of wrong and assertions of right we feel ourselves to be intimate partners of all the governments and peoples associated together against the Imperialists. We cannot be separated in interest or divided in purpose. We stand together until the end. For such arrangements and covenants we are willing to fight and to continue to fight until they are achieved; but only because we wish the right to prevail and desire a just and stable peace such as can be secured only by removing the chief provocations to war, which this program does remove. We have no jealousy of German greatness, and there is nothing in this program that impairs it. We grudge her no achievement or distinction of learning or of pacific enterprise such as have made her record very bright and very enviable. We do not wish to injure her or to block in any way her legitimate influence or power. We do not wish to fight her either with arms or with hostile arrangements of trade if she is willing to associate herself with us and the other peace-loving nations of the world in covenants of justice and law and fair dealing. We wish her only to accept a place of equality among the peoples of the world,—the new world in which we now live—instead of a place of mastery.

Neither do we presume to suggest to her any alteration or modification of her institutions. But it is necessary, we must frankly say, and necessary as a preliminary to any intelligent dealings with her on our part, that we should know whom her spokesmen speak for when they speak to us, whether for the Reichstag majority or for the military party and the men whose creed is imperial domination.

We have spoken now, surely, in terms too concrete to admit of any further doubt or question. An evident principle runs through the whole program I have outlined. It is the principle of justice to all peoples and nationalities, and their right to live on equal terms of liberty and safety with one another, whether they be strong or weak.

Unless this principle be made its foundation no part of the structure of international justice can stand. The people of the United States could act upon no other principle; and to the vindication of this principle they are ready to devote their lives, their honor, and everything they possess. The moral climax of this the culminating and final war for human liberty has come, and they are ready to put their own strength, their own highest purpose, their own integrity and devotion to the test.

32: Gandhi Gives Voice to Non-Violence and Non-Cooperation

Abmadabad, India, March 18, 1922

IN SEEKING TO GIVE WORLD WAR I—KNOWN AT THE TIME AS THE GREAT War—a higher purpose, U.S. President Woodrow Wilson inspired hope among the world's colonized peoples that they, too, would enjoy the Wilsonian dream of self-determination. When the war ended, British-controlled India was among the nations seeking a place in the new world order that Wilson envisioned. Some of the various ethnic, geographic and religious strains of Indian nationalism coalesced around a demand for dominion status within the British empire, which would have allowed India a home-rule government and the ability to govern its domestic affairs.

In early 1919, just weeks after the armistice of November 11, 1918 took effect, the British government in India introduced a series of laws designed to crack down on the subcontinent's nationalist movement. Under the legislation, recommended by a panel led by British judge Sidney Rowlatt, police were given greater power to restrict the activities of those suspected of sedition, and could arrest suspects without cause. In addition, it allowed the Raj to continue to imprison thousands thrown into jail because of their anti-government activities.

The legislation, called the Rowlatt Act, took effect in March, 1919 and immediately inspired unrest. One of the country's foremost nationalists, a lawyer named Mohandas K. Gandhi, was seriously ill at the time and believed he might be dying. But the Rowlatt Act restored his energy, leading him to announce a nationwide general strike—known as a "hartal"—on April 6, 1919 to protest the government's policy. The hartal was designed to be peaceful, in keeping with Gandhi's belief in non-violence, but the protest led not only to work stoppages and prayer but confrontation with British authorities. Riots broke out in many villages and cities, leading to an assault on a British schoolteacher in the Punjabi city of Amristar. The teacher survived the attack, but the British military ordered an end to public meetings in the city. Thousands defied the ban on April 13. Troops under the command of Brigadier General Reginald Dyer opened fire on the unarmed civilians, killing four hundred and injuring more than a thousand. After the slaughter, Dyer ordered Indians to crawl when they passed the place where the teacher was attacked, and told his troops to flog any Indians who failed to properly salute a Briton. The Jallianwalla Bagh massacre, as Indians called it, and its aftermath were a turning point in Anglo-Indian relations.

Gandhi, grieving over the deadly turn of events, believed he bore some of the blame for the deaths. The Indian people, he concluded, were not prepared to face the blunt force of British repression. When the British offered a peace offering in the form of civil service jobs and increased opportunities in local governments, Gandhi seized the initiative and asked Indians to stop cooperating with authorities. Indians, he said, should remain outside the governing structures of the British Raj, and, in fact, should stop speaking the conqueror's tongue, English. Non-cooperation offered a non-violent, non-confrontational means of rallying Indians to the nationalist cause.

The Indian National Congress, the dominant voice of Indian nationalism, supported Gandhi's campaign of non-cooperation. Gandhi himself moved from city to city, village to village, to rally the Indian masses, becoming in the process not just a radical political figure but a moral leader. His austere, pious and simple manner won the hearts of his countrymen. And that made him a dangerous figure, indeed.

Britain's Prince of Wales (the future King Edward VIII) arrived in India for a state visit in November, 1921. The visit was poorly timed, for it incited another round of unrest. Gandhi and other Indian nationalists urged a boycott of the Prince's visit, but once again, his calls for non-violent protest went unheard as demonstrations led to violence and murder, this time in Bombay and, several weeks later, in Chauri Chaura, where more than twenty police officers were slain.

On March 10, 1922, Gandhi was arrested and charged with writing several articles deemed seditious in the weekly newspaper he edited, *Young India*. The case was brought to court at noon on March 18 in the city of Abmadabad. After the charges were read—he was accused of attempting to "excite . . . disaffection towards His Majesty's Government"—Gandhi entered his plea: Guilty. Before the judge pronounced his sentence, Gandhi addressed the court. He had a prepared statement, which recounted his life's struggles and his foiled wishes for an accommodation with Britain. But before he began reading, he improvised remarks in which he took full blame for anti-British violence. He said he knew he was playing with fire, but that he would do the same again—strong words from a man the world remembers for his moral authority and devotion to peaceful resistance.

After his speech, Gandhi was sentenced to six years in prison, but he was released in 1924. He remained out of politics for several years, but by 1928, he had resumed his place at the head of the Indian freedom movement.

▼ ▼ ▼

BEFORE I read this statement I would like to state that I entirely endorse the learned Advocate-General's remarks in connection with my humble self. I think that he has made, because it is very true and I have no desire whatsoever to conceal from this court the fact that to preach disaffection towards the existing system of Government has become almost a passion with me, and the Advocate-General is entirely in the right when he says that my preaching of disaffection did not commence with my connection with Young India but that it commenced much earlier, and in the statement that I am about to read, it will be my painful duty to admit before this court that it commenced much earlier than the period stated by the Advocate-General. It is a painful duty with me but I have to discharge that duty knowing the responsibility that rests upon my shoulders, and I wish to endorse all the blame that the learned Advocate-General has thrown on my shoulders in connection with the Bombay occurrences, Madras occurrences and the Chauri Chuara occurrences. Thinking over these things deeply and sleeping over them night after night, it is impossible for me to dissociate myself from the diabolical crimes of Chauri Chaura or the mad outrages of Bombay. He is quite right when he says, that as a man of responsibility, a man having received a fair share of education, having had a fair share of experience of this world, I should have known the consequences of every one of my acts. I know them. I knew that I was playing with fire. I ran the risk and if I was set free I would still do the same. I have felt it this morning that I would have failed in my duty, if I did not say what I said here just now.

I wanted to avoid violence. Non-violence is the first article of my faith. It is also the last article of my creed. But I had to make my choice. I had either to submit to a system which I considered had done an irreparable harm to my country, or incur the risk of the mad fury of my people bursting forth when they understood the truth from my lips. I know that my people have sometimes gone mad. I am deeply sorry for it and I am, therefore, here to submit not to a light penalty but to the highest penalty. I do not ask for mercy. I do not plead any extenuating act. I am here, therefore, to invite and cheerfully submit to the highest penalty that can be inflicted upon me for what in law is a deliberate crime, and what appears to me to be the highest duty of a citizen. The only course open to you, the Judge, is, as I am going to say in my statement, either to resign your post, or inflict on me the severest penalty if you believe that the system and law you are assisting to administer are good for the people. I do not expect that kind of conversion. But by the time I have finished with my statement you will have a glimpse of what is raging within my breast to run this maddest risk which a sane man can run.

I owe it perhaps to the Indian public and to the public in England, to placate which this prosecution is mainly taken up, that I should explain why from a staunch loyalist and co-operator, I have become an uncompromising disaffectionist and non-cooperator. To the court too I should say why I plead guilty to the charge of promoting disaffection towards the Government established by law in India.

My public life began in 1893 in South Africa in troubled weather. My first contact with British authority in that country was not of a happy character. I discovered that as a man and an Indian, I had no rights. More correctly I discovered that I had no rights as a man because I was an Indian.

But I was not baffled. I thought that this treatment of Indians was an excrescence upon a system that was intrinsically and mainly good. I gave the Government my voluntary and hearty cooperation, criticizing it freely where I felt it was faulty but never wishing its destruction.

Consequently when the existence of the Empire was threatened in 1899 by the Boer challenge, I offered my services to it, raised a volunteer ambulance corps and served at several actions that took place for the relief of Ladysmith. Similarly in 1906, at the time of the Zulu "revolt," I raised a stretcher bearer party and served till the end of the "rebellion." On both the occasions I received medals and was even mentioned in dispatches. For my work in South Africa I was given by Lord Hardinge a Kaisar-i-Hind gold medal. When the war broke out in 1914 between England and Germany, I raised a volunteer ambulance corps in London, consisting of the then resident Indians in London, chiefly students. Its work was acknowledged by the authorities to be valuable. Lastly, in India when a special appeal was made at the War Conference in Delhi in 1918 by Lord Chelmsford for recruits, I struggled at the cost of my health to raise a corps in Kheda, and the response was being made when the hostilities ceased and orders were received that no more recruits were wanted. In all these efforts at service, I was actuated by the belief that it was possible by such services to gain a status of full equality in the Empire for my countrymen.

The first shock came in the shape of the Rowlatt Act-a law designed to rob the people of all real freedom. I felt called upon to lead an intensive agitation against it. Then followed the Punjab horrors beginning with the massacre at Jallianwala Bagh and culminating in crawling orders, public flogging and other indescribable humiliations. I discovered too that the plighted word of the Prime Minister to the Mussalmans of India regarding the integrity of Turkey and the holy places of Islam was not likely to be fulfilled. But in spite of the forebodings and the grave warnings of friends, at the Amritsar Congress in 1919, I fought for cooperation and working of the Montagu-Chemlmsford reforms, hoping that the Prime Minister would redeem his promise to the Indian Mussalmans, that the Punjab wound would be healed, and that the reforms, inadequate and unsatisfactory though they were, marked a new era of hope in the life of India.

But all that hope was shattered. The Khilafat promise was not to be redeemed. The Punjab crime was whitewashed and most culprits went not only unpunished but remained in service, and some continued to draw pensions from the Indian revenue and in some cases were even rewarded. I saw too that not only did the reforms not mark a change of heart, but they were only a method of further draining India of her wealth and of prolonging her servitude.

I came reluctantly to the conclusion that the British connection had made India more helpless than she ever was before, politically and economically. A disarmed India has no power of resistance against any aggressor if she wanted to engage in an armed conflict with him. So much is this the case that some of our best men consider that India must take generations, before she can achieve Dominion Status. She has become so poor that she has little power of resisting famines. Before the British advent India spun and wove in her millions of cottages, just the supplement she needed for adding to her meager agricultural resources. This cottage industry, so vital for India's existence, has been ruined by incredibly heartless and inhuman processes as described by English witnesses. Little do town dwellers know how the semi-starved masses of India are slowly sinking to lifelessness. Little do they know that their miserable comfort represents the brokerage they get for the work they do for the foreign exploiter, that the profits and the brokerage are sucked from the masses. Little do they realize that the Government established by law in British India is carried on for this exploitation of the masses. No sophistry, no jugglery in figures, can explain away the evidence that the skeletons in many villages present to the naked eye. I have no doubt whatsoever that both England and the town dweller of India will have to answer, if there is a God above, for this crime against humanity, which is perhaps unequalled in history. The law itself in this country has been used to serve the foreign exploiter. My unbiased examination of the Punjab Martial Law cases has led me to believe that at least ninety-five per cent of convictions were wholly bad. My experience of political cases in India leads me to the conclusion, in nine out of every ten, the condemned men were totally innocent. Their crime consisted in the love of their country. In ninety-nine cases out of hundred, justice has been denied to Indians as against Europeans in the courts of India. This is not an exaggerated picture. It is the experience of almost every Indian who has had anything to do with such cases. In my opinion, the administration of the law is thus prostituted, consciously or unconsciously, for the benefit of the exploiter.

The greater misfortune is that the Englishmen and their Indian associates in the administration of the country do not know that they are engaged in the crime I have attempted to describe. I am satisfied that many Englishmen and Indian officials honestly systems devised in the world, and that India is making steady, though slow, progress. They do not know, a subtle but effective system of terrorism and an organized display of force on the one hand, and the deprivation of all powers of retaliation or self-defense on the other, has emasculated the people and induced in them the habit of simulation. This awful habit has added to the ignorance and the self-deception of the administrators. Section 124 A, under which I am happily charged, is perhaps the prince among the political sections of the Indian Penal Code designed to suppress the liberty of the citizen. Affection cannot be manufactured or regulated by law. If one has no affection for a person or system, one should be free to give the fullest expression to his disaffection, so long as he does not contemplate, promote, or incite to violence. But the section under which mere promotion of disaffection is a crime. I have studied some of the cases tried under it; I know that some of the most loved of India's patriots have been convicted under it. I consider it a privilege, therefore, to be charged under that section. I have endeavored to give in their briefest outline the reasons for my disaffection. I have no personal ill-will against any single administrator, much less can I have any disaffection towards the King's person. But I hold it to be a virtue to be disaffected towards a Government which in its totality has done more harm to India than any previous system. India is less manly under the British rule than she ever was before. Holding such a belief, I consider it to be a sin to have affection for the system. And it has been a precious privilege for me to be able to write what I have in the various articles tendered in evidence against me.

In fact, I believe that I have rendered a service to India and England by showing in non-cooperation the way out of the unnatural state in which both are living. In my opinion, non-cooperation with evil is as much a duty as is cooperation with good. But in the past, non-cooperation has been deliberately expressed in violence to the evil-doer. I am endeavoring to show to my countrymen that violent non-cooperation only multiplies evil, and that as evil can only be sustained by violence, withdrawal of support of evil requires complete abstention from violence. Non-violence implies voluntary submission to the penalty for non-cooperation with evil. I am here, therefore, to invite and submit cheerfully to the highest penalty that can be inflicted upon me for what in law is deliberate crime, and what appears to me to be the highest duty of a citizen. The only course open to you, the Judge and the assessors, is either to resign your posts and thus dissociate yourselves from evil, if you feel that the law you are called upon to administer is an evil, and that in reality I am innocent, or to inflict on me the severest penalty, if you believe that the system and the law you are assisting to administer are good for the people of this country, and that my activity is, therefore, injurious to the common weal.

33: Sun Yat-sen Pleads for Pan-Asian Resistance to Western Imperialism

Kobe, Japan: November 28, 1924

CHINESE COMMUNISTS AND NATIONALISTS AGREED ON VERY LITTLE IN THE twentieth century, but both sides recognized Sun Yat-sen as one of their country's greatest statesmen. A founder of the Republic of China and an ardent opponent of Western imperialism in Asia, Sun was a revolutionary, a nationalist, and a social democrat who rejected Marxist theory but who welcomed the Bolshevik victory in Russia.

Sun was a physician who grew disillusioned with the calcified Qing dynasty as a young man in the late nineteenth century. After plotting, and failing, to overthrow the dynasty in 1895, Sun was forced into exile for more than fifteen years. A renewed rebellion against China's imperial family succeeded in 1911, and Sun returned to his native land to become the provisional president of the new Republic of China in 1912. His term was short-lived, however, and the republic was weak, representing only China's southern provinces. After losing a power struggle, Sun went into exile again, this time in Japan. He returned to China in 1917 and began an effort to unify the nation through his political movement, the Kuomintang.

Sun drew political inspiration from several Western figures, including Abraham Lincoln, Karl Marx and Henry George. His ideology was a bewildering amalgamation of ideologies and dogma, but what was clear was his belief that not only China but all of Asia ought to shake itself loose from the exploitation of European powers. He gained a European ally when the new Bolshevik government took power in Russia in 1918. Comintern, the international communist organization founded in Moscow in 1919, offered assistance to Sun and his Kuomintang movement. While Sun was not a communist, he admired the Soviet system and believed that the Kuomintang ought to model itself on the Soviet Communist Party.[1]

He also admired Japan, which had so recently shocked Europe with its victory over Czarist Russia in the Russo-Japanese War in 1904-05. He proposed an alliance between Japan and China at the outset of World War I, promising Japan access to Chinese markets in exchange for aid in Sun's efforts to re-establish control over the country's government. Japan did not reply to Sun.

In 1924, an ailing Sun and the Kuomintang were attempting once again to unify the northern and southern provinces of China. One area of common interest, he believed, was the inequity of trade treaties with the Western powers having access if not outright control over Asian markets. In late November, 1924, Sun traveled to Kobe, Japan, to deliver a remarkable speech in which he condemned the inequity of Western treaties, praised Japan for abolishing all such treaties, and urged a united Asian effort to rid the continent of European and American exploitation. In this clash of civilizations, Sun argued that Asia held the moral high ground, for the West ruled by force, while Asian nations embraced justice and humanity.

Sun's speech was a strong, pan-nationalist polemic, delivered by a man who was suffering from liver cancer that would kill him just four months later, in March, 1925. It did not succeed in bringing China and Japan closer. In fact, in less than a decade Japan invaded China in the first battle of what became World War II. Ironically, one of Japan's war aims was the establishment of what it called a "Greater East Asian Co-Prosperity Sphere," an anti-Western alliance led, of course, by the Japanese.

GENTLEMEN: I highly appreciate this cordial reception with which you are honoring me today. The topic of the day is "Pan-Asianism," but before we touch upon the subject, we must first have a clear conception of Asia's place in the world. Asia, in my opinion, is the cradle of the world's oldest civilization. Several thousand years ago, its peoples had already attained an advanced civilization; even the ancient civilizations of the West, of Greece and Rome, had their origins on Asiatic soil. In Ancient Asia we had a philosophic, religious, logical and industrial civilization. The origins of the various civilizations of the modern world can be traced back to Asia's ancient civilization. It is only during the last few centuries that the countries and races of Asia have gradually degenerated and become weak, while the European countries have gradually developed their resources and become powerful. After the latter had fully developed their strength, they turned their attention to, and penetrated into, East Asia, where they either destroyed or pressed hard upon each and every one of the Asiatic nations, so that thirty years ago there existed, so to speak, no independent country in the whole of Asia. With this, we may say, the low water mark had been reached.

When Asia reached this point, the tide started to turn, and the turn meant the regeneration of Asia. It started thirty years ago when Japan abolished all the Unequal Treaties that she had entered into with the foreign countries. The day when the Unequal Treaties were abolished by Japan was a day of regeneration for all Asiatic peoples. After the abolition of the Unequal Treaties, Japan became the first independent country in Asia. The remaining countries, such as China, India, Persia, Afghanistan, Arabia, and Turkey were not independent, that is to say, they were still dominated, and treated as colonies, by Europe. Thirty years ago, Japan was also a colony of the European countries. But the Japanese were far-sighted. They realized that the only way to power was to struggle with the Europeans and to abolish all Unequal Treaties, which they did, thus turning Japan into an independent country. Since Japan has become an independent country in East Asia, the various nations in this part of the world have been buoyed up with a new hope. They realized that since Japan has been able to achieve her independence through the abolition of the Unequal Treaties, they could do the same. So once again they have mustered courage to conduct their various independent activities with the hope of shaking off the yoke of European restriction and domination and regaining their own rightful position in Asia. This has been the prevailing thought in Asia during the past thirty years, which indeed gives ground for optimism.

Thirty years ago the idea was different. Men thought and believed that European civilization was a progressive one-in science, industry, manufacture, and armament-and that Asia had nothing to compare with it. Consequently, they assumed that Asia could never resist Europe, that European oppression could never be shaken off. Such was the idea prevailing thirty years ago. It was a pessimistic idea. Even after Japan abolished the Unequal Treaties and attained the status of an independent country, Asia, with the exception of a few countries situated near Japan, was little influenced. Ten years later, however, the Russo-Japanese war broke out and Russia was defeated by Japan. For the first time in the history of the last several hundred years, an Asiatic country has defeated a European Power.

The effect of this victory immediately spread over the whole of Asia, and gave a new hope to all Asiatic peoples. In the year of the outbreak of the Russo-Japanese war I was in Europe. One day news came that Admiral Togo had defeated the Russian navy, annihilating in the Japan Sea the fleet newly dispatched from Europe to Vladivostock. The population of the whole continent was taken aback. Britain was Japan's Ally, yet most of the British people were painfully surprised, for in their eyes Japan's victory over Russia was certainly not a blessing for the White peoples. "Blood," after all, "is thicker than water." Later on I sailed for Asia. When the steamer passed the Suez Canal a number of natives came to see me. All of them wore smiling faces, and asked me whether I was a Japanese. I replied that I was a Chinese and inquired what was in their minds, and why they were so happy. They said they had just heard the news that Japan had completely destroyed the Russian fleet recently dispatched from Europe, and were wondering how true the story was. Some of them, living on both banks of the Canal, had witnessed Russian hospital ships, with wounded on board, passing through the Canal from time to time. That was surely a proof of the Russian defeat, they added.

In former days, the colored races in Asia, suffering from the oppression of the Western peoples, thought that emancipation was impossible. We regarded that Russian defeat by Japan as the defeat of the West by the East. We regarded the Japanese victory as our own victory. It was indeed a happy event. Did not therefore this news of Russia's defeat by Japan affect the peoples of the whole of Asia? Was not its effect tremendous? While it may not have seemed so important and consequently have had only a slight effect on the peoples living in East Asia, it had a great effect on the peoples living in West Asia and in the neighborhood of Europe who were in constant touch with Europeans and subject to their oppression daily. The suffering of these Asiatic peoples was naturally greater than that of those living in the further East, and they were therefore more quick to respond to the news of this great victory.

Since the day of Japan's victory over Russia, the peoples of Asia have cherished the hope of shaking off the yoke of European oppression, a hope which has given rise to a series of independence movements-in Egypt, Persia, Turkey, Afghanistan, and finally in India. Therefore, Japan's defeat of Russia gave rise to a great hope for the independence of Asia. From the inception of this hope to the present day only twenty years have elapsed. The Egyptian, Turkish, Persian, Afghan, and Arabian independence movements have already materialized, and even the independence movement in India has, with the passage of time, been gaining ground. Such facts are concrete proofs of the progress of the nationalist idea in Asia. Until this idea reaches its full maturity, no unification or independence movement of the Asiatic peoples as a whole is possible. In East Asia, China and Japan are the two greatest peoples. China and Japan are the driving force of this nationalist movement. What will be the consequences of this driving force still remains to be seen. The present tide of events seems to indicate that not only China and Japan but all the peoples in East Asia will unite together to restore the former status of Asia.

Such a tendency is clearly evident to the eyes of Europe and America. One American scholar[2] has written a book to discuss the rise of the colored peoples, where he maintains that Japan's defeat of Russia amounts to a victory of the Yellow race over the White race, and that such a tendency, if unchecked, will result in the unification of the entire Yellow race, which will be a calamity for the White peoples, and ways and means should therefore be devised to prevent it. Subsequently, he wrote another book in which he described all emancipation movements as Revolts against Civilization. In his view, emancipation movements in Europe should be regarded as revolts against civilization; even more so should such emancipation movements in Asia be regarded. Such views are common among the privileged classes of people in both Europe and America. A minority, they oppress the majority in their own continent or country. Now they wish to extend their evil practice to Asia, with a view to suppressing the nine hundred million people of Asia, and treating them as their slaves. This American scholar considers the awakening of the Asiatic peoples as a revolt against civilization. Thus, the Westerners consider themselves as the only ones possessed and worthy of true culture and civilization; other peoples with any culture or independent ideas are considered as Barbarians in revolt against Civilization. When comparing Occidental with Oriental civilization they only consider their own civilization logical and humanitarian.

From the aspect of cultural development during the last several hundred years, the material civilization of Europe has reached its height while Oriental civilization has remained stagnant. Outwardly, Europe is superior to Asia. Fundamentally, European civilization during the last several hundred years is one of scientific materialism. Such a civilization, when applied to society, will mean the cult of force, with aeroplanes, bombs, and cannons as its outstanding features. Recently, this cult of force has been repeatedly employed by the Western peoples to oppress Asia, and as a consequence, there is no progress in Asia. To oppress others with the cult of force, in the language of the Ancients, is the rule of Might. Therefore, European civilization is nothing but the rule of Might. The rule of Might has always been looked down upon by the Orient. There is another kind of civilization superior to the rule of Might. The fundamental characteristics of this civilization are benevolence, justice and morality: This civilization makes people respect, not fear, it. Such a civilization is, in the language of the Ancients, the rule of Right or the Kingly Way. One may say, therefore, that Oriental civilization is one of the rule of Right. Since the development of European materialistic civilization and the cult of Might, the morality of the world has been on the decline. Even in Asia, morality in several countries has degenerated. Of late, a number of European and American scholars have begun to study Oriental civilization and they realize that, while materially the Orient is far behind the Occident, morally the Orient is superior to the Occident.

Which civilization, the rule of Might or the rule of Right, will prove to be beneficial to justice and humanity, to nations and countries? You can give your own answer to this question.

I may cite an example here to illustrate the point. For instance, between five hundred and two thousand years ago, there was a period of a thousand years when China was supreme in the world. Her status in the world then was similar to that of Great Britain and America today. What was the situation of the weaker nations toward China then? They respected China as their superior and sent annual tribute to China by their own will, regarding it as an honor to be allowed to do so. They wanted, of their own free will, to be dependencies of China. Those countries which sent tribute to China were not only situated in Asia but in distant Europe as well. But in what way did China maintain her prestige among so many small and weaker nations? Did she send her army or navy, i.e. use Might, to compel them to send their contributions? Not at all. It was not her rule of Might that forced the weaker nations to send tribute to China. It was the influence of her rule of Right. Once they were influenced by the "Kingly Way" of China they continued to send tribute, not merely once or twice, but the practice was carried on from generation to generation. This influence is felt even at the present moment; there are still traces and evidences of it.

There are two small countries situated to the north of India, namely, Bhutan and Nepal. These countries are small in size, but are inhabited by a brave, strong, and warlike people. During the present British rule of India, Britain often went to Nepal in search of soldiers in order to rule the Indians. A great deal of money by way of subsidies had to be spent before Britain was allowed to dispatch a political observer to Nepal. Even a great Power such as Great Britain had to respect her; Nepal was, in fact, a great Power in Asia. But what is the attitude of Nepal toward Great Britain during the past hundred years? Over a hundred years ago India was conquered by Great Britain, and during this period Nepal was able to live peacefully on the border of the British colony. Although a hundred years have passed, Nepal has never sent tribute to Great Britain. Great Britain, on the other hand, has to spend a large sum by way of subsidies to Nepal. But what is the attitude of Nepal toward China? The status of China has deteriorated to such an extent that it is now inferior even to that of a British colony. Though far away from China Proper and separated from her by Tibet, Nepal considered China as her suzerain State and up to 1911 Nepal sent annual tribute to China via Tibet. In that year, however, when the Nepal commissioners reached Szechuan and found communications interrupted, they returned to their country. The different attitudes of Nepal toward Great Britain and toward China is due to the difference between the Oriental and Occidental civilization. China has degenerated during the last several hundred years, yet Nepal still respects her as a superior State. Great Britain, on the other hand, is a powerful country, but Nepal has been influenced by Chinese civilization, which, in her eyes, is the true civilization, while that of Britain is nothing but the rule of Might.

Now, what is the problem that underlies Pan-Asianism, the Principle of Greater Asia, which we are discussing here today?

Briefly, it is a cultural problem, a problem of comparison and conflict between the Oriental and Occidental culture and civilization. Oriental civilization is the rule of Right; Occidental civilization is the rule of Might. The rule of Right respects benevolence and virtue, while the rule of Might only respects force and utilitarianism. The rule of Right always influences people with justice and reason, while the rule of Might always oppresses people with brute force and military measures. People who are influenced by justice and virtue will never forget their superior State, even if that country has become weak. So Nepal even now willingly respects China as a superior State. People who are oppressed by force never submit entirely to the oppressor State. The relations of Great Britain with Egypt and India form a typical example. Although under British rule, Egypt and India have always entertained the thought of independence and separation from Great Britain. If Great Britain becomes weaker some day, Egypt and India will overthrow British rule and regain their independence within five years. You should now realize which is the superior civilization, the Oriental or the Occidental?

If we want to realize Pan-Asianism in this new world, what should be its foundation if not our ancient civilization and culture? Benevolence and virtue must be the foundations of Pan-Asianism. With this as a sound foundation we must then learn science from Europe for our industrial development and the improvement of our armaments, not, however, with a view to oppressing or destroying other countries and peoples as the Europeans have done, but purely for our self-defense.

Japan is the first nation in Asia to completely master the military civilization of Europe. Japan's military and naval forces are her own creation, independent of European aid or assistance. Therefore, Japan is the only completely independent country in East Asia. There is another country in Asia who joined with the Central Powers during the European War and was partitioned after her final defeat. After the war, however, she was not only able to regain her territory, but to expel all Europeans from that territory. Thus she attained her status of complete independence. This is Turkey. At present Asia has only two independent countries, Japan in the East and Turkey in the West. In other words, Japan and Turkey are the Eastern and Western barricades of Asia. Now Persia, Afghanistan, and Arabia are also following the European example in arming themselves, with the result that the Western peoples dare not look down on them. China at present also possesses considerable armaments, and when her unification is accomplished she too will become a great Power. We advocate Pan-Asianism in order to restore the status of Asia. Only by the unification of all the peoples in Asia on the foundation of benevolence and virtue can they become strong and powerful.

But to rely on benevolence alone to influence the Europeans in Asia to relinquish the privileges they have acquired in China would be an impossible dream. If we want to regain our rights we must resort to force. In the matter of armaments, Japan has already accomplished her aims, while Turkey has recently also completely armed herself. The other Asiatic races, such as the peoples of Persia, Afghanistan, and Arabia are all war-like peoples. China has a population of four hundred millions, and although she needs to modernize her armament and other equipment, and her people are a peace-loving people, yet when the destiny of their country is at stake the Chinese people will also fight with courage and determination. Should all Asiatic peoples thus unite together and present a united front against the Occidentals, they will win the final victory. Compare the populations of Europe and Asia: China has a population of four hundred millions, India three hundred and fifty millions, Japan several scores of millions, totaling, together with other peoples, no less than nine hundred millions. The population in Europe is somewhere around four hundred millions. For the four hundred millions to oppress the nine hundred millions is an intolerable injustice, and in the long run the latter will be defeated. What is more, among the four hundred millions some of them have already been influenced by us. Judging from the present tendency of civilization, even in Great Britain and America, there are people who advocate the principles of benevolence and justice. Such an advocacy also exists in some of the barbarian countries. Thus, we realize that the Western civilization of utilitarianism is submitting to the influence of the Oriental civilization of benevolence and justice. That is to say the rule of Might gives way to the rule of Right, presaging a bright future for world civilization.

At present there is a new country in Europe which has been looked down upon and expelled from the Family of Nations by the White races of the whole of Europe. Europeans consider it as a poisonous snake or some brutal animal, and dare not approach it. Such a view is also shared by some countries in Asia. This country is Russia. At present, Russia is attempting to separate from the White peoples in Europe. Why? Because she insists on the rule of Right and denounces the rule of Might. She advocates the principle of benevolence and justice and refuses to accept the principles of utilitarianism and force. She maintains Right and opposes the oppression of the majority by the minority. From this point of view, recent Russian civilization is similar to that of our ancient civilization. Therefore, she joins with the Orient and separates from the West. The new principles of Russia were considered as intolerable by Europeans. They are afraid that these principles, when put into effect, would overthrow their rule of Might. Therefore they do not accept the Russian way, which is in accord with the principles of benevolence and justice, but denounce it as contrary to world principles.

What problem does Pan-Asianism attempt to solve? The problem is how to terminate the sufferings of the Asiatic peoples and how to resist the aggression of the powerful European countries. In a word, Pan-Asianism represents the cause of the oppressed Asiatic peoples. Oppressed peoples

are found not only in Asia, but in Europe as well. Those countries that practice the rule of Might do not only oppress the weaker people outside their
continent, but also those within their own continent. Pan-Asianism is based
on the principle of the rule of Right, and justifies the avenging of the
wrongs done to others. An American scholar considers all emancipation
movements as revolts against civilization. Therefore now we advocate the
avenging of the wrong done to those in revolt against the civilization of the
rule of Might, with the aim of seeking a civilization of peace and equality
and the emancipation of all races. Japan today has become acquainted with
the Western civilization of the rule of Might, but retains the characteristics
of the Oriental civilization of the rule of Right. Now the question remains
whether Japan will be the hawk of the Western civilization of the rule of
Might, or the tower of strength of the Orient. This is the choice which lies
before the people of Japan.

34: Haile Selassie Pleads
for His Country
Geneva, June 30, 1936

THE ITALIAN INVASION OF ETHIOPIA ON OCTOBER 3, 1935, CAME AS LITTLE surprise to anyone involved, least of all Ethiopia's emperor, Haile Selassie. As the ruler of one of Africa's very few independent nations, he watched with considerable anxiety as the Italian duce, Benito Mussolini, built up his armed forces in east Africa after a clash between Ethiopian and Italian troops near the city of Wal Wal in Ethiopia in late 1934. The Italians controlled Eritrea, which shared a border with Ethiopia to the northwest, and Somalia, to the east of Ethiopia.

Equally overt were Mussolini's ambitions. He promised Italians a return to imperial glory, a place in the sun, he said, with the other great powers of Europe. That sunny place required colonial possessions and military conquest. Ethiopia was an obvious target for several reasons: It had not been colonized by other European powers, its northern and eastern frontiers were vulnerable to assault from Italian troops already operating in East Africa, and Ethiopia had defeated Italy in 1896 when Italians first set their eyes on this African prize.

By early fall, 1935, Italy had assembled more than a half-million troops in East Africa. They had at their disposal tanks, warplanes, heavy artillery and other implements of mechanized war. Opposing them, on paper anyway, was an army of about 750,000, but few were experienced soldiers. Ethiopia's air force was negligible; the army relied on camels and mules to transport men and material. But as Ethiopia prepared for war, its emperor believed it had one important means of defense: The power and influence of the League of Nations.

The League, based in Geneva, Switzerland, was founded to avoid a repeat of the catastrophe of World War I. The crisis in East Africa in 1935 tested the League's power to intervene on behalf of one member, Ethiopia, threatened by another, Italy. In September, 1935, Ethiopia's representative to the League delivered an impassioned plea on his country's behalf. "The League is the conscience of mankind," said Gaston Jeze. "Ethiopia makes a supreme appeal to that conscience."[1]

Great Britain indicated that it would support League measures, including military sanctions, against Italy. Privately, however, both Britain and France were worried about the rising influence of Adolf Hitler in Germany. The British and French believed Mussolini's Italy might yet be part of an anti-German coalition, and so were reluctant to confront Italian aggression in Africa, a continent on which both powers also had colonies. The League appointed a committee of thirteen members to devise a plan to conciliate Italy and to modernize Ethiopia. It issued a report just days before the Italian onslaught began, with no formal declaration of war, on October 3.

Ethiopian resistance was stronger than expected, slowing the Italian advance through late 1935. Mussolini authorized the use of mustard gas against Ethiopian soldiers and civilians alike. The League of Nations declared Italy an aggressor and imposed a series of sanctions on the Fascist government, but the Italians were not denied important supplies, especially oil. By the end of March, the invaders defeated the main Ethiopian army under the personal command of the Emperor himself. Haile Selassie left the country on May 2, and the Italians marched into the Ethiopian capital, Addis Ababa, three days later. Mussolini declared Italian King Victor Emanuel to be emperor of Italian East Africa; shortly thereafter, he ordered his troops in Ethiopia to murder any prisoners they took during the war.

Selassie, enraged by the crime against his country, was not content to go into quiet exile. Determined to bring his nation's case to the world's attention, he traveled first to London, where he was given asylum, and then to Geneva to address the League of Nations on June 30, 1935.

The Swiss capital was a tense, depressed place in the aftermath of the Italian victory and the League's abject failure to prevent it or to punish the aggressors. Before Selassie addressed the League's representatives, the body's president read a letter from Mussolini indicating that he had no further territorial ambitions. Then Haile Selassie, dressed in a white tunic and cape, was introduced as the Emperor of Ethiopia. Italian journalists in the hall began jeering and whistling, with one shouting "Murderer!" at the emperor. The demonstration went on for ten minutes, with Haile Selassie standing in front of the crowd, silent in the face of the abuse. League officials ordered the journalists removed from the hall, allowing Selassie to begin.

Exhausted by war and his recent travels, the deposed Emperor delivered a stirring, impassioned appeal to the world's conscience. He reprised the events leading to the war, emphasized the degree to which his country appealed to the League for intervention, and made the case against Italy as an aggressor. The Emperor's defiance and dignity won him many admirers in the democratic world, turning him into a symbol of resistance against the expansion of totalitarianism. Ultimately, however, his speech was a eulogy for the League of Nations, which allowed Ethiopia to bleed to death.

▼ ▼ ▼

"I, HAILE SELASSIE I, Emperor of Ethiopia, am here today to claim that justice which is due to my people, and the assistance promised to it eight months ago, when fifty nations asserted that aggression had been committed in violation of international treaties.

There is no precedent for a Head of State himself speaking in this assembly. But there is also no precedent for a people being victim of such injustice and being at present threatened by abandonment to its aggressor. Also, there has never before been an example of any Government proceeding to the systematic extermination of a nation by barbarous means, in violation of the most solemn promises made by the nations of the earth that there should not be used against innocent human beings the terrible poison of harmful gases. It is to defend a people struggling for its age-old independence that the head of the Ethiopian Empire has come to Geneva to fulfill this supreme duty, after having himself fought at the head of his armies.

I pray to Almighty God that He may spare nations the terrible sufferings that have just been inflicted on my people, and of which the chiefs who accompany me here have been the horrified witnesses.

It is my duty to inform the Governments assembled in Geneva, responsible as they are for the lives of millions of men, women and children, of the deadly peril which threatens them, by describing to them the fate which has been suffered by Ethiopia. It is not only upon warriors that the Italian Government has made war. It has above all attacked populations far removed from hostilities, in order to terrorize and exterminate them.

At the beginning, towards the end of 1935, Italian aircraft hurled upon my armies bombs of tear-gas. Their effects were but slight. The soldiers learned to scatter, waiting until the wind had rapidly dispersed the poison-

ous gases. The Italian aircraft then resorted to mustard gas. Barrels of liquid were hurled upon armed groups. But this means also was not effective;
the liquid affected only a few soldiers, and barrels upon the ground were
themselves a warning to troops and to the population of the danger.

It was at the time when the operations for the encircling of Makalle were
taking place that the Italian command, fearing a rout, followed the procedure
which it is now my duty to denounce to the world. Special sprayers were
installed on board aircraft so that they could vaporize, over vast areas of territory, a fine, death-dealing rain. Groups of nine, fifteen, eighteen aircraft followed one another so that the fog issuing from them formed a continuous
sheet. It was thus that, as from the end of January, 1936, soldiers, women,
children, cattle, rivers, lakes and pastures were drenched continually with this
deadly rain. In order to kill off systematically all living creatures, in order to
more surely poison waters and pastures, the Italian command made its aircraft pass over and over again. That was its chief method of warfare.

The very refinement of barbarism consisted in carrying ravage and terror into the most densely populated parts of the territory, the points farthest
removed from the scene of hostilities. The object was to scatter fear and
death over a great part of the Ethiopian territory. These fearful tactics succeeded. Men and animals succumbed. The deadly rain that fell from the
aircraft made all those whom it touched fly shrieking with pain. All those
who drank the poisoned water or ate the infected food also succumbed in
dreadful suffering. In tens of thousands, the victims of the Italian mustard
gas fell. It is in order to denounce to the civilized world the tortures inflicted upon the Ethiopian people that I resolved to come to Geneva. None
other than myself and my brave companions in arms could bring the
League of Nations the undeniable proof. The appeals of my delegates
addressed to the League of Nations had remained without any answer; my
delegates had not been witnesses. That is why I decided to come myself to
bear witness against the crime perpetrated against my people and give
Europe a warning of the doom that awaits it, if it should bow before the
accomplished fact.

Is it necessary to remind the Assembly of the various stages of the
Ethiopian drama? For twenty years past, either as Heir Apparent, Regent
of the Empire, or as Emperor, I have never ceased to use all my efforts to
bring my country the benefits of civilization, and in particular to establish
relations of good neighborliness with adjacent powers. In particular I succeeded in concluding with Italy the Treaty of Friendship of 1928, which

absolutely prohibited the resort, under any pretext whatsoever, to force of arms, substituting for force and pressure the conciliation and arbitration on which civilized nations have based international order.

In its report of October, 193S, the Committee of Thirteen recognized my effort and the results that I had achieved. The Governments thought that the entry of Ethiopia into the League, whilst giving that country a new guarantee for the maintenance of her territorial integrity and independence, would help her to reach a higher level of civilization. It does not seem that in Ethiopia today there is more disorder and insecurity than in the year of the committee of Thirteen's report. On the contrary, the country is more united and the central power is better obeyed.

I should have procured still greater results for my people if obstacles of every kind had not been put in the way by the Italian Government, the Government which stirred up revolt and armed the rebels. Indeed the Rome Government, as it has today openly proclaimed, has never ceased to prepare for the conquest of Ethiopia. The Treaties of Friendship it signed with me were not sincere; their only object was to hide its real intention from me. The Italian Goverment asserts that for fourteen years it has been preparing for its present conquest. It therefore recognizes today that when it supported the admission of Ethiopia to the League of Nations in 1923, when it concluded the Treaty of Friendship in 1928, when it signed the Pact of Paris outlawing war, it was deceiving the whole world. The Ethiopian Government was, in these solemn treaties, given additional guarantees of security which would enable it to achieve further progress along the specific path of reform on which it had set its feet, and to which it was devoting all its strength and all its heart.

The Wal-Wal incident, in December, 1934, came as a thunderbolt to me. The Italian provocation was obvious and I did not hesitate to appeal to the League of Nations. I invoked the provisions of the treaty of 1928, the principles of the Covenant; I urged the procedure of conciliation and arbitration. Unhappily for Ethiopia this was the time when a certain Government considered that the European situation made it imperative at all costs to obtain the friendship of Italy. The price paid was the abandonment of Ethiopian independence to the greed of the Italian Government. This secret agreement, contrary to the obligations of the Covenant, has exerted a great influence over the course of events. Ethiopia and the whole world have suffered and are still suffering today its disastrous consequences.

This first violation of the Covenant was followed by many others. Feeling itself encouraged in its policy against Ethiopia, the Rome Government feverishly made war preparations, thinking that the concerted pressure which was beginning to be exerted on the Ethiopian Government might perhaps not overcome the resistance of my people to Italian domination. The time had to come, thus all sorts of difficulties were placed in the way with a view to breaking up the procedure of conciliation and arbitration. All kinds of obstacles were placed in the way of that procedure. Governments tried to prevent the Ethiopian Government from finding arbitrators amongst their nationals: when once the arbitral tribunal was set up pressure was exercised so that an award favorable to Italy should be given.

All this was in vain: the arbitrators, two of whom were Italian officials, were forced to recognize unanimously that in the Wal-Wal incident, as in the subsequent incidents, no international responsibility was to be attributed to Ethiopia.

Following on this award, the Ethiopian Government sincerely thought that an era of friendly relations might be opened with Italy. I loyally offered my hand to the Roman Government. The Assembly was informed by the report of the Committee of Thirteen, dated October, 1935, of the details of the events which occurred after the month of December, 1934, and up to October, 1935.

It will be sufficient if I quote a few of the conclusions of that report, Nos. 24, 25 and 26: "The Italian memorandum (containing the complaints made by Italy) was laid on the Council table on September, 1935, whereas Ethiopia's first appeal to the Council had been made on December, 1934. In the interval between these two dates, the Italian Government opposed the consideration of the question by the Council on the ground that the only appropriate procedure was that provided for in the Italo-Ethiopian Treaty of 1928. Throughout the whole of that period, moreover, the despatch of Italian troops to East Africa was proceeding. These shipments of troops were represented to the Council by the Italian Government as necessary for the defense of its colonies menaced by Ethiopia's preparations. Ethiopia, on the contrary, drew attention to the official pronouncements made in Italy which, in its opinion, left no doubt as to the hostile intentions of the Italian Government.

From the outset of the dispute, the Ethiopian Government has sought a settlement by peaceful means. It has appealed to the procedures of the Covenant. The Italian Government desiring to keep strictly to the procedures of the Italo-Ethiopian Treaty of 1928, the Ethiopian Government assented. It invariably stated that it would faithfully carry out the arbitral award even if the decision went against it. It agreed that the question of the ownership of Wal-Wal should not be dealt with by the arbitrators, because the Italian Government would not agree to such a course. It asked the Council to despatch neutral observers and offered to lend itself to any inquiries upon which the Council might decide.

Once the Wal-Wal dispute had been settled by arbitration, however, the Italian Government submitted its detailed memorandum to the Council in support of its claim to liberty of action. It asserted that a case like that of Ethiopia cannot be settled by the means provided by the Covenant. It stated that, 'since this question affects vital interest and is of primary importance to Italian security and civilization' it 'would be failing in its most elementary duty, did it not cease once and for all to place any confidence in Ethiopia, reserving full liberty to adopt any measures that may become necessary to ensure the safety of its colonies and to safeguard its own interests.'

Those are the terms of the report of the Committee of Thirteen. The Council and the Assembly unanimously adopted the conclusion that the Italian Government had violated the Covenant and was in a state of aggression. I did not hesitate to declare that I did not wish for war, that it was imposed upon me, and I should struggle solely for the independence and integrity of my people, and that in that struggle I was the defender of the cause of all small States exposed to the greed of a powerful neighbor.

In October, 1935, the fifty-two nations who are listening to me today gave me an assurance that the aggressor would not triumph, that the resources of the Covenant would be employed in order to ensure the reign of right and the failure of violence.

I ask the fifty-two nations not to forget today the policy upon which they embarked eight months ago, and on faith of which I directed the resistance of my people against the aggressor whom they had denounced to the world. Despite the inferiority of my weapons, the complete lack of aircraft, artillery, munitions, hospital services, my confidence in the League was absolute. I thought it to be impossible that fifty-two nations, including the most powerful in the world, should be successfully opposed by a single aggressor. Counting on the faith due to treaties, I had made no preparation for war, and that is the case with certain small countries in Europe.

When the danger became more urgent, being aware of my responsibilities towards my people, during the first six months of 1935 I tried to acquire armaments. Many Governments proclaimed an embargo to prevent my doing so, whereas the Italian Government, through the Suez Canal, was given all facilities for transporting without cessation and without protest, troops, arms, and munitions.

On October, 1935, the Italian troops invaded my territory. A few hours later only I decreed general mobilization. In my desire to maintain peace I had, following the example of a great country in Europe on the eve of the Great War, caused my troops to withdraw thirty kilometers so as to remove any pretext of provocation.

War then took place in the atrocious conditions which I have laid before the Assembly. In that unequal struggle between a Government commanding more than forty-two million inhabitants, having at its disposal financial, industrial and technical means which enabled it to create unlimited quantities of the most death-dealing weapons, and, on the other hand, a small people of twelve million inhabitants, without arms, without resources having on its side only the justice of its own cause and the promise of the League of Nations. What real assistance was given to Ethiopia by the fifty-two nations who had declared the Rome Government guilty of a breach of the Covenant and had undertaken to prevent the triumph of the aggressor? Has each of the States Members, as it was its duty to do in virtue of its signature appended to Article 15 of the Covenant, considered the aggressor as having committed an act of war personally directed against itself? I had placed all my hopes in the execution of these undertakings. My confidence had been confirmed by the repeated declarations made in the Council to the effect that aggression must not be rewarded, and that force would end by being compelled to bow before right.

In December, 1935, the Council made it quite clear that its feelings were in harmony with those of hundreds of millions of people who, in all parts of the world, had protested against the proposal to dismember Ethiopia. It was constantly repeated that there was not merely a conflict between the Italian Government and the League of Nations, and that is why I personally refused all proposals to my personal advantage made to me by the Italian Government, if only I would betray my people and the Covenant of the League of Nations. I was defending the cause of all small peoples who are threatened with aggression.

What have become of the promises made to me as long ago as October, 1935? I noted with grief, but without surprise that three Powers considered their undertakings under the Covenant as absolutely of no value. Their connections with Italy impelled them to refuse to take any measures whatsoever in order to stop Italian aggression. On the contrary, it was a profound disappointment to me to learn the attitude of a certain Government which, whilst ever protesting its scrupulous attachment to the Covenant, has tirelessly used all its efforts to prevent its observance. As soon as any measure which was likely to be rapidly effective was proposed, various pretexts were devised in order to postpone even consideration of the measure. Did the secret agreements of January, 1935, provide for this tireless obstruction?

The Ethiopian Government never expected other Governments to shed their soldiers' blood to defend the Covenant when their own immediately personal interests were not at stake. Ethiopian warriors asked only for means to defend themselves. On many occasions I have asked for financial assistance for the purchase of arms. That assistance has been constantly refused me. What, then, in practice, is the meaning of Article 16 of the Covenant and of collective security?

The Ethiopian Government's use of the railway from Djibouti to Addis Ababa was in practice a hazardous regards transport of arms intended for the Ethiopian forces. At the present moment this is the chief, if not the only means of supply of the Italian armies of occupation. The rules of neutrality should have prohibited transports intended for Italian forces, but there is not even neutrality since Article 16 lays upon every State Member of the League the duty not to remain a neutral but to come to the aid not of the aggressor but of the victim of aggression. Has the Covenant been respected? Is it today being respected?

Finally a statement has just been made in their Parliaments by the Governments of certain Powers, amongst them the most influential members of the League of Nations, that since the aggressor has succeeded in occupying a large part of Ethiopian territory they propose not to continue the application of any economic and financial measures that may have been decided upon against the Italian Government. These are the circumstances in which at the request of the Argentine Government, the Assembly of the League of Nations meets to consider the situation created by Italian aggression. I assert that the problem submitted to the Assembly today is a much wider one. It is not merely a question of the settlement of Italian aggression.

LEAGUE THREATENED

It is collective security: it is the very existence of the League of Nations. It is the confidence that each State is to place in international treaties. It is the value of promises made to small States that their integrity and their independence shall be respected and ensured. It is the principle of the equality of States on the one hand, or otherwise the obligation laid upon small Powers to accept the bonds of vassalship. In a word, it is international morality that is at stake. Have the signatures appended to a Treaty value only in so far as the signatory Powers have a personal, direct and immediate interest involved?

No subtlety can change the problem or shift the grounds of the discussion. It is in all sincerity that I submit these considerations to the Assembly. At a time when my people are threatened with extermination, when the support of the League may ward off the final blow, may I be allowed to speak with complete frankness, without reticence, in all directness such as is demanded by the rule of equality as between all States Members of the League?

Apart from the Kingdom of the Lord there is not on this earth any nation that is superior to any other. Should it happen that a strong Government finds it may with impunity destroy a weak people, then the hour strikes for that weak people to appeal to the League of Nations to give its judgment in all freedom. God and history will remember your judgment.

I have heard it asserted that the inadequate sanctions already applied have not achieved their object. At no time, and under no circumstances could sanctions that were intentionally inadequate, intentionally badly applied, stop an aggressor. This is not a case of the impossibility of stopping an aggressor but of the refusal to stop an aggressor. When Ethiopia requested and requests that she should be given financial assistance, was that a measure which it was impossible to apply whereas financial assistance of the League has been granted, even in times of peace, to two countries and exactly to two countries who have refused to apply sanctions against the aggressor?

Faced by numerous violations by the Italian Government of all international treaties that prohibit resort to arms, and the use of barbarous methods of warfare, it is my painful duty to note that the initiative has today been taken with a view to raising sanctions. Does this initiative not mean in practice the abandonment of Ethiopia to the aggressor? On the very eve of the day when I was about to attempt a supreme effort in the defense of my people before this Assembly does not this initiative deprive Ethiopia of one of her last chances to succeed in obtaining the support and guarantee of States Members? Is that the guidance the League of Nations and each of the

States Members are entitled to expect from the great Powers when they assert their right and their duty to guide the action of the League? Placed by the aggressor face to face with the accomplished fact, are States going to set up the terrible precedent of bowing before force?

Your Assembly will doubtless have laid before it proposals for the reform of the Covenant and for rendering more effective the guarantee of collective security. Is it the Covenant that needs reform? What undertakings can have any value if the will to keep them is lacking? It is international morality which is at stake and not the Articles of the Covenant. On behalf of the Ethiopian people, a member of the League of Nations, I request the Assembly to take all measures proper to ensure respect for the Covenant. I renew my protest against the violations of treaties of which the Ethiopian people has been the victim. I declare in the face of the whole world that the Emperor, the Government and the people of Ethiopia will not bow before force; that they maintain their claims that they will use all means in their power to ensure the triumph of right and the respect of the Covenant.

I ask the fifty-two nations, who have given the Ethiopian people a promise to help them in their resistance to the aggressor, what are they willing to do for Ethiopia? And the great Powers who have promised the guarantee of collective security to small States on whom weighs the threat that they may one day suffer the fate of Ethiopia, I ask what measures do you intend to take?

Representatives of the world, I have come to Geneva to discharge in your midst the most painful of the duties of the head of a State. What reply shall I have to take back to my people?

35. Franklin Roosevelt Sees the Ill-Housed, Ill-Clad, Ill-Nourished

Washington, January 20, 1937

WHEN HE CAMPAIGNED FOR THE PRESIDENCY IN 1932, FRANKLIN ROOSEVELT'S theme song was "Happy Days Are Here Again." It was an expression of hope for a disillusioned and angry nation in the throes of an historic economic depression. The stock market crash of 1929 brought the prosperity of the Roaring Twenties to an abrupt and painful end. Unemployment rose from 3.2 percent in 1930 to more than 23 percent in 1932 as businesses and banks collapsed. The misery spread around the globe, leading to the rise of fascism and militarism in Europe.

Roosevelt defeated incumbent President Herbert Hoover in 1932 and then set in motion an energetic, government-led response to the crisis. New government agencies were created to regulate the financial industry, stimulate development and put people to work. By 1936, when Roosevelt campaigned for a second term, the jobless rate had fallen to about 17 percent, and the nation's gross domestic product was growing at an annual rate of 14 percent.

Happy days? Perhaps not quite yet, but as the nation went to the polls in November, 1936, to give Roosevelt a breathtaking victory—FDR defeated Alf Landon of Kansas in every state except Maine and Vermont—prosperity seemed to be within the nation's grasp.

As he prepared his second inaugural address, Franklin Roosevelt had reason to celebrate the accomplishments of his first term and the victories of the New Deal he had famously promised the American people in 1932. But the President was not in an especially triumphant mood, despite his success and his landslide victory. He was furious with the Supreme Court, which had declared important parts of his economic recovery package unconstitutional. He had grown to despise the nation's business community, which he had envisioned as part of a cross-class solution to the nation's devastating economic problems. By 1936, however, he had abandoned those hopes. During his re-election campaign, Roosevelt unleashed a volley of criticism against the nation's "economic royalists" who represented the forces of "organized money." He knew the nation's industrialists hated him, he said, "and I welcome their hatred."[1]

Roosevelt's smashing victory over Landon, coming despite the business community's "hatred," inspired his supporters to dream big. The New Republic, a reliable proponent of the New Deal, announced that FDR's re-election was "the greatest revolution in our political history."[2] With his huge mandate, FDR had the support he needed to find an even greater place for state power in American society. Or so his supporters believed.

An historic victory inspired elevated expectations. But Roosevelt understood, as some of his more enthusiastic backers did not, that happy days had not returned. The depression was not over. Huge swaths of the population remained impoverished. Government action had put some of the pieces back together again, but the economy still was broken.

On a dreary Wednesday morning in January, 1937, Roosevelt took the oath of office for the second time, becoming the first President sworn in on January 20, rather than March 4. The twentieth amendment to the Constitution, ratified in 1933, changed the date of the presidential inauguration to January, shortening the interval between Election Day and the start of a new administration.

Roosevelt was ready to go. As thousands huddled under umbrellas on the east side of the Capitol, FDR delivered an inaugural address that reminded listeners of how far the nation had come in four years, but also how far it still needed to travel. The President gave voice to his inner populist, assailing the nation's financiers who, he had decided, bore much of the blame for the Depression. Government, he declared, ought to "find practical controls over blind economic forces and blindly selfish men." Given his attacks on the nation's financial elites during the '36 campaign, there was no mistaking the reference to the "blindly selfish."

The inaugural address was a far more starkly ideological and partisan document than his first one, which sought to bring the nation together to face the financial emergency. With the nation solidly behind him, Roosevelt and his more liberal aides felt free to articulate not just a series of emergency measures, but a new way of imagining the power and scope of government and of society. Touting the achievements of the New Deal thus far, Roosevelt said: "We refused to leave the problems of our common welfare to be solved by the winds of chance and the hurricanes of disaster." In a stirring few sentences, Roosevelt suggested that the storms had not passed; indeed, they continued to buffet portions of the nation. In a phrase that would become one of the most famous in presidential oratory, FDR said: "I see one-third of a nation ill-housed, ill-clad, ill-nourished." It was a reminder that misery remained unconquered despite the exertions of his first term.

But there were questions about how much more Roosevelt would be able to achieve despite his popularity. The Supreme Court, stacked with aging jurists who did not share FDR's belief in activist government, presented a formidable obstacle to a greater government presence in the economy. A few weeks before Inauguration Day, Roosevelt and his aides discussed the ways in which they could reshape the Court to gain a pro-New Deal majority. Roosevelt recalled a similar crisis in Great Britain in 1911, when then-Prime Minister Herbert Asquith threatened to create dozens more members of the House of Lords to prevent that body from vetoing legislation. A plan to pack the Court with new justices began to take shape.

In his inaugural address, there is a hint of his ambitions. "The Constitution of 1787," he said, almost cryptically, "did not make our democracy impotent." A more vital, activist government, in fact, was fully in keeping with democratic ideals, for government had begun to rein in what he called "private autocratic powers"—that is, big business—in the interests of the people.

These were big and important themes, and Roosevelt knew it. A few weeks after delivering the speech, the President unveiled his plan to change the federal judiciary. For every judge over the age of 70 with 10 years experience or more, he wished Congressional authority to appoint another judge, including up to six on the Supreme Court. The court-packing scheme turned out to be a political disaster, a classic example of second-term overreach. In the end, however, FDR got what he wanted: The Court suddenly showed more sympathy for new federal programs, and justices began to retire.

But by the end of 1937, the nation's recovery from the crash of '29 fell apart. The economy returned to recession, and unemployment rose to 19 percent by the beginning of 1938. Only the coming of war returned the nation to prosperity and full employment.

Roosevelt's inaugural address in 1937, then, was the high point of the New Deal. By the time he delivered another, the nation was faced not with economic distress, but with a world at war.

▼ ▼ ▼

WHEN four years ago we met to inaugurate a President, the Republic, single-minded in anxiety, stood in spirit here. We dedicated ourselves to the fulfillment of a vision—to speed the time when there would be for all the people that security and peace essential to the pursuit of happiness. We of the Republic pledged ourselves to drive from the temple of our ancient faith those who had profaned it; to end by action, tireless and unafraid, the stagnation and despair of that day. We did those first things first.

Our covenant with ourselves did not stop there. Instinctively we recognized a deeper need—the need to find through government the instrument of our united purpose to solve for the individual the ever-rising problems of a complex civilization. Repeated attempts at their solution without the aid of government had left us baffled and bewildered. For, without that aid, we had been unable to create those moral controls over the services of science which are necessary to make science a useful servant instead of a ruthless master of mankind. To do this we knew that we must find practical controls over blind economic forces and blindly selfish men.

We of the Republic sensed the truth that democratic government has innate capacity to protect its people against disasters once considered inevitable, to solve problems once considered unsolvable. We would not admit that we could not find a way to master economic epidemics just as, after centuries of fatalistic suffering, we had found a way to master epidemics of disease. We refused to leave the problems of our common welfare to be solved by the winds of chance and the hurricanes of disaster.

In this we Americans were discovering no wholly new truth; we were writing a new chapter in our book of self-government.

This year marks the one hundred and fiftieth anniversary of the Constitutional Convention which made us a nation. At that Convention our forefathers found the way out of the chaos which followed the Revolutionary War; they created a strong government with powers of united action sufficient then and now to solve problems utterly beyond individual or local solution. A century and a half ago they established the Federal Government in order to promote the general welfare and secure the blessings of liberty to the American people.

Today we invoke those same powers of government to achieve the same objectives.

Four years of new experience have not belied our historic instinct. They hold out the clear hope that government within communities, government within the separate States, and government of the United States can do the things the times require, without yielding its democracy. Our tasks in the last four years did not force democracy to take a holiday.

Nearly all of us recognize that as intricacies of human relationships increase, so power to govern them also must increase—power to stop evil; power to do good. The essential democracy of our Nation and the safety of our people depend not upon the absence of power, but upon lodging it with those whom the people can change or continue at stated intervals through an honest and free system of elections. The Constitution of 1787 did not make our democracy impotent.

In fact, in these last four years, we have made the exercise of all power more democratic; for we have begun to bring private autocratic powers into their proper subordination to the public's government. The legend that they were invincible—above and beyond the processes of a democracy—has been shattered. They have been challenged and beaten.

Our progress out of the depression is obvious. But that is not all that you and I mean by the new order of things. Our pledge was not merely to do a patchwork job with secondhand materials. By using the new materials of social justice we have undertaken to erect on the old foundations a more enduring structure for the better use of future generations.

In that purpose we have been helped by achievements of mind and spirit. Old truths have been relearned; untruths have been unlearned. We have always known that heedless self-interest was bad morals; we know now that it is bad economics. Out of the collapse of a prosperity whose builders boasted their practicality has come the conviction that in the long run economic morality pays. We are beginning to wipe out the line that divides the practical from the ideal; and in so doing we are fashioning an instrument of unimagined power for the establishment of a morally better world.

This new understanding undermines the old admiration of worldly success as such. We are beginning to abandon our tolerance of the abuse of power by those who betray for profit the elementary decencies of life.

In this process evil things formerly accepted will not be so easily condoned. Hard-headedness will not so easily excuse hardheartedness. We are moving toward an era of good feeling. But we realize that there can be no era of good feeling save among men of good will.

For these reasons I am justified in believing that the greatest change we have witnessed has been the change in the moral climate of America.

Among men of good will, science and democracy together offer an ever-richer life and ever-larger satisfaction to the individual. With this change in our moral climate and our rediscovered ability to improve our economic order, we have set our feet upon the road of enduring progress.

Shall we pause now and turn our back upon the road that lies ahead? Shall we call this the promised land? Or, shall we continue on our way? For "each age is a dream that is dying, or one that is coming to birth."

Many voices are heard as we face a great decision. Comfort says, "Tarry a while." Opportunism says, "This is a good spot." Timidity asks, "How difficult is the road ahead?"

True, we have come far from the days of stagnation and despair. Vitality has been preserved. Courage and confidence have been restored. Mental and moral horizons have been extended.

But our present gains were won under the pressure of more than ordinary circumstances. Advance became imperative under the goad of fear and suffering. The times were on the side of progress.

To hold to progress today, however, is more difficult. Dulled conscience, irresponsibility, and ruthless self-interest already reappear. Such symptoms of prosperity may become portents of disaster! Prosperity already tests the persistence of our progressive purpose.

Let us ask again: Have we reached the goal of our vision of that fourth day of March 1933? Have we found our happy valley?

I see a great nation, upon a great continent, blessed with a great wealth of natural resources. Its hundred and thirty million people are at peace among themselves; they are making their country a good neighbor among the nations. I see a United States which can demonstrate that, under democratic methods of government, national wealth can be translated into a spreading volume of human comforts hitherto unknown, and the lowest standard of living can be raised far above the level of mere subsistence.

But here is the challenge to our democracy: In this nation I see tens of millions of its citizens—a substantial part of its whole population—who at this very moment are denied the greater part of what the very lowest standards of today call the necessities of life.

I see millions of families trying to live on incomes so meager that the pall of family disaster hangs over them day by day.

I see millions whose daily lives in city and on farm continue under conditions labeled indecent by a so-called polite society half a century ago.

I see millions denied education, recreation, and the opportunity to better their lot and the lot of their children.

I see millions lacking the means to buy the products of farm and factory and by their poverty denying work and productiveness to many other millions.

I see one-third of a nation ill-housed, ill-clad, ill-nourished.

It is not in despair that I paint you that picture. I paint it for you in hope—because the Nation, seeing and understanding the injustice in it, proposes to paint it out. We are determined to make every American citizen the subject of his country's interest and concern; and we will never regard any faithful law-abiding group within our borders as superfluous. The test of our progress is not whether we add more to the abundance of those who have much; it is whether we provide enough for those who have too little.

If I know aught of the spirit and purpose of our Nation, we will not listen to Comfort, Opportunism, and Timidity. We will carry on.

Overwhelmingly, we of the Republic are men and women of good will; men and women who have more than warm hearts of dedication; men and women who have cool heads and willing hands of practical purpose as well. They will insist that every agency of popular government use effective instruments to carry out their will.

Government is competent when all who compose it work as trustees for the whole people. It can make constant progress when it keeps abreast of all the facts. It can obtain justified support and legitimate criticism when the people receive true information of all that government does.

If I know aught of the will of our people, they will demand that these conditions of effective government shall be created and maintained. They will demand a nation uncorrupted by cancers of injustice and, therefore, strong among the nations in its example of the will to peace.

Today we reconsecrate our country to long-cherished ideals in a suddenly changed civilization. In every land there are always at work forces that drive men apart and forces that draw men together. In our personal ambitions we are individualists. But in our seeking for economic and political progress as a nation, we all go up, or else we all go down, as one people.

To maintain a democracy of effort requires a vast amount of patience in dealing with differing methods, a vast amount of humility. But out of the confusion of many voices rises an understanding of dominant public need. Then political leadership can voice common ideals, and aid in their realization.

In taking again the oath of office as President of the United States, I assume the solemn obligation of leading the American people forward along the road over which they have chosen to advance.

While this duty rests upon me I shall do my utmost to speak their purpose and to do their will, seeking Divine guidance to help us each and every one to give light to them that sit in darkness and to guide our feet into the way of peace.

36: Adolf Hitler Denounces Umbrella-Carrying Types

Weimar, November 6, 1938

THE RISE OF ADOLF HITLER AND HIS NAZI MOVEMENT IN THE 1930'S RAISED the specter of renewed conflict on a continent, Europe, where the fresh graves of millions bore silent witness to the killing power of modern warfare. Hitler came to power in 1932 with a promise to return Germany to its stolen glory, and soon he publicly identified those who stood in the way of a revived Aryan race: Europe's Jews. The Nuremburg Laws, which passed the Reichstag in 1935, marked the beginning of a state-sanctioned campaign against Germany's Jewish community, a campaign that would move rapidly from internal repression to continent-wide extermination.

As Hitler made little secret of his intentions, whether by fomenting anti-Semitic hatred or by re-arming his country in violation of the Treaty of Versailles, war-weary Great Britain and France looked on with anxiety and a desperate wish to avoid another worldwide slaughter. Both nations had lost a generation in World War I, as had Germany. But unlike the German masses whipped up by Nazi propaganda, the British and French populations were unwilling to contemplate another war.

And so Hitler re-armed. His troops re-occupied the Rhineland in 1936 without opposition, even though the Treaty of Versailles insisted that the region remain demilitarized. In March, 1938, the country of Hitler's birth, Austria, joined the German Reich. Hitler then turned his attention to portions of the new nation of Czechoslovakia, created at Versailles when the former Austro-Hungarian empire broke up. About three million Germans lived in border areas with Germany and Austria called the Sudetenland, and Hitler made himself into their champion, demanding that they be returned to his Reich. The Czech army mobilized in May, and the French and British governments, pledged by treaty to aid Czechoslovakia against aggression, feared that events would spiral out of control as they had in August, 1914. Hitler, however, had no such fears, for he wished not for peace but for war.

"It is my unshakeable will to wipe Czechoslovakia off the map," he told top aides and military commanders, some of whom believed the German army was not strong enough to resist a military response from Britain and France if they came to Czechoslovakia's aid.[1]

British Prime Minister Neville Chamberlain was determined to appease Hitler rather than confront him, a course that history now condemns as short-sighted and morally reprehensible. At the time, however, the mass murder of Jews had not yet begun, and while Hitler clearly was dangerous and possibly mad, Chamberlain was desperate to avoid a confrontation that might lead to another bloody cataclysm.

In the fall of 1936, Chamberlain, the very personification of British ruling-class sensibilities and manners, met in Munich with Hitler, clad in a brown coat and a Nazi armband, to resolve the Sudetenland crisis peacefully. French Prime Minister Edouard Dadalier—who was more suspicious of Hitler than Chamberlain was—and Italian dictator Benito Mussolini also were in attendance, but not Eduard Benes, the president of Czechoslovakia. He had no say in the four-power agreement to cede a portion of his country to Hitler.

Chamberlain returned to Britain and famously announced that he had achieved "peace in our time." Crowds roared in approval, as they did in Paris and even in Germany, where the agreement was seen for what it was, a concession to Hitler and an affirmation of Germany's aggression. Hitler himself was not so pleased. He despised Chamberlain as ineffectual and weak, representing an exhausted nation whose time in the imperial sun had set. He wished to overthrow the order Chamberlain represented, not negotiate with it. Munich got him the territory he craved, but the process left him angry and dissatisfied.

On November 6, Hitler traveled to the city of Weimar, birthplace of the post-World War I republic which he overturned, to address a crowd of supporters. He had followed debates in the British House of Commons over the Munich Agreement and took note of ferocious criticism from Winston Churchill, who predicted that the agreement was "the first foretaste of a bitter cup which will be proffered to us year by year unless by a supreme recovery of moral health and martial vigor, we arise again and take our stand for freedom as in the olden time."

With Churchill's defiance and Chamberlain's Old World manners in mind, Hitler assailed the very nation, Great Britain, which had chosen not to challenge him, which had, in fact, acquiesced in his plan to wipe Czechoslovakia off the map. The speech included personal attacks on

Churchill, but Hitler saved his greatest contempt for a man unmentioned in the text. As his audience roared in approval, knowing precisely who his target was, Hitler announced that the "umbrella-carrying types of our former bourgeois world of parties are extinguished and they will never return." Chamberlain was often photographed carrying an umbrella, a handy instrument in British weather but, in Hitler's hands, a symbol of a defanged British ruling class seeking to take cover rather than defy the elements arraigned against it.

This was post-Munich Hitler's victory speech in which he confirmed Churchill's analysis of Munich, which he described as a "military defeat without a war." From now on, he said, Germany would pay heed only to Germans, not to world opinion or international bodies. And Germany would proceed from strength, for every German would be "the first soldier in the world."

The speech is filled with lies—Hitler described himself as a "lover of peace"—and invective, most of it aimed at Churchill. But within days of the speech, another target would face an onslaught of a different sort. On the night of November 7, 1938, a French Jew named Herschel Grynszpan shot and wounded a German diplomat in Paris. When the German died of his wounds on November 9, anti-Semitic riots broke out in several cities. The authorities stood by as violence intensified. Jewish businesses were attacked, and dozens of Jews killed or injured. History would remember the violence as Crystal Night, the night of broken glass, the night when Hitler's supporters delivered another "foretaste of a bitter cup" to come.

WHAT seems to us almost a miracle as we look back upon it is nothing else than the reward for infinite and unwearying labor.... And now for that labor we have received from Providence our reward, just as the Germany of 1918 received its reward. At that time Germany shared in those blessings which we think of under the collective idea Democracy. But Germany has learned that democracy in practice is a different thing from democracy in theory.

If today at times in foreign countries Parliamentarians or politicians venture to maintain that Germany has not kept her treaties, then we can give as our answer to these men: the greatest breach of a treaty that ever was practiced on the German people. Every promise which had been made to Germany in the Fourteen Points—those promises on the faith of which Germany had laid down her arms—was afterwards broken. In 1932 Germany was faced with final collapse. The German Reich and people both seemed lost. And then came the German resurrection. It began with a change of faith. While all the German parties before us believed in forces and ideals which lay outside of the German Reich and outside of our people, we National Socialists have resolutely championed belief in our own people, starting from that watchword of eternal validity: God helps only those who are prepared and determined to help themselves. In the place of all those international factors—Democracy, the Conscience of Peoples, the Conscience of the World, the League of Nations, and the like—we have set a single factor—our own people. . . .

We were all convinced that a true community of the people is not produced overnight—it is not attained through theories or programs—but that through many decades, yes, and perhaps always and for all time the individual must be trained for this community. This work of education we have carried through ever since the Party was founded and especially since we came into power. But nothing is perfect in this world and no success can be felt to be finally satisfying. And so, even today, we have no wish to maintain that our achievement is already the realization of our ideal. We have an ideal which floats before our minds and in accordance with that ideal we educate Germans, generation after generation. So National Socialism will continually be transformed from a profession of political faith to a real education of the people. . . .

The umbrella-carrying types of our former bourgeois world of parties are extinguished and they will never return . . .

From the very first day I have proclaimed as a fundamental principle: "the German is either the first soldier in the world or he is no soldier at all." No soldiers at all we cannot be, and we do not wish to be. Therefore we shall be only the first. As one who is a lover of peace I have endeavored to create for the German people such an army and such munitions as are calculated to convince others, too, to seek peace.

There are, it is true, people who abuse the hedgehog because it has spines. But they have only got to leave the animal in peace. No hedgehog has ever attacked anyone unless he was first threatened. That should be our position, too. Folk must not come too near us. We want nothing else than to be left in peace; we want the possibility of going on with our work, we claim for our people the right to live, the same right which others claim for

themselves. And that the democratic States above all others should grasp
and understand, for they never stop talking about equality of rights. If they
keep talking about the rights of small peoples, how can they be outraged if
in its turn a great people claims the same right? Our National Socialist
Army serves to secure and guarantee this claim of right.

It is with this in view that in foreign policy also I have initiated a change
in our attitude and have drawn closer to those who like us were compelled
to stand up for their rights.

And when today I examine the results of this action of ours, then I am
able to say: Judge all of you for yourselves: Have we not gained enormous-
ly through acting on these principles?

But precisely for this reason we do not wish that we should ever forget
what has made these successes of ours possible. When certain foreign newspapers write: "But all that you could have gained by the way of negotiation,"
we know very well that Germany before our day did nothing but negotiate
continuously. For fifteen years they only negotiated and they lost everything
for their pains. I, too, am ready to negotiate but I leave no one in any doubt
that neither by way of negotiation nor by any other way will I allow the rights
of Germany to be cut down. Never forget, German people, to what it is you
owe your successes—to what Movement, to what ideas, and to what principles! And in the second place: always be cautious, be ever on your guard!

It is very fine to talk of international peace and international disarmament, but I am mistrustful of a disarmament in weapons of war so long as
there has been no disarmament of the spirit.

There has been formed in the world the curious custom of dividing
peoples into so-called "authoritarian" States, that is disciplined States, and
democratic States. In the authoritarian, that is, the disciplined States, it
goes without saying that one does not abuse foreign peoples, does not lie
about them, does not incite to war. But the democratic States are precisely
"democratic," that is, that all this can happen there. In the authoritarian
States a war—agitation is of course impossible, for their Governments are
under an obligation to see to it that there is no such thing. In the democracies, on the other hand, the Governments have only one duty: to maintain
democracy, and that means the liberty, if necessary, to incite to war. . . .

Mr. Churchill had stated his view publicly, namely that the present
regime in Germany must be overthrown with the aid of forces within
Germany which would gladly cooperate. If Mr. Churchill would but spend
less of his time in *émigré* circles, that is with traitors to their country main-

tained and paid abroad, and more of his time with Germans, then he would realize the utter madness and stupidity of his idle chatter. I can only assure this gentleman, who would appear to be living in the moon, of one thing: there is no such force in Germany which could turn against the present regime.

I will not refuse to grant to this gentleman that, naturally we have no right to demand that the other peoples should alter their constitutions. But, as leader of the Germans, I have the duty to consider this constitution of theirs and the possibilities which result from it. When a few days ago in the House of Commons the Deputy Leader of the Opposition declared that he made no secret of the fact that he would welcome the destruction of Germany and Italy, then, of course, I cannot prevent it if perhaps this man on the basis of the democratic rules of the game should in fact with his party in one or two years become the Government. But of one thing I can assure him: I can prevent him from destroying Germany. And just as I am convinced that the German people will take care that the plans of these gentlemen so far as Germany is concerned will never succeed, so in precisely the same way Fascist Italy will, I know, take care for itself!

I believe that for us all these international hopes can only teach us to stand firm together and to cling to our friends. The more that we in Germany form a single community, the less favorable will be the prospects of these inciters to war, and the closer we unite ourselves in particular with the State which is in a position similar to ours, with Italy, the less desire they will have to pick a quarrel with us! . . .

Germany has become greater by the most natural way, by a way which could not be more morally unassailable. . . . When the rest of the world speaks of disarmament, then we too are ready for disarmament, but under one condition: the war-agitation must first be disarmed!

So long as the others only talk of disarmament, while they infamously continue to incite to war, we must presume that they do but wish to steal from us our arms, in order once more to prepare for us the fate of 1918-19. And in that case, my only answer to Mr. Churchill and his like must be: That happens once only and it will not be repeated! . . .

37: Lou Gehrig, the "Luckiest Man on the Face of the Earth"

Yankee Stadium, the Bronx, July 4, 1939

ON THE AFTERNOON OF MAY 2, 1939, LOU GEHRIG, THE CAPTAIN OF THE New York Yankees, told his manager, Joe McCarthy, that he was taking himself out of the lineup for a rest. Gehrig had played in two thousand, one hundred and thirty consecutive games dating back to 1925, when he replaced a slumping Wally Pipp as the Yankees' first baseman. He would never play another, for he was suffering from amyotrophic lateral sclerosis (ALS), an incurable disease of the central nervous system.

Gehrig, who turned 36 in 1939, was one of baseball's greatest stars, a superb defensive first baseman who hit for power and average. He was part of the great Yankee teams of the late 1920s, batting fourth in the lineup after the great Babe Ruth. Gehrig, a native New Yorker and graduate of Columbia University, did not have the larger-than-life personality of his famous teammate, but baseball fans knew that he was just as important to the team's astonishing success in the 20's and 30's. He won the Triple Crown in 1934, leading the American League in batting average (.363), home runs (49) and runs batted in (165) and had a record twenty-three grand-slam home runs. As a leader and a superstar, he also helped to bridge the gap between Ruth's departure from the Yankees in 1934 and the arrival of Joe DiMaggio in 1936.

Gehrig suffered through a miserable spring training in 1939 and things only became worse when the season opened in April. While his batting eye was as good as ever—he struck out only once in twenty-eight at-bats through May 1—he had only four hits. And even casual fans noticed that he struggled in the field. When pitcher Johnny Murphy complimented him after making a routine play against the Washington Senators, Gehrig decided he had to sit. So, on May 2, he remained on the bench when his teammates took the field to play the Detroit Tigers in Detroit. Babe Dahlgren took his place at first base. Gehrig continued to suit up, but he was out of the lineup through May and into June.

In mid-June, Gehrig and his wife of five years, Eleanor, went to the Mayo Clinic in Minnesota for a series of tests. Doctors returned with their diagnosis: the indestructible Lou Gehrig was dying of ALS. He announced his retirement on June 21.

On July 4, 1939, the Yankees honored their captain with a ceremony between games of a doubleheader at Yankee Stadium. Members of the great Yankee team of 1927, including Babe Ruth, joined with current Yankees, politicians and other dignitaries in showering tributes on the stricken man. Joe McCarthy presented Gehrig, hatless but wearing his Yankee pinstripes, with a trophy from his current teammates. After McCarthy and others spoke, Gehrig stepped in front of a battery of microphones to deliver one of the twentieth century's most-quoted speeches, certainly the century's most famous speech by an American athlete. His words echoing around the stadium, Gehrig described himself as "the luckiest man on the face of the earth." The famous phrase is remembered as the emotional climax of Gehrig's career, but it was not the climax of the speech. Gehrig went on to pay tribute to his teammates, his manager, his wife and family, and to life itself. "I may have had a tough break," he said, "but I have an awful lot to live for."

When he finished, as 61,000 fans roared their appreciation for one of baseball's great gentlemen, Gehrig stepped away from the microphones, bowed his head and wiped tears from his eyes. Babe Ruth stepped forward and wrapped his big arms around his old teammate. "I wanted to laugh and cheer him up," Ruth later said. "I wound up crying like a baby."[1]

Surprisingly, Lou Gehrig Day did not mark the dying man's last appearance in a Yankee uniform. Although retired and increasingly ill, Gehrig was on the bench when his team defeated the Cincinnati Reds for the 1939 World Championship, the team's fourth straight Series title.

Lou Gehrig died on June 2, 1941, just a few weeks before his 38th birthday.

▼ ▼ ▼

FANS, for the past two weeks you have been reading about a bad break I got. Yet today I consider myself the luckiest man on the face of the earth. I have been in ballparks for seventeen years and have never received anything but kindness and encouragement from you fans.

Look at these grand men. Which of you wouldn't consider it the highlight of his career to associate with them for even one day?

Sure, I'm lucky. Who wouldn't consider it an honor to have known Jacob Ruppert—also the builder of baseball's greatest empire, Ed Barrow—to have spent the next nine years with that wonderful little fellow Miller Huggins—then to have spent the next nine years with that outstanding leader, that smart student of psychology—the best manager in baseball today, Joe McCarthy!

Sure, I'm lucky. When the New York Giants, a team you would give your right arm to beat, and vice versa, sends you a gift, that's something! When everybody down to the groundskeepers and those boys in white coats remember you with trophies, that's something.

When you have a wonderful mother-in-law who takes sides with you in squabbles against her own daughter, that's something. When you have a father and mother who work all their lives so that you can have an education and build your body, it's a blessing! When you have a wife who has been a tower of strength and shown more courage than you dreamed existed, that's the finest I know.

So I close in saying that I might have had a tough break—but I have an awful lot to live for!

38: Winston Churchill, First Speech as Prime Minister

"Blood, Toil, Tears and Sweat"

London, May 13, 1940

THE GREAT NATIONS OF EUROPE WERE AT WAR WITH EACH OTHER AGAIN IN the spring of 1940, although the capitals of the warring nations—Britain, France, Germany and Italy—seemed surprisingly placid. After the German conquest of Poland, launched in coordination with the Red Army of the Soviet Union on September 1, 1939, a strange sort of tranquility descended along the western front.

To the north, however, the allied armies of Britain and France were engaged with the Germans in a struggle over Norway. The Germans needed the Norwegian port city of Narvik to ensure a steady supply of iron for its armed forces. The allies were well aware of the city's strategic importance, and Britain's First Lord of the Admiralty, Winston Churchill, dispatched the mighty Royal Navy north to meet an expected German attack on Norway.

The German assault came on April 9, 1940. A confident Churchill told the House of Commons that "Herr Hitler has committed a grave strategic error," but it was Churchill's judgment, not Hitler's, that was open to question.[1] The British made a botch of its challenge to the German invasion. Their troops were ill-prepared for the fight, and, not coincidentally, they suffered heavy casualties. British politicians and opinion leaders whispered complaints about Churchill's management of the campaign. The main opposition party, Labor, demanded a major debate on the Norwegian disaster and the direction of the war beginning on Tuesday, May 7. The very competence of Prime Minister Neville Chamberlain and his Conservative government was to be put on trial. The embattled Prime Minister assured allies that his "enemies" would not succeed in overthrowing him.[2] Even as military disaster unfolded above the Arctic Circle, Chamberlain could not help but view his critics not as concerned fellow Britons, but as enemies of the government.

He said as much on the House floor during the debate, demanding a show of "who is with us and who is against us." Those were the words of a desperate man unaware that the power he sought to retain was about to be torn from his grasp.[3] Eighty-year-old David Lloyd George, the man who had helped lead Britain through the horrors of World War I, rose to reply to Chamberlain. The House grew silent as the great old man began to speak. The issue was not about the Prime Minister's friends, he said. The issue was leadership. The Prime Minister himself had called for sacrifice. "I say solemnly that the Prime Minister should give an example of sacrifice, because there is nothing which can contribute more to victory in this war than that he should sacrifice the seals of office."[4]

Churchill gamely defended the Prime Minister and the government, but for Neville Chamberlain, the battle was lost. As politicians left the House that night and began to discuss the possibility of forming a national, all-party government to unify the country, Labor made it clear it would not serve in any Cabinet with Chamberlain as Prime Minister.

Behind closed doors in the Palace of Westminster on May 9, the elected representatives of the British people discussed the nation's future leadership. On the Continent, German forces moved into position near the borders with France, Belgium, and the Netherlands. Some two million troops, marvelously equipped and superbly trained, were about to put an end to the so-called "phony war" on the Western front.

With just hours to go before the surprise assault, Neville Chamberlain, who had sought so desperately and so inadequately to avoid another European war, decided he could no longer remain as Prime Minister. He offered his position not to Churchill, but to Lord Halifax, the government's Foreign Minister. Halifax declined, noting that he was a member of the House of Lords, which would bar him from leading the government in the House of Commons. Halifax recommended Churchill, the man who had so bitterly condemned Chamberlain's policy of appeasing Hitler, who had warned of the threat from Hitler for so long and with so little effect.

The following day, as German troops rampaged through the Low Countries in a lightning attack, King George VI sent for sixty-five year-old Winston Churchill and commissioned him to form a new government. In as grave a moment as Britain has ever known, it fell to Winston Churchill, so recently considered yesterday's man fighting yesterday's battles, to lead the fight against the forces of industrial slaughter.

"At last I had the authority to give directions over the whole scene," Churchill later wrote. "I felt as if I were walking with destiny, and that all my past life had been put a preparation for this hour and for this trial."[5]

He went to work immediately, taking personal command of the war effort, issuing directives from his bed, meeting with commanders who were directing British troops engaged in the defense of France. He brought to Downing Street not only the energy and passion of a British patriot, but the words of a man who studied the English language and considered it one of the world's treasures.

On May 13, Churchill addressed the House of Commons for the first time as Prime Minister. He faced no opposition in the benches that faced him, for his Cabinet included all parties. In this moment of peril, the nation was united. But victory was not assured. The only certainties were grief, and sacrifice, and loss. But those burdens had to be borne if Britain were to survive.

Churchill's speech was short, and was designed not simply to inspire, but to address a practical concern. He asked for a vote of confidence in the new government. He made that request in phrases that schoolchildren a half-century later recognize. He told his nation that he had little to offer. But he promised them that he had but one goal in mind: Victory.

▼ ▼ ▼

O N Friday evening last I received from His Majesty the mission to form a new administration. It was the evident will of' Parliament and the nation that this should be conceived on the broadest possible basis and that it should include all parties.

I have already completed the most important part of this task.

A war cabinet has been formed of five members, representing, with the Labor, Opposition, and Liberals, the unity of the nation. It was necessary that this should be done in one single day on account of the extreme urgency and rigor of events. Other key positions were filled yesterday. I am submitting a further list to the king tonight. I hope to complete the appointment of principal ministers during tomorrow.

The appointment of other ministers usually takes a little longer. I trust when Parliament meets again this part of my task will be completed and that the administration will be complete in all respects. I considered it in the public interest to suggest to the Speaker that the House should be summoned today. At the end of today's proceedings, the adjournment of the House will be proposed until May 21 with provision for earlier meeting if need be. Business for that will be notified to MPs at the earliest opportunity.

I now invite the House by a resolution to record its approval of the steps taken and declare its confidence in the new government.

The resolution:

"That this House welcomes the formation of a government representing the united and inflexible resolve of the nation to prosecute the war with Germany to a victorious conclusion."

To form an administration of this scale and complexity is a serious undertaking in itself. But we are in the preliminary phase of one of the greatest battles in history. We are in action at many other points-in Norway and in Holland-and we have to be prepared in the Mediterranean. The air battle is continuing, and many preparations have to be made here at home.

In this crisis I think I may be pardoned if I do not address the House at any length today, and I hope that any of my friends and colleagues or former colleagues who are affected by the political reconstruction will make all allowances for any lack of ceremony with which it has been necessary to act.

I say to the House as I said to ministers who have joined this government, I have nothing to offer but blood, toil, tears, and sweat. We have before us an ordeal of the most grievous kind. We have before us many, many months of struggle and suffering.

You ask, what is our policy? I say it is to wage war by land, sea, and air. War with all our might and with all the strength God has given us, and to wage war against a monstrous tyranny never surpassed in the dark and lamentable catalogue of human crime. That is our policy.

You ask, what is our aim? I can answer in one word. It is victory. Victory at all costs—Victory in spite of all terrors—Victory, however long and hard the road may be, for without victory there is no survival.

Let that be realized. No survival for the British Empire, no survival for all that the British Empire has stood for, no survival for the urge, the impulse of the ages, that mankind shall move forward toward his goal.

I take up my task in buoyancy and hope. I feel sure that our cause will not be suffered to fail among men. I feel entitled at this juncture, at this time, to claim the aid of all and to say, "Come then, let us go forward together with our united strength."

39: Franklin Roosevelt's D-Day Prayer
"They Fight to End Conquest"
Washington, June 6, 1944

IN EARLY JUNE, 1944, U.S. PRESIDENT FRANKLIN ROOSEVELT RETREATED TO Charlottesville, Virginia, for a weekend at the home of his longtime aide Edwin "Pa" Watson. Aides searched his face for signs of anxiety, and they found them. Roosevelt biographer James MacGregor Burns wrote that FDR's secretary, Grace Tully, saw tension in every move the President made that weekend.

The President's mood was understandable, for he was privy to one of the best-kept secrets in military history, the date and location of an Allied invasion of northern France. It was to be June 5, at dawn, on the beaches of Normandy. But while FDR knew the precise details, his aides, his enemies, and anybody who read a newspaper or listened to a radio knew that the invasion was imminent, and that it promised to be a furious and perhaps decisive battle in the crusade to rid Europe of Nazi domination.

Across the Atlantic, along the coast of southern England, tens of thousands of American, British, Canadian troops were boarding transports for the hundred-mile journey across the English Channel, where they would assault Adolf Hitler's formidable Fortress Europe. The German army, under the command of the legendary Field Marshal Erwin Rommel, knew that the Allies were coming, although they could not be sure when and, more to the point, where. The most likely place seemed to be Calais, near the Belgian border, where the Channel was just 25 miles wide. Germans monitored the movements and radio traffic of the First U.S. Army Group, under the command of General George Patton and based in eastern England. The Germans didn't realize that the vast force was pure fiction, "created" by elaborate ruses to keep attention diverted from the buildup in southern England.

Intense planning and complicated negotiations were about to reach a climax as Roosevelt prepared to announce the invasion to the American people. He consulted the Book of Common Prayer, a traditional source of spiritual meditation for Episcopalians, as he wrote a prayer of his own for the occasion. As he did, however, an intense storm battered the staging areas of southern England, the Channel and the landing sites of Normandy. The Supreme Commander of the invasion force, Dwight Eisenhower, ordered a postponement. Ships already out to see were forced to return to base.

Roosevelt was back in Washington on Monday, June 5, to deliver his twenty-ninth fireside chat that evening. Rome, the capital of Fascist Italy, had fallen into Allied hands a day earlier, and FDR announced the news on the radio. "The first of the Axis capitals is now in our hands," he said. "One up and two to go!"

Even as he spoke, he knew that Allied soldiers, sailors and airmen were crossing or preparing to cross the Channel to begin a campaign aimed at a second Axis capital, Berlin. Eisenhower ordered the invasion to proceed that night even though the weather was far from perfect, and the Allies had never before launched an invasion in less-than-ideal conditions. Further postponements, however, threatened the invasion's security, so Eisenhower, relying on weather reports from the North Atlantic showing a break in the storms in the morning, gave the go-ahead. An armada of five thousands ships crossed the Channel that night, undetected. The secret was revealed only when dawn broke in Normandy, as German defenders were awakened by a ferocious pre-invasion bombardment from the sea and air. The first wave hit the beaches at about 6:30 a.m.

This was the crucial moment of the war in the west. A successful invasion would build on gains the Red Army had made in the east after the Battle of Stalingrad in 1943. If the invaders were thrown back into the sea, however, it would take many months to recover from the blow. Eisenhower prepared a statement he planned to release if the invasion failed, accepting full responsibility for the failure.

For several fateful hours, the battle hung in the balance as American forces were pinned down on a beach code-named Omaha. It was a vital sector, because if the Germans had prevailed and continued to hold the high ground above the beach, they could have turned their guns on the other invasion beaches, code-named Gold, Sword, Juno and Utah. By mid-day, however, the tide had begun to turn at Omaha. Eventually, about 125,000 Allied troops would land on the beaches and begin their assault on Nazi-occupied Europe.

For the second time in as many nights, Roosevelt spoke to the American people via radio. During his long tenure as president—he was elected in 1932 and would run for a fourth term later in 1944—Roosevelt became a master of the medium. With a fine baritone voice and an aristocratic, Old World-New York accent that seemed exotic to millions of his fellow citizens, Roosevelt used radio to transform himself from President of the United States to a chatty, genial neighbor and friend. He understood the medium's intimacy and its informality—during one fireside chat, he complained about Washington's heat, asked an aide for a glass of water, and promptly took an audible swallow while live on the air.

On the night of June 6, 1944, long after darkness had fallen on the beaches and landing grounds of northern France, Franklin Roosevelt addressed the nation with a short statement and a prayer he wrote for the young men of America who were taking part in a crusade to rid the Old World of unspeakable tyranny. Roosevelt's speech defined the moral parameters of the war. In speaking of the GIs in France, he said: "They fight not for the lust of conquest. They fight to end conquest." His imagery, his empathy for the families of the troops, and his acknowledgement that victory would not come without sacrifice make this a poignant as well as an historic speech. Spoken in a grave but steady voice, Roosevelt's prayer stated the moral imperatives of the war as most Americans understood them.

▼ ▼ ▼

MY Fellow Americans:
　　　　Last night, when I spoke with you about the fall of Rome, I knew at that moment that troops of the United States and our Allies were crossing the Channel in another and greater operation. It has come to pass with success thus far.

And so, in this poignant hour, I ask you to join with me in prayer:

Almighty God: Our sons, pride of our nation, this day have set upon a mighty endeavor, a struggle to preserve our Republic, our religion, and our civilization, and to set free a suffering humanity.

Lead them straight and true; give strength to their arms, stoutness to their hearts, steadfastness in their faith.

They will need Thy blessings. Their road will be long and hard. For the enemy is strong. He may hurl back our forces. Success may not come with rushing speed, but we shall return again and again; and we know that by Thy grace, and by the righteousness of our cause, our sons will triumph.

They will be sore tried, by night and by day, without rest—until the victory is won. The darkness will be rent by noise and flame. Men's souls will be shaken with the violences of war.

For these men are lately drawn from the ways of peace. They fight not for the lust of conquest. They fight to end conquest. They fight to liberate. They fight to let justice arise, and tolerance and goodwill among all Thy people. They yearn but for the end of battle, for their return to the haven of home.

Some will never return. Embrace these, Father, and receive them, Thy heroic servants, into Thy kingdom.

And for us at home—fathers, mothers, children, wives, sisters, and brothers of brave men overseas, whose thoughts and prayers are ever with them—help us, Almighty God, to rededicate ourselves in renewed faith in Thee in this hour of great sacrifice.

Many people have urged that I call the nation into a single day of special prayer. But because the road is long and the desire is great, I ask that our people devote themselves in a continuance of prayer. As we rise to each new day, and again when each day is spent, let words of prayer be on our lips, invoking Thy help to our efforts.

Give us strength, too—strength in our daily tasks, to redouble the contributions we make in the physical and the material support of our armed forces.

And let our hearts be stout, to wait out the long travail, to bear sorrows that may come, to impart our courage unto our sons wheresoever they may be.

And, O Lord, give us faith. Give us faith in Thee; faith in our sons; faith in each other; faith in our united crusade. Let not the keenness of our spirit ever be dulled. Let not the impacts of temporary events, of temporal matters of but fleeting moment—let not these deter us in our unconquerable purpose.

With Thy blessing, we shall prevail over the unholy forces of our enemy. Help us to conquer the apostles of greed and racial arrogances. Lead us to the saving of our country, and with our sister nations into a world unity that will spell a sure peace—a peace invulnerable to the schemings of unworthy men. And a peace that will let all of men live in freedom, reaping the just rewards of their honest toil.

Thy will be done, Almighty God.

Amen.

40: Emperor Hirohito Addresses His Subjects
"We Have Resolved to Pave the Way to a Grand Peace"
Tokyo, August 15, 1945

THE CITIES OF HIROSHIMA AND NAGASAKI WERE IN ASHES, TENS OF THOUSANDS vaporized in a moment unlike any other in the sad history of human conflict. The dead were the lucky ones. Tens of thousands survived the blasts and the fireball but were burned beyond saving. Their unknowable agonies lasted until they, too, were dead. The poisoned lived for a time, their sufferings unprecedented in the annals of human misery. And they died, too. And then there were those who would be born long after bombs fell, born to parents exposed to massive doses of radiation. Disfigured and impaired, they would not count in the long register of the war's wounded, but they surely were victims all the same.

No nation on earth had suffered such a calamity as Japan did on August 6, 1945, when an American warplane named the Enola Gay dropped an atomic bomb over Hiroshima. It would take hours for news of the devastation to reach Tokyo and Emperor Hirohito, the man worshiped as not just a ruler but as a living deity, the source of all political power and the symbol of the nation itself. The stunned Emperor told an aide that the war must come to an end. But other government officials resisted, holding out hope not for victory but for the preservation of the Emperor and his line. During a conference with Soviet leader Josef Stalin in Potsdam, the Americans and British released a statement demanding unconditional surrender of Japan's armed services, but said nothing about the future of the nation's supreme ruler. The war must go on, the hardliners said, for the sake of the Emperor.

So there was no peace after Hiroshima. The Soviet Union declared war on Japan, ending Japanese hopes that the Russians might mediate a more honorable end to the war than unconditional surrender. Another nuclear weapon fell on August 9 on Nagasaki. In the United States, a spirited debate unfolded among policymakers and ordinary citizens about the Emperor's future in a vanquished Japan. After Nagasaki, Japan signaled that it was willing to accept the Anglo-American terms outlined in Potsdam with the condition that the Emperor retain his role as sovereign ruler. President Truman, however, rejected the overture. In his view, one shared by many Americans, Japanese reverence for the Emperor contributed not only to the war, but to their suicidal resistance. The cult of the Emperor was inseparable from Japanese militarism, at least according to Truman and many of his advisors.

The United States, however, was weary of war, and feared the implications of a Soviet advance in Manchuria. Continued stalemate over the terms of surrender might leave the United States with no choice but to invade Japan and absorb hundreds of thousands of casualties, the very scenario Washington sought to avoid by dropping the atomic bombs. The British persuaded Truman and his advisors to drop a demand that the Emperor himself sign the instruments of surrender, thus sparing Hirohito the humiliation.

American incendiary bombs continued to fall on Tokyo, burning what was left of the capital. Hirohito and his government, meeting in bomb shelters, debated the latest American terms, communicated by Secretary of State James Byrnes. The document made no mention of the Emperor's future, simply endorsing the notion of a new government that would have the support of the Japanese people. Hirohito believed the language did not rule out, in fact, might well strengthen, a continued role for the Imperial family.

On the morning of August 14, Emperor Hirohito, wearing a military uniform and white gloves, took his place at the head of an emergency Cabinet meeting. The government still was divided. The nation's top military commanders argued that the Americans had not offered specific guarantees about the Imperial family and its role in a conquered Japan. They pleaded against surrender.

Hirohito, his eyes never meeting those of his commanders, rose from his throne to address his divided counselors. He acknowledged the hardliners' arguments. He explained that he had studied the Byrnes note and concluded that it did not conflict with Japan's expressed condition that the Emperor retain his sovereignty. "I cannot endure the thought of letting my people suffer any longer," he said. Continued resistance would only lead to thousands more dead. "How then," he asked, "could I carry on the wishes of my Imperial ancestors?"[1]

It was time to end the war. He told his government that he would deliver an address on radio to inform his subjects of his decision. The voice of the Emperor had never been heard over the airwaves. Worshipped as a god, he kept his distance from his subjects. Until now.

The document Hirohito wished to read on the air was subjected to a thorough vetting by his government. The word "surrender" was not mentioned. The attacked on Hiroshima and Nagasaki, and the continued fire-bombing of Tokyo, were similarly unspoken. When the government was satisfied, the text of Hirohito's speech was sent to a calligrapher who spent hours transforming the text into a formal imperial document.

Hirohito would not deliver such a momentous speech live. Instead, at eleven o'clock on the night of August 14, the Emperor spoke into a microphone in his office as his words were recorded on a phonograph record. Nervous and unfamiliar with the recording process, he shouted at first, until an aide told him to speak in a conversational tone. After completing the speech, Hirohito asked to read the speech again so that there was a back-up recording, just in case.

Even as he spoke a second time, a group of officers attempted to stage a coup to prevent a surrender. They heard, correctly, that a photograph recording of the Emperor's speech had been created, and they invaded a radio station and the Imperial Palace itself in search of it. But they searched in vain. When they were confronted the following morning, they admitted their guilt, apologized for questioning the Emperor's wisdom, and killed themselves.

Just before noon on August 15, the recording of Emperor Hirohito's voice was transmitted via radiowaves to the Japanese people. They had never heard his voice before. He told them not that the war was lost, but that "the war situation has developed not necessarily to our advantage." The stilted, clumsy, and ultimately tragic wording hardly mattered. The Emperor himself was speaking, and he was telling the Japanese people, in his own tortured way, that their worst nightmare had come to pass. They were defeated. Japan officially surrendered to General Douglas MacArthur aboard the battleship *U.S.S. Missouri* on September 2, 1945.

Hirohito continued to reign, but in a mostly ceremonial role, for more than forty years. The imperial family still plays an important role in Japanese culture and in its national identity. In the end, the United States found a role for the Emperor, and perhaps not coincidentally, Japan remained in America's sphere of influence during the Cold War.

▼ ▼ ▼

T0 our good and loyal subjects: After pondering deeply the general trends of the world and the actual conditions obtaining in our empire today, we have decided to effect a settlement of the present situation by resorting to an extraordinary measure.

We· have ordered our Government to communicate to the Governments of the United States, Great Britain, China and the Soviet Union that our empire accepts the provisions of their joint declaration.

To strive for the common prosperity and happiness of all nations as well as the security and well-being of our subjects is the solemn obligation which has been handed down by our imperial ancestors and which we lay close to the heart.

Indeed, we declared war on America and Britain out of our sincere desire to insure Japan's self-preservation and the stabilization of East Asia, it being far from our thought either to infringe upon the sovereignty of other nations or to embark upon territorial aggrandizement.

But now the war has lasted for nearly four years. Despite the best that has been done by everyone—the gallant fighting of our military and naval forces, the diligence and assiduity of our servants of the State and the devoted service of our 100,000,000 people—the war situation has developed not necessarily to Japan's advantage, while the general trends of the world have all turned against her interest.

Moreover, the enemy has begun to employ a new and most cruel bomb, the power of which to do damage is, indeed, incalculable, taking the toll of many innocent lives.   Should we continue to fight, it would not only result in an ultimate collapse and obliteration of the Japanese nation, but also it would lead to the total extinction of human civilization.

Such being the case, how are we to save the millions of our subjects, or to atone ourselves before the hallowed spirits of our imperial ancestors? This is the reason why we have ordered the acceptance of the provisions of the joint declaration of the powers.

We cannot but express the deepest sense of regret to our allied nations of East Asia, who have consistently cooperated with the Empire toward the emancipation of East Asia.

The thought of those officers and men as well as others who have fallen in the fields of battle, those who died at their posts of duty, or those who met death [otherwise] and all their bereaved families, pains our heart night and day.

The welfare of the wounded and the war sufferers and of those who lost their homes and livelihood is the object of our profound solicitude. The hardships and sufferings to which our nation is to be subjected hereafter will be certainly great.

We are keenly aware of the inmost feelings of all of you, our subjects. However, it is according to the dictates of time and fate that we have resolved to pave the way for a grand peace for all the generations to come by enduring the [unavoidable] and suffering what is unsufferable. Having been able to save and maintain the structure of the Imperial State, we are always with you, our good and loyal subjects, relying upon your sincerity and integrity.

Beware most strictly of any outbursts of emotion that may engender needless complications, of any fraternal contention and strife that may create confusion, lead you astray and cause you to lose the confidence of the world.

Let the entire nation continue as one family from generation to generation, ever firm in its faith in the imperishableness of its divine land, and mindful of its heavy burden of responsibilities, and the long road before it. Unite your total strength to be devoted to the construction for the future. Cultivate the ways of rectitude, nobility of spirit, and work with resolution so that you may enhance the innate glory of the Imperial State and keep pace with the progress of the world.

41: Ho Chi Minh Declares Independence for Vietnam

Ba Dinh Square, September 2, 1945

IN THE CLOSING MONTHS OF WORLD WAR II IN THE PACIFIC, AS JAPAN MOVED ever closer to defeat, a Vietnamese nationalist who called himself Ho Chi Minh (meaning "Enlightener") saw that peace would create a power vacuum in Indochina, including Vietnam. Ho believed that after Japan surrendered, the old European colonial powers as well as nationalist China would seek to regain their influence over the region.

Ho, whose given name was Nguyen Tat Thanh, spent the war fighting a guerilla campaign against the Vichy French, the Nazi collaborators who controlled the country during most of the war, and the Japanese, who installed a puppet regime in early 1945. He was well-traveled, having spent time in France, Great Britain, China, and the United States as a young man. Ho's father was a Vietnamese patriot who resigned from a government position in disgust over France's colonial domination of his country. Ho was not only a nationalist, but a communist as well. He helped found a Communist Party in France in the years following World War I, and worked with Chinese communists in the early 1930's as he sought to win independence for Vietnam.

Karl Marx was not, however, the only influence on his political development. Ho found much to admire in both the American and French revolutions. In late 1943, when a U.S. pilot was downed near the Chinese-Vietnamese border, he was rescued by Ho's comrades, known as the Viet Minh. The pilot shouted "Viet Minh!" when the guerillas approached, and they replied, "America! Roosevelt!"[1]

Ho's biographer, William J. Duiker, believes Ho "undoubtedly" knew of Franklin Roosevelt's distaste for European colonialism in general, and, in particular, French colonial rule in Indochina.

Ho and the Viet Minh turned over the pilot to U.S. forces in China, leading to a series of contacts between the movement and personnel from the U.S. Office of Strategic Services. Ho met with General Claire Chennault, commander of the U.S. 14th Air Force in China, in an effort to win American trust and, hopefully, support for his campaign against the Japanese occupiers of Vietnam. In the spring of 1945, some OSS officials advocated for a covert alliance with the Viet Minh despite Ho's embrace of communism. When Ho became ill with malaria in the fall of 1945, he was treated by an OSS nurse, although another account credits Ho's recovery to a folk remedy.

Despite his illness, the fifty-four-year-old Ho was prepared to seize the initiative when the Japanese finally surrendered. As news of the atomic bombing of Hiroshima and Nagasaki filtered east, Ho urged his colleagues to prepare for an insurrection against the Japanese-supported government. During a meeting of the Vietnamese Communist Party held days before the Japanese surrender, an order went out to the Viet Minh to begin an armed takeover of the country.

The well-organized movement used mass protests as well as the threat of armed conflict to seize the initiative. Thousands of Vietnamese civilians demonstrated in cities and villages on behalf of the Viet Minh and against a new, non-communist government that seized power in Saigon, in the southern part of the country, after the Japanese surrender. That pressure led the country's putative ruler, Emperor Bao Dai, who served under both French and Japanese occupiers, to abdicate his throne.

Ho's path to power seemed to be clear. Several possible opponents on both the right and the left were rounded up and summarily executed. A revolutionary group called the National Liberation Committee elected Ho as chairman of the provisional government of the Democratic Republic of Vietnam in Hanoi on August 27. He set to work on writing a speech in which he would declare his nation's independence, a task he later described as "the happiest moments" he'd ever known.[2]

On September 2, the speech was ready and Hanoi took on the atmosphere of a great national carnival. With years of war seemingly behind them and long-sought independence a reality, Vietnamese civilians flocked into the city for a planned celebration of the Viet Minh victory and the foundation of a new national government. Workplaces and school closed. Men and women carried banners expressing their support for the government and denouncing colonialism.

Ho was scheduled to speak at two o'clock. Workers constructed a wooden platform in a square called Place Puginier by the French, but eventually renamed Ba Dinh Square. As the hour approached, Ho was nervous and concerned about his appearance. He looked far older than his fifty-five years, indeed, he had been called an "old man" or "old Ho" for years. But his main concern was his clothing—as the hour approached, he finally settled on a khaki suit.

The square was jammed, and the afternoon was brutally hot. Ho was delayed by the sheer crush of civilians gathered to hear him. When he finally mounted the podium, he waited while his comrade, Vo Nguyen Giap, introduced him as the country's new president.

His first words were a direct quotation from America's Declaration of Independence. He knew his translation was correct, because he checked it with an OSS officer. In a speech notable for his effort to link his cause with that of two nations he would have to fight to win full independence, Ho denounced the evils of imperialism in language that read like a modern version of Thomas Jefferson's list of grievances against King George III.

In the end, of course, his citations would earn him no support from either the French or the Americans. He died in 1969 after humiliating the French and in the midst of bleeding the United States.

▼ ▼ ▼

"ALL men are created equal. They are endowed by their Creator with certain unalienable Rights; among these are Life, Liberty, and the pursuit of Happiness."

This immortal statement was made in the Declaration of Independence of the United States of America in 1776. In a broader sense, this means: All the peoples on the earth are equal from birth, all the peoples have a right to live, to be happy and free.

The Declaration of the French Revolution made in 1791 on the Rights of Man and the citizen also states: "All men are born free and with equal rights, and must always remain free and have equal rights."

These are undeniable truths.

Nevertheless, for more than eighty years, the French imperialists, abusing the standard of Liberty, Equality, and Fraternity, have violated our Fatherland and oppressed our fellow citizens. They have acted contrary to the ideals of humanity and justice.

In the field of politics, they have deprived our people of every democratic liberty.

They have enforced inhuman laws; they have set up three distinct political regimes in the North, the Center, and the South of Viet-Nam in order to wreck our national unity and prevent our people from being united.

They have built more prisons than schools. They have mercilessly slain our patriots; they have drowned our uprisings in rivers of blood.

They have fettered public opinion; they have practiced obscurantism against our people.

To weaken our race they have forced us to use opium and alcohol.

In the field of economics, they have fleeced us to the backbone, impoverished our people and devastated our land.

They have robbed us of our rice fields, our mines, our forests, and our raw materials. They have monopolized the issuing of bank notes and the export trade.

They have invented numerous unjustifiable taxes and reduced our people, especially our peasantry, to a state of extreme poverty.

They have hampered the prospering of our national bourgeoisie; they have mercilessly exploited our workers.

In the autumn of 1940, when the Japanese fascists violated Indochina's territory to establish new bases in their fight against the Allies, the French imperialists went down on their bended knees and handed over our country to them.

Thus, from that date, our people were subjected to the double yoke of the French and the Japanese. Their sufferings and miseries increased. The result was that, from the end of last year to the beginning of this year, from Quang Tri Province to the North of Viet-Nam, more than two million of our fellow citizens died from starvation. On March 9 [1945], the French troops were disarmed by the Japanese. The French colonialists either fled or surrendered, showing that not only were they incapable of "protecting" us, but that, in the span of five years, they had twice sold our country to the Japanese.

On several occasions before March 9, the Viet Minh League urged the French to ally themselves with it against the Japanese. Instead of agreeing to this proposal, the French colonialists so intensified their terrorist activities against the Viet Minh members, that before fleeing they massacred a great number of our political prisoners detained at Yen Bay and Cao Bang.

Notwithstanding all this, our fellow citizens have always manifested toward the French a tolerant and humane attitude. Even after the Japanese Putsch of March, 1945, the Viet Minh League helped many Frenchmen to cross the frontier, rescued some of them from Japanese jails, and protected French lives and property.

From the autumn of 1940, our country had in fact ceased to be a

French colony and had become a Japanese possession.

After the Japanese had surrendered to the Allies, our whole people rose to regain our national sovereignty and to found the Democratic Republic of Viet-Nam.

The truth is that we have wrested our independence from the Japanese and not from the French.

The French have fled, the Japanese have capitulated, Emperor Bao Dai has abdicated. Our people have broken the chains which for nearly a century have fettered them and have won independence for the Fatherland. Our people at the same time have overthrown the monarchic regime that has reigned supreme for dozens of centuries. In its place has been established the present Democratic Republic.

For these reasons, we, members of the Provisional Government, representing the whole Vietnamese people, declare that from now on we break off all relations of a colonial character with France; we repeal all the international obligations that France has so far subscribed to on behalf of Viet-Nam, and we abolish all the special rights the French have unlawfully acquired in our Fatherland.

The whole Vietnamese people, animated by a common purpose, are determined to fight to the bitter end against any attempt by the French colonialists to reconquer their country.

We are convinced that the Allied nations, which at Teheran and San Francisco have acknowledged the principles of self-determination and equality of nations, will not refuse to acknowledge the independence of Viet-Nam.

A people who have courageously opposed French domination for more than eighty years, a people who have fought side by side with the Allies against the fascists during these last years, such a people must be free and independent.

For these reasons, we, members of the Provisional Government of the Democratic Republic of Viet-Nam, solemnly declare to the world that Viet-Nam has the right to be a free and independent country—and in fact it is so already. The entire Vietnamese people are determined to mobilize all their physical and mental strength, to sacrifice their lives and property in order to safeguard their independence and liberty.

42: Winston Churchill's Iron Curtain Speech

Fulton, Missouri, March 5, 1946

RARELY IN THE FIELD OF HUMAN CONFLICT HAVE POWERFUL ALLIES DIS-agreed on so much so shortly after their triumph. Such was the fate of the alliance among the United States, Great Britain and the Soviet Union after World War II.

Tensions among the victors predated the end of the war. In the summer of 1945, after the German surrender and days before Hiroshima and Nagasaki were obliterated, Winston Churchill, Harry Truman (Franklin Roosevelt's successor) and Soviet leader Josef Stalin met in Potsdam, Germany, to plan for post-war administration of Europe. Although the conference produced a joint statement of postwar aims, it also revealed fault lines among the allies. Truman learned of the successful test of an atomic bomb during the conference's early sessions, and with that knowledge as his trump card, he demanded that the Soviets relinquish demands for $10 billion in reparations from Germany. An economically vital Germany was the key to reconstruction of Western Europe, an American priority. In Truman's view, the Soviet claim would set back German recovery and perhaps foil American plans for reconstruction.

At the same time, the Americans distanced themselves from British concerns over Stalin's ambitions in Eastern Europe, although both Churchill and Truman objected to Soviet attempts to push the western border of Poland into territory formerly part of Germany. Eventually, however, Truman acquiesced, but only after Churchill left the stage, defeated in Britain's first general election since the war began and replaced at the conference by a new prime minister, Clement Attlee. The American concession did not necessarily ease relations between Washington and Moscow. During the conference, U.S. Admiral William Leahy referred to Stalin privately as a "liar and a crook."[1]

Before Churchill left the conference, never to return, he spoke with

Truman about a closer Anglo-American relationship, one that would allow both nations to share defense facilities around the world—and one which he envisioned as a buffer against Soviet expansionism. Truman was amenable, but insisted that any such *defacto* alliance would have to be conducted within the framework of the fledgling United Nations organization.

Truman was more optimistic about Stalin's behavior than Churchill was, but in the months following Japan's surrender, some State Department and military officials advised the White House to be more wary of Soviet designs. When Stalin delivered a speech in February, 1946, declaring that capitalism and communism could not co-exist, hardliners in Washington warned of a new conflict with America's one-time ally. American policy began to take a more confrontational turn.

Winston Churchill was in the United States in the late winter and early spring of 1946. He was no longer prime minister, of course, but he still was a Member of Parliament, serving as leader of the opposition in the House of Commons. At age seventy-one, he had no plans to remain on the sidelines as the postwar world emerged from the ashes of Europe's great cities.

Truman invited Churchill to speak at Westminster College in Fulton, Missouri, in March. The former prime minister saw an opportunity to define conflicts between the West and the Soviets in much the same way as he defined the conflict between the Allies and the Axis, and to sound a warning about the Soviets and Stalin just as he had warned the world of the depredations of Hitler's Germany in the 1930s.

After spending some time in Florida and Cuba, which he had last visited in 1895, before the Spanish-American war, Churchill flew to Washington on February 10 for dinner with Truman, Truman's Secretary of State James Byrnes and other officials. According to Churchill biographer Martin Gilbert, the former prince minister gave the Americans a preview of the speech he was preparing for delivery in Missouri. Admiral Leahy, who attended the dinner, noted in his diary that Churchill spoke about the need for "full military collaboration" between the United States and Britain to preserve world peace. Leahy observed that the Soviets might well object to "our having a bilateral military association."[2] Truman, however, voiced no such concerns, according to Churchill.

The Englishman spent the next several days consulting friends and colleagues about the speech. The prospect of a major address and a global audience helped him forget, if only for a moment, the bitter memory of his defeat at the polls months earlier. On March 1, as Churchill continued to polish the speech, Washington learned that the Soviets would not remove troops from northern Iran as promised, prompting greater unease in Washington about Stalin's designs. Churchill could not have asked for a better context for his speech. Days later, the U.S. dispatched the battleship *U.S.S. Missouri* to the Mediterranean as a show of force.

Truman and Churchill traveled to Missouri together by train. Even now, Churchill continued to revise the speech, according to biographer Gilbert. He showed Truman the finished version before they arrived in Fulton. The President, according to Churchill, liked what he saw, although he conceded that it "would make a stir."[3]

That surely was the point. Churchill entitled his speech, "The Sinews of Peace," for he regarded it not as a warning of imminent war—in fact, he insisted that there was no immediate threat of war—but as a framework for peace. Anglo-American cooperation, he said, was the key to keeping the peace.

But the speech has gone down in history not as a peaceful document, but as a founding statement of the Cold War. Churchill famously asserted that an "iron curtain" had descended across Europe, separating the free West from the totalitarian East. Lost in that famous formula was Churchill's warm words for the Soviet Union and its people. He said he would "welcome constant, frequent and growing contacts between the Russian people and our own people on both sides of the Atlantic."

Nevertheless, as Truman predicted, the speech created a stir. Biographer Gilbert noted that press reaction focused on the "iron curtain" remark, but not on his more positive comments about the Soviets. Ninety-three members of the House of Commons from the Labor Party signed a document condemning Churchill's speech as a threat to world peace.

Today, the speech is regarded as yet another example of Churchill's moral clarity and his ability to construct a memorable phrase.

I AM glad to come to Westminster College this afternoon, and am complimented that you should give me a degree. The name "Westminster" is somehow familiar to me. I seem to have heard of it before. Indeed, it was at Westminster that I received a very large part of my education in politics, dialectic, rhetoric, and one or two other things. In fact we have both been educated at the same, or similar, or, at any rate, kindred establishments.

It is also an honor, perhaps almost unique, for a private visitor to be introduced to an academic audience by the President of the United States. Amid his heavy burdens, duties, and responsibilities—unsought but not recoiled from—the President has travelled a thousand miles to dignify and magnify our meeting here today and to give me an opportunity of addressing this kindred nation, as well as my own countrymen across the ocean, and perhaps some other countries too. The President has told you that it is his wish, as I am sure it is yours, that I should have full liberty to give my true and faithful counsel in these anxious and baffling times. I shall certainly avail myself of this freedom, and feel the more right to do so because any private ambitions I may have cherished in my younger days have been satisfied beyond my wildest dreams. Let me, however, make it clear that I have no official mission or status of any kind, and that I speak only for myself. There is nothing here but what you see.

I can therefore allow my mind, with the experience of a lifetime, to play over the problems which beset us on the morrow of our absolute victory in arms, and to try to make sure with what strength I have that what has been gained with so much sacrifice and suffering shall be preserved for the future glory and safety of mankind.

The United States stands at this time at the pinnacle of world power. It is a solemn moment for the American Democracy. For with primacy in power is also joined an awe-inspiring accountability to the future. If you look around you, you must feel not only the sense of duty done but also you must feel anxiety lest you fall below the level of achievement. Opportunity is here now, clear and shining for both our countries. To reject it or ignore it or fritter it away will bring upon us all the long reproaches of the aftertime. It is necessary that constancy of mind, persistency of purpose, and the grand simplicity of decision shall guide and rule the conduct of the English-speaking peoples in peace as they did in war. We must, and I believe we shall, prove ourselves equal to this severe requirement.

When American military men approach some serious situation they are wont to write at the head of their directive the words "over-all strategic concept." There is wisdom in this, as it leads to clarity of thought. What then is the over-all strategic concept which we should inscribe today? It is nothing less than the safety and welfare, the freedom and progress, of all the homes and families of all the men and women in all the lands. And here I speak particularly of the myriad cottage or apartment homes where the wage-earner strives amid the accidents and difficulties of life to guard his wife and children from privation and bring the family up in the fear of the Lord, or upon ethical conceptions which often play their potent part.

To give security to these countless homes, they must be shielded from the two giant marauders, war and tyranny. We all know the frightful disturbances in which the ordinary family is plunged when the curse of war swoops down upon the bread-winner and those for whom he works and contrives. The awful ruin of Europe, with all its vanished glories, and of large parts of Asia glares us in the eyes. When the designs of wicked men or the aggressive urge of mighty States dissolve over large areas the frame of civilized society, humble folk are confronted with difficulties with which they cannot cope. For them all is distorted, all is broken, even ground to pulp.

When I stand here this quiet afternoon I shudder to visualise what is actually happening to millions now and what is going to happen in this period when famine stalks the earth. None can compute what has been called "the unestimated sum of human pain." Our supreme task and duty is to guard the homes of the common people from the horrors and miseries of another war. We are all agreed on that.

Our American military colleagues, after having proclaimed their "overall strategic concept" and computed available resources, always proceed to the next step—namely, the method. Here again there is widespread agreement. A world organization has already been erected for the prime purpose of preventing war; UNO, the successor of the League of Nations, with the decisive addition of the United States and all that that means, is already at work. We must make sure that its work is fruitful, that it is a reality and not a sham, that it is a force for action, and not merely a frothing of words, that it is a true temple of peace in which the shields of many nations can some day be hung up, and not merely a cockpit in a Tower of Babel. Before we cast away the solid assurances of national armaments for self-preservation we must be certain that our temple is built, not upon shifting sands or quagmires, but upon the rock. Anyone can see with his eyes open that our path will be difficult and also long, but if we persevere together as we did in the two world wars—though not, alas, in the interval between them—I cannot doubt that we shall achieve our common purpose in the end.

I have, however, a definite and practical proposal to make for action. Courts and magistrates may be set up but they cannot function without sheriffs and constables. The United Nations Organization must immediately begin to be equipped with an international armed force. In such a matter we can only go step by step, but we must begin now. I propose that each of the Powers and States should be invited to delegate a certain number of air squadrons to the service of the world organization. These squadrons would be trained and prepared in their own countries, but would move around in rotation from one country to another. They would wear the uniform of their own countries but with different badges. They would not be required to act against their own nation, but in other respects they would be directed by the world organization. This might be started on a modest scale and would grow as confidence grew. I wished to see this done after the first world war, and I devoutly trust it may be done forthwith.

It would nevertheless be wrong and imprudent to entrust the secret knowledge or experience of the atomic bomb, which the United States, Great Britain, and Canada now share, to the world organization, while it is still in its infancy. It would be criminal madness to cast it adrift in this still agitated and un-united world. No one in any country has slept less well in their beds because this knowledge and the method and the raw materials to apply it, are at present largely retained in American hands. I do not believe we should all have slept so soundly had the positions been reversed and if some Communist or neo-Fascist State monopolized for the time being these dread agencies. The fear of them alone might easily have been used to enforce total-itarian systems upon the free democratic world, with consequences appalling to human imagination. God has willed that this shall not be and we have at least a breathing space to set our house in order before this peril has to be encountered: and even then, if no effort is spared, we should still possess so formidable a superiority as to impose effective deterrents upon its employ-ment, or threat of employment, by others. Ultimately, when the essential brotherhood of man is truly embodied and expressed in a world organization with all the necessary practical safeguards to make it effective, these powers would naturally be confided to that world organization.

Now I come to the second danger of these two marauders which threat-ens the cottage, the home, and the ordinary people—namely, tyranny. We cannot be blind to the fact that the liberties enjoyed by individual citizens throughout the British Empire are not valid in a considerable number of countries, some of which are very powerful. In these States control is enforced upon the common people by various kinds of all-embracing police governments. The power of the State is exercised without restraint, either by dictators or by compact oligarchies operating through a privileged party and a political police. It is not our duty at this time when difficulties are so numerous to interfere forcibly in the internal affairs of countries which we have not conquered in war. But we must never cease to proclaim in fearless tones the great principles of freedom and the rights of man which are the joint inheritance of the English-speaking world and which through Magna Carta, the Bill of Rights, the Habeas Corpus, trial by jury, and the English common law find their most famous expression in the American Declaration of Independence.

All this means that the people of any country have the right, and should have the power by constitutional action, by free unfettered elections, with secret ballot, to choose or change the character or form of government under which they dwell; that freedom of speech and thought should reign; that courts of justice, independent of the executive, unbiased by any party, should administer laws which have received the broad assent of large majorities or are consecrated by time and custom. Here are the title deeds of freedom which should lie in every cottage home. Here is the message of the British and American peoples to mankind. Let us preach what we practise—let us practise what we preach.

I have now stated the two great dangers which menace the homes of the people: War and Tyranny. I have not yet spoken of poverty and privation which are in many cases the prevailing anxiety. But if the dangers of war and tyranny are removed, there is no doubt that science and cooperation can bring in the next few years to the world, certainly in the next few decades newly taught in the sharpening school of war, an expansion of material well-being beyond anything that has yet occurred in human experience. Now, at this sad and breathless moment, we are plunged in the hunger and distress which are the aftermath of our stupendous struggle; but this will pass and may pass quickly, and there is no reason except human folly of sub-human crime which should deny to all the nations the inauguration and enjoyment of an age of plenty. I have often used words which I learned fifty years ago from a great Irish-American orator, a friend of mine, Mr. Bourke Cockran. "There is enough for all. The earth is a generous mother; she will provide in plentiful abundance food for all her children if they will but cultivate her soil in justice and in peace." So far I feel that we are in full agreement.

Now, while still pursuing the method of realizing our overall strategic concept, I come to the crux of what I have travelled here to say. Neither the sure prevention of war, nor the continuous rise of world organization will be gained without what I have called the fraternal association of the English-speaking peoples. This means a special relationship between the British

Commonwealth and Empire and the United States. This is no time for generalities, and I will venture to be precise. Fraternal association requires not only the growing friendship and mutual understanding between our two vast but kindred systems of society, but the continuance of the intimate relationship between our military advisers, leading to common study of potential dangers, the similarity of weapons and manuals of instructions, and to the interchange of officers and cadets at technical colleges. It should carry with it the continuance of the present facilities for mutual security by the joint use of all Naval and Air Force bases in the possession of either country all over the world. This would perhaps double the mobility of the American Navy and Air Force. It would greatly expand that of the British Empire Forces and it might well lead, if and as the world calms down, to important financial savings. Already we use together a large number of islands; more may well be entrusted to our joint care in the near future.

The United States has already a Permanent Defence Agreement with the Dominion of Canada, which is so devotedly attached to the British Commonwealth and Empire. This Agreement is more effective than many of those which have often been made under formal alliances. This principle should be extended to all British Commonwealths with full reciprocity. Thus, whatever happens, and thus only, shall we be secure ourselves and able to work together for the high and simple causes that are dear to us and bode no ill to any. Eventually there may come—I feel eventually there will come—the principle of common citizenship, but that we may be content to leave to destiny, whose outstretched arm many of us can already clearly see.

There is however an important question we must ask ourselves. Would a special relationship between the United States and the British Commonwealth be inconsistent with our over-riding loyalties to the World Organization? I reply that, on the contrary, it is probably the only means by which that organization will achieve its full stature and strength. There are already the special United States relations with Canada which I have just mentioned, and there are the special relations between the United States and the South American Republics. We British have our twenty years' Treaty of Collaboration and Mutual Assistance with Soviet Russia. I agree with Mr. Bevin, the Foreign Secretary of Great Britain, that it might well be a fifty years' Treaty so far as we are concerned. We aim at nothing but mutual assistance and collaboration. The British have an alliance with Portugal unbroken since 1384, and which produced fruitful results at critical moments in the late war. None of these clash with the general interest of a world agreement, or a world organization; on the contrary they help it. "In my father's house are many mansions." Special associations between members of the United Nations which have no aggressive point against any other country, which harbor no design incompatible with the Charter of the United Nations, far from being harmful, are beneficial and, as I believe, indispensable.

I spoke earlier of the Temple of Peace. Workmen from all countries must build that temple. If two of the workmen know each other particularly well and are old friends, if their families are inter-mingled, and if they have "faith in each other's purpose, hope in each other's future and charity towards each other's shortcomings"—to quote some good words I read here the other day—why cannot they work together at the common task as friends and partners? Why cannot they share their tools and thus increase each other's working powers? Indeed they must do so or else the temple may not be built, or, being built, it may collapse, and we shall all be proved again unteachable and have to go and try to learn again for a third time in a school of war, incomparably more rigorous than that from which we have just been released. The dark ages may return, the Stone Age may return on the gleaming wings of science, and what might now shower immeasurable material blessings upon mankind, may even bring about its total destruction. Beware, I say; time may be short. Do not let us take the course of allowing events to drift along until it is too late. If there is to be a fraternal association of the kind I have described, with all the extra strength and security which both our countries can derive from it, let us make sure that that great fact is known to the world, and that it plays its part in steadying and stabilizing the foundations of peace. There is the path of wisdom. Prevention is better than cure.

A shadow has fallen upon the scenes so lately lighted by the Allied victory. Nobody knows what Soviet Russia and its Communist international organization intends to do in the immediate future, or what are the limits, if any, to their expansive and proselytizing tendencies. I have a strong admiration and regard for the valiant Russian people and for my wartime comrade, Marshal Stalin. There is deep sympathy and goodwill in Britain—and I doubt not here also—towards the peoples of all the Russias and a resolve to persevere through many differences and rebuffs in establishing lasting friendships. We understand the Russian need to be secure on her western frontiers by the removal of all possibility of German aggression. We welcome Russia to her rightful place among the leading nations of the world.

We welcome her flag upon the seas. Above all, we welcome constant, frequent and growing contacts between the Russian people and our own people on both sides of the Atlantic. It is my duty however, for I am sure you would wish me to state the facts as I see them to you, to place before you certain facts about the present position in Europe.

From Stettin in the Baltic to Trieste in the Adriatic, an iron curtain has descended across the Continent. Behind that line lie all the capitals of the ancient states of Central and Eastern Europe. Warsaw, Berlin, Prague, Vienna, Budapest, Belgrade, Bucharest and Sofia, all these famous cities and the populations around them lie in what I must call the Soviet sphere, and all are subject in one form or another, not only to Soviet influence but to a very high and, in many cases, increasing measure of control from Moscow. Athens alone—Greece with its immortal glories—is free to decide its future at an election under British, American and French observation. The Russian-dominated Polish Government has been encouraged to make enormous and wrongful inroads upon Germany, and mass expulsions of millions of Germans on a scale grievous and undreamed-of are now taking place. The Communist parties, which were very small in all these Eastern States of Europe, have been raised to pre-eminence and power far beyond their numbers and are seeking everywhere to obtain totalitarian control. Police governments are prevailing in nearly every case, and so far, except in Czechoslovakia, there is no true democracy.

Turkey and Persia are both profoundly alarmed and disturbed at the claims which are being made upon them and at the pressure being exerted by the Moscow Government. An attempt is being made by the Russians in Berlin to build up a quasi-Communist party in their zone of Occupied Germany by showing special favors to groups of left-wing German leaders. At the end of the fighting last June, the American and British Armies withdrew westwards, in accordance with an earlier agreement, to a depth at some points of 150 miles upon a front of nearly four hundred miles, in order to allow our Russian allies to occupy this vast expanse of territory which the Western Democracies had conquered.

If now the Soviet Government tries, by separate action, to build up a pro-Communist Germany in their areas, this will cause new serious difficulties in the British and American zones, and will give the defeated Germans the power of putting themselves up to auction between the Soviets and the Western Democracies. Whatever conclusions may be drawn from these facts—and facts they are—this is certainly not the Liberated Europe we fought to build up. Nor is it one which contains the essentials of permanent peace.

The safety of the world requires a new unity in Europe, from which no nation should be permanently outcast. It is from the quarrels of the strong parent races in Europe that the world wars we have witnessed, or which occurred in former times, have sprung. Twice in our own lifetime we have seen the United States, against their wishes and their traditions, against arguments, the force of which it is impossible not to comprehend, drawn by irresistible forces, into these wars in time to secure the victory of the good cause, but only after frightful slaughter and devastation had occurred. Twice the United States has had to send several millions of its young men across the Atlantic to find the war; but now war can find any nation, wherever it may dwell between dusk and dawn. Surely we should work with conscious purpose for a grand pacification of Europe, within the structure of the United Nations and in accordance with its Charter. That I feel is an open cause of policy of very great importance.

In front of the iron curtain which lies across Europe are other causes for anxiety. In Italy the Communist Party is seriously hampered by having to support the Communist-trained Marshal Tito's claims to former Italian territory at the head of the Adriatic. Nevertheless the future of Italy hangs in the balance. Again one cannot imagine a regenerated Europe without a strong France. All my public life I have worked for a strong France and I never lost faith in her destiny, even in the darkest hours. I will not lose faith now. However, in a great number of countries, far from the Russian frontiers and throughout the world, Communist fifth columns are established and work in complete unity and absolute obedience to the directions they receive from the Communist center. Except in the British Commonwealth and in the United States where Communism is in its infancy, the Communist parties or fifth columns constitute a growing challenge and peril to Christian civilization. These are somber facts for anyone to have to recite on the morrow of a victory gained by so much splendid comradeship in arms and in the cause of freedom and democracy; but we should be most unwise not to face them squarely while time remains.

The outlook is also anxious in the Far East and especially in Manchuria. The Agreement which was made at Yalta, to which I was a party, was extremely favourable to Soviet Russia, but it was made at a time when no one could say that the German war might not extend all through the summer and autumn of 1945 and when the Japanese war was expected to last

for a further 18 months from the end of the German war. In this country
you are all so well-informed about the Far East, and such devoted friends
of China, that I do not need to expatiate on the situation there.

I have felt bound to portray the shadow which, alike in the west and in
the east, falls upon the world. I was a high minister at the time of the
Versailles Treaty and a close friend of Mr. Lloyd-George, who was the head
of the British delegation at Versailles. I did not myself agree with many
things that were done, but I have a very strong impression in my mind of
that situation, and I find it painful to contrast it with that which prevails
now. In those days there were high hopes and unbounded confidence that
the wars were over, and that the League of Nations would become all-powerful. I do not see or feel that same confidence or even the same hopes in
the haggard world at the present time.

On the other hand I repulse the idea that a new war is inevitable; still
more that it is imminent. It is because I am sure that our fortunes are still
in our own hands and that we hold the power to save the future, that I feel
the duty to speak out now that I have the occasion and the opportunity to
do so. I do not believe that Soviet Russia desires war. What they desire is
the fruits of war and the indefinite expansion of their power and doctrines.
But what we have to consider here to-day while time remains, is the permanent prevention of war and the establishment of conditions of freedom and
democracy as rapidly as possible in all countries. Our difficulties and dangers will not be removed by closing our eyes to them. They will not be
removed by mere waiting to see what happens; nor will they be removed by
a policy of appeasement. What is needed is a settlement, and the longer this
is delayed, the more difficult it will be and the greater our dangers will
become.

From what I have seen of our Russian friends and Allies during the war,
I am convinced that there is nothing they admire so much as strength, and
there is nothing for which they have less respect than for weakness, especially military weakness. For that reason the old doctrine of a balance of
power is unsound. We cannot afford, if we can help it, to work on narrow
margins, offering temptations to a trial of strength. If the Western
Democracies stand together in strict adherence to the principles of the
United Nations Charter, their influence for furthering those principles will
be immense and no one is likely to molest them. If however they become
divided or falter in their duty and if these all-important years are allowed to
slip away then indeed catastrophe may overwhelm us all.

Last time I saw it all coming and cried aloud to my own fellow-country-men and to the world, but no one paid any attention. Up till the year 1933 or even 1935, Germany might have been saved from the awful fate which has overtaken her and we might all have been spared the miseries Hitler let loose upon mankind. There never was a war in all history easier to prevent by timely action than the one which has just desolated such great areas of the globe. It could have been prevented in my belief without the firing of a single shot, and Germany might be powerful, prosperous and honored today; but no one would listen and one by one we were all sucked into the awful whirlpool. We surely must not let that happen again. This can only be achieved by reaching now, in 1946, a good understanding on all points with Russia under the general authority of the United Nations Organization and by the maintenance of that good understanding through many peaceful years, by the world instrument, supported by the whole strength of the English-speaking world and all its connections. There is the solution which I respectfully offer to you in this Address to which I have given the title "The Sinews of Peace."

Let no man underrate the abiding power of the British Empire and Commonwealth. Because you see the 46 millions in our island harassed about their food supply, of which they only grow one half, even in war-time, or because we have difficulty in restarting our industries and export trade after six years of passionate war effort, do not suppose that we shall not come through these dark years of privation as we have come through the glorious years of agony, or that half a century from now, you will not see 70 or 80 millions of Britons spread about the world and united in defence of our traditions, our way of life, and of the world causes which you and we espouse. If the population of the English-speaking Commonwealths be added to that of the United States with all that such cooperation implies in the air, on the sea, all over the globe and in science and in industry, and in moral force, there will be no quivering, precarious balance of power to offer its temptation to ambition or adventure. On the contrary, there will be an overwhelming assurance of security. If we adhere faithfully to the Charter of the United Nations and walk forward in sedate and sober strength seeking no one's land or treasure, seeking to lay no arbitrary control upon the thoughts of men; if all British moral and material forces and convictions are joined with your own in fraternal association, the high-roads of the future will be clear, not only for us but for all, not only for our time, but for a century to come.

43: Nikita Khrushchev's Secret Speech

Moscow: February 25, 1956

JOSEF STALIN DIED ON MARCH 5, 1953, AFTER PRESIDING OVER THE SOVIET Union for thirty years. During his long and murderous reign, millions of Soviet citizens were dispatched to their graves on his whim. On the day he died, more than two million more were living, if such a life could be described as "living," in brutal labor camps, victims of one of the twentieth century's most repressive governments.

In the decades to come, the name of Stalin would be linked with that of the man his nation fought so heroically, Adolf Hitler, during World War II. But at the time of his death, Stalin was a hero of the Soviet Union despite his crimes. Biographer William Taubman noted that when news of Stalin's death reached the camps he built to house dissidents, some prisoners broke down in tears.[1] British journalist John Rettie, who was based in Moscow as a correspondent for *The Observer* newspaper, noted that most Soviet citizens saw Stalin "as a divine father."[2]

His colleagues in the Communist Party leadership were grief-stricken as well. During Stalin's funeral ceremony in Moscow's Hall of Columns, a portly, bald figure standing with Communist Party dignitaries wept openly. His name was Nikita Khrushchev, the son of Russian peasants who rose to power and prominence under Stalin. He willingly served Stalin in the Ukraine after World War II, when the Soviets brutally suppressed a fledgling independence movement

In the power struggle that began to unfold even as Stalin was breathing his last, Khrushchev emerged victorious, outmaneuvering rivals to seize control of the Central Committee of the Soviet Communist Party. In early 1956, as the party prepared for its first general congress since Stalin's death, Nikita Khrushchev was the most powerful man in the Soviet Union.

The congress was the Soviet party's twentieth, a gathering that brought more than twelve hundred communists from around the world to the Kremlin. The congress was designed to be the governing body of the Communist Party, but it quickly became little more than a conscripted audience for the dictates of Lenin and Stalin. During Stalin's tenure, the congress met only sporadically, and when it did, it simply ratified the dictator's agenda.

Stalin's last congress, the 19th such gathering, met in 1952—its first meeting in a dozen years. The 20th congress figured to be as prosaic as its predecessors. Participation would be limited to the party's elite; most delegates were there to applaud. The agenda featured long speeches about the Soviet economy, international relations, and other matters.

As First Secretary of the Soviet party, Khrushchev opened the congress, noting in his introductory remarks that since the congress last met, the communist world had lost "distinguished leaders."[3] He listed three names: Stalin, Klement Gottwald of Czechoslovakia, and Kyuchi Tokuda, a Japanese communist.

The linkage of Stalin with the obscure Gottwald and the practically unknown Tokuda did not pass without notice in the hall. Surely the great Stalin deserved a more prominent mention and a greater tribute than to be lumped together with two extremely minor figures.

The more prominent mention was yet to come, and it would hardly be what the delegates were expecting.

The congress lasted for ten days, during which Khrushchev consolidated his power. His speeches invariably were greeted with great applause, standing ovations, and loud approval, according to the party organ, *Pravda*. He dominated the stage, delivering several speeches and reports, signaling that he was very much in charge.

On the night of February 24, as the congress drew to a close and delegates were preparing to return home, journalists gathered outside noticed that the lights were on in the Central Committee's Kremlin office and there seemed to be an extraordinary amount of activity in and around the Kremlin. The reporters found this curious, as *The Observer*'s John Rettie recalled years later.[4]

It was more than curious. It was nothing short of history in the making. That night, Soviet leaders learned that Khrushchev intended to deliver a long attack on Stalin the following morning. Stunned, the party's leaders argued long into the night in Central Committee headquarters about the speech. Khrushchev intended to not simply criticize a beloved predecessor, but to indict him as a monster who was responsible for the deaths of millions of innocents, who built a regime based on terror and paranoia, and who created a cult of personality which subsumed the general good to his own mania for power and control.

The following morning, delegates were hurriedly summoned to a secret session of the congress. They arrived to find Khrushchev in his usual place on center stage surrounded by grim-faced party officials. He began by explaining that he wished to discuss "how the cult of the person of Stalin had been gradually growing," and why this cult represented a grave departure from the teachings of Marx and Lenin himself, a man who, Khrushchev was quick to remind his listeners, considered Stalin to be an "excessively rude" person who "abuses his power."

Having claimed Marx and Lenin as his allies in absentia, Khrushchev outlined his case against Stalin in a twenty-six-thousand word speech that took four hours to deliver. Stalin, he said, used "extreme methods and mass repressions" against the Soviet people, he "trampled on the Leninist principle of collective party leadership" and ordered executions and mass arrests that "caused tremendous harm to our country." He revealed that Winston Churchill, no friend of the Soviet state, had warned Stalin in 1941 to expect a German invasion, but "Stalin took no heed of these warnings," leading to horrendous losses in the early fighting on the Eastern front. He called Stalin a "coward" who refused to visit the front lines during the war.

As Khrushchev spoke, delegates put their faces in their hands. One delegate with a weak heart reached for his medication, fearing he would suffer a heart attack on the spot. When Khrushchev interrupted his presentation for an intermission, his shocked listeners could barely speak to one another.

Khrushchev concluded his speech with a pledge to return the Soviet Union to the principles of Lenin, whose memory Stalin had defiled. The speech's conclusion prompted prolonged applause, but the rest of the speech inspired only despair, shock, and, for those who had hated Stalin all along, quiet joy. Journalist Rettie, writing on the fiftieth anniversary of the speech, noted that top Soviet leaders were so distraught that they failed to appear at diplomatic functions for weeks afterwards. In Georgia, Stalin's birthplace, riots broke out when a text of Khrushchev's speech was read to workers.

Although Khrushchev pledged his listeners to secrecy, Western reporters soon heard rumors of the assault on Stalin. The Central Intelligence Agency got its hands on an edited version of the speech through Polish sources, and that version was published in *The New York Times* and *The Observer* in London. *The Observer* later received a full version of the speech and printed it, all twenty-six thousand words of it, in June.

The speech marked the beginning of Khrushchev's campaign to purge the Soviet Union of the cult of Stalin and of the dictator's brutal excesses. Prisoners jailed by Stalin were set free. Dissidents were rehabilitated by the thousands. Meanwhile, in Eastern Europe, reformers and anti-Soviet nationalists took the speech as a signal to step up their opposition. Hungary and Poland were in a ferment by the summer of 1956, an unintended consequence of the secret speech. Fearing that the two satellite regimes would break from the Soviet orbit, Khrushchev ordered troops and tanks into Hungary in October to crush the dissident movement. Twenty thousand Hungarians were killed, and the fledgling revolt was crushed.

Decades later, after the Soviet Union ceased to exist, historians pointed to the secret speech as the beginning of the end for a regime that proved incapable of purging Stalin from its DNA. The Soviet Union was never quite the same after Khrushchev's bold words. Mikhail Gorbachev, a college student and young communist activist in 1956, tried to finish the process Khrushchev began, but it was too late.

Khrushchev himself survived an attempt to oust him as First Secretary of the party in 1957, but was not so lucky the second time around, in 1964CK. But the words he spoke in 1956 outlasted his critics and enemies. On that day in Moscow, he dared to speak the truth, and in doing so, changed the course of history.

▼ ▼ ▼

COMRADES! In the Party Central Committee's report at the 20th Congress and in a number of speeches by delegates to the Congress, as also formerly during Plenary CC/CPSU [Central Committee of the Communist Party of the Soviet Union] sessions, quite a lot has been said about the cult of the individual and about its harmful consequences.

After Stalin's death, the Central Committee began to implement a policy of explaining concisely and consistently that it is impermissible and foreign to the spirit of Marxism-Leninism to elevate one person, to transform him into a superman possessing supernatural characteristics, akin to those of a god. Such a man supposedly knows everything, sees everything, thinks for everyone, can do anything, is infallible in his behavior.

Such a belief about a man, and specifically about Stalin, was cultivated among us for many years. The objective of the present report is not a thorough evaluation of Stalin's life and activity. Concerning Stalin's merits, an entirely sufficient number of books, pamphlets and studies had already been written in his lifetime. Stalin's role in the preparation and execution of the Socialist Revolution, in the Civil War, and in the fight for the construction of socialism in our country, is universally known. Everyone knows it well.

At present, we are concerned with a question which has immense importance for the Party now and for the future—with how the cult of the person of Stalin has been gradually growing, the cult which became at a certain specific stage the source of a whole series of exceedingly serious and grave perversions of Party principles, of Party democracy, of revolutionary legality.

Because not all as yet realize fully the practical consequences resulting from the cult of the individual, [or] the great harm caused by violation of the principle of collective Party direction and by the accumulation of immense and limitless power in the hands of one person, the Central Committee considers it absolutely necessary to make material pertaining to this matter available to the 20th Congress of the Communist Party of the Soviet Union.

Allow me first of all to remind you how severely the classics of Marxism-Leninism denounced every manifestation of the cult of the individual. In a letter to the German political worker Wilhelm Bloss, [Karl] Marx stated: "From my antipathy to any cult of the individual, I never made public during the existence of the [first] International the numerous addresses from various countries which recognized my merits and which annoyed me. I did not even reply to them, except sometimes to rebuke their authors. [Fredrich] Engels and I first joined the secret society of Communists on the condition that everything making for superstitious worship of authority would be deleted from its statute. [Ferdinand] Lassalle subsequently did quite the opposite."

Sometime later Engels wrote: "Both Marx and I have always been against any public manifestation with regard to individuals, with the exception of cases when it had an important purpose. We most strongly opposed such manifestations which during our lifetime concerned us personally."

The great modesty of the genius of the Revolution, Vladimir Ilyich Lenin, is known. Lenin always stressed the role of the people as the creator of history, the directing and organizational roles of the Party as a living and creative organism, and also the role of the Central Committee.

Marxism does not negate the role of the leaders of the working class in directing the revolutionary liberation movement.

While ascribing great importance to the role of the leaders and organizers of the masses, Lenin at the same time mercilessly stigmatized every manifestation of the cult of the individual, inexorably combated [any] foreign-to-Marxism views about a "hero" and a "crowd," and countered all efforts to oppose a "hero" to the masses and to the people.

Lenin taught that the Party's strength depends on its indissoluble unity with the masses, on the fact that behind the Party follows the people—workers, peasants, and the intelligentsia. Lenin said, "Only he who believes in the people, [he] who submerges himself in the fountain of the living creativeness of the people, will win and retain power."

Lenin spoke with pride about the Bolshevik Communist Party as the leader and teacher of the people. He called for the presentation of all the most important questions before the opinion of knowledgeable workers, before the opinion of their Party. He said: "We believe in it, we see in it the wisdom, the honor, and the conscience of our epoch."

Lenin resolutely stood against every attempt aimed at belittling or weakening the directing role of the Party in the structure of the Soviet state. He worked out Bolshevik principles of Party direction and norms of Party life, stressing that the guiding principle of Party leadership is its collegiality. Already during the pre-Revolutionary years, Lenin called the Central Committee a collective of leaders and the guardian and interpreter of Party principles. "During the period between congresses," Lenin pointed out, "the Central Committee guards and interprets the principles of the Party."

Underlining the role of the Central Committee and its authority, Vladimir Ilyich pointed out: "Our Central Committee constituted itself as a closely centralized and highly authoritative group."

During Lenin's life the Central Committee was a real expression of collective leadership: of the Party and of the nation. Being a militant Marxist-revolutionist, always unyielding in matters of principle, Lenin never imposed his views upon his co-workers by force. He tried to convince. He patiently explained his opinions to others. Lenin always diligently saw to it that the norms of Party life were realized, that Party statutes were enforced, that Party congresses and Plenary sessions of the Central Committee took place at their proper intervals.

In addition to V. I. Lenin's great accomplishments for the victory of the working class and of the working peasants, for the victory of our Party and for the application of the ideas of scientific Communism to life, his acute mind expressed itself also in this. [Lenin] detected in Stalin in time those negative characteristics which resulted later in grave consequences. Fearing the future fate of the Party and of the Soviet nation, V. I. Lenin made a completely correct characterization of Stalin. He pointed out that it was necessary to consider transferring Stalin from the position of [Party] General Secretary because Stalin was excessively rude, did not have a proper attitude toward his comrades, and was capricious and abused his power.

In December 1922, in a letter to the Party Congress, Vladimir Ilyich wrote: "After taking over the position of General Secretary, comrade Stalin accumulated immeasurable power in his hands and I am not certain whether he will be always able to use this power with the required care."

This letter—a political document of tremendous importance, known in the Party's history as Lenin's "Testament"— was distributed among [you] delegates to [this] 20th Party Congress. You have read it and will undoubtedly read it again more than once. You might reflect on Lenin's plain words, in which expression is given to Vladimir Ilyich's anxiety concerning the Party, the people, the state, and the future direction of Party policy.

Vladimir Ilyich said:

"Stalin is excessively rude, and this defect, which can be freely tolerated in our midst and in contacts among us Communists, becomes a defect which cannot be tolerated in one holding the position of General Secretary. Because of this, I propose that the comrades consider the method by which Stalin would be removed from this position and by which another man would be selected for it, a man who, above all, would differ from Stalin in only one quality, namely, greater tolerance, greater loyalty, greater kindness and a more considerate attitude toward the comrades, a less capricious temper, etc."

This document of Lenin's was made known to the delegates at the 13th Party Congress, who discussed the question of transferring Stalin from the position of General Secretary. The delegates declared themselves in favor of retaining Stalin in this post, hoping that he would heed Vladimir Ilyich's critical remarks and would be able to overcome the defects which caused Lenin serious anxiety.

Comrades! The Party Congress should become acquainted with two new documents, which confirm Stalin's character as already outlined by Vladimir Ilyich Lenin in his "Testament." These documents are a letter from Nadezhda Konstantinovna Krupskaya to [Lev] Kamenev, who was at that time head of the Politbiuro, and a personal letter from Vladimir Ilyich Lenin to Stalin.

I will now read these documents:

"LEV BORISOVICH!

"Because of a short letter which I had written in words dictated to me by Vladimir Ilyich by permission of the doctors, Stalin allowed himself yesterday an unusually rude outburst directed at me.

This is not my first day in the Party. During all these thirty years I have never heard one word of rudeness from any comrade. The Party's and Ilyich's business is no less dear to me than to Stalin. I need maximum self-control right now. What one can and what one cannot discuss with Ilyich I know better than any doctor, because I know what makes him nervous and what does not. In any case I know [it] better than Stalin. I am turning to you and to Grigory [Zinoviev] as much closer comrades of V[ladimir] I[lyich]. I beg you to protect me from rude interference with my private life and from vile invectives and threats. I have no doubt what the Control Commission's unanimous decision [in this matter], with which Stalin sees fit to threaten me, will be. However I have neither strength nor time to waste on this foolish quarrel. And I am a human being and my nerves are strained to the utmost.

"N. KRUPSKAYA"

Nadezhda Konstantinovna wrote this letter on December 23, 1922. After two and a half months, in March 1923, Vladimir Ilyich Lenin sent Stalin the following letter:

"TO COMRADE STALIN (COPIES FOR: KAMENEV AND ZINOVIEV):

"Dear comrade Stalin!

"You permitted yourself a rude summons of my wife to the telephone and a rude reprimand of her. Despite the fact that she told you that she agreed to forget what was said, nevertheless Zinoviev and Kamenev heard about it from her. I have no intention to forget so easily that which is being done against me. I need not stress here that I consider as directed against me that which is being done against my wife. I ask you, therefore, that you weigh carefully whether you are agreeable to retracting your words and apologizing, or whether you prefer the severance of relations between us.

"SINCERELY: LENIN, MARCH 5, 1923

(Commotion in the hall.)

Comrades! I will not comment on these documents. They speak eloquently for themselves. Since Stalin could behave in this manner during Lenin's life, could thus behave toward Nadezhda Konstantinovna

Krupskaya—whom the Party knows well and values highly as a loyal friend of Lenin and as an active fighter for the cause of the Party since its creation—we can easily imagine how Stalin treated other people. These negative characteristics of his developed steadily and during the last years acquired an absolutely insufferable character.

As later events have proven, Lenin's anxiety was justified. In the first period after Lenin's death, Stalin still paid attention to his advice, but later he began to disregard the serious admonitions of Vladimir Ilyich. When we analyze the practice of Stalin in regard to the direction of the Party and of the country, when we pause to consider everything which Stalin perpetrated, we must be convinced that Lenin's fears were justified. The negative characteristics of Stalin, which, in Lenin's time, were only incipient, transformed themselves during the last years into a grave abuse of power by Stalin, which caused untold harm to our Party.

We have to consider seriously and analyze correctly this matter in order that we may preclude any possibility of a repetition in any form whatever of what took place during the life of Stalin, who absolutely did not tolerate collegiality in leadership and in work, and who practiced brutal violence, not only toward everything which opposed him, but also toward that which seemed, to his capricious and despotic character, contrary to his concepts.

Stalin acted not through persuasion, explanation and patient cooperation with people, but by imposing his concepts and demanding absolute submission to his opinion. Whoever opposed these concepts or tried to prove his [own] viewpoint and the correctness of his [own] position was doomed to removal from the leadership collective and to subsequent moral and physical annihilation. This was especially true during the period following the 17th Party Congress, when many prominent Party leaders and rank-and-file Party workers, honest and dedicated to the cause of Communism, fell victim to Stalin's despotism.

We must affirm that the Party fought a serious fight against the Trotskyites, rightists and bourgeois nationalists, and that it disarmed ideologically all the enemies of Leninism. This ideological fight was carried on successfully, as a result of which the Party became strengthened and tempered. Here Stalin played a positive role.

The Party led a great political-ideological struggle against those in its own ranks who proposed anti-Leninist theses, who represented a political line hostile to the Party and to the cause of socialism. This was a stubborn and a difficult fight but a necessary one, because the political line of both the Trotskyite-Zinovievite bloc and of the Bukharinites led actually toward the restoration of capitalism and toward capitulation to the world bourgeoisie. Let us consider for a moment what would have happened if in 1928-1929 the political line of right deviation had prevailed among us, or orientation toward "cotton-dress industrialization," or toward the kulak, etc. We would not now have a powerful heavy industry; we would not have the kolkhozes; we would find ourselves disarmed and weak in a capitalist encirclement.

It was for this reason that the Party led an inexorable ideological fight, explaining to all [its] members and to the non-Party masses the harm and the danger of the anti-Leninist proposals of the Trotskyite opposition and the rightist opportunists. And this great work of explaining the Party line bore fruit. Both the Trotskyites and the rightist opportunists were politically isolated. An overwhelming Party majority supported the Leninist line, and the Party was able to awaken and organize the working masses to apply the Leninist line and to build socialism.

A fact worth noting is that extreme repressive measures were not used against the Trotskyites, the Zinovievites, the Bukharinites, and others during the course of the furious ideological fight against them. The fight [in the 1920's] was on ideological grounds. But some years later, when socialism in our country was fundamentally constructed, when the exploiting classes were generally liquidated, when Soviet social structure had radically changed, when the social basis for political movements and groups hostile to the Party had violently contracted, when the ideological opponents of the Party were long since defeated politically—then repression directed against them began. It was precisely during this period (1935-1937-1938) that the practice of mass repression through the Government apparatus was born, first against the enemies of Leninism—Trotskyites, Zinovievites, Bukharinites, long since politically defeated by the Party—and subsequently also against many honest Communists, against those Party cadres who had borne the heavy load of the Civil War and the first and most difficult years of industrialization and collectivization, who had fought actively against the Trotskyites and the rightists for the Leninist Party line.

Stalin originated the concept "enemy of the people." This term automatically made it unnecessary that the ideological errors of a man or men engaged in a controversy be proven. It made possible the use of the cruelest repression, violating all norms of revolutionary legality, against anyone who in any way disagreed with Stalin, against those who were only suspected of hostile intent, against those who had bad reputations. The concept "enemy of the people" actually eliminated the possibility of any kind of ideological fight or the making of one's views known on this or that issue, even [issues] of a practical nature. On the whole, the only proof of guilt actually used, against all norms of current legal science, was the "confession" of the accused himself. As subsequent probing has proven, "confessions" were acquired through physical pressures against the accused. This led to glaring violations of revolutionary legality and to the fact that many entirely innocent individuals—[persons] who in the past had defended the Party line— became victims.

We must assert that, in regard to those persons who in their time had opposed the Party line, there were often no sufficiently serious reasons for their physical annihilation. The formula "enemy of the people" was specifically introduced for the purpose of physically annihilating such individuals.

It is a fact that many persons who were later annihilated as enemies of the Party and people had worked with Lenin during his life. Some of these persons had made errors during Lenin's life, but, despite this, Lenin benefited by their work; he corrected them and he did everything possible to retain them in the ranks of the Party; he induced them to follow him.

In this connection the delegates to the Party Congress should familiarize themselves with an unpublished note by V. I. Lenin directed to the Central Committee's Politburo in October 1920. Outlining the duties of the [Party] Control Commission, Lenin wrote that the Commission should be transformed into a real "organ of Party and proletarian conscience."

"As a special duty of the Control Commission there is recommended a deep, individualized relationship with, and sometimes even a type of therapy for, the representatives of the so-called opposition—those who have experienced a psychological crisis because of failure in their Soviet or Party career. An effort should be made to quiet them, to explain the matter to them in a way used among comrades, to find for them (avoiding the method of issuing orders) a task for which they are psychologically fitted. Advice and rules relating to this matter are to be formulated by the Central Committee's Organizational Bureau, etc."

Everyone knows how irreconcilable Lenin was with the ideological enemies of Marxism, with those who deviated from the correct Party line. At the same time, however, Lenin, as is evident from the given document, in his practice of directing the Party demanded the most intimate Party contact with people who had shown indecision or temporary non-conform ity with the Party line, but whom it was possible to return to the Party path. Lenin advised that such people should be patiently educated without the application of extreme methods.

Lenin's wisdom in dealing with people was evident in his work with cadres.

An entirely different relationship with people characterized Stalin. Lenin's traits—patient work with people, stubborn and painstaking education of them, the ability to induce people to follow him without using compulsion, but rather through the ideological influence on them of the whole collective—were entirely foreign to Stalin. He discarded the Leninist method of convincing and educating, he abandoned the method of ideological struggle for that of administrative violence, mass repressions and terror. He acted on an increasingly larger scale and more stubbornly through punitive organs, at the same time often violating all existing norms of morality and of Soviet laws.

Arbitrary behavior by one person encouraged and permitted arbitrariness in others. Mass arrests and deportations of many thousands of people, execution without trial and without normal investigation created conditions of insecurity, fear and even desperation.

This, of course, did not contribute toward unity of the Party ranks and of all strata of working people, but, on the contrary, brought about annihilation and the expulsion from the Party of workers who were loyal but inconvenient to Stalin.

Our Party fought for the implementation of Lenin's plans for the construction of socialism. This was an ideological fight. Had Leninist principles been observed during the course of this fight, had the Party's devotion to principles been skillfully combined with a keen and solicitous concern for people, had they not been repelled and wasted but rather drawn to our side, we certainly would not have had such a brutal violation of revolutionary legality and many thousands of people would not have fallen victim to the method of terror. Extraordinary methods would then have been resorted to only against those people who had in fact committed criminal acts against the Soviet system.

Let us recall some historical facts.

In the days before the October Revolution, two members of the Central Committee of the Bolshevik Party—Kamenev and Zinoviev—declared themselves against Lenin's plan for an armed uprising. In addition, on October 18 they published in the Menshevik newspaper, *Novaya Zhizn,* a statement declaring that the Bolsheviks were making preparations for an uprising and that they considered it adventuristic. Kamenev and Zinoviev thus disclosed to the enemy the decision of the Central Committee to stage the uprising, and that the uprising had been organized to take place within the very near future.

This was treason against the Party and against the Revolution. In this connection, V. I. Lenin wrote: "Kamenev and Zinoviev revealed the decision of the Central Committee of their Party on the armed uprising to [Mikhail] Rodzyanko and [Alexander] Kerensky.... He put before the Central Committee the question of Zinoviev's and Kamenev's expulsion from the Party.

However, after the Great Socialist October Revolution, as is known, Zinoviev and Kamenev were given leading positions. Lenin put them in positions in which they carried out the most responsible Party tasks and participated actively in the work of the leading Party and Soviet organs. It is known that Zinoviev and Kamenev committed a number of other serious errors during Lenin's life. In his "Testament" Lenin warned that "Zinoviev's and Kamenev's October episode was of course not an accident." But Lenin did not pose the question of their arrest and certainly not their shooting.

Or, let us take the example of the Trotskyites. At present, after a sufficiently long historical period, we can speak about the fight with the Trotskyites with complete calm and can analyze this matter with sufficient objectivity. After all, around Trotsky were people whose origin cannot by any means be traced to bourgeois society. Part of them belonged to the Party intelligentsia and a certain part were recruited from among the workers. We can name many individuals who, in their time, joined the Trotskyites; however, these same individuals took an active part in the workers' movement before the Revolution, during the Socialist October Revolution itself, and also in the consolidation of the victory of this greatest of revolutions. Many of them broke with Trotskyism and returned to Leninist positions. Was it necessary to annihilate such people? We are deeply convinced that, had Lenin lived, such an extreme method would not have been used against any of them.

Such are only a few historical facts. But can it be said that Lenin did not decide to use even the most severe means against enemies of the Revolution when this was actually necessary? No; no one can say this. Vladimir Ilyich demanded uncompromising dealings with the enemies of the Revolution and of the working class and when necessary resorted ruthlessly to such methods. You will recall only V. I. Lenin's fight with the Socialist Revolutionary organizers of the anti-Soviet uprising, with the counterrevolutionary kulaks in 1918 and with others, when Lenin without hesitation used the most extreme methods against the enemies. Lenin used such methods, however, only against actual class enemies and not against those who blunder, who err, and whom it was possible to lead through ideological influence and even retain in the leadership. Lenin used severe methods only in the most necessary cases, when the exploiting classes were still in existence and were vigorously opposing the Revolution, when the struggle for survival was decidedly assuming the sharpest forms, even including a Civil War.

Stalin, on the other hand, used extreme methods and mass repressions at a time when the Revolution was already victorious, when the Soviet state was strengthened, when the exploiting classes were already liquidated and socialist relations were rooted solidly in all phases of national economy, when our Party was politically consolidated and had strengthened itself both numerically and ideologically.

It is clear that here Stalin showed in a whole series of cases his intolerance, his brutality and his abuse of power. Instead of proving his political correctness and mobilizing the masses, he often chose the path of repression and physical annihilation, not only against actual enemies, but also against individuals who had not committed any crimes against the Party and the Soviet Government. Here we see no wisdom but only a demonstration of the brutal force which had once so alarmed V. I. Lenin.

Lately, especially after the unmasking of the Beria gang, the Central Committee looked into a series of matters fabricated by this gang. This revealed a very ugly picture of brutal willfulness connected with the incorrect behavior of Stalin. As facts prove, Stalin, using his unlimited power, allowed himself many abuses, acting in the name of the Central Committee, not asking for the opinion of the Committee members nor even of the members of the Central Committee's Politburo; often he did not inform them about his personal decisions concerning very important Party and government matters.

Considering the question of the cult of an individual, we must first of all show everyone what harm this caused to the interests of our Party.

Vladimir Ilyich Lenin had always stressed the Party's role and significance in the direction of the socialist government of workers and peasants; he saw in this the chief precondition for a successful building of socialism in our country. Pointing to the great responsibility of the Bolshevik Party, as ruling Party of the Soviet state, Lenin called for the most meticulous observance of all norms of Party life; he called for the realization of the principles of collegiality in the direction of the Party and the state.

Collegiality of leadership flows from the very nature of our Party, a Party built on the principles of democratic centralism. "This means," said Lenin, "that all Party matters are accomplished by all Party members—directly or through representatives—who, without any exceptions, are subject to the same rules; in addition, all administrative members, all directing collegia, all holders of Party positions are elective, they must account for their activities and are recallable."

It is known that Lenin himself offered an example of the most careful observance of these principles. There was no matter so important that Lenin himself decided it without asking for advice and approval of the majority of the Central Committee members or of the members of the Central Committee's Politbiuro. In the most difficult period for our Party and our country, Lenin considered it necessary regularly to convoke Congresses, Party Conferences and Plenary sessions of the Central Committee at which all the most important questions were discussed and where resolutions, carefully worked out by the collective of leaders, were approved.

We can recall, for an example, the year 1918 when the country was threatened by the attack of the imperialistic interventionists. In this situation the 7th Party Congress was convened in order to discuss a vitally important matter which could not be postponed—the matter of peace. In 1919, while the Civil War was raging, the 8th Party Congress convened which adopted a new Party program, decided such important matters as the relationship with the peasant masses, the organization of the Red Army, the leading role of the Party in the work of the soviets, the correction of the social composition of the Party, and other matters. In 1920 the 9th Party Congress was convened which laid down guiding principles pertaining to the Party's work in the sphere of economic construction. In 1921 the 10th Party Congress accepted Lenin's New Economic Policy and the historic resolution called "On Party Unity."

During Lenin's life, Party congresses were convened regularly; always, when a radical turn in the development of the Party and the country took place, Lenin considered it absolutely necessary that the Party discuss at length all the basic matters pertaining to internal and foreign policy and to questions bearing on the development of Party and government.

It is very characteristic that Lenin addressed to the Party Congress as the highest Party organ his last articles, letters and remarks. During the period between congresses, the Central Committee of the Party, acting as the most authoritative leading collective, meticulously observed the principles of the Party and carried out its policy.

So it was during Lenin's life. Were our Party's holy Leninist principles observed after the death of Vladimir Ilyich?

Whereas, during the first few years after Lenin's death, Party Congresses and Central Committee Plenums took place more or less regularly, later, when Stalin began increasingly to abuse his power, these principles were brutally violated. This was especially evident during the last fifteen years of his life. Was it a normal situation when over thirteen years elapsed between the 18th and 19th Party Congresses, years during which our Party and our country had experienced so many important events? These events demanded categorically that the Party should have passed resolutions pertaining to the country's defense during the [Great] Patriotic War and to peacetime construction after the war.

Even after the end of the war a Congress was not convened for over seven years. Central Committee Plenums were hardly ever called. It should be sufficient to mention that during all the years of the Patriotic War not a single Central Committee Plenum took place. It is true that there was an attempt to call a Central Committee Plenum in October 1941, when Central Committee members from the whole country were called to Moscow. They waited two days for the opening of the Plenum, but in vain. Stalin did not even want to meet and talk to the Central Committee members. This fact shows how demoralized Stalin was in the first months of the war and how haughtily and disdainfully he treated the Central Committee members.

In practice, Stalin ignored the norms of Party life and trampled on the Leninist principle of collective Party leadership.

Stalin's willfulness vis-à-vis the Party and its Central Committee became fully evident after the 17th Party Congress, which took place in 1934.

Having at its disposal numerous data showing brutal willfulness toward Party cadres, the Central Committee has created a Party commission under the control of the Central Committee's Presidium. It has been charged with investigating what made possible mass repressions against the majority of the Central Committee members and candidates elected at the 17th Congress of the All-Union Communist Party (Bolsheviks).

The commission has become acquainted with a large quantity of materials in the NKVD archives and with other documents. It has established many facts pertaining to the fabrication of cases against Communists, to false accusations, [and] to glaring abuses of socialist legality, which resulted in the death of innocent people. It became apparent that many Party, Soviet and economic activists who in 1937-1938 were branded "enemies" were actually never enemies, spies, wreckers, etc., but were always honest Communists. They were merely stigmatized [as enemies]. Often, no longer able to bear barbaric tortures, they charged themselves (at the order of the investigative judges/falsifiers) with all kinds of grave and unlikely crimes.

The commission has presented to the Central Committee's Presidium lengthy and documented materials pertaining to mass repressions against the delegates to the 17th Party Congress and against members of the Central Committee elected at that Congress. These materials have been studied by the Presidium.

It was determined that of the 139 members and candidates of the Central Committee who were elected at the 17th Congress, 98 persons, i.e., 70 per cent, were arrested and shot (mostly in 1937-1938). (Indignation in the hall.) What was the composition of the delegates to the 17th Congress? It is known that 80 per cent of the voting participants of the 17th Congress joined the Party during the years of conspiracy before the Revolution and during the Civil War, i.e. meaning before 1921. By social origin the basic mass of the delegates to the Congress were workers (60 per cent of the voting members).

For this reason, it is inconceivable that a Congress so composed could have elected a Central Committee in which a majority [of the members] would prove to be enemies of the Party. The only reasons why 70 per cent of the Central Committee members and candidates elected at the 17th Congress were branded as enemies of the Party and of the people were because honest Communists were slandered, accusations against them were fabricated, and revolutionary legality was gravely undermined.

The same fate met not only Central Committee members but also the majority of the delegates to the 17th Party Congress. Of 1,966 delegates with either voting or advisory rights, 1,108 persons were arrested on charges of anti-revolutionary crimes, i.e., decidedly more than a majority. This very fact shows how absurd, wild and contrary to common sense were the charges of counterrevolutionary crimes made out, as we now see, against a majority of participants at the 17th Party Congress.

(Indignation in the hall.)

We should recall that the 17th Party Congress is known historically as the Congress of Victors. Delegates to the Congress were active participants in the building of our socialist state; many of them suffered and fought for Party interests during the pre-Revolutionary years in the conspiracy and at the civil-war fronts; they fought their enemies valiantly and often nerveless-ly looked into the face of death.

How, then, can we believe that such people could prove to be "two-faced" and had joined the camps of the enemies of socialism during the era after the political liquidation of Zinovievites, Trotskyites and rightists and after the great accomplishments of socialist construction? This was the result of the abuse of power by Stalin, who began to use mass terror against Party cadres.

What is the reason that mass repressions against activists increased more and more after the 17th Party Congress? It was because at that time Stalin had so elevated himself above the Party and above the nation that he ceased to consider either the Central Committee or the Party.

Stalin still reckoned with the opinion of the collective before the 17th Congress. After the complete political liquidation of the Trotskyites, Zinovievites and Bukharinites, however, when the Party had achieved unity, Stalin to an ever greater degree stopped considering the members of the Party's Central Committee and even the members of the Politburo. Stalin thought that now he could decide all things alone and that all he needed were statisticians. He treated all others in such a way that they could only listen to him and praise him.

After the criminal murder of Sergey M. Kirov, mass repressions and brutal acts of violation of socialist legality began. On the evening of December 1, 1934 on Stalin's initiative (without the approval of the Politburo —which was given two days later, casually), the Secretary of the Presidium of the Central Executive Committee, [Abel] Yenukidze, signed the following directive:

"1. Investigative agencies are directed to speed up the cases of those accused of the preparation or execution of acts of terror.

2. Judicial organs are directed not to hold up the execution of death sentences pertaining to crimes of this category in order to consider the pos-sibility of pardon, because the Presidium of the Central Executive

Committee of the USSR does not consider as possible the receiving of petitions of this sort.

3. The organs of the Commissariat of Internal Affairs [NKVD] are directed to execute the death sentences against criminals of the above-mentioned category immediately after the passage of sentences."

This directive became the basis for mass acts of abuse against socialist legality. During many of the fabricated court cases, the accused were charged with "the preparation" of terroristic acts; this deprived them of any possibility that their cases might be re-examined, even when they stated before the court that their "confessions" were secured by force, and when, in a convincing manner, they disproved the accusations against them.

It must be asserted that to this day the circumstances surrounding Kirov's murder hide many things which are inexplicable and mysterious and demand a most careful examination. There are reasons for the suspicion that the killer of Kirov, [Leonid] Nikolayev, was assisted by someone from among the people whose duty it was to protect the person of Kirov.

A month and a half before the killing, Nikolayev was arrested on the grounds of suspicious behavior but he was released and not even searched. It is an unusually suspicious circumstance that when the Chekist assigned to protect Kirov was being brought for an interrogation, on December 2, 1934, he was killed in a car "accident" in which no other occupants of the car were harmed. After the murder of Kirov, top functionaries of the Leningrad NKVD were given very light sentences, but in 1937 they were shot. We can assume that they were shot in order to cover up the traces of the organizers of Kirov's killing.

(Movement in the hall.)

Mass repressions grew tremendously from the end of 1936 after a telegram from Stalin and [Andrey] Zhdanov, dated from Sochi on September 25, 1936, was addressed to [Lazar] Kaganovich, [Vyacheslav] Molotov and other members of the Politburo. The content of the telegram was as follows:

"We deem it absolutely necessary and urgent that comrade [Nikolay] Yezhov be nominated to the post of People's Commissar for Internal Affairs. [Genrikh] Yagoda definitely has proven himself incapable of unmasking the Trotskyite-Zinovievite bloc. The OGPU is four years behind in this matter. This is noted by all Party workers and by the majority of the representatives of the NKVD."

Strictly speaking, we should stress that Stalin did not meet with and, therefore, could not know the opinion of Party workers.

This Stalinist formulation that the "NKVD is four years behind" in applying mass repression and that there is a necessity for "catching up" with the neglected work directly pushed the NKVD workers on the path of mass arrests and executions.

We should state that this formulation was also forced on the February-March Plenary session of the Central Committee of the All-Union Communist Party (Bolsheviks) in 1937. The Plenary resolution approved it on the basis of Yezhov's report, "Lessons flowing from the harmful activity, diversion and espionage of the Japanese-German-Trotskyite agents," stating:

"The Plenum of the Central Committee of the All-Union Communist Party (Bolsheviks) considers that all facts revealed during the investigation into the matter of an anti-Soviet Trotskyite center and of its followers in the provinces show that the People's Commissariat of Internal Affairs has fallen behind at least four years in the attempt to unmask these most inexorable enemies of the people.

The mass repressions at this time were made under the slogan of a fight against the Trotskyites. Did the Trotskyites at this time actually constitute such a danger to our Party and to the Soviet state? We should recall that in 1927, on the eve of the 15th Party Congress, only some 4,000 [Party] votes were cast for the Trotskyite-Zinovievite opposition while there were 724,000 for the Party line. During the ten years which passed between the 15th Party Congress and the February-March Central Committee Plenum, Trotskyism was completely disarmed. Many former Trotskyites changed their former views and worked in the various sectors building socialism. It is clear that in the situation of socialist victory there was no basis for mass terror in the country.

Stalin's report at the February-March Central Committee Plenum in 1937, "Deficiencies of Party work and methods for the liquidation of the Trotskyites and of other two-facers," contained an attempt at theoretical justification of the mass terror policy under the pretext that class war must allegedly sharpen as we march forward toward socialism. Stalin asserted that both history and Lenin taught him this.

Actually Lenin taught that the application of revolutionary violence is necessitated by the resistance of the exploiting classes, and this referred to the era when the exploiting classes existed and were powerful. As soon as the nation's political situation had improved, when in January 1920 the Red Army took Rostov and thus won a most important victory over [General A.

I.] Denikin, Lenin instructed [Felix] Dzerzhinsky to stop mass terror and to abolish the death penalty. Lenin justified this important political move of the Soviet state in the following manner in his report at the session of the All-Union Central Executive Committee on February 2, 1920:

"We were forced to use terror because of the terror practiced by the Entente, when strong world powers threw their hordes against us, not avoiding any type of conduct. We would not have lasted two days had we not answered these attempts of officers and White Guardists in a merciless fashion; this meant the use of terror, but this was forced upon us by the terrorist methods of the Entente.

"But as soon as we attained a decisive victory, even before the end of the war, immediately after taking Rostov, we gave up the use of the death penalty and thus proved that we intend to execute our own program in the manner that we promised. We say that the application of violence flows out of the decision to smother the exploiters, the big landowners and the capitalists; as soon as this was accomplished we gave up the use of all extraordinary methods. We have proved this in practice."

Stalin deviated from these clear and plain precepts of Lenin. Stalin put the Party and the NKVD up to the use of mass terror when the exploiting classes had been liquidated in our country and when there were no serious reasons for the use of extraordinary mass terror.

This terror was actually directed not at the remnants of the defeated exploiting classes but against the honest workers of the Party and of the Soviet state; against them were made lying, slanderous and absurd accusations concerning "two-facedness," "espionage," "sabotage," preparation of fictitious "plots," etc.

At the February-March Central Committee Plenum in 1937 many members actually questioned the rightness of the established course regarding mass repressions under the pretext of combating "two-facedness."

Comrade [Pavel] Postyshev most ably expressed these doubts. He said:

"I have philosophized that the severe years of fighting have passed. Party members who have lost their backbones have broken down or have joined the camp of the enemy; healthy elements have fought for the Party. These were the years of industrialization and collectivization. I never thought it possible that after this severe era had passed Karpov and people like him would find themselves in the camp of the enemy. (Karpov was a worker in the Ukrainian Central Committee whom Postyshev knew well.)

And now, according to the testimony, it appears that Karpov was recruited in 1934 by the Trotskyites. I personally do not believe that in 1934 an honest Party member who had trod the long road of unrelenting fight against enemies for the Party and for socialism would now be in the camp of the enemies. I do not believe it.... I cannot imagine how it would be possible to travel with the Party during the difficult years and then, in 1934, join the Trotskyites. It is an odd thing...."

(Movement in the hall.)

Using Stalin's formulation, namely, that the closer we are to socialism the more enemies we will have, and using the resolution of the February-March Central Committee Plenum passed on the basis of Yezhov's report, the provocateurs who had infiltrated the state-security organs together with conscienceless careerists began to protect with the Party name the mass terror against Party cadres, cadres of the Soviet state, and ordinary Soviet citizens. It should suffice to say that the number of arrests based on charges of counterrevolutionary crimes had grown ten times between 1936 and 1937.

It is known that brutal willfulness was practiced against leading Party workers. The [relevant] Party statute, approved at the 17th Party Congress, was based on Leninist principles expressed at the 10th Party Congress. It stated that, in order to apply an extreme method such as exclusion from the Party against a Central Committee member, against a Central Committee candidate or against a member of the Party Control Commission, "it is necessary to call a Central Committee Plenum and to invite to the Plenum all Central Committee candidate members and all members of the Party Control Commission"; only if two-thirds of the members of such a general assembly of responsible Party leaders found it necessary, only then could a Central Committee member or candidate be expelled.

The majority of those Central Committee's members and candidates who were elected at the 17th Congress and arrested in 1937-1938 were expelled from the Party illegally through brutal abuse of the Party statute, because the question of their expulsion was never studied at the Central Committee Plenum.

Now, when the cases of some of these so-called "spies" and "saboteurs" were examined, it was found that all their cases were fabricated. The confessions of guilt of many of those arrested and charged with enemy activity were gained with the help of cruel and inhuman tortures.

At the same time, Stalin, as we have been informed by members of the

Politburo of that time, did not show them the statements of many accused political activists when they retracted their confessions before the military tribunal and asked for an objective examination of their cases. There were many such declarations, and Stalin doubtless knew of them.

The Central Committee considers it absolutely necessary to inform the Congress of many such fabricated "cases" against the members of the Party's Central Committee elected at the 17th Party Congress.

An example of vile provocation, of odious falsification and of criminal violation of revolutionary legality is the case of the former candidate for the Central Committee Politburo, one of the most eminent workers of the Party and of the Soviet Government, comrade [Robert] Eikhe, who had been a Party member since 1905.

(Commotion in the hall.)

Comrade Eikhe was arrested on April 29, 1938 on the basis of slander-ous materials, without the sanction of the [State] Prosecutor of the USSR. This was finally received 15 months after the arrest.

The investigation of Eikhe's case was made in a manner which most brutally violated Soviet legality and was accompanied by willfulness and fal-sification.

Under torture, Eikhe was forced to sign a protocol of his confession prepared in advance by the investigative judges. In it, he and several other eminent Party workers were accused of anti-Soviet activity.

On October 1, 1939 Eikhe sent his declaration to Stalin in which he cat-egorically denied his guilt and asked for an examination of his case. In the declaration he wrote: "There is no more bitter misery than to sit in the jail of a government for which I have always fought."

A second declaration of Eikhe has been preserved, which he sent to Stalin on October 27, 1939. In it [Eikhe] cited facts very convincingly and countered the slanderous accusations made against him, arguing that this provocatory accusation was on one hand the work of real Trotskyites whose arrests he had sanctioned as First Secretary of the West Siberian Regional Party Committee and who conspired in order to take revenge on him, and, on the other hand, the result of the base falsification of materials by the investigative judges.

Eikhe wrote in his declaration:

". . . On October 25 of this year I was informed that the investigation in my case has been concluded and I was given access to the materials of this investigation. Had I been guilty of only one hundredth of the crimes with which I am charged, I would not have dared to send you this pre-execution declaration. However I have not been guilty of even one of the things with which I am charged and my heart is clean of even the shadow of baseness. I have never in my life told you a word of falsehood, and now, finding both feet in the grave, I am still not lying. My whole case is a typical example of provocation, slander and violation of the elementary basis of revolutionary legality. . . .

". . . The confessions which were made part of my file are not only absurd but contain slander toward the Central Committee of the All-Union Communist Party (Bolsheviks) and toward the Council of People's Commissars. [This is] because correct resolutions of the Central Committee of the All-Union Communist Party (Bolsheviks) and of the Council of People's Commissars which were not made on my initiative and [were promulgated] without my participation are presented as hostile acts of counterrevolutionary organizations made at my suggestion.

"I am now alluding to the most disgraceful part of my life and to my really grave guilt against the Party and against you. This is my confession of counterrevolutionary activity . . . . The case is as follows: Not being able to suffer the tortures to which I was submitted by [Z.] Ushakov and Nikolayev—especially by the former, who utilized the knowledge that my broken ribs have not properly mended and have caused me great pain—I have been forced to accuse myself and others.

"The majority of my confession has been suggested or dictated by Ushakov. The rest is my reconstruction of NKVD materials from Western Siberia for which I assumed all responsibility. If some part of the story which Ushakov fabricated and which I signed did not properly hang together, I was forced to sign another variation. The same thing was done to [Moisey] Rukhimovich, who was at first designated as a member of the reserve net and whose name later was removed without telling me anything about it. The same also was done with the leader of the reserve net, supposedly created by Bukharin in 1935. At first I wrote my [own] name in, and then I was instructed to insert [Valery] Mezhlauk's. There were other similar incidents.

". . . I am asking and begging you that you again examine my case, and this not for the purpose of sparing me but in order to unmask the vile provocation which, like a snake, wound itself around many persons in a great degree due to my meanness and criminal slander. I have never betrayed you or the Party. I know that I perish because of vile and mean work of enemies of the Party and of the people, who have fabricated the provocation against me."

It would appear that such an important declaration was worth an examination by the Central Committee. This, however, was not done. The declaration was transmitted to Beria while the terrible maltreatment of the Politburo candidate, comrade Eikhe, continued.

On February 2, 1940, Eikhe was brought before the court. Here he did not confess any guilt and said as follows:

"In all the so-called confessions of mine there is not one letter written by me with the exception of my signatures under the protocols, which were forced from me. I have made my confession under pressure from the investigative judge, who from the time of my arrest tormented me. After that I began to write all this nonsense.... The most important thing for me is to tell the court, the Party and Stalin that I am not guilty. I have never been guilty of any conspiracy. I will die believing in the truth of Party policy as I have believed in it during my whole life."

On February 4, Eikhe was shot.

(Indignation in the hall.)

It has been definitely established now that Eikhe's case was fabricated. He has been rehabilitated posthumously.

Comrade [Yan] Rudzutak, a candidate-member of the Politburo, a member of the Party since 1905 who spent ten years in a Tsarist hard-labor camp, completely retracted in court the confession forced from him. The protocol of the session of the Collegium of the Supreme Military Court contains the following statement by Rudzutak:

". . . The only plea which [the defendant] places before the court is that the Central Committee of the All-Union Communist Party (Bolsheviks) be informed that there is in the NKVD an as yet not liquidated center which is craftily manufacturing cases, which forces innocent persons to confess. There is no opportunity to prove one's non-participation in crimes to which the confessions of various persons testify. The investigative methods are such that they force people to lie and to slander entirely innocent persons in addition to those who already stand accused. [The defendant] asks the Court that he be allowed to inform the Central Committee of the All-Union Communist Party (Bolsheviks) about all this in writing. He assures the Court that he personally had never any evil designs in regard to the policy of our Party because he has always agreed with Party policy concerning all spheres of economic and cultural activity."

This declaration of Rudzutak was ignored, despite the fact that Rudzutak was in his time the head of the Central Control Commission—which had been called into being, in accordance with Lenin's conception, for the purpose of fighting for Party unity. In this manner fell the head of this highly authoritative Party organ, a victim of brutal willfulness. He was not even called before the Politburo because Stalin did not want to talk to him. Sentence was pronounced on him in twenty minutes and he was shot.

(Indignation in the hall.)

After careful examination of the case in 1955, it was established that the accusation against Rudzutak was false and that it was based on slanderous materials. Rudzutak has been rehabilitated posthumously.

The way in which the former NKVD workers manufactured various fictitious "anti-Soviet centers" and "blocs" with the help of provocatory methods is seen from the confession of comrade Rozenblum, a Party member since 1906, who was arrested in 1937 by the Leningrad NKVD.

During the examination in 1955 of the Komarov case, Rozenblum revealed the following fact: When Rozenblum was arrested in 1937, he was subjected to terrible torture during which he was ordered to confess false information concerning himself and other persons. He was then brought to the office of [Leonid] Zakovsky, who offered him freedom on condition that he make before the court a false confession fabricated in 1937 by the NKVD concerning "sabotage, espionage and diversion in a terroristic center in Leningrad." (Movement in the hall.) With unbelievable cynicism, Zakovsky told about the vile "mechanism" for the crafty creation of fabricated "anti-Soviet plots."

"In order to illustrate it to me," stated Rozenblum, "Zakovsky gave me several possible variants of the organization of this center and of its branches. After he detailed the organization to me, Zakovsky told me that the NKVD would prepare the case of this center, remarking that the trial would be public. Before the court were to be brought 4 or 5 members of this center: [Mikhail] Chudov, [Fyodor] Ugarov, [Pyotr] Smorodin, [Boris] Pozern, Chudov's wife [Liudmilla] Shaposhnikova and others together with two or three members from the branches of this center. . . .

". . . The case of the Leningrad center has to be built solidly, and for this reason witnesses are needed. Social origin (of course, in the past) and the Party standing of the witness will play more than a small role. 'You, yourself,' said Zakovsky, 'will not need to invent anything. The NKVD will prepare for you a ready outline for every branch of the center. You will have to study it carefully, and remember well all questions the Court might ask and their answers. This case will be ready in four or five months, perhaps in half a year. During all this time you will be preparing yourself so that you will not compromise the investigation and yourself. Your future will depend on how the trial goes and on its results. If you begin to lie and to testify falsely, blame yourself. If you manage to endure it, you will save your head and we will feed and clothe you at the Government's cost until your death.'"

This is the kind of vile thing practiced then.

(Movement in the hall.)

Even more widely was the falsification of cases practiced in the provinces. The NKVD headquarters of the Sverdlov Province "discovered" a so-called "Ural uprising staff"—an organ of the bloc of rightists, Trotskyites, Socialist Revolutionaries, and church leaders—whose chief supposedly was the Secretary of the Sverdlov Provincial Party Committee and member of the Central Committee, All-Union Communist Party (Bolsheviks), [Ivan] Kabakov, who had been a Party member since 1914. Investigative materials of that time show that in almost all regions, provinces and republics there supposedly existed "rightist Trotskyite, espionage-terror and diversionary-sabotage organizations and centers" and that the heads of such organizations as a rule—for no known reason—were First Secretaries of provincial or republican Communist Party committees or Central Committees.

Many thousands of honest and innocent Communists have died as a result of this monstrous falsification of such "cases," as a result of the fact that all kinds of slanderous "confessions" were accepted, and as a result of the practice of forcing accusations against oneself and others. In the same manner were fabricated the "cases" against eminent Party and state workers—[Stanislav] Kosior, [Vlas] Chubar, [Pavel] Postyshev, [Alexander] Kosarev, and others.

In those years repressions on a mass scale were applied which were based on nothing tangible and which resulted in heavy cadre losses to the Party.

The vicious practice was condoned of having the NKVD prepare lists of persons whose cases were under the jurisdiction of the Military Collegium and whose sentences were prepared in advance. Yezhov would send these [execution] lists to Stalin personally for his approval of the proposed punishment. In 1937-1938, 383 such lists containing the names of many thousands of Party, Soviet, Komsomol, Army, and economic workers were sent to Stalin. He approved these lists.

A large part of these cases are being reviewed now. A great many are being voided because they were baseless and falsified. Suffice it to say that from 1954 to the present time the Military Collegium of the Supreme Court has rehabilitated 7,679 persons, many of whom have been rehabilitated posthumously.

Mass arrests of Party, Soviet, economic and military workers caused tremendous harm to our country and to the cause of socialist advancement.

Mass repressions had a negative influence on the moral-political condition of the Party, created a situation of uncertainty, contributed to the spreading of unhealthy suspicion, and sowed distrust among Communists. All sorts of slanderers and careerists were active.

Resolutions of the January, 1938 Central Committee Plenum brought some measure of improvement to Party organizations. However, widespread repression also existed in 1938.

Only because our Party has at its disposal such great moral-political strength was it possible for it to survive the difficult events in 1937-1938 and to educate new cadres. There is, however, no doubt that our march forward toward socialism and toward the preparation of the country's defense would have been much more successful were it not for the tremendous loss in the cadres suffered as a result of the baseless and false mass repressions in 1937-1938.

We are accusing Yezhov justly for the degenerate practices of 1937. But we have to answer these questions: Could Yezhov have arrested Kosior, for instance, without Stalin's knowledge? Was there an exchange of opinions or a Politburo decision concerning this?

No, there was not, as there was none regarding other cases of this type. Could Yezhov have decided such important matters as the fate of such eminent Party figures?

No, it would be a display of naiveté to consider this the work of Yezhov alone. It is clear that these matters were decided by Stalin, and that without his orders and his sanction Yezhov could not have done this.

We have examined these cases and have rehabilitated Kosior, Rudzutak, Postyshev, Kosarev and others. For what causes were they arrested and sentenced? Our review of evidence shows that there was no reason for this. They, like many others, were arrested without prosecutorial knowledge.

In such a situation, there is no need for any sanction, for what sort of a sanction could there be when Stalin decided everything? He was the chief prosecutor in these cases. Stalin not only agreed to arrest orders but issued them on his own initiative. We must say this so that the delegates to the Congress can clearly undertake and themselves assess this and draw the proper conclusions.

Facts prove that many abuses were made on Stalin's orders without reckoning with any norms of Party and Soviet legality. Stalin was a very distrustful man, sickly suspicious. We know this from our work with him. He could look at a man and say: "Why are your eyes so shifty today?" or "Why are you turning so much today and avoiding to look me directly in the eyes?" The sickly suspicion created in him a general distrust even toward eminent Party workers whom he had known for years. Everywhere and in everything he saw "enemies," "two-facers" and "spies." Possessing unlimited power, he indulged in great willfulness and stifled people morally as well as physically. A situation was created where one could not express one's own volition.

When Stalin said that one or another should be arrested, it was necessary to accept on faith that he was an "enemy of the people." Meanwhile, Beria's gang, which ran the organs of state security, outdid itself in proving the guilt of the arrested and the truth of materials which it falsified. And what proofs were offered? The confessions of the arrested, and the investigative judges accepted these "confessions." And how is it possible that a person confesses to crimes which he has not committed? Only in one way —because of the application of physical methods of pressuring him, tortures, bringing him to a state of unconsciousness, deprivation of his judgment, taking away of his human dignity. In this manner were "confessions" acquired.

The wave of mass arrests began to recede in 1939. When the leaders of territorial Party organizations began to accuse NKVD workers of using methods of physical pressure on the arrested, Stalin dispatched a coded telegram on January 20, 1939 to the committee secretaries of provinces and regions, to the central committees of republican Communist parties, to the [republican] People's Commissars of Internal Affairs and to the heads of NKVD organizations. This telegram stated:

"The Central Committee of the All-Union Communist Party (Bolsheviks) explains that the application of methods of physical pressure in NKVD practice is permissible from 1937 on in accordance with permission of the Central Committee of the All-Union Communist Party (Bolsheviks) ... It is known that all bourgeois intelligence services use methods of physical influence against representatives of the socialist proletariat and that they use them in their most scandalous forms.

"The question arises as to why the socialist intelligence service should be more humanitarian against the mad agents of the bourgeoisie, against the deadly enemies of the working class and of kolkhoz workers. The Central Committee of the All-Union Communist Party (Bolsheviks) considers that physical pressure should still be used obligatorily, as an exception applicable to known and obstinate enemies of the people, as a method both justifiable and appropriate."

Thus, Stalin had sanctioned in the name of the Central Committee of the All-Union Communist Party (Bolsheviks) the most brutal violation of socialist legality, torture and oppression, which led as we have seen to the slandering and to the self-accusation of innocent people.

Not long ago—only several days before the present Congress—we called to the Central Committee Presidium session and interrogated the investigative judge Rodos, who in his time investigated and interrogated Kosior, Chubar and Kosarev. He is a vile person, with the brain of a bird, and completely degenerate morally. It was this man who was deciding the fate of prominent Party workers. He also was making judgments concerning the politics in these matters, because, having established their "crime," he thereby provided materials from which important political implications could be drawn.

The question arises whether a man with such an intellect could—by himself—have conducted his investigations in a manner proving the guilt of people such as Kosior and others. No, he could not have done it without proper directives. At the Central Committee Presidium session he told us: "I was told that Kosior and Chubar were people's enemies and for this reason I, as an investigative judge, had to make them confess that they were enemies."

(Indignation in the hall.)

He would do this only through long tortures, which he did, receiving detailed instructions from Beria. We must say that at the Central Committee Presidium session he cynically declared: "I thought that I was executing the orders of the Party." In this manner, Stalin's orders concerning the use of methods of physical pressure against the arrested were carried out in practice.

These and many other facts show that all norms of correct Party solution of problems were [in]validated and that everything was dependent upon the willfulness of one man.

The power accumulated in the hands of one person, Stalin, led to serious consequences during the Great Patriotic War.

When we look at many of our novels, films and historical-scientific studies, the role of Stalin in the Patriotic War appears to be entirely improbable. Stalin had foreseen everything. The Soviet Army, on the basis of a strategic plan prepared by Stalin long before, used the tactics of so-called "active defense," i.e., tactics which, as we know, allowed the Germans to come up to Moscow and Stalingrad. Using such tactics, the Soviet Army, supposedly thanks only to Stalin's genius, turned to the offensive and subdued the enemy. The epic victory gained through the armed might of the land of the Soviets, through our heroic people, is ascribed in this type of novel, film and "scientific study" as being completely due to the strategic genius of Stalin.

We have to analyze this matter carefully because it has a tremendous significance not only from the historical, but especially from the political, educational and practical points of view. What are the facts of this matter?

Before the war, our press and all our political-educational work was characterized by its bragging tone: When an enemy violates the holy Soviet soil, then for every blow of the enemy we will answer with three, and we will battle the enemy on his soil and we will win without much harm to ourselves. But these positive statements were not based in all areas on concrete facts, which would actually guarantee the immunity of our borders.

During the war and after the war, Stalin advanced the thesis that the tragedy our nation experienced in the first part of the war was the result of an "unexpected" attack by the Germans against the Soviet Union. But, comrades, this is completely untrue. As soon as Hitler came to power in Germany he assigned to himself the task of liquidating Communism. The fascists were saying this openly. They did not hide their plans.

In order to attain this aggressive end, all sorts of pacts and blocs were created, such as the famous Berlin-Rome-Tokyo Axis. Many facts from the prewar period clearly showed that Hitler was going all out to begin a war against the Soviet state, and that he had concentrated large armies, together with armored units, near the Soviet borders.

Documents which have now been published show that [as early as] April 3, 1941 Churchill, through his ambassador to the USSR, [Sir Stafford] Cripps, personally warned Stalin that the Germans had begun regrouping their armed units with the intent of attacking the Soviet Union.

It is self-evident that Churchill did not do this at all because of his friendly feeling toward the Soviet nation. He had in this his own imperialistic goals—to bring Germany and the USSR into a bloody war and thereby to strengthen the position of the British Empire.

All the same, Churchill affirmed in his writings that he sought to "warn Stalin and call his attention to the danger which threatened him." Churchill stressed this repeatedly in his dispatches of April 18 and on the following days. However, Stalin took no heed of these warnings. What is more, Stalin ordered that no credence be given to information of this sort, so as not to provoke the initiation of military operations.

We must assert that information of this sort concerning the threat of German armed invasion of Soviet territory was coming in also from our own military and diplomatic sources. However, because the leadership was conditioned against such information, such data was dispatched with fear and assessed with reservation. Thus, for instance, information sent from Berlin on May 6, 1941 by the Soviet military (sic) attaché, Captain (sic) Vorontsov, stated: "Soviet citizen Bozer ... communicated to the Deputy naval attaché that, according to a statement of a certain German officer from Hitler's headquarters, Germany is preparing to invade the USSR on May 14 through Finland, the Baltic countries and Latvia. At the same time Moscow and Leningrad will be heavily raided and paratroopers landed in border cities. . . ."

In his report of May 22, 1941, the Deputy Military Attaché in Berlin, Khlopov, communicated that "...the attack of the German Army is reportedly scheduled for June 15, but it is possible that it may begin in the first days of June . . ."

A cable from our London Embassy dated June 18, 1941 stated: "As of now Cripps is deeply convinced of the inevitability of armed conflict between Germany and the USSR, which will begin not later than the middle of June. According to Cripps, the Germans have presently concentrated 147 divisions (including air force and service units) along the Soviet borders. . . ."

Despite these particularly grave warnings, the necessary steps were not taken to prepare the country properly for defense and to prevent it from being caught unawares.

Did we have time and the capabilities for such preparations? Yes, we had the time and the capability. Our industry was already so developed that it was capable of supplying fully the Soviet Army with everything that it needed. This is proven by the fact that, although during the war we lost almost half of our industry and important industrial and food-production areas as the result of enemy occupation of the Ukraine, Northern Caucasus and other western parts of the country, the Soviet nation was still able to organize the production of military equipment in the eastern parts of the country, to install there equipment taken from the western industrial areas, and to supply our armed forces with everything necessary to destroy the enemy.

Had our industry been mobilized properly and in time to supply the Army with the necessary *materiel*, our wartime losses would have been decidedly smaller. However such mobilization had not been started in time. And already in the first days of the war it became evident that our Army was badly armed. We did not have enough artillery, tanks and planes to throw the enemy back.

Soviet science and technology produced excellent models of tanks and artillery pieces before the war. But mass production of all this was not organized. As a matter of fact, we started to modernize our military equipment only on the eve of the war. As a result, when the enemy invaded Soviet territory we did not have sufficient quantities either of old machinery which was no longer used for armament production or of new machinery which we had planned to introduce into armament production.

The situation with anti-aircraft artillery was especially bad. We did not organize the production of anti-tank ammunition. Many fortified regions proved to be indefensible as soon as they were attacked, because their old arms had been withdrawn and new ones were not yet available there.

This pertained, alas, not only to tanks, artillery and planes. At the outbreak of the war we did not even have sufficient numbers of rifles to arm the mobilized manpower. I recall that in those days I telephoned from Kiev to comrade [Georgy] Malenkov and told him, "People have volunteered for the new Army [units] and are demanding weapons. You must send us arms."

Malenkov answered me, "We cannot send you arms. We are sending all our rifles to Leningrad and you have to arm yourselves."

(Movement in the hall.)

Such was the armament situation.

In this connection we cannot forget, for instance, the following fact: Shortly before the invasion of the Soviet Union by Hitler's army, [Colonel-General M. P.] Kirponos, who was chief of the Kiev Special Military District (he was later killed at the front), wrote to Stalin that German armies were at the Bug River, were preparing for an attack and in the very near future would probably start their offensive. In this connection, Kirponos proposed that a strong defense be organized, that 300,000 people be evacuated from the border areas and that several strong points be organized there: anti-tank ditches, trenches for the soldiers, etc.

Moscow answered this proposition with the assertions that this would be a provocation, that no preparatory defensive work should be undertaken at the borders, and that the Germans were not to be given any pretext for the initiation of military action against us. Thus our borders were insufficiently prepared to repel the enemy.

When the fascist armies had actually invaded Soviet territory and military operations began, Moscow issued an order that German fire was not to be returned. Why? It was because Stalin, despite the self-evident facts, thought that the war had not yet started, that this was only a provocative action on the part of several undisciplined sections of the German Army, and that our reaction might serve as a reason for the Germans to begin the war.

The following fact is also known: On the eve of the invasion of Soviet territory by Hitler's army, a certain German citizen crossed our border and stated that the German armies had received orders to start [their] offensive against the Soviet Union on the night of June 22 at 3 o'clock. Stalin was informed about this immediately, but even this warning was ignored.

As you see, everything was ignored: warnings of certain Army commanders, declarations of deserters from the enemy army, and even the open hostility of the enemy. Is this an example of the alertness of the chief of the Party and of the state at this particularly significant historical moment?

And what were the results of this carefree attitude, this disregard of clear facts? The result was that already in the first hours and days the enemy had destroyed in our border regions a large part of our Air Force, our artillery and other military equipment. [Stalin] annihilated large numbers of our military cadres and disorganized our military leadership. Consequently we could not prevent the enemy from marching deep into the country.

Very grievous consequences, especially with regard to the beginning of the war, followed Stalin's annihilation of many military commanders and political workers during 1937-1941 because of his suspiciousness and through slanderous accusations. During these years repressions were instituted against certain parts of our military cadres beginning literally at the company- and battalion-commander levels and extending to higher military centers. During this time, the cadre of leaders who had gained military experience in Spain and in the Far East was almost completely liquidated.

The policy of large-scale repression against military cadres led also to undermined military discipline, because for several years officers of all ranks and even soldiers in Party and Komsomol cells were taught to "unmask" their superiors as hidden enemies.

(Movement in the hall.)

It is natural that this caused a negative influence on the state of military discipline in the initial stage of the war.

And, as you know, we had before the war excellent military cadres which were unquestionably loyal to the Party and to the Fatherland. Suffice it to say that those of them who managed to survive, despite severe tortures to which they were subjected in the prisons, have from the first war days shown themselves real patriots and heroically fought for the glory of the Fatherland. I have here in mind such [generals] as: [Konstantin] Rokossovsky (who, as you know, had been jailed); [Alexander] Gorbatov; [Kiril] Meretskov (who is a delegate at the present Congress); [K. P.] Podlas (he was an excellent commander who perished at the front); and many, many others. However, many such commanders perished in the camps and the jails and the Army saw them no more.

All this brought about a situation at the beginning of the war that was a great threat to our Fatherland.

It would be wrong to forget that, after [our] severe initial disaster[s] and defeat[s] at the front, Stalin thought that it was the end. In one of his [declarations] in those days he said: "Lenin left us a great legacy and we've lost it forever."

After this Stalin for a long time actually did not direct military operations and ceased to do anything whatsoever. He returned to active leadership only when a Politburo delegation visited him and told him that steps needed to be taken immediately so as to improve the situation at the front.

Therefore, the threatening danger which hung over our Fatherland in the initial period of the war was largely due to Stalin's very own faulty methods of directing the nation and the Party.

However, we speak not only about the moment when the war began, which led to our Army's serious disorganization and brought us severe losses. Even after the war began, the nervousness and hysteria which Stalin demonstrated while interfering with actual military operations caused our Army serious damage.

Stalin was very far from understanding the real situation that was developing at the front. This was natural because, during the whole Patriotic War, he never visited any section of the front or any liberated city except for one short ride on the Mozhaisk highway during a stabilized situation at the front. To this incident were dedicated many literary works full of fantasies of all sorts and so many paintings. Simultaneously, Stalin was interfering with operations and issuing orders which did not take into consideration the real situation at a given section of the front and which could not help but result in huge personnel losses.

I will allow myself in this connection to bring out one characteristic fact which illustrates how Stalin directed operations at the fronts. Present at this Congress is Marshal [Ivan] Bagramyan, who was once the head of operations in the Southwestern Front Headquarters and who can corroborate what I will tell you.

When an exceptionally serious situation for our Army developed in the Kharkov region in 1942, we correctly decided to drop an operation whose objective was to encircle [the city]. The real situation at that time would have threatened our Army with fatal consequences if this operation were continued.

We communicated this to Stalin, stating that the situation demanded changes in [our] operational plans so that the enemy would be prevented from liquidating a sizable concentration of our Army.

Contrary to common sense, Stalin rejected our suggestion. He issued the order to continue the encirclement of Kharkov, despite the fact that at this time many [of our own] Army concentrations actually were threatened with encirclement and liquidation.

I telephoned to [Marshal Alexander] Vasilevsky and begged him: "Alexander Mikhailovich, take a map"—Vasilevsky is present here—"and show comrade Stalin the situation that has developed." We should note that Stalin planned operations on a globe.

(Animation in the hall.)

Yes, comrades, he used to take a globe and trace the front line on it. I said to comrade Vasilevsky: "Show him the situation on a map. In the present situation we cannot continue the operation which was planned. The old decision must be changed for the good of the cause."

Vasilevsky replied, saying that Stalin had already studied this problem. He said that he, Vasilevsky, would not see Stalin further concerning this matter, because the latter didn't want to hear any arguments on the subject of this operation.

After my talk with Vasilevsky, I telephoned to Stalin at his *dacha*. But Stalin did not answer the phone and Malenkov was at the receiver. I told comrade Malenkov that I was calling from the front and that I wanted to speak personally to Stalin. Stalin informed me through Malenkov that I should speak with Malenkov. I stated for the second time that I wished to inform Stalin personally about the grave situation which had arisen for us at the front. But Stalin did not consider it convenient to pick up the phone and again stated that I should speak to him through Malenkov, although he was only a few steps from the telephone.

After "listening" in this manner to our plea, Stalin said: "Let everything remain as it is!"

And what was the result of this? The worst we had expected. The Germans surrounded our Army concentrations and as a result [of the Kharkov counterattack] we lost hundreds of thousands of our soldiers. This is Stalin's military "genius." This is what it cost us.

(Movement in the hall.)

On one occasion after the war, during a meeting [between] Stalin [and] members of the Politburo, Anastas Ivanovich Mikoyan mentioned that Khrushchev must have been right when he telephoned concerning the Kharkov operation and that it was unfortunate that his suggestion had not been accepted.

You should have seen Stalin's fury! How could it be admitted that he, Stalin, had not been right! He is after all a "genius," and a genius cannot help but be right! Everyone can err, but Stalin considered that he never erred, that he was always right. He never acknowledged to anyone that he, made any mistake, large or small, despite the fact that he made more than a few in matters of theory and in his practical activity. After the Party Congress we shall probably have to re-evaluate many [of our] wartime military operations and present them in their true light.

The tactics on which Stalin insisted—without knowing the basics of conducting battle operations—cost much blood until we succeeded in stopping the opponent and going over to the offensive.

The military knows that as late as the end of 1941, instead of great operational maneuvers flanking [our] opponent and penetrating behind his back, Stalin was demanding incessant frontal [counter-]attacks and the [re-]capture of one village after another.

Because of this, we paid with great losses—until our generals, upon whose shoulders the whole weight of conducting the war rested, succeeded in altering the situation and shifting to flexible-maneuver operations. [This] immediately brought serious changes at the front [that were] favorable to us.

All the more shameful was the fact that after our great victory over the enemy, which cost us so dearly, Stalin began to downgrade many of the commanders who had contributed so much to it. [This was] because Stalin ruled out any chance that services rendered at the front might be credited to anyone but himself.

Stalin was very much interested in assessments of comrade [Grigory] Zhukov as a military leader. He asked me often for my opinion of Zhukov. I told him then, "I have known Zhukov for a long time. He is a good general and a good military leader."

After the war Stalin began to tell all kinds of nonsense about Zhukov. Among it [was] the following: "You praised Zhukov, but he does not deserve it. They say that before each operation at the front Zhukov used to behave as follows: He used to take a handful of earth, smell it and say, 'We can begin the attack,' or its opposite, 'The planned operation cannot be carried out.'" I stated at the time, "Comrade Stalin, I do not know who invented this, but it is not true."

It is possible that Stalin himself invented these things for the purpose of minimizing the role and military talents of Marshal Zhukov.

In this connection, Stalin very energetically popularized himself as a great leader. In various ways he tried to inculcate the notion that the victories gained by the Soviet nation during the Great Patriotic War were all due to the courage, daring, and genius of Stalin and of no one else. Just like [a] Kuzma Kryuchkov, he put one dress on seven people at the same time.

(Animation in the hall.)

In the same vein, let us take for instance our historical and military films and some [of our] literary creations. They make us feel sick. Their true objective is propagating the theme of praising Stalin as a military genius. Let us recall the film, *The Fall of Berlin*. Here only Stalin acts. He issues orders in a hall in which there are many empty Chairs. Only only one man approaches him to report something to him—it is [Alexander] Poskrebyshev, his loyal shield-bearer.

(Laughter in the hall.)

And where is the military command? Where is the Politburo? Where is the Government? What are they doing, and with what are they engaged?

There is nothing about them in the film. Stalin acts for everybody, he does not reckon with anyone. He asks no one for advice. Everything is shown to the people in this false light. Why? To surround Stalin with glory— contrary to the facts and contrary to historical truth.

The question arises: Where is the military, on whose shoulders rested the burden of the war? It is not in the film. With Stalin's inclusion, there was no room left for it.

Not Stalin, but the Party as a whole, the Soviet Government, our heroic Army, its talented leaders and brave soldiers, the whole Soviet nation— these are the ones who assured victory in the Great Patriotic War.

(Tempestuous and prolonged applause.)

Central Committee members, Ministers, our economic leaders, the leaders of Soviet culture, directors of territorial-party and Soviet organizations, engineers, and technicians—every one of them in his own place of work generously gave of his strength and knowledge toward ensuring victory over the enemy.

Exceptional heroism was shown by our hard core—surrounded by glory are our whole working class, our kolkhoz peasantry, the Soviet intelligentsia, who under the leadership of Party organizations overcame untold hardships and bearing the hardships of war, and devoted all their strength to the cause of the Fatherland's defense.

Our Soviet women accomplished great and brave deeds during the war. They bore on their backs the heavy load of production work in the factories, on the kolkhozes, and in various economic and cultural sectors. Many women participated directly in the Great Patriotic War at the front. Our brave youth contributed immeasurably, both at the front and at home, to the defense of the Soviet Fatherland and to the annihilation of the enemy.

The services of Soviet soldiers, of our commanders and political workers of all ranks are immortal. After the loss of a considerable part of the Army in the initial war months, they did not lose their heads and were able to reorganize during the course of combat. Over the course of the war they created and toughened a strong, heroic Army. They not only withstood [our] strong and cunning enemy's pressure but smashed him.

The magnificent, heroic deeds of hundreds of millions of people of the East and of the West during the fight against the threat of fascist subjugation which loomed before us will live for centuries, [indeed] for millennia in the memory of thankful humanity.

(Thunderous applause.)

The main roles and the main credit for the victorious ending of the war belong to our Communist Party, to the armed forces of the Soviet Union, and to the tens of millions of Soviet people uplifted by the Party.

(Thunderous and prolonged applause.)

Comrades, let us reach for some other facts. The Soviet Union justly is considered a model multinational state because we have assured in practice the equality and friendship of all [of the] peoples living in our great Fatherland.

All the more monstrous are those acts whose initiator was Stalin and which were rude violations of the basic Leninist principles [behind our] Soviet state's nationalities policies. We refer to the mass deportations of entire nations from their places of origin, together with all Communists and Komsomols without any exception. This deportation was not dictated by any military considerations.

Thus, at the end of 1943, when there already had been a permanent change of fortune at the front in favor of the Soviet Union, a decision concerning the deportation of all the Karachai from the lands on which they lived was taken and executed.

In the same period, at the end of December, 1943, the same lot befell the [Kalmyks] of the Kalmyk Autonomous Republic. In March, 1944, all the Chechens and Ingushi were deported and the Chechen-Ingush Autonomous Republic was liquidated. In April, 1944, all Balkars were deported from the territory of the Kabardino-Balkar Autonomous Republic to faraway places and their Republic itself was renamed the Autonomous Kabardian Republic.

Ukrainians avoided meeting this fate only because there were too many of them and there was no place to which to deport them. Otherwise, [Stalin] would have deported them also.

(Laughter and animation in the hall.)

No Marxist-Leninist, no man of common sense can grasp how it is possible to make whole nations responsible for inimical activity, including women, children, old people, Communists and Komsomols, to use mass repression against them, and to expose them to misery and suffering for the hostile acts of individual persons or groups of persons.

After the conclusion of the Patriotic War, the Soviet nation proudly stressed the magnificent victories gained through [our] great sacrifices and tremendous efforts. The country experienced a period of political enthusiasm. The Party came out of the war even more united. Its cadres were tempered and hardened by the fire of the war. Under such conditions nobody could have even thought of the possibility of some plot in the Party.

And it was precisely at this time that the so-called "Leningrad affair" was born. As we have now proven, this case was fabricated. Those who innocently lost their lives included: comrades [Nikolay] Voznesensky, [Aleksey] Kuznetsov, [Mikhail] Rodionov, [Pyotr] Popkov, and others.

As is known, Voznesensky and Kuznetsov were talented and eminent leaders. Once they stood very close to Stalin. It is sufficient to mention that Stalin made Voznesensky First Deputy to the Chairman of the Council of Ministers and Kuznetsov was elected Secretary of the Central Committee. The very fact that Stalin entrusted Kuznetsov with the supervision of the state-security organs shows the trust which he enjoyed.

How did it happen that these persons were branded as enemies of the people and liquidated?

Facts prove that the "Leningrad affair" is also the result of willfulness which Stalin exercised against Party cadres. Had a normal situation existed in the Party's Central Committee and in the Central Committee Politburo, affairs of this nature would have been examined there in accordance with Party practice, and all pertinent facts assessed; as a result, such an affair as well as others would not have happened.

We must state that, after the war, the situation became even more complicated. Stalin became even more capricious, irritable and brutal. In particular, his suspicion grew. His persecution mania reached unbelievable dimensions. Many workers became enemies before his very eyes. After the war, Stalin separated himself from the collective even more. Everything was decided by him alone without any consideration for anyone or anything.

This unbelievable suspicion was cleverly taken advantage of by the abject provocateur and vile enemy, Beria, who murdered thousands of Communists and loyal Soviet people. The elevation of Voznesensky and Kuznetsov alarmed Beria. As we have now proven, it had been precisely Beria who had "suggested" to Stalin the fabrication by him and by his confidants of materials in the form of declarations and anonymous letters, and in the form of various rumors and talks.

The Party's Central Committee has examined this so-called "Leningrad affair;" persons who innocently suffered are now rehabilitated and honor has been restored to the glorious Leningrad Party organization. [V. S.] Abakumov and others who had fabricated this affair were brought before a court; their trial took place in Leningrad and they received what they deserved.

The question arises: Why is it that we see the truth of this affair only now, and why did we not do something earlier, during Stalin's life, in order to prevent the loss of innocent lives? It was because Stalin personally supervised the "Leningrad affair," and the majority of the Politburo members did not, at that time, know all of the circumstances in these matters and could not therefore intervene.

When Stalin received certain materials from Beria and Abakumov, without examining these slanderous materials he ordered an investigation of the "affair" of Voznesensky and Kuznetsov. With this, their fate was sealed.

Similarly instructive is the case of the Mingrelian nationalist organization which supposedly existed in Georgia. As is known, resolutions by the Central Committee, Communist Party of the Soviet Union, were made concerning this case in November 1951 and in March 1952. These resolutions were made without prior discussion with the Politburo. Stalin had personally dictated them. They made serious accusations against many loyal Communists. On the basis of falsified documents, it was proven that there existed in Georgia a supposedly nationalistic organization whose objective was the liquidation of the Soviet power in that republic with the help of imperialist powers.

In this connection, a number of responsible Party and Soviet workers were arrested in Georgia. As was later proven, this was a slander directed against the Georgian Party organization.

We know that there have been at times manifestations of local bourgeois nationalism in Georgia as in several other republics. The question arises: Could it be possible that, in the period during which the resolutions referred to above were made, nationalist tendencies grew so much that there was a danger of Georgia's leaving the Soviet Union and joining Turkey?

(Animation in the hall, laughter).

This is, of course, nonsense. It is impossible to imagine how such assumptions could enter anyone's mind. Everyone knows how Georgia has developed economically and culturally under Soviet rule. Industrial production in the Georgian Republic is 27 times greater than it was before the Revolution. Many new industries have arisen in Georgia which did not exist there before the Revolution: iron smelting, an oil industry, a machine-construction industry, etc. Illiteracy has long since been liquidated, which, in pre-Revolutionary Georgia, included 78 per cent of the population.

Could the Georgians, comparing the situation in their republic with the hard situation of the working masses in Turkey, be aspiring to join Turkey? In 1955, Georgia produced 18 times as much steel per person as Turkey. Georgia produces 9 times as much electrical energy per person as Turkey. According to the available 1950 census, 65 per cent of Turkey's total population is illiterate, and 80 per cent of its women. Georgia has 19 institutions of higher learning which have about 39,000 students; this is 8 times more than in Turkey (for each 1,000 inhabitants). The prosperity of the working people has grown tremendously in Georgia under Soviet rule.

It is clear that, as the economy and culture develop, and as the socialist consciousness of the working masses in Georgia grows, the source from which bourgeois nationalism draws its strength evaporates.

As it developed, there was no nationalistic organization in Georgia. Thousands of innocent people fell victim to willfulness and lawlessness. All of this happened under the "genius" leadership of Stalin, "the great son of the Georgian nation," as Georgians like to refer to him.

(Animation in the hall.)

The willfulness of Stalin showed itself not only in decisions concerning the internal life of the country but also in the international relations of the Soviet Union.

The July Plenum of the Central Committee studied in detail the reasons for the development of conflict with Yugoslavia. It was a shameful role which Stalin played here. The "Yugoslav affair" contained no problems which could not have been solved through Party discussions among comrades. There was no significant basis for the development of this "affair." It was completely possible to have prevented the rupture of relations with that country. This does not mean, however, that Yugoslav leaders made no mistakes or had no shortcomings. But these mistakes and shortcomings were magnified in a monstrous manner by Stalin, resulting in the breakoff of relations with a friendly country.

I recall the first days when the conflict between the Soviet Union and Yugoslavia began to be blown up artificially. Once, when I came from Kiev to Moscow, I was invited to visit Stalin, who, pointing to the copy of a letter recently sent to [Yugoslavian President Marshal Joseph] Tito, asked me, "Have you read this?"

Not waiting for my reply, he answered, "I will shake my little finger—and there will be no more Tito. He will fall."

We have paid dearly for this "shaking of the little finger." This statement reflected Stalin's mania for greatness, but he acted just that way: "I will shake my little finger—and there will be no Kosior"; "I will shake my little finger once more and Postyshev and Chubar will be no more"; "I will shake my little finger again—and Voznesensky, Kuznetsov and many others will disappear."

But this did not happen to Tito. No matter how much or how little Stalin shook, not only his little finger but everything else that he could shake, Tito did not fall. Why? The reason was that, in this instance of disagreement with [our] Yugoslav comrades, Tito had behind him a state and a people who had had a serious education in fighting for liberty and independence, a people who gave support to its leaders.

You see what Stalin's mania for greatness led to. He completely lost consciousness of reality. He demonstrated his suspicion and haughtiness not only in relation to individuals in the USSR, but in relation to whole parties and nations.

We have carefully examined the case of Yugoslavia. We have found a proper solution which is approved by the peoples of the Soviet Union and of Yugoslavia as well as by the working masses of all the people's democracies and by all progressive humanity. The liquidation of [our] abnormal relationship with Yugoslavia was done in the interest of the whole camp of socialism, in the interest of strengthening peace in the whole world.

Let us also recall the "affair of the doctor-plotters."

(Animation in the hall.)

Actually there was no "affair" outside of the declaration of the woman doctor [Lidiya] Timashuk, who was probably influenced or ordered by someone (after all, she was an unofficial collaborator of the organs of state security) to write Stalin a letter in which she declared that doctors were applying supposedly improper methods of medical treatment.

Such a letter was sufficient for Stalin to reach an immediate conclusion that there are doctor-plotters in the Soviet Union. He issued orders to arrest a group of eminent Soviet medical specialists. He personally issued advice on the conduct of the investigation and the method of interrogation of the arrested persons. He said that academician [V. N.] Vinogradov should be put in chains, and that another one [of the alleged plotters] should be beaten. The former Minister of State Security, comrade [Semyen] Ignatiev, is present at this Congress as a delegate. Stalin told him curtly, "If you do not obtain confessions from the doctors we will shorten you by a head."

(Tumult in the hall.)

Stalin personally called the investigative judge, gave him instructions, and advised him on which investigative methods should be used. These methods were simple—beat, beat and beat again.

Shortly after the doctors were arrested, we members of the Politburo received protocols with the doctors' confessions of guilt. After distributing these protocols, Stalin told us, "You are blind like young kittens. What will happen without me? The country will perish because you do not know how to recognize enemies."

The case was presented so that no one could verify the facts on which the investigation was based. There was no possibility of trying to verify facts by contacting those who had made the confessions of guilt.

We felt, however, that the case of the arrested doctors was questionable. We knew some of these people personally because they had once treated us. When we examined this "case" after Stalin's death, we found it to have been fabricated from beginning to end.

This ignominious "case" was set up by Stalin. He did not, however, have the time in which to bring it to an end (as he conceived that end), and for this reason the doctors are still alive. All of them have been rehabilitated. They are working in the same places they were working before. They are treating top individuals, not excluding members of the Government. They have our full confidence; and they execute their duties honestly, as they did before.

In putting together various dirty and shameful cases, a very base role was played by a rabid enemy of our Party, an agent of a foreign intelligence service—Beria, who had stolen into Stalin's confidence. How could this provocateur have gained such a position in the Party and in the state, so as to become the First Deputy Chair of the Council of Ministers of the Soviet Union and a Politburo member? It has now been established that this villain climbed up the Government ladder over an untold number of corpses.

Were there any signs that Beria was an enemy of the Party? Yes, there were. Already in 1937, at a Central Committee Plenum, former People's Commissar of Health [Grigory] Kaminsky said that Beria worked for the Musavat intelligence service. But the Plenum had barely concluded when Kaminsky was arrested and then shot. Had Stalin examined Kaminsky's statement? No, because Stalin believed in Beria, and that was enough for him. And when Stalin believed in anyone or anything, then no one could say anything that was contrary to his opinion. Anyone daring to express opposition would have met the same fate as Kaminsky.

There were other signs, also. The declaration which comrade [A. V.] Snegov made to the Party's Central Committee is interesting. (Parenthetically speaking, he was also rehabilitated not long ago, after seventeen years in prison camps.) In this declaration, Snegov writes:

"In connection with the proposed rehabilitation of the former Central Committee member, [Lavrenty] Kartvelishvili-Lavrentiev, I have entrusted to the hands of the representative of the Committee of State Security a detailed deposition concerning Beria's role in the disposition of the Kartvelishvili case and concerning the criminal motives by which Beria was guided.

"In my opinion, it is indispensable to recall an important fact pertaining to this case and to communicate it to the Central Committee, because I did not consider it as proper to include in the investigation documents.

"On October 30, 1931, at a session of the Organizational Bureau of the Central Committee of the All-Union Communist Party (Bolsheviks), Kartvelishvili, Secretary of the Transcaucasian Regional Committee, made a report. All members of the executive of the Regional Committee were present. Of them I alone am now alive.

"During this session, J. V. Stalin made a motion at the end of his speech concerning the organization of the secretariat of the Transcaucasian Regional Committee composed of the following: First Secretary, Kartvelishvili; Second Secretary, Beria (it was then, for the first time in the Party's history, that Beria's name was mentioned as a candidate for a Party position). Kartvelishvili answered that he knew Beria well and for that reason refused categorically to work together with him. Stalin proposed then that this matter be left open and that it be solved in the process of the work itself. Two days later a decision was arrived at that Beria would receive the Party post and that Kartvelishvili would be deported from the Transcaucasus.

"This fact can be confirmed by comrades Mikoyan and Kaganovich, who were present at that session."

The long, unfriendly relations between Kartvelishvili and Beria were widely known. They date back to the time when comrade Sergo [Ordzhonikidze] was active in the Transcaucasus. Kartvelishvili was the closest assistant of Sergo. The unfriendly relationship impelled Beria to fabricate a "case" against Kartvelishvili. It is characteristic that Kartvelishvili was charged with a terroristic act against Beria in this "case."

The indictment in the Beria case contains a discussion of his crimes.

Some things should, however, be recalled, especially since it is possible that not all delegates to the Congress have read this document. I wish to recall Beria's bestial disposition of the cases of [Mikhail] Kedrov, [V.] Golubev, and Golubev's adopted mother, Baturina—persons who wished to inform the Central Committee concerning Beria's treacherous activity. They were shot without any trial and the sentence was passed ex post facto, after the execution.

Here is what the old Communist, comrade Kedrov, wrote to the Central Committee through comrade [Andrey] Andreyev (comrade Andreyev was then a Central Committee Secretary):

"I am calling to you for help from a gloomy cell of the Lefortovo prison. Let my cry of horror reach your ears; do not remain deaf, take me under your protection; please, help remove the nightmare of interrogations and show that this is all a mistake.

"I suffer innocently. Please believe me. Time will testify to the truth. I am not an agent provocateur of the Tsarist Okhrana. I am not a spy, I am not a member of an anti-Soviet organization of which I am being accused on the basis of denunciations. I am also not guilty of any other crimes against the Party and the Government. I am an old Bolshevik, free of any stain; I have honestly fought for almost forty years in the ranks of the Party for the good and prosperity of the nation. . . .

". . . Today I, a 62-year-old man, am being threatened by the investigative judges with more severe, cruel and degrading methods of physical pressure. They (the judges) are no longer capable of becoming aware of their error and of recognizing that their handling of my case is illegal and impermissible. They try to justify their actions by picturing me as a hardened and raving enemy and are demanding increased repressions. But let the Party know that I am innocent and that there is nothing which can turn a loyal son of the Party into an enemy, even right up to his last dying breath.

"But I have no way out. I cannot divert from myself the hastily approaching new and powerful blows.

"Everything, however, has its limits. My torture has reached the extreme. My health is broken, my strength and my energy are waning, the end is drawing near. To die in a Soviet prison, branded as a vile traitor to the Fatherland—what can be more monstrous for an honest man? And how monstrous all this is! Unsurpassed bitterness and pain grips my heart. No! No! This will not happen; this cannot be, I cry. Neither the Party, nor the Soviet Government, nor the People's Commissar, L. P. Beria, will permit this cruel, irreparable injustice. I am firmly certain that, given a quiet, objective examination, without any foul rantings, without any anger and without the fearful tortures, it would be easy to prove the baselessness of the charges. I believe deeply that truth and justice will triumph. I believe. I believe."

The old Bolshevik, comrade Kedrov, was found innocent by the Military Collegium. But, despite this, he was shot at Beria's order.

(Indignation in the hall.)

Beria also handled cruelly the family of comrade Ordzhonikidze. Why? Because Ordzhonikidze had tried to prevent Beria from realizing his shameful plans. Beria had cleared from his way all persons who could possibly interfere with him. Ordzhonikidze was always an opponent of Beria, which he told to Stalin. Instead of examining this affair and taking appropriate steps, Stalin allowed the liquidation of Ordzhonikidze's brother and brought Ordzhonikidze himself to such a state that he was forced to shoot himself.

(Indignation in the hall.)

Beria was unmasked by the Party's Central Committee shortly after Stalin's death. As a result of particularly detailed legal proceedings, it was established that Beria had committed monstrous crimes and Beria was shot.

The question arises why Beria, who had liquidated tens of thousands of Party and Soviet workers, was not unmasked during Stalin's life. He was not unmasked earlier because he had utilized very skillfully Stalin's weaknesses; feeding him with suspicions, he assisted Stalin in everything and acted with his support.

Comrades: The cult of the individual acquired such monstrous size chiefly because Stalin himself, using all conceivable methods, supported the glorification of his own person. This is supported by numerous facts. One of the most characteristic examples of Stalin's self-glorification and of his lack of even elementary modesty is the edition of his *Short Biography*, which was published in 1948 (sic).

This book is an expression of the most dissolute flattery, an example of making a man into a godhead, of transforming him into an infallible sage, "the greatest leader, sublime strategist of all times and nations." Finally, no other words could be found with which to lift Stalin up to the heavens.

We need not give here examples of the loathsome adulation filling this book. All we need to add is that they all were approved and edited by Stalin personally. Some of them were added in his own handwriting to the draft text of the book.

What did Stalin consider essential to write into this book? Did he want to cool the ardor of the flatterers who were composing his *Short Biography*? No! He marked the very places where he thought that the praise of his services was insufficient. Here are some examples characterizing Stalin's activity, added in Stalin's own hand:

"In this fight against the skeptics and capitulators, the Trotskyites, Zinovievites, Bukharinites and Kamenevites, there was definitely welded together, after Lenin's death, that leading core of the Party... that upheld the great banner of Lenin, rallied the Party behind Lenin's behests, and brought the Soviet people onto the broad paths of industrializing the country and collectivizing the rural economy. The leader of this core and the guiding force of the Party and the state was comrade Stalin."

Thus writes Stalin himself! Then he adds:

"Although he performed his tasks as leader of the Party and the people with consummate skill, and enjoyed the unreserved support of the entire Soviet people, Stalin never allowed his work to be marred by the slightest hint of vanity, conceit or self-adulation."

Where and when could a leader so praise himself? Is this worthy of a leader of the Marxist-Leninist type? No. Precisely against this did Marx and Engels take such a strong position. This always was sharply condemned also by Vladimir Ilyich Lenin.

In the draft text of [Stalin's] book appeared the following sentence: "Stalin is the Lenin of today." This sentence appeared to Stalin to be too weak. Thus, in his own handwriting, he changed it to read: "Stalin is the worthy continuer of Lenin's work, or, as it is said in our Party, Stalin is the Lenin of today." You see how well it is said, not by the nation but by Stalin himself.

It is possible to offer many such self-praising appraisals written into the draft text of that book in Stalin's hand. He showers himself especially generously with praises regarding his military genius and his talent for strategy. I will cite one more insertion made by Stalin on the theme: "The advanced Soviet science of war received further development," he writes, "at Comrade Stalin's hands. Comrade Stalin elaborated the theory of the permanent operating factors that decide the issue of wars, of active defense and the laws of counteroffensive and offensive, of the cooperation of all services and arms in modern warfare, of the role of big tank masses and air forces in modern war, and of the artillery as the most formidable of the armed services. At various stages of the war, Stalin's genius found correct solutions that took into account all the circumstances of the situation."

(Movement in the hall.)

Further, Stalin writes: "Stalin's military mastership was displayed both in defense and on offense. Comrade Stalin's genius enabled him to divine the enemy's plans and defeat them. The battles in which comrade Stalin directed the Soviet armies are brilliant examples of operational military skill."

This is how Stalin was praised as a strategist. Who did this? Stalin himself, not in his role as a strategist but in the role of an author-editor, one of the main creators of his [own] self-adulatory biography. Such, comrades, are the facts. Or should be said, rather, the shameful facts.

One additional fact from the same *Short Biography* of Stalin: As is known, the *History of the All-Union Communist Party (Bolsheviks), Short Course* was written by a commission of the Party Central Committee.

This book, parenthetically, was also permeated with the cult of the individual and was written by a designated group of authors. This fact was reflected in the following formulation on the proof copy of the *Short Biography* of Stalin: "A commission of the Central Committee, All-Union Communist Party (Bolsheviks), under the direction of comrade Stalin and with his most active personal participation, has prepared a *History of the All-Union Communist Party (Bolsheviks), Short Course*."

But even this phrase did not satisfy Stalin: The following sentence replaced it in the final version of the *Short Biography*: "In 1938, the book *History of the All-Union Communist Party (Bolsheviks), Short Course* appeared, written by comrade Stalin and approved by a commission of the Central Committee, All-Union Communist Party (Bolsheviks)." Can one add anything more?

(Animation in the hall.)

As you see, a surprising metamorphosis changed the work created by a group into a book written by Stalin. It is not necessary to state how and why this metamorphosis took place.

A pertinent question comes to our mind: If Stalin is the author of this book, why did he need to praise the person of Stalin so much and to transform the whole post-October historical period of our glorious Communist Party solely into an action of "the Stalin genius?"

Did this book properly reflect the efforts of the Party in the socialist transformation of the country, in the construction of socialist society, in the industrialization and collectivization of the country, and also other steps taken by the Party which undeviatingly traveled the path outlined by Lenin? This book speaks principally about Stalin, about his speeches, about his reports. Everything without the smallest exception is tied to his name.

And when Stalin himself asserts that he himself wrote the *Short Course*, this calls at least for amazement. Can a Marxist-Leninist thus write about himself, praising his own person to the heavens?

Or let us take the matter of the Stalin Prizes.

(Movement in the hall.)

Not even the Tsars created prizes which they named after themselves.

Stalin recognized as the best a text of the national anthem of the Soviet Union which contains not a word about the Communist Party; it contains, however, the following unprecedented praise of Stalin: "Stalin brought us up in loyalty to the people. He inspired us to great toil and deeds."

In these lines of the anthem, the whole educational, directional and inspirational activity of the great Leninist Party is ascribed to Stalin. This is, of course, a clear deviation from Marxism-Leninism, a clear debasing and belittling of the role of the Party. We should add for your information that the Presidium of the Central Committee has already passed a resolution concerning the composition of a new text of the anthem, which will reflect the role of the people and the role of the Party.

(Loud, prolonged applause.)

And was it without Stalin's knowledge that many of the largest enterprises and towns were named after him? Was it without his knowledge that Stalin monuments were erected in the whole country—these "memorials to the living"? It is a fact that Stalin himself had signed on July 2, 1951 a resolution of the USSR Council of Ministers concerning the erection on the Volga-Don Canal of an impressive monument to Stalin; on September 4 of the same year he issued an order making 33 tons of copper available for the construction of this impressive monument.

Anyone who has visited the Stalingrad area must have seen the huge statue which is being built there, and that on a site which hardly any people frequent. Huge sums were spent to build it at a time when people of this area had lived since the war in huts. Consider, yourself, was Stalin right when he wrote in his biography that ". . . he did not allow in himself . . . even a shadow of conceit, pride, or self-adoration"?

At the same time Stalin gave proofs of his lack of respect for Lenin's memory. It is not a coincidence that, despite the decision taken over thirty years ago to build a Palace of Soviets as a monument to Vladimir Ilyich, this palace was not built, its construction was always postponed and the project allowed to lapse.

We cannot forget to recall the Soviet Government resolution of August 14, 1925 concerning "the founding of Lenin prizes for educational work." This resolution was published in the press, but until this day there are no Lenin prizes. This, too, should be corrected.

(Tumultuous, prolonged applause.)

During Stalin's life—thanks to known methods which I have mentioned, and quoting facts, for instance, from the *Short Biography* of Stalin—all events were explained as if Lenin played only a secondary role, even during the October Socialist Revolution. In many films and in many literary works the figure of Lenin was incorrectly presented and inadmissibly depreciated.

Stalin loved to see the film *The Unforgettable Year of 1919*, in which he was shown on the steps of an armored train and where he was practically vanquishing the foe with his own saber. Let Klimenty Yefremovich [Voroshilov], our dear friend, find the necessary courage and write the truth about Stalin; after all, he knows how Stalin had fought. It will be difficult for comrade Voroshilov to undertake this, but it would be good if he did it. Everyone will approve of it, both the people and the Party. Even his grandsons will thank him.

(Prolonged applause.)

In speaking about the events of the October Revolution and about the Civil War, the impression was created that Stalin always played the main role, as if everywhere and always Stalin had suggested to Lenin what to do and how to do it. However, this is slander of Lenin.

(Prolonged applause.)

I will probably not sin against the truth when I say that 99 per cent of the persons present here heard and knew very little about Stalin before the year 1924, while Lenin was known to all. He was known to the whole Party, to the whole nation, from children all the way up to old men.

(Tumultuous, prolonged applause.)

All this has to be thoroughly revised so that history, literature and the fine arts properly reflect V. I. Lenin's role and the great deeds of our Communist Party and of the Soviet people—a creative people.

(Applause.)

Comrades! The cult of the individual caused the employment of faulty principles in Party work and in economic activity. It brought about rude violation of internal Party and Soviet democracy, sterile administration, deviations of all sorts, cover-ups of shortcomings, and varnishings of reality. Our nation bore forth many flatterers and specialists in false optimism and deceit.

We should also not forget that, due to the numerous arrests of Party, Soviet and economic leaders, many workers began to work uncertainly, showed overcautiousness, feared all which was new, feared their own shadows, and began to show less initiative in their work.

Take, for instance, Party and Soviet resolutions. They were prepared in a routine manner, often without considering the concrete situation. This went so far that Party workers, even during the smallest sessions, read [prepared] speeches. All this produced the danger of formalizing the Party and Soviet work and of bureaucratizing the whole apparatus.

Stalin's reluctance to consider life's realities, and the fact that he was not aware of the real state of affairs in the provinces, can be illustrated by his direction of agriculture.

All those who interested themselves even a little in the national situation saw the difficult situation in agriculture, but Stalin never even noted it. Did we tell Stalin about this? Yes, we told him, but he did not support us. Why? Because Stalin never traveled anywhere, did not meet city and kolkhoz workers. He did not know the actual situation in the provinces.

He knew the country and agriculture only from films. And these films dressed up and beautified the existing situation in agriculture. Many films pictured kolkhoz life such that [farmhouse] tables groaned from the weight of turkeys and geese. Evidently, Stalin thought that it was actually so.

Vladimir Ilyich Lenin looked at life differently. He always was close to the people. He used to receive peasant delegates and often spoke at factory gatherings. He used to visit villages and talk with the peasants.

Stalin separated himself from the people and never went anywhere. This lasted ten years. The last time he visited a village was in January, 1928, when he visited Siberia in connection with grain procurements. How then could he have known the situation in the provinces?

Once, [Stalin] was told during a discussion that our situation on the land was a difficult one and that the situation in cattle breeding and meat production was especially bad. [From this] there came a commission charged with the preparation of a resolution called "Measures toward the further development of animal husbandry in kolkhozes and sovkhozes." We worked out this project.

Of course, our proposals at that time did not cover all the possibilities. However we did chart ways in which animal husbandry on kolkhozes and sovkhozes could be boosted. We proposed to raise livestock prices so as to create material incentives for kolkhoz, MTS [machine-tractor station] and sovkhoz workers in developing breeding. But our project was not accepted. In February 1953 it was laid aside entirely.

What is more, while reviewing this project Stalin proposed that the taxes paid by kolkhozes and by kolkhoz workers should be raised by 40 billion rubles. According to him, the peasants were well off and a kolkhoz worker would need to sell only one more chicken to pay his tax in full.

Think about what this implied. Forty billion rubles is a sum which [these workers] did not realize for *all* the products which they sold to the State. In 1952, for instance, kolkhozes and kolkhoz workers received 26,280 million rubles for all products delivered and sold to the State.

Did Stalin's position, then, rest on data of any sort whatever? Of course not. In such cases facts and figures did not interest him. If Stalin said anything, it meant it was so—after all, he was a "genius," and a genius does not need to count, he only needs to look and can immediately tell how it should be. When he expresses his opinion, everyone has to repeat it and to admire his wisdom.

But how much wisdom was contained in the proposal to raise the agricultural tax by 40 billion rubles? None, absolutely none, because the proposal was not based on an actual assessment of the situation but on the fantastic ideas of a person divorced from reality.

We are currently beginning slowly to work our way out of a difficult agricultural situation. The speeches of the delegates to the Twentieth Congress please us all. We are glad that many delegates have delivered speeches [to the effect] that conditions exist for fulfilling the sixth Five-Year Plan for animal husbandry [early]: not in five years, but within two to three years. We are certain that the commitments of the new Five-Year Plan will be accomplished successfully.

(Prolonged applause.)

Comrades! If we sharply criticize today the cult of the individual which was so widespread during Stalin's life, and if we speak about the many negative phenomena generated by this cult (which is so alien to the spirit of Marxism-Leninism), some may ask: How could it be? Stalin headed the

Party and the country for 30 years and many victories were gained during his lifetime. Can we deny this? In my opinion, the question can be asked in this manner only by those who are blinded and hopelessly hypnotized by the cult of the individual, only by those who do not understand the essence of the revolution and of the Soviet state, only by those who do not understand, in a Leninist manner, the role of the Party and of the nation in the development of the Soviet society.

[Our] Socialist Revolution was attained by the working class and by the poor peasantry with the partial support of middle-class peasants. It was attained by the people under the leadership of the Bolshevik Party. Lenin's great service consisted of the fact that he created a militant Party of the working class, but he was armed with Marxist understanding of the laws of social development and with the science of proletarian victory in the fight with capitalism, and he steeled this Party in the crucible of the revolutionary struggle of the masses of the people.

During this fight the Party consistently defended the interests of the people and became its experienced leader. [The Party] led the working masses to power, to the creation of the first socialist state. You remember well the wise words of Lenin: that the Soviet state is strong because of the awareness of the masses that history is created by the millions and tens of millions of people.

Our historical victories were attained thanks to the Party's organizational work, to the many provincial organizations, and to the self-sacrificing work of our great nation. These victories are the result of the great drive and activity of the nation and of the Party as a whole. They are not at all the fruit of Stalin's leadership, which is how the situation was pictured during the period of the cult of the individual.

If we are to consider this matter as Marxists and as Leninists, then we have to state unequivocally that the leadership practices which came into being during the last years of Stalin's life became a serious obstacle in the path of Soviet social development. Stalin often failed for months to take up some unusually important problems, concerning the life of the Party and of the State, whose solution could not be postponed. During Stalin's leadership our peaceful relations with other nations were often threatened, because one-man decisions could cause, and often did cause, great complications.

In the past [few] years, [after] we managed to free ourselves of the harmful practice of the cult of the individual and took several proper steps in terms of [both] internal and external policies, everyone [has been able to see] how activity has grown before our very eyes, how the creative activity of the broad working masses has developed, and how favorably all this has acted upon economic and cultural development.

(Applause.)

Some comrades may ask us: Where were the members of the Politburo? Why did they not assert themselves against the cult of the individual in time? And why is this being done only now? First of all, we have to consider the fact that the members of the Politburo viewed these matters in a different way at different times. Initially, many of them backed Stalin actively because he was one of the strongest Marxists and his logic, his strength and his will greatly influenced [Party] cadres and Party work.

It is known that after Lenin's death, especially during the first years, Stalin actively fought for Leninism against the enemies of Leninist theory and against those who deviated. Beginning with Leninist theory, the Party, with its Central Committee at the head, started on a great scale work on the socialist industrialization of the country, on agricultural collectivization, and on cultural revolution. At that time Stalin gained great popularity, sympathy and support. The Party had to fight those who tried to lead the country away from the correct Leninist path. It had to fight Trotskyites, Zinovievites and rightists, and bourgeois nationalists. This fight was indispensable.

Later, however, Stalin, abusing his power more and more, began to fight eminent Party and Government leaders and to use terroristic methods against honest Soviet people. As we have already shown, Stalin thus handled such eminent Party and State leaders as Kosior, Rudzutak, Eikhe, Postyshev and many others.

Attempts to oppose groundless suspicions and charges resulted in the opponent's falling victim to the repression. This characterized the fall of comrade Postyshev.

In one of his [exchanges] Stalin expressed his dissatisfaction with Postyshev and asked him, "What are you actually?"

Postyshev answered clearly, "I am a Bolshevik, comrade Stalin, a Bolshevik."

At first, this assertion was considered to show [merely] a lack of respect for Stalin. Later it was considered a harmful act. Eventually it resulted in Postyshev's annihilation and castigation as an "enemy of the people."

In the situation which then prevailed, I often talked with Nikolay Alexandrovich Bulganin. Once when we two were traveling in a car, he said,

"It has happened sometimes that a man goes to Stalin on his invitation as a friend. And when he sits with Stalin, he does not know where he will be sent next—home or to jail."

It is clear that such conditions put every member of the Politburo in a very difficult situation. And, when we also consider the fact that in the last years Central Committee Plenary sessions were not convened and that sessions of the Politburo occurred only occasionally, from time to time, then we will understand how difficult it was for any member of the Politburo to take a stand against one or another unjust or improper procedure, against serious errors and shortcomings in leadership practices.

As we have already shown, many decisions were taken either by one person or in a roundabout way, without collective discussion. The sad fate of Politburo member comrade Voznesensky, who fell victim to Stalin's repressions, is known to all. Characteristically, the decision to remove him from the Politburo was never discussed but was reached in a devious fashion. In the same way came the decision regarding Kuznetsov's and Rodionov's removals from their posts.

The importance of the Central Committee's Politburo was reduced and its work was disorganized by the creation within the Politburo of various commissions—the so-called "quintets," "sextets," "septets" and "nonets." Here is, for instance, a Politburo resolution from October 3, 1946:

"Stalin's proposal:

"1.The Politburo Commission for Foreign Affairs ('Sextet') is to concern itself in the future, in addition to foreign affairs, also with matters of internal construction and domestic policy.

"2.The Sextet is to add to its roster the Chairman of the State Commission of Economic Planning of the USSR, comrade Voznesensky, and is to be known as a Septet.

"Signed: Secretary of the Central Committee, J. Stalin."

What [sophistry]!

(Laughter in the hall.)

It is clear that the creation within the Politburo of this type of commissions—"quintets," "sextets," "septets" and "nonets"—was against the principle of collective leadership. The result of this was that some members of the Politburo were in this way kept away from participation in reaching the most important state matters.

One of the oldest members of our Party, Klimenty Yefremovich Voroshilov, found himself in an almost impossible situation. For several years he was actually deprived of the right of participation in Politburo sessions. Stalin forbade him to attend Politburo sessions and to receive documents. When the Politburo was in session and comrade Voroshilov heard about it, he telephoned each time and asked whether he would be allowed to attend. Sometimes Stalin permitted it, but always showed his dissatisfaction.

Because of his extreme suspicion, Stalin toyed also with the absurd and ridiculous suspicion that Voroshilov was an English agent.

(Laughter in the hall.)

It's true—an English agent. A special tap was installed in his home to listen to what was said there.

(Indignation in the hall.)

By unilateral decision, Stalin had also separated one other man from the work of the Politburo—Andrey Andreyevich Andreyev. This was one of the most unbridled acts of willfulness.

Let us consider the first Central Committee Plenum after the 19th Party Congress. Stalin, in his talk at the Plenum, characterized Vyacheslav Mikhailovich Molotov and Anastas Ivanovich Mikoyan and suggested that these old workers of our Party were guilty of some baseless charges. We cannot rule out the possibility that had Stalin remained at the helm for another several months, Comrades Molotov and Mikoyan probably would not have delivered any speeches at this [20th] Congress.

Stalin evidently had plans to finish off the older members of the Politburo. He often stated that Politburo members should be replaced by new ones. His proposal after the 19th Congress to elect 25 persons to the Central Committee Presidium was aimed at the removal of old Politburo members and at bringing in less experienced persons so that these would extol him in all sorts of ways.

We can assume that this was also a design for the future annihilation of the old Politburo members and, in this way, a cover for all shameful acts of Stalin, acts which we are now considering.

Comrades! So as not to repeat errors of the past, the Central Committee has declared itself resolutely against the cult of the individual. We consider that Stalin was extolled to excess. However, in the past Stalin undoubtedly performed great services to the Party, to the working class and to the international workers' movement.

This question is complicated by the fact that all this which we have just discussed was done during Stalin's life under his leadership and with his concurrence; here Stalin was convinced that this was necessary for the defense of the interests of the working classes against the plotting of enemies and against the attack of the imperialist camp.

He saw this from the position of the interest of the working class, of the interest of the laboring people, of the interest of the victory of socialism and communism. We cannot say that these were the deeds of a giddy despot. He considered that this should be done in the interest of the Party, of the working masses, in the name of the defense of the revolution's gains. In this lies the whole tragedy!

Comrades! Lenin had often stressed that modesty is an absolutely integral part of a real Bolshevik. Lenin himself was the living personification of the greatest modesty. We cannot say that we have been following this Leninist example in all respects.

It is enough to point out that many towns, factories and industrial enterprises, kolkhozes and sovkhozes, Soviet institutions and cultural institutions have been referred to by us with a title if I may express it so—of private property of the names of these or those Government or Party leaders who were still active and in good health. Many of us participated in the action of assigning our names to various towns, rayons, enterprises and kolkhozes. We must correct this.

(Applause.)

But this should be done calmly and slowly. The Central Committee will discuss this matter and consider it carefully in order to prevent errors and excesses. I can remember how Ukraine learned about Kosior's arrest. Kiev radio used to start its programs thus: "This is Radio Kosior." When one day the programs began without mentioning Kosior, everyone was quite certain that something had happened to him and that he probably had been arrested.

Thus, if today we begin to change the signs everywhere and to rename things, people will think that these comrades in whose honor the given enterprises, kolkhozes or cities are named also met some bad fate and that they have also been arrested.

(Animation in the hall.)

How is the authority and the importance of this or that leader judged? On the basis of how many towns, industrial enterprises and factories, kolkhozes and sovkhozes carry his name. Is it not about time that we eliminate this "private property" and "nationalize" the factories, the industrial enterprises, the kolkhozes and the sovkhozes?

(Laughter, applause, voices: "That is right.")

This will benefit our cause. After all, the cult of the individual is manifested also in this way.

We should, in all seriousness, consider the question of the cult of the individual. We cannot let this matter get out of the Party, especially not to the press. It is for this reason that we are considering it here at a closed Congress session. We should know the limits; we should not give ammunition to the enemy; we should not wash our dirty linen before their eyes. I think that the delegates to the Congress will understand and assess properly all these proposals.

(Tumultuous applause.)

Comrades! We must abolish the cult of the individual decisively, once and for all; we must draw the proper conclusions concerning both ideological-theoretical and practical work. It is necessary for this purpose:

First, in a Bolshevik manner to condemn and to eradicate the cult of the individual as alien to Marxism-Leninism and not consonant with the principles of Party leadership and the norms of Party life, and to fight inexorably all attempts at bringing back this practice in one form or another.

To return to and actually practice in all our ideological work the most important theses of Marxist-Leninist science about the people as the creator of history and as the creator of all material and spiritual good of humanity, about the decisive role of the Marxist Party in the revolutionary fight for the transformation of society, about the victory of communism.

In this connection we will be forced to do much work in order to examine critically from the Marxist-Leninist viewpoint and to correct the widely spread erroneous views connected with the cult of the individual in the spheres of history, philosophy, economy and of other sciences, as well as in literature and the fine arts. It is especially necessary that in the immediate future we compile a serious textbook of the history of our Party which will be edited in accordance with scientific Marxist objectivism, a textbook of the history of Soviet society, a book pertaining to the events of the Civil War and the Great Patriotic War.

Second, to continue systematically and consistently the work done by the Party's Central Committee during the last years, a work characterized by minute observation in all Party organizations, from the bottom to the top, of the Leninist principles of Party leadership, characterized, above all, by the main principle of collective leadership, characterized by the observance of the norms of Party life described in the statutes of our Party, and, finally, characterized by the wide practice of criticism and self-criticism.

Third, to restore completely the Leninist principles of Soviet socialist democracy, expressed in the Constitution of the Soviet Union, to fight willfulness of individuals abusing their power. The evil caused by acts violating revolutionary socialist legality which have accumulated during a long time as a result of the negative influence of the cult of the individual has to be completely corrected.

Comrades! The 20th Congress of the Communist Party of the Soviet Union has manifested with a new strength the unshakable unity of our Party, its cohesiveness around the Central Committee, its resolute will to accomplish the great task of building communism.

(Tumultuous applause.)

And the fact that we present in all their ramifications the basic problems of overcoming the cult of the individual which is alien to Marxism-Leninism, as well as the problem of liquidating its burdensome consequences, is evidence of the great moral and political strength of our Party.

(Prolonged applause.)

We are absolutely certain that our Party, armed with the historical resolutions of the 20th Congress, will lead the Soviet people along the Leninist path to new successes, to new victories.

(Tumultuous, prolonged applause.)

Long live the victorious banner of our Party—Leninism!

44: John Kennedy in Berlin
"Ich bein ein Berliner!"
Berlin, June 26, 1963

DURING HIS THOUSAND DAYS AS U.S. PRESIDENT, JOHN F. KENNEDY GAVE several memorable speeches, elegantly written and impeccably delivered. His inaugural address in 1961 was a political version of the script for the film "Casablanca"—every sentence, it seemed, was a gem. More than two years after his inaugural, he delivered three more extraordinary speeches in the space of less than a month. One June 10, 1963, speaking at American University in Washington, D.C., Kennedy asserted that that it was time to put aside the antagonism between the U.S. and the Soviet Union in the interests of peace. The following day, as Governor George Wallace of Alabama barred the doors of his state's university to African-American students, Kennedy told the nation that it faced a moral crisis over civil rights.

Less than two weeks later, on June 26, standing near the Berlin Wall and in front of hundreds of thousands of West Berliners, Kennedy delivered his third important speech of the month. This one was destined to become one of the great texts of the Cold War.

The Berlin Wall speech, remembered best for a single, grammatically imprecise line in German—*Ich bin ein Berliner*, lacked the brilliant word pictures and smooth execution of Kennedy's inaugural. It was raw and ragged, a work born not of Kennedy's cool detachment but of passionate engagement. That is why it was and remains such a spectacular oratorical achievement. The Berlin speech is Kennedy unleashed, Kennedy freed from the soft edges of diplomatic-speak, Kennedy giving voice to his inner rage. But while the speech's spontaneity is part of its power, it was not devoid of calculation and intrigue. And much of it had to do not with the apparent targets of Kennedy's invective—the Soviet Union and East Germany—but with two of Washington's allies, West Germany and France.

John Kennedy was not the first foreign dignitary to charm Germans by speaking a few sentences in their native tongue. In September, 1962,

French President Charles de Gaulle paid a state visit to West Germany as part of an effort to build a strategic partnership between the free German state and France. During the visit, the proud de Gaulle surprised his German audience by speaking several phrases in German, no small concession from a French nationalist. His mission to West Germany was deemed a smashing diplomatic success.

Kennedy and British Prime Minister Harold Macmillan distrusted de Gaulle and believed he was trying to build a counter-weight to Anglo-American domination of Western Europe. Their distrust turned to hostility when, in January, 1963, de Gaulle vetoed Britain's application for membership in the European Common Market. Macmillan had expended enormous political capital trying to persuade Britons that their future was with continental Europe, and Kennedy viewed British membership in the Common Market as essential for American interests. Ironically, that was precisely how de Gaulle viewed it, and thus, the French veto.

The prospective Franco-West German partnership was very much on Kennedy's mind when he flew to Bonn, the West's capital, on June 22. During the long trans-Atlantic flight, Kennedy thought about what he might say to the citizens of West Berlin, trapped as they were behind the Iron Curtain in the heart of Soviet-controlled East Germany. On the way to Germany, he was reminded of the famous boast of the Roman empire— *civis Romanus sum*, or I am a citizen of Rome. He summoned McGeorge Bundy, his national security adviser, and asked him to come up with an appropriate phrase in German. Bundy gave Kennedy the line by which the speech became famous: *Ich bin ein Berliner*—I am a Berliner. Kennedy wrote down the phrase on an index card, spelling it phonetically.

Berlin, more so than Cuba, loomed as the most dangerous site of East-West confrontation in the early 1960s. The Soviets regarded U.S. control of half the city as a constant provocation, while the U.S. saw West Berlin as an island fortress in a sea of communist red. Mass defections from the communist east to the democratic west led the Soviets and East Germany to build a wall in late 1961 to prevent further flight. Ironically, the wall helped ease tensions between Moscow and Washington because it stopped the flow of human traffic, which was a sore point between the two superpowers.

Nevertheless, the wall was a brutal symbol of Soviet rule, and the sight of it enraged Kennedy when he arrived in the city on June 26. During a tour of the divided city, after he peered over the wall into grey, lifeless East Berlin, Kennedy showed General James Polke, U.S. commander in the city, a copy of the speech he was scheduled to deliver later in the day. Polke told Kennedy the speech was terrible. It was dull, careful and diplomatic—but it was in keeping with Kennedy's speech on June 10 when he challenged his fellow Americans to change their views about the Soviets and the Cold War.

Kennedy didn't like the speech, either. He discarded it and instead gave vent to his emotions. In so doing, his short address transcended Cold War rivalries and internecine Atlantic politics. But after it was over, after Kennedy denounced those who "say we can work with the communists," his staff reminded him that at that very moment, his administration was negotiating with the Soviets on a treaty to limit the testing of nuclear weapons. Kennedy winced, and later that day he gave a more-measured speech about East-West relations.

That speech, of course, is long forgotten. His speech at the Berlin Wall remains a memorable moment in twentieth century history, a rare glimpse of a president giving vent to his emotions, speaking the truth as he saw it.

Those five hundred words also had a more practical effect. On the trip home, Bundy told Kennedy that a German poll showed him besting de Gaulle in the battle for West German's hearts and minds. "But his popularity was then, and yours is now," Bundy said.[1] Kennedy was assassinated five months later.

▼ ▼ ▼

I AM proud to come to this city as the guest of your distinguished Mayor, who has symbolized throughout the world the fighting spirit of West Berlin. And I am proud to visit the Federal Republic with your distinguished Chancellor who for so many years has committed Germany to democracy and freedom and progress, and to come here in the company of my fellow American, General Clay, who has been in this city during its great moments of crisis and will come again if ever needed.

Two thousand years ago the proudest boast was "civis Romanus sum." Today, in the world of freedom, the proudest boast is "Ich bin ein Berliner."

I appreciate my interpreter translating my German!

There are many people in the world who really don't understand, or say they don't, what is the great issue between the free world and the Communist world. Let them come to Berlin. There are some who say that communism is the wave of the future. Let them come to Berlin. And there are some who say in Europe and elsewhere we can work with the Communists.

Let them come to Berlin. And there are even a few who say that it is true that communism is an evil system, but it permits us to make economic progress. Lass' sie nach Berlin kommen. Let them come to Berlin.

Freedom has many difficulties and democracy is not perfect, but we have never had to put a wall up to keep our people in, to prevent them from leaving us. I want to say, on behalf of my countrymen, who live many miles away on the other side of the Atlantic, who are far distant from you, that they take the greatest pride that they have been able to share with you, even from a distance, the story of the last 18 years. I know of no town, no city, that has been besieged for 18 years that still lives with the vitality and the force, and the hope and the determination of the city of West Berlin. While the wall is the most obvious and vivid demonstration of the failures of the Communist system, for all the world to see, we take no satisfaction in it, for it is, as your Mayor has said, an offense not only against history but an offense against humanity, separating families, dividing husbands and wives and brothers and sisters, and dividing a people who wish to be joined together.

What is true of this city is true of Germany—real, lasting peace in Europe can never be assured as long as one German out of four is denied the elementary right of free men, and that is to make a free choice. In 18 years of peace and good faith, this generation of Germans has earned the right to be free, including the right to unite their families and their nation in lasting peace, with good will to all people. You live in a defended island of freedom, but your life is part of the main. So let me ask you as I close, to lift your eyes beyond the dangers of today, to the hopes of tomorrow, beyond the freedom merely of this city of Berlin, or your country of Germany, to the advance of freedom everywhere, beyond the wall to the day of peace with justice, beyond yourselves and ourselves to all mankind.

Freedom is indivisible, and when one man is enslaved, all are not free. When all are free, then we can look forward to that day when this city will be joined as one and this country and this great Continent of Europe in a peaceful and hopeful globe. When that day finally comes, as it will, the people of West Berlin can take sober satisfaction in the fact that they were in the front lines for almost two decades.

All free men, wherever they may live, are citizens of Berlin, and, therefore, as a free man, I take pride in the words "Ich bin ein Berliner."

45: Barbara Jordan Addresses the House Judiciary Committee
"Today I Am an Inquisitor"
Washington, July 24, 1974

ON THE MORNING OF JULY 24, 1974, THE PRESIDENT OF THE UNITED STATES learned the limits of his powers. The Supreme Court that morning announced its decision in a case known as United States v. Nixon—the people v. their president. Without a dissenting vote, the Court ruled that Richard Nixon could not withhold tape recordings of White House meetings from investigators looking into possible criminal conduct by the President and his aides. The tapes, Nixon knew, damning evidence about his

It was a devastating blow to Nixon's frantic effort to retain the presidency. Since taking the oath of office for the second time in January, 1973, Nixon had stared down a series of scandals and investigations stemming from a botched break-in of the Democratic National Committee's headquarters in the Watergate Hotel in 1972. His most-trusted advisors, H.R. Haldeman and John Ehrlichman, resigned at the President's request on April 30, 1973. Nixon hoped the resignations would ease pressure on the White House, but, in fact, pressure was only beginning to build. Two weeks later, on May 10, Nixon's attorney general and campaign manager, John Mitchell, was indicted on election-law charges, as was his campaign treasurer, Maurice Stans. Over the summer, the nation watched on live television as current and former Nixon officials testified in front of a U.S. Senate panel investigating a series of scandals that fell under the umbrella term of "Watergate." In early October, Nixon's vice president, Spiro Agnew, resigned amid charges that he accepted bribes while he was governor of Maryland. In late October, Nixon fired a special prosecutor, Archibald Cox, who was investigating the Watergate scandals.

The Nixon presidency no longer was engulfed in a mere scandal. It was now the center of a constitutional crisis, the most serious since the post-Civil War impeachment of Abraham Lincoln's successor, Andrew Johnson. Nixon saw the crisis as the "campaign of my life,"[1] but for the country, it was a demoralizing spectacle, the latest in a series of national traumas beginning with the assassination of John Kennedy in 1963. The endless war in Vietnam, the killings of Martin Luther King Jr. and Robert Kennedy in 1968, the urban riots and violent demonstrations of the late Sixties all suggested that the nation, once so confident, was speeding in the wrong direction. Watergate seemed to be a fittingly dispiriting capstone to a decade that produced only bitterness and disappointment.

In late October, after Agnew's resignation and Nixon's firing of Cox, the drama shifted to Capitol Hill. The musty machinery of impeachment—the grave process by which a president could be forced to stand trial in the Senate and possible removed from office—was dusted off in the House of Representatives. No president since Johnson had been threatened so seriously with possible removal. By the end of the month, the House Judiciary Committee, where the process would begin, had nearly two dozen articles of impeachment to consider. Members of the committee would decide whether or not the accusations, ranging from abuse of office to tax evasion, merited the attention of the full House.

Among those considering the case against Nixon was a first-term congresswoman from Texas named Barbara Jordan. Elected in 1972, Jordan was the first African-American to represent Texas in the House since Reconstruction. She was the daughter of a Baptist preacher, the product of a segregated schools system, and the holder of a law degree from Boston University.

Jordan was blessed with a thunderous, deep voice and the ability to use it to great effect. Her knowledge of the Constitution, her scholarly demeanor, and her compelling life story made for a formidable presence on the committee despite her inexperience.

The Judiciary Committee deliberated into 1974 as the White House scandals deepened. In April, the Committee issued a subpoena for more than forty tape recordings of meetings in the White House. Nixon desperately sought to retain possession of the tapes by offering instead edited transcripts of the recorded conversations, arguing that the transcripts proved that he did not attempt to coverup the Watergate burglary.

By the spring of 1974, however, the burglary was just one of several scandals that imperiled Nixon's presidency. The public, grown accustomed to deception and worse from the White House and other elected leaders, nevertheless was shocked when the transcripts were published. The conversations among Nixon and his advisors were profane and cynical, which even a demoralized public found hard to take. One newspaper compared Nixon and his aides to gangsters. The president lost supporters in the press and in his own party. But the worst was yet to come.

Leon Jaworski, who succeeded Cox as special prosecutor, wanted his investigators to hear recordings of sixty-four meetings. Nixon again refused to turn over the tapes, even when ordered to do so by federal Judge John Sirica. Nixon appealed Sirica's decision to the Supreme Court. While the Court deliberated, the House Judiciary Committee continued its own demands for access to the tapes. Nixon continued to claim executive privilege.

One of the tapes in question was from meetings on June 23, 1972. When the Court ruled that Nixon must surrender the tapes, the public learned why he had fought to hard to keep them away from investigators. During meetings that day, June 23, with former chief of staff H.R. Halderman, Nixon approved plans to block the FBI's investigation of the Watergate burglary. It was the smoking gun.

Hours after the Court's ruling, the House Judiciary Committee met for its most extraordinary session in more than a century. Television sets across the country were tuned into the proceedings as senior committee members offered opening remarks in a crowded committee room in the Rayburn House Office Building.

Freshman Representative Barbara Jordan, one of forty committee members, was reluctant to give a speech, despite the presence of television and a national audience. She thought the deliberations were far too grave for political grandstanding. But after listening to her more experienced colleagues during the opening session, she decided to compose remarks to be delivered the following day.

She took as her cue several citations of the Constitution's famous preamble, which began with the words, "We the people." It occurred to her that those who wrote the document did not include people like her, a woman and an African-American, in their definition of "the people." And yet here she was, sitting in judgment of a president.

Her words on July 25, 1974, have been compared favorably to the power and eloquence of Winston Churchill. Speaking with barely contained emotion, she placed the narrative of impeachment in the story of America's struggle to achieve true equality. And she laid out, with rich, righteous language, the Constitutional case against Richard Nixon.

The committee voted two days later to recommend impeachment. Nixon resigned on August 9.

▼ ▼ ▼

T HANK you, Mr. Chairman.

Mr. Chairman, I join my colleague Mr. Rangel in thanking you for giving the junior members of this committee the glorious opportunity of sharing the pain of this inquiry. Mr. Chairman, you are a strong man, and it has not been easy but we have tried as best we can to give you as much assistance as possible.

Earlier today, we heard the beginning of the Preamble to the Constitution of the United States: "We, the people." It's a very eloquent beginning. But when that document was completed on the seventeenth of September in 1787, I was not included in that "We, the people." I felt somehow for many years that George Washington and Alexander Hamilton just left me out by mistake. But through the process of amendment, interpretation, and court decision, I have finally been included in "We, the people."

Today I am an inquisitor. An hyperbole would not be fictional and would not overstate the solemness that I feel right now. My faith in the Constitution is whole; it is complete; it is total. And I am not going to sit here and be an idle spectator to the diminution, the subversion, the destruction, of the Constitution.

"Who can so properly be the inquisitors for the nation as the representatives of the nation themselves?" "The subjects of its jurisdiction are those offenses which proceed from the misconduct of public men."? And that's what we're talking about. In other words, [the jurisdiction comes] from the abuse or violation of some public trust.

It is wrong, I suggest, it is a misreading of the Constitution for any member here to assert that for a member to vote for an article of impeachment means that that member must be convinced that the President should be removed from office. The Constitution doesn't say that. The powers relating to impeachment are an essential check in the hands of the body of the legislature against and upon the encroachments of the executive. The division between the two branches of the legislature, the House and the Senate, assigning to the one the right to accuse and to the other the right to judge, the framers of this Constitution were very astute. They did not make the accusers and the judges the same person.

We know the nature of impeachment. We've been talking about it awhile now. It is chiefly designed for the President and his high ministers to somehow be called into account. It is designed to "bridle" the executive if he engages in excesses. "It is designed as a method of national inquest into the conduct of public men."? The framers confided in the Congress the power if need be, to remove the President in order to strike a delicate balance between a President swollen with power and grown tyrannical, and preservation of the independence of the executive.

The nature of impeachment: a narrowly channeled exception to the separation-of-powers maxim. The Federal Convention of 1787 said that. It limited impeachment to high crimes and misdemeanors and discounted and opposed the term "maladministration." "It is to be used only for great misdemeanors," so it was said in the North Carolina ratification convention. And in the Virginia ratification convention: "We do not trust our liberty to a particular branch. We need one branch to check the other."

"No one need be afraid"—the North Carolina ratification convention—"No one need be afraid that officers who commit oppression will pass with immunity." "Prosecutions of impeachments will seldom fail to agitate the passions of the whole community," said Hamilton in the Federalist Papers, number 65. "We divide into parties more or less friendly or inimical to the accused."? I do not mean political parties in that sense.

The drawing of political lines goes to the motivation behind impeachment; but impeachment must proceed within the confines of the constitutional term "high crime[s] and misdemeanors." Of the impeachment process, it was Woodrow Wilson who said that "Nothing short of the grossest offenses against the plain law of the land will suffice to give them speed and effectiveness. Indignation so great as to overgrow party interest may secure a conviction; but nothing else can."

Common sense would be revolted if we engaged upon this process for petty reasons. Congress has a lot to do: Appropriations, Tax Reform, Health Insurance, Campaign Finance Reform, Housing, Environmental Protection, Energy Sufficiency, Mass Transportation. Pettiness cannot be allowed to stand in the face of such overwhelming problems. So today we are not being petty. We are trying to be big, because the task we have before us is a big one.

This morning, in a discussion of the evidence, we were told that the evidence which purports to support the allegations of misuse of the CIA by the President is thin. We're told that that evidence is insufficient. What that recital of the evidence this morning did not include is what the President did know on June the 23rd, 1972.

The President did know that it was Republican money, that it was money from the Committee for the Re-Election of the President, which was found in the possession of one of the burglars arrested on June the 17th. What the President did know on the 23rd of June was the prior activities of E. Howard Hunt, which included his participation in the break-in of Daniel Ellsberg's psychiatrist, which included Howard Hunt's participation in the Dita Beard ITT affair, which included Howard Hunt's fabrication of cables designed to discredit the Kennedy Administration.

We were further cautioned today that perhaps these proceedings ought to be delayed because certainly there would be new evidence forthcoming from the President of the United States. There has not even been an obfuscated indication that this committee would receive any additional materials from the President. The committee subpoena is outstanding, and if the President wants to supply that material, the committee sits here. The fact is that on yesterday, the American people waited with great anxiety for eight hours, not knowing whether their President would obey an order of the Supreme Court of the United States.

At this point, I would like to juxtapose a few of the impeachment criteria with some of the actions the President has engaged in. Impeachment criteria: James Madison, from the Virginia ratification convention. "If the President be connected in any suspicious manner with any person and there be grounds to believe that he will shelter him, he may be impeached."

We have heard time and time again that the evidence reflects the payment to defendants money. The President had knowledge that these funds were being paid and these were funds collected for the 1972 presidential campaign. We know that the President met with Mr. Henry Petersen twenty-seven times to discuss matters related to Watergate, and immediately thereafter met with the very persons who were implicated in the information Mr. Petersen was receiving. The words are: "If the President is connected in any suspicious manner with any person and there be grounds to believe that he will shelter that person, he may be impeached."

Justice Story: "Impeachment" is intended for occasional and extraordinary cases where a superior power acting for the whole people is put into operation to protect their rights and rescue their liberties from violations." We know about the Huston plan. We know about the break-in of the psychiatrist's office. We know that there was absolute complete direction on September 3rd when the President indicated that a surreptitious entry had been made in Dr. Fielding's office, after having met with Mr. Ehrlichman and Mr. Young. "Protect their rights." "Rescue their liberties from violation."

The Carolina ratification convention impeachment criteria: those are impeachable "who behave amiss or betray their public trust."4 Beginning shortly after the Watergate break-in and continuing to the present time, the President has engaged in a series of public statements and actions designed to thwart the lawful investigation by government prosecutors. Moreover, the President has made public announcements and assertions bearing on the Watergate case, which the evidence will show he knew to be false. These assertions, false assertions, impeachable, those who misbehave. Those who "behave amiss or betray the public trust."

James Madison again at the Constitutional Convention: "A President is impeachable if he attempts to subvert the Constitution." The Constitution charges the President with the task of taking care that the laws be faithfully executed, and yet the President has counseled his aides to commit perjury, willfully disregard the secrecy of grand jury proceedings, conceal surreptitious entry, attempt to compromise a federal judge, while publicly displaying his cooperation with the processes of criminal justice. "A President is impeachable if he attempts to subvert the Constitution."

If the impeachment provision in the Constitution of the United States will not reach the offenses charged here, then perhaps that eighteenth century Constitution should be abandoned to a twentieth century paper shredder.

Has the President committed offenses, and planned, and directed, and acquiesced in a course of conduct which the Constitution will not tolerate? That's the question. We know that. We know the question. We should now forthwith proceed to answer the question. It is reason, and not passion, which must guide our deliberations, guide our debate, and guide our decision.

I yield back the balance of my time, Mr. Chairman.

46: Anwar Sadat Addresses
the Israeli Knesset
"A bold Drive Towards New Horizons"
Jerusalem, November 20, 1977

On October 21, 1977, U.S. President Jimmy Carter met with his top foreign policy and national security aides over breakfast to discuss the latest turn in a winding road that Carter hoped would lead to peace in the Middle East. In the months since taking office in January, Carter had made the Middle East one of his top priorities, seeking to invite all parties—including the Palestinians—for comprehensive talks in Geneva, Switzerland. Carter's broad approach represented a change in American policy towards the Middle East. Previously, Washington had sought to act as a mediator in bi-lateral talks between Israel and neighboring Arab nations.

Carter's approach was complicated, all the more so because it envisioned the U.S. and the Soviet Union and its allies as partners in the mediation process. The Middle East had served as one of many global stages for Cold War conflict; Carter hoped the two superpowers could now use their influence to achieve stability in a region in which both nations had vital interests.

The Carter Administration's road map to Geneva was strewn with obstacles, making progress slow and painful. A U.S.-authored working paper outlining the proposed talks met with suspicion in the Arab world because it was perceived to be a collaborative effort with the Israelis and not a disinterested statement of principles. Among those who rejected to the working paper was Egypt's President, Anwar el-Sadat.

Sadat, the son of a poor Egyptian family, rose to power during the regime of Gamal Abdel Nassar, the charismatic army officer who helped throw off British rule in Egypt after World War II and later seized the Suez Canal in defiance of Britain and France. Sadat succeeded Nassar as Egypt's president in 1970, purged the government of many of his mentor's allies, and won immense popularity in 1973 when Egypt and Syria attacked Israel in 1973 in an attempt to recapture land lost during the Six Day War in 1967.

Egypt won several early victories before being pushed back in the Sinai peninsula, marking the country and its leader as a formidable power in the region.

Four years later, and more than thirty years after the Arab world tried in vain to crush Israel at birth in 1948, Anwar el-Sadat was growing impatient with the status quo and with the broad American attempt to change that status quo. Carter was aware of Sadat's dissatisfaction and of the importance of Egypt in any attempt to bring multiple parties to Geneva. So, on October 22, after Carter met with aides to discuss the prospects for Geneva, the president composed a hand-written note to Sadat asking for his support for the U.S.-led effort. "The time has now come to move forward," Carter wrote, "and your early public endorsement of our approach is extremely important . . ."[1]

Carter's letter was hand-delivered to Sadat, who, unknown to Carter and the Americans, already was engaged in secret conversations with Israel. In later years, Sadat said that Carter's letter inspired him to think about an entirely different way of moving forward. Even as the letter led to further communications between Cairo and Washington over the proposed Geneva conference, Sadat focused on his own solution to the stalemate: An official visit to Jerusalem, the capital of Israel.

At the time, no Arab nation recognized Israel and the partition of Palestine which had created the Jewish state in 1948. Four wars between Israel and its neighbors resulted in humiliating defeats for the more numerous Arabs, but no formal concessions and no peace treaties. Sadat sent a message to Washington in late October promising of a "bold step."[2] Several days later, he elaborated with a proposal to convene an extraordinary conference in East Jerusalem—where most of the city's Arab's lived—that would include the leaders of the Soviet Union and communist China as well as regional representatives. He said he would make a formal announcement of his plan when he spoke to Egypt's legislature on November 9. But Carter rejected Sadat's proposal, re-emphasizing the U.S. push for a meeting in Geneva.

Sadat gave his speech anyway, but it did not contain the East Jerusalem proposal. Instead, he offered a far more dramatic gesture. Emphasizing the need for regional peace, he said: "Israel will be astonished when it hears me saying now before you that I am ready to go to their house, to the Knesset itself, and to talk to them."[3]

Israel was astonished, indeed. And so was the rest of the world, especially Sadat's fellow Arabs. Sadat's daughter, Camelia Sadat, later noted that in "the Arab world . . . many voices were raised against Father's 'treachery.' Reportedly, even Syrian government officials called for his assassination."[4] Outrage spread beyond the Middle East; several Eastern-bloc nations aligned with the Soviet Union threatened war with Egypt if Sadat made a separate peace with America's ally, Israel.

In Jerusalem, amid the astonishment, Israeli Prime Minister Menahem Begin seized on the opportunity. Begin was a one-time guerilla commander whose campaign of terrorism helped persuade the British to withdraw its troops from Palestine in 1948, leading to Israel's creation. He envisioned a greater Israel that included Jewish settlements in areas seized from Arabs during the 1967 war. His response to Sadat was, then, carefully measured. Israel would not withdraw from those seized territories, nor would it accept a separate Palestinian state, as Sadat suggested in his November 9 speech. As long as Sadat understood Israel's position, Begin said, he would be welcome to visit Jerusalem. In an extraordinary radio address to Sadat's people, Begin said Israel wanted no further wars with Egypt. "It will be a pleasure to welcome and receive your President with the traditional hospitality you and we have inherited from our common father, Abraham," Begin said.[5]

The opening was made. But details were lacking. The Carter Administration found itself on the sidelines after months of trying to arrange a regional conference. Instead, Israel and Egypt embarked on a course of their own.

Three days after Begin's radio speech, Sadat appeared on American television, interviewed by the nation's leading broadcast journalist, Walter Cronkite. Sadat told him that he was ready to make the trip to Jerusalem within a week of receiving an official invitation.

That invitation arrived the following day, on November 15. The date was set: Arrival at Ben-Gurion Airport on Saturday, November 19, followed by a speech to the Knesset the following afternoon.

The weekend visit inspired scenes few thought possible, even after Sadat's speech of November 9. Israeli crowds waved Egyptian flags, and an Israeli band played the Egyptian national anthem at official ceremonies. Begin, an unreconstructed Zionist, and Sadat, who helped launch a surprise attack on Israel in 1973, met privately to discuss a bilateral peace process. Israeli dignitaries and security officers escorted Sadat to the Al Aqsa mosque in East Jerusalem and Yad Vashem, a monument to Holocaust victims.

Sadat arrived at the Knesset at around four o'clock on Sunday, November 20. Legislators rose to their feet and cheered him, acknowledging his courage in taking a step no other Arab leader dared make. His hour-long speech, delivered in Arabic, did not entirely please his audience. Sadat demanded that Israel abandon territory it gained in the 1967 war and he advocated a Palestinian state at a time when Israel was opposed to such an entity. Still, his overall message of the need for peace, indeed, his very presence in Israel, provided the inspiration for historic talks at Camp David, Maryland, in 1978 and the signing of a treaty between Israel and Egypt, the first of its kind between the Jewish state and an Arab neighbor.

Sadat's courage cost him his life. He was assassinated in 1981 by hardliners in the Egyptian army.

▼ ▼ ▼

IN the name of God, Mr. Speaker of the Knesset, ladies and gentlemen, allow me first to thank deeply the Speaker of the Knesset for affording me this opportunity to address you....

I come to you today on solid ground to shape a new life and to establish peace. We all love this land, the land of God, we all, Moslems, Christians and Jews, all worship God....

I do not blame all those who received my decision when I announced it to the entire world before the Egyptian People's Assembly. I do not blame all those who received my decision with surprise and even with amazement, some gripped even by violent surprise. Still others interpreted it as political, to camouflage my intentions of launching a new war.

I would go so far as to tell you that one of my aides at the presidential office contacted me at a late hour following my return home from the People's Assembly and sounded worried as he asked me: "Mr. President, what would be our reaction if Israel actually extended an invitation to you?"

I replied calmly: "I would accept it immediately. I have declared that I would go to the end of the earth. I would go to Israel, for I want to put before the people of Israel all the facts...." No one could have ever conceived that the president of the biggest Arab state, which bears the heaviest burden and the main responsibility pertaining to the cause of war and peace in the Middle East, should declare his readiness to go to the land of the adversary while we were still in a state of war.

We all still bear the consequences of four fierce wars waged within thirty years. All this at the time when the families of the 1973 October war are still mourning under the cruel pain of bereavement of father, son, husband and brother.

As I have already declared, I have not consulted as far as this decision is concerned with any of my colleagues or brothers, the Arab heads of state or the confrontation states.

Most of those who contacted me following the declaration of this decision expressed their objection because of the feeling of utter suspicion and absolute lack of confidence between the Arab states and the Palestine people on the one hand and Israel on the other that still surges in us all.

Many months in which peace could have been brought about have been wasted over differences and fruitless discussions on the procedure of convening the Geneva conference. All have shared suspicion and absolute lack of confidence.

But to be absolutely frank with you, I took this decision after long thought, knowing that it constitutes a great risk, for God Almighty has made it my fate to assume responsibility on behalf of the Egyptian people, to share in the responsibility of the Arab nation, the main duty of which, dictated by responsibility, is to exploit all and every means in a bid to save my Egyptian Arab people and the pan-Arab nation from the horrors of new suffering and destructive wars, the dimensions of which are foreseen only by God Himself.

After long thinking, I was convinced that the obligation of responsibility before God and before the people make it incumbent upon me that I should go to the far corners of the world, even to Jerusalem to address members of the Knesset and acquaint them with all the facts surging in me, then I would let you decide for yourselves....

Ladies and gentlemen, there are moments in the lives of nations and peoples when it is incumbent upon those known for their wisdom and clarity of vision to survey the problem, with all its complexities and vain memories, in a bold drive towards new horizons.

Those who like us are shouldering the same responsibilities entrusted to us are the first who should have the courage to make determining decisions that are consonant with the magnitude of the circumstances. We must all rise above all forms of obsolete theories of superiority, and the most important thing is never to forget that infallibility is the prerogative of God alone.

If I said that I wanted to avert from all the Arab people the horrors of shocking and destructive wars I must sincerely declare before you that I have the same feelings and bear the same responsibility towards all and every man on earth, and certainly towards the Israeli people.

Any life that is lost in war is a human life be it that of an Arab or an Israeli. A wife who becomes a widow is a human being entitled to a happy family life, whether she be an Arab or an Israeli.

Innocent children who are deprived of the care and compassion of their parents are ours. They are ours, be they living on Arab or Israeli land.

They command our full responsibility to afford them a comfortable life today and tomorrow.

For the sake of them all, for the sake of the lives of all our sons and brothers, for the sake of affording our communities the opportunity to work for the progress and happiness of man, feeling secure and with the right to a dignified life, for the generations to come, for a smile on the face of every child born in our land, for all that I have taken my decision to come to you, despite all the hazards, to deliver my address.

I have shouldered the prerequisites of the historic responsibility and therefore I declared on February 4, 1971, that I was willing to sign a peace agreement with Israel. This was the first declaration made by a responsible Arab official since the outbreak of the Arab-Israeli conflict. Motivated by all these factors dictated by the responsibilities of leadership, on October 16, 1973, before the Egyptian People's Assembly, I called for an international conference to establish permanent peace based on justice. I was not heard.

I was in the position of a man pleading for peace or asking for a cease-fire. Motivated by the duties of history and leadership, I signed the first disengagement agreement, followed by the second disengagement agreement at Sinai.

Then we proceeded, trying both open and closed doors in a bid to find a certain road leading to a durable and just peace.

We opened our heart to the peoples of the entire world to make them understand our motivations and objectives and actually to convince them of the fact that we are advocates of justice and peacemakers. Motivated by all these factors, I also decided to come to you with an open mind and an open heart and with a conscious determination so that we might establish permanent peace based on justice....

Ladies and gentlemen, let us be frank with each other. Using straightforward words and a clear conception with no ambiguity, let us be frank with each other today while the entire world, both East and West, follows these unparalleled moments, which could prove to be a radical turning point in the history of this part of the world if not in the history of the world as a whole.

Let us be frank with each other, let us be frank with each other as we answer this important question.

How can we achieve permanent peace based on justice? Well, I have come to you carrying my clear and frank answer to this big question, so that the people in Israel as well as the entire world may hear it....

Before I proclaim my answer, I wish to assure you that in my clear and frank answer I am availing myself of a number of facts that no one can deny.

The first fact is that no one can build his happiness at the expense of the misery of others.

The second fact: never have I spoken, nor will I ever speak, with two tongues; never have I adopted, nor will I ever adopt, two policies. I never deal with anyone except in one tongue, one policy and with one face.

The third fact: direct confrontation is the nearest and most successful method to reach a clear objective.

The fourth fact: the call for permanent and just peace based on respect for United Nations resolutions has now become the call of the entire world. It has become the expression of the will of the international community, whether in official capitals where policies are made and decisions taken, or at the level of the world public opinion, which influences policymaking and decision-taking.

The fifth fact, and this is probably the clearest and most prominent, is that the Arab nation, in its drive for permanent peace based on justice, does not proceed from a position of weakness. On the contrary, it has the power and stability for a sincere will for peace. The Arab declared intention stems from an awareness prompted by a heritage of civilization, that to avoid an inevitable disaster that will befall us, you and the whole world, there is no alternative to the establishment of permanent peace based on justice, peace that is not swayed by suspicion or jeopardized by ill intentions.

In the light of these facts, which I meant to place before you the way I see them, I would also wish to warn you, in all sincerity I warn you, against some thoughts that could cross your minds.

Frankness makes it incumbent upon me to tell you the following:

First, I have not come here for a separate agreement between Egypt and Israel. This is not part of the policy of Egypt. The problem is not that of Egypt and Israel.An interim peace between Egypt and Israel, or between any Arab confrontation state and Israel, will not bring permanent peace based on justice in the entire region.Rather, even if peace between all the confrontation states and Israel were achieved in the absence of a just solution of the Palestinian problem, never will there be that durable and just peace upon which the entire world insists.

Second, I have not come to you to seek a partial peace, namely to terminate the state of belligerency at this stage and put off the entire problem to a subsequent stage. This is not the radical solution that would steer us to permanent peace.Equally, I have not come to you for a third disengagement agreement in Sinai or in Golan or the West Bank.For this would mean that we are merely delaying the ignition of the fuse. It would also mean that we are lacking the courage to face peace, that we are too weak to shoulder the burdens and responsibilities of a durable peace based upon justice.

I have come to you so that together we should build a durable peace based on justice to avoid the shedding of one single drop of blood by both sides. It is for this reason that I have proclaimed my readiness to go to the farthest corner of the earth.

Here I would go back to the big question.

How can we achieve a durable peace based on justice? In my opinion, and I declare it to the whole world, from this forum, the answer is neither difficult nor is it impossible despite long years of feuds, blood, faction, strife, hatreds and deep-rooted animosity....

You want to live with us, in this part of the world.

In all sincerity I tell you we welcome you among us with full security and safety. This in itself is a tremendous turning point, one of the landmarks of a decisive historical change. We used to reject you. We had our reasons and our fears, yes.

We refused to meet with you, anywhere, yes.

We were together in international conferences and organizations and our representatives did not, and still do not, exchange greetings with you. Yes. This has happened and is still happening.

It is also true that we used to set as a precondition for any negotiations with you a mediator who would meet separately with each party.

Yes. Through this procedure the talks of the first and second disengagement agreements took place.

Our delegates met in the first Geneva conference without exchanging a direct word, yes, this has happened.

Yet today I tell you, and I declare it to the whole world, that we accept to live with you in permanent peace based on justice. We do not want to encircle you or be encircled ourselves by destructive missiles ready for launching, nor by the shells of grudges and hatreds.

I have announced on more than one occasion that Israel has become a fait accompli, recognized by the world, and that the two superpowers have undertaken the responsibility for its security and the defense of its existence. As we really and truly seek peace we really and truly welcome you to live among us in peace and security.

There was a huge wall between us that you tried to build up over a quarter of a century but it was destroyed in 1973. It was the wall of an implacable and escalating psychological warfare.

It was a wall of the fear of the force that could sweep the entire Arab nation. It was a wall of propaganda that we were a nation reduced to immobility. Some of you have gone as far as to say that even for 50 years to come, the Arabs will not regain their strength. It was a wall that always threatened with a long arm that could reach and strike anywhere. It was a wall that warned us of extermination and annihilation if we tried to use our legitimate rights to liberate the occupied territories.

Together we have to admit that that wall fell and collapsed in 1973. Yet, there remains another wall. This wall constitutes a psychological barrier between us, a barrier of suspicion, a barrier of rejection; a barrier of fear, or deception, a barrier of hallucination without any action, deed or decision.

A barrier of distorted and eroded interpretation of every event and statement. It is this psychological barrier that I described in official statements as constituting 70 percent of the whole problem.

Today, through my visit to you, I ask why don't we stretch out our hands with faith and sincerity so that together we might destroy this barrier? Why shouldn't our and your will meet with faith and sincerity so that together we might remove all suspicion of fear, betrayal and bad intentions?

Why don't we stand together with the courage of men and the boldness of heroes who dedicate themselves to a sublime aim? Why don't we stand together with the same courage and daring to erect a huge edifice of peace?

An edifice that builds and does not destroy. An edifice that serves as a beacon for generations to come with the human message for construction, development and the dignity of man.

Ladies and gentlemen, to tell you the truth, peace cannot be worth its name unless it is based on justice and not on the occupation of the land of others. It would not be right for you to demand for yourselves what you deny to others. With all frankness and in the spirit that has prompted me to come to you today, I tell you you have to give up once and for all the dreams of conquest and give up the belief that force is the best method for dealing with the Arabs.

' You should clearly understand the lesson of confrontation between you and us. Expansion does not pay. To speak frankly, our land does not yield itself to bargaining, it is not even open to argument....

We cannot accept any attempt to take away or accept to seek one inch of it nor can we accept the principle of debating or bargaining over it.

I sincerely tell you also that before us today lies the appropriate chance for peace. If we are really serious in our endeavor for peace, it is a chance that may never come again. It is a chance that if lost or wasted, the resulting slaughter would bear the curse of humanity and of history.

What is peace for Israel? It means that Israel lives in the region with her Arab neighbors in security and safety. Is that logical? I say yes. It means that Israel lives within its borders, secure against any aggression. Is that logical? And I say yes. It means that Israel obtains all kinds of guarantees that will ensure these two factors. To this demand, I say yes.

Beyond that we declare that we accept all the international guarantees you envisage and accept. We declare that we accept all the guarantees you want from the two superpowers or from either of them or from the Big Five or from some of them. Once again, I declare clearly and unequivocally that we agree to any guarantees you accept, because in return we shall receive the same guarantees.

In short then, when we ask what is peace for Israel, the answer would be that Israel lives within her borders, among her Arab neighbors in safety and security, within the framework of all the guarantees she accepts and that are offered to her.

But, how can this be achieved? How can we reach this conclusion that would lead us to permanent peace based on justice? There are facts that should be faced with courage and clarity. There are Arab territories that Israel has occupied and still occupies by force. We insist on complete withdrawal from these territories, including Arab Jerusalem.

I have come to Jerusalem, the city of peace, which will always remain as a living embodiment of coexistence among believers of the three religions. It is inadmissible that anyone should conceive the special status of the city of Jerusalem within the framework of annexation or expansionism. It should be a free and open city for all believers.

Above all, this city should not be severed from those who have made it their abode for centuries. Instead of reviving the precedent of the Crusades, we should revive the spirit of Omar Ibn al-Khattab and Saladin, namely the spirit of tolerance and respect for right.

The holy shrines of Islam and Christianity are not only places of worship but a living testimony of our interrupted presence here. Politically, spiritually and intellectually, here let us make no mistake about the importance and reverence we Christians and Moslems attach to Jerusalem.

Let me tell you without the slightest hesitation that I have not come to you under this roof to make a request that your troops evacuate the occupied territories. Complete withdrawal from the Arab territories occupied after 1967 is a logical and undisputed fact. Nobody should plead for that. Any talk about permanent peace based on justice and any move to ensure our coexistence in peace and security in this part of the world would become meaningless while you occupy Arab territories by force of arms.

For there is no peace that could be built on the occupation of the land of others, otherwise it would not be a serious peace. Yet this is a foregone conclusion that is not open to the passion of debate if intentions are sincere or if endeavors to establish a just and durable peace for our and for your generations to come are genuine.

As for the Palestine cause, nobody could deny that it is the crux of the entire problem. Nobody in the world could accept today slogans propagated here in Israel, ignoring the existence of a Palestinian people and questioning even their whereabouts. Because the Palestinian people and their legitimate rights are no longer denied today by anybody; that is nobody who has the ability of judgment can deny or ignore it. It is an acknowledged fact, perceived by the world community, both in the East and in the West, with support and recognition in international documents and official statements. It is of no use to anybody to turn deaf ears to its resounding voice, which is being heard day and night, or to overlook its historical reality.

Even the United States of America, your first ally, which is absolutely committed to safeguard Israel's security and existence and which offered and still offers Israel every moral, material and military support. I say, even the United States has opted to face up to reality and admit that the Palestinian people are entitled to legitimate rights and that the Palestine problem is the cause and essence of the conflict and that so long as it continues to be unresolved, the conflict will continue to aggravate, reaching new dimensions.

In all sincerity I tell you that there can be no peace without the Palestinians. It is a grave error of unpredictable consequences to overlook or brush aside this cause.

I shall not indulge in past events such as the Balfour Declaration sixty years ago. You are well acquainted with the relevant text. If you have found the moral and legal justification to set up a national home on a land that did not all belong to you, it is incumbent upon you to show understanding of the insistence of the people of Palestine for establishment once again of a state on their land. When some extremists ask the Palestinians to give up the sublime objective, this in fact means asking them to renounce their identity and every hope for the future.

I hail the Israeli voices that called for the recognition of the Palestinian people's right to achieve and safeguard peace.

Here I tell you, ladies and gentlemen, that it is no use to refrain from recognizing the Palestinian people and their right to statehood as their right of return. We, the Arabs, have faced this experience before with you. And with the reality of the Israeli existence, the struggle that took us from war to war, from victims to more victims, until you and we have today reached the edge of a horrible abyss and a terrifying disaster unless, together, we seize this opportunity today of a durable peace based on justice.

You have to face reality bravely, as I have done. There can never be any solution to a problem by evading it or turning a deaf ear to it. Peace cannot last if attempts are made to impose fantasy concepts on which the world has turned its back and announced its unanimous call for the respect of rights and facts....

Direct confrontation and straightforwardness are the shortcuts and the most successful way to reach a clear objective. Direct confrontation concerning the Palestinian problem and tackling it in one single language with a view to achieving a durable and just peace lie in the establishment of that peace. With all the guarantees you demand, there should be no fear of a newly born state that needs the assistance of all countries of the world.

When the bells of peace ring there will be no hands to beat the drums of war. Even if they existed, they would be stilled.

Conceive with me a peace agreement in Geneva that we would herald to a world thirsting for peace. A peace agreement based on the following points.

Ending the occupation of the Arab territories occupied in 1967.

Achievement of the fundamental rights of the Palestinian people and their right to self-determination, including their right to establish their own state.

The right of all states in the area to live in peace within their boundaries, their secure boundaries, which will be secured and guaranteed through procedures to be agreed upon, which will provide appropriate security to international boundaries in addition to appropriate international guarantees.

Commitment of all states in the region to administer the relations among them in accordance with the objectives and principles of the United Nations Charter. Particularly the principles concerning the non-use of force and a solution of differences among them by peaceful means.

Ending the state of belligerence in the region.

Ladies and gentlemen, peace is not a mere endorsement of written lines. Rather it is a rewriting of history. Peace is not a game of calling for peace to defend certain whims or hide certain admissions. Peace in its essence is a dire struggle against all and every ambition and whim.

Perhaps the example taken and experienced, taken from ancient and modern history, teaches that missiles, warships and nuclear weapons cannot establish security. Instead they destroy what peace and security build.

For the sake of our peoples and for the sake of the civilization made by man, we have to defend man everywhere against rule by the force of arms so that we may endow the rule of humanity with all the power of the values and principles that further the sublime position of mankind.

Allow me to address my call from this rostrum to the people of Israel. I pledge myself with true and sincere words to every man, woman and child in Israel. I tell them, from the Egyptian people who bless this sacred mission of peace, I convey to you the message of peace of the Egyptian people, who do not harbor fanaticism and whose sons, Moslems, Christians and Jews, live together in a state of cordiality, love and tolerance.

This is Egypt, whose people have entrusted me with their sacred message. A message of security, safety and peace to every man, woman and child in Israel. I say, encourage your leadership to struggle for peace. Let all endeavors be channeled towards building a huge stronghold for peace instead of building destructive rockets.

Introduce to the entire world the image of the new man in this area so that he might set an example to the man of our age, the man of peace everywhere. Ring the bells for your sons. Tell them that those wars were the last of wars and the end of sorrows. Tell them that we are entering upon a new beginning, a new life, a life of love, prosperity, freedom and peace.

You, sorrowing mother, you, widowed wife, you, the son who lost a brother or a father, all the victims of wars, fill the air and space with recitals of peace, fill bosoms and hearts with the aspirations of peace. Make a reality that blossoms and lives. Make hope a code of conduct and endeavor....

I have chosen to set aside all precedents and traditions known by warring countries. In spite of the fact that occupation of Arab territories is still there, the declaration of my readiness to proceed to Israel came as a great surprise that stirred many feelings and confounded many minds. Some of them even doubted its intent.

Despite all that, the decision was inspired by all the clarity and purity of belief and with all the true passions of my people's will and intentions, and I have chosen this road, considered by many to be the most difficult road.

I have chosen to come to you with an open heart and an open mind. I have chosen to give this great impetus to all international efforts exerted for peace. I have chosen to present to you, in your own home, the realities, devoid of any scheme or whim. Not to maneuver, or win a round, but for us to win together, the most dangerous of rounds embattled in modern history, the battle of permanent peace based on justice.

It is not my battle alone. Nor is it the battle of the leadership in Israel alone. It is the battle of all and every citizen in all our territories, whose right it is to live in peace. It is the commitment of conscience and responsibility in the hearts of millions.

When I put forward this initiative, many asked what is it that I conceived as possible to achieve during this visit and what my expectations were. And as I answer the questions, I announce before you that I have not thought of carrying out this initiative from the precepts of what could be achieved during this visit. And I have come here to deliver a message. I have delivered the message and may God be my witness. . . .

I come to you today on solid ground to shape a new life and to establish peace. We all love this land, the land of God, we all, Moslems, Christians and Jews, all worship God. . . .

I do not blame all those who received my decision when I announced it to the entire world before the Egyptian People's Assembly. I do not blame all those who received my decision with surprise and even with amazement, some gripped even by violent surprise. Still others interpreted it as political, to camouflage my intentions of launching a new war.

I would go so far as to tell you that one of my aides at the presidential office contacted me at a late hour following my return home from the People's Assembly and sounded worried as he asked me: "Mr. President, what would be our reaction if Israel actually extended an invitation to you?"

I replied calmly: "I would accept it immediately. I have declared that I would go to the end of the earth. I would go to Israel, for I want to put before the people of Israel all the facts...." No one could have ever conceived that the president of the biggest Arab state, which bears the heaviest burden and the main responsibility pertaining to the cause of war and peace in the Middle East, should declare his readiness to go to the land of the adversary while we were still in a state of war.

We all still bear the consequences of four fierce wars waged within 30 years. All this at the time when the families of the 1973 October war are still mourning under the cruel pain of bereavement of father, son, husband and brother.

As I have already declared, I have not consulted as far as this decision is concerned with any of my colleagues or brothers, the Arab heads of state or the confrontation states.

Most of those who contacted me following the declaration of this decision expressed their objection because of the feeling of utter suspicion and absolute lack of confidence between the Arab states and the Palestine people on the one hand and Israel on the other that still surges in us all.

Many months in which peace could have been brought about have been wasted over differences and fruitless discussions on the procedure of convening the Geneva conference. All have shared suspicion and absolute lack of confidence.

But to be absolutely frank with you, I took this decision after long thought, knowing that it constitutes a great risk, for God Almighty has made it my fate to assume responsibility on behalf of the Egyptian people, to share in the responsibility of the Arab nation, the main duty of which, dictated by responsibility, is to exploit all and every means in a bid to save my Egyptian Arab people and the pan-Arab nation from the horrors of new suffering and destructive wars, the dimensions of which are foreseen only by God Himself.

After long thinking, I was convinced that the obligation of responsibility before God and before the people make it incumbent upon me that I should go to the far corners of the world, even to Jerusalem to address members of the Knesset and acquaint them with all the facts surging in me, then I would let you decide for yourselves. . . .

Ladies and gentlemen, there are moments in the lives of nations and peoples when it is incumbent upon those known for their wisdom and clarity of vision to survey the problem, with all its complexities and vain memories, in a bold drive towards new horizons.

Those who like us are shouldering the same responsibilities entrusted to us are the first who should have the courage to make determining decisions that are consonant with the magnitude of the circumstances. We must all rise above all forms of obsolete theories of superiority, and the most important thing is never to forget that infallibility is the prerogative of God alone.

If I said that I wanted to avert from all the Arab people the horrors of shocking and destructive wars I must sincerely declare before you that I have the same feelings and bear the same responsibility towards all and every man on earth, and certainly towards the Israeli people.

Any life that is lost in war is a human life be it that of an Arab or an Israeli. A wife who becomes a widow is a human being entitled to a happy family life, whether she be an Arab or an Israeli.

Innocent children who are deprived of the care and compassion of their parents are ours. They are ours, be they living on Arab or Israeli land.

They command our full responsibility to afford them a comfortable life today and tomorrow.

For the sake of them all, for the sake of the lives of all our sons and brothers, for the sake of affording our communities the opportunity to work for the progress and happiness of man, feeling secure and with the right to a dignified life, for the generations to come, for a smile on the face of every child born in our land, for all that I have taken my decision to come to you, despite all the hazards, to deliver my address.

I have shouldered the prerequisites of the historic responsibility and therefore I declared on Feb. 4, 1971, that I was willing to sign a peace agreement with Israel. This was the first declaration made by a responsible Arab official since the outbreak of the Arab- Israeli conflict. Motivated by all these factors dictated by the responsibilities of leadership, on Oct. 16, 1973, before the Egyptian People's Assembly, I called for an international conference to establish permanent peace based on justice. I was not heard.

I was in the position of a man pleading for peace or asking for a cease-fire. Motivated by the duties of history and leadership, I signed the first disengagement agreement, followed by the second disengagement agreement at Sinai.

Then we proceeded, trying both open and closed doors in a bid to find a certain road leading to a durable and just peace.

We opened our heart to the peoples of the entire world to make them understand our motivations and objectives and actually to convince them of the fact that we are advocates of justice and peacemakers. Motivated by all these factors, I also decided to come to you with an open mind and an open heart and with a conscious determination so that we might establish permanent peace based on justice. . . .

Ladies and gentlemen, let us be frank with each other. Using straightforward words and a clear conception with no ambiguity, let us be frank with each other today while the entire world, both East and West, follows these unparalleled moments, which could prove to be a radical turning point in the history of this part of the world if not in the history of the world as a whole.

Let us be frank with each other, let us be frank with each other as we answer this important question.

How can we achieve permanent peace based on justice? Well, I have come to you carrying my clear and frank answer to this big question, so that the people in Israel as well as the entire world may hear it. . . .

Before I proclaim my answer, I wish to assure you that in my clear and frank answer I am availing myself of a number of facts that no one can deny.

The first fact is that no one can build his happiness at the expense of the misery of others.

The second fact: never have I spoken, nor will I ever speak, with two tongues; never have I adopted, nor will I ever adopt, two policies. I never deal with anyone except in one tongue, one policy and with one face.

The third fact: direct confrontation is the nearest and most successful method to reach a clear objective.

The fourth fact: the call for permanent and just peace based on respect for United Nations resolutions has now become the call of the entire world. It has become the expression of the will of the international community, whether in official capitals where policies are made and decisions taken, or at the level of the world public opinion, which influences policymaking and decision-taking.

The fifth fact, and this is probably the clearest and most prominent, is that the Arab nation, in its drive for permanent peace based on justice, does not proceed from a position of weakness. On the contrary, it has the power and stability for a sincere will for peace. The Arab declared intention stems from an awareness prompted by a heritage of civilization, that to avoid an inevitable disaster that will befall us, you and the whole world, there is no alternative to the establishment of permanent peace based on justice, peace that is not swayed by suspicion or jeopardized by ill intentions.

In the light of these facts, which I meant to place before you the way I see them, I would also wish to warn you, in all sincerity I warn you, against some thoughts that could cross your minds.

Frankness makes it incumbent upon me to tell you the following:

First, I have not come here for a separate agreement between Egypt and Israel. This is not part of the policy of Egypt. The problem is not that of Egypt and Israel. An interim peace between Egypt and Israel, or between any Arab confrontation state and Israel, will not bring permanent peace based on justice in the entire region. Rather, even if peace between all the confrontation states and Israel were achieved in the absence of a just solution of the Palestinian problem, never will there be that durable and just peace upon which the entire world insists.

Second, I have not come to you to seek a partial peace, namely to terminate the state of belligerency at this stage and put off the entire problem to a subsequent stage. This is not the radical solution that would steer us to permanent peace. Equally, I have not come to you for a third disengagement agreement in Sinai or in Golan or the West Bank. For this would mean that we are merely delaying the ignition of the fuse. It would also mean that we are lacking the courage to face peace, that we are too weak to shoulder the burdens and responsibilities of a durable peace based upon justice.

I have come to you so that together we should build a durable peace based on justice to avoid the shedding of one single drop of blood by both sides. It is for this reason that I have proclaimed my readiness to go to the farthest corner of the earth.

Here I would go back to the big question.

How can we achieve a durable peace based on justice? In my opinion, and I declare it to the whole world, from this forum, the answer is neither difficult nor is it impossible despite long years of feuds, blood, faction, strife, hatreds and deep-rooted animosity. . . .

You want to live with us, in this part of the world.

In all sincerity I tell you we welcome you among us with full security and safety. This in itself is a tremendous turning point, one of the landmarks of a decisive historical change. We used to reject you. We had our reasons and our fears, yes.

We refused to meet with you, anywhere, yes.

We were together in international conferences and organizations and our representatives did not, and still do not, exchange greetings with you. Yes. This has happened and is still happening.

It is also true that we used to set as a precondition for any negotiations with you a mediator who would meet separately with each party.

Yes. Through this procedure the talks of the first and second disengagement agreements took place.

Our delegates met in the first Geneva conference without exchanging a direct word, yes, this has happened.

Yet today I tell you, and I declare it to the whole world, that we accept to live with you in permanent peace based on justice. We do not want to encircle you or be encircled ourselves by destructive missiles ready for launching, nor by the shells of grudges and hatreds.

I have announced on more than one occasion that Israel has become a fait accompli, recognized by the world, and that the two superpowers have undertaken the responsibility for its security and the defense of its existence. As we really and truly seek peace we really and truly welcome you to live among us in peace and security.

There was a huge wall between us that you tried to build up over a quarter of a century but it was destroyed in 1973. It was the wall of an implacable and escalating psychological warfare.

It was a wall of the fear of the force that could sweep the entire Arab nation. It was a wall of propaganda that we were a nation reduced to immobility. Some of you have gone as far as to say that even for 50 years to come, the Arabs will not regain their strength. It was a wall that always threatened with a long arm that could reach and strike anywhere. It was a wall that warned us of extermination and annihilation if we tried to use our legitimate rights to liberate the occupied territories.

Together we have to admit that that wall fell and collapsed in 1973. Yet, there remains another wall. This wall constitutes a psychological barrier between us, a barrier of suspicion, a barrier of rejection; a barrier of fear, or deception, a barrier of hallucination without any action, deed or decision.

A barrier of distorted and eroded interpretation of every event and statement. It is this psychological barrier that I described in official statements as constituting 70 percent of the whole problem.

Today, through my visit to you, I ask why don't we stretch out our hands with faith and sincerity so that together we might destroy this barrier? Why shouldn't our and your will meet with faith and sincerity so that together we might remove all suspicion of fear, betrayal and bad intentions?

Why don't we stand together with the courage of men and the boldness of heroes who dedicate themselves to a sublime aim? Why don't we stand together with the same courage and daring to erect a huge edifice of peace?

An edifice that builds and does not destroy. An edifice that serves as a beacon for generations to come with the human message for construction, development and the dignity of man.

Ladies and gentlemen, to tell you the truth, peace cannot be worth its name unless it is based on justice and not on the occupation of the land of others. It would not be right for you to demand for yourselves what you deny to others. With all frankness and in the spirit that has prompted me to come to you today, I tell you you have to give up once and for all the dreams of conquest and give up the belief that force is the best method for dealing with the Arabs.

You should clearly understand the lesson of confrontation between you and us. Expansion does not pay. To speak frankly, our land does not yield itself to bargaining, it is not even open to argument. . . .

We cannot accept any attempt to take away or accept to seek one inch of it nor can we accept the principle of debating or bargaining over it.

I sincerely tell you also that before us today lies the appropriate chance for peace. If we are really serious in our endeavor for peace, it is a chance that may never come again. It is a chance that if lost or wasted, the resulting slaughter would bear the curse of humanity and of history.

What is peace for Israel? It means that Israel lives in the region with her Arab neighbors in security and safety. Is that logical? I say yes. It means that Israel lives within its borders, secure against any aggression. Is that logical? And I say yes. It means that Israel obtains all kinds of guarantees that will ensure these two factors. To this demand, I say yes.

Beyond that we declare that we accept all the international guarantees you envisage and accept. We declare that we accept all the guarantees you want from the two superpowers or from either of them or from the Big Five or from some of them. Once again, I declare clearly and unequivocally that we agree to any guarantees you accept, because in return we shall receive the same guarantees.

In short then, when we ask what is peace for Israel, the answer would be that Israel lives within her borders, among her Arab neighbors in safety and security, within the framework of all the guarantees she accepts and that are offered to her.

But, how can this be achieved? How can we reach this conclusion that would lead us to permanent peace based on justice? There are facts that should be faced with courage and clarity. There are Arab territories that Israel has occupied and still occupies by force. We insist on complete withdrawal from these territories, including Arab Jerusalem.

I have come to Jerusalem, the city of peace, which will always remain as a living embodiment of coexistence among believers of the three religions. It is inadmissible that anyone should conceive the special status of the city of Jerusalem within the framework of annexation or expansionism. It should be a free and open city for all believers.

Above all, this city should not be severed from those who have made it their abode for centuries. Instead of reviving the precedent of the Crusades, we should revive the spirit of Omar Ibn al-Khattab and Saladin, namely the spirit of tolerance and respect for right.

The holy shrines of Islam and Christianity are not only places of worship but a living testimony of our interrupted presence here. Politically, spiritually and intellectually, here let us make no mistake about the importance and reverence we Christians and Moslems attach to Jerusalem.

Let me tell you without the slightest hesitation that I have not come to you under this roof to make a request that your troops evacuate the occupied territories. Complete withdrawal from the Arab territories occupied after 1967 is a logical and undisputed fact. Nobody should plead for that. Any talk about permanent peace based on justice and any move to ensure our coexistence in peace and security in this part of the world would become meaningless while you occupy Arab territories by force of arms.

For there is no peace that could be built on the occupation of the land of others, otherwise it would not be a serious peace. Yet this is a foregone conclusion that is not open to the passion of debate if intentions are sincere or if endeavors to establish a just and durable peace for our and for your generations to come are genuine.

As for the Palestine cause, nobody could deny that it is the crux of the entire problem. Nobody in the world could accept today slogans propagated here in Israel, ignoring the existence of a Palestinian people and questioning even their whereabouts. Because the Palestine people and their legitimate rights are no longer denied today by anybody; that is nobody who has the ability of judgment can deny or ignore it. It is an acknowledged fact, perceived by the world community, both in the East and in the West, with support and recognition in international documents and official statements.

It is of no use to anybody to turn deaf ears to its resounding voice, which is being heard day and night, or to overlook its historical reality.

Even the United States of America, your first ally, which is absolutely committed to safeguard Israel's security and existence and which offered and still offers Israel every moral, material and military support. I say, even the United States has opted to face up to reality and admit that the Palestinian people are entitled to legitimate rights and that the Palestine problem is the cause and essence of the conflict and that so long as it continues to be unresolved, the conflict will continue to aggravate, reaching new dimensions.

In all sincerity I tell you that there can be no peace without the Palestinians. It is a grave error of unpredictable consequences to overlook or brush aside this cause.

I shall not indulge in past events such as the Balfour Declaration 60 years ago. You are well acquainted with the relevant text. If you have found the moral and legal justification to set up a national home on a land that did not all belong to you, it is incumbent upon you to show understanding of the insistence of the people of Palestine for establishment once again of a state on their land. When some extremists ask the Palestinians to give up the sublime objective, this in fact means asking them to renounce their identity and every hope for the future.

I hail the Israeli voices that called for the recognition of the Palestinian people's right to achieve and safeguard peace.

Here I tell you, ladies and gentlemen, that it is no use to refrain from recognizing the Palestinian people and their right to statehood as their right of return. We, the Arabs, have faced this experience before with you. And with the reality of the Israeli existence, the struggle that took us from war to war, from victims to more victims, until you and we have today reached the edge of a horrible abyss and a terrifying disaster unless, together, we seize this opportunity today of a durable peace based on justice.

You have to face reality bravely, as I have done. There can never be any solution to a problem by evading it or turning a deaf ear to it. Peace cannot last if attempts are made to impose fantasy concepts on which the world has turned its back and announced its unanimous call for the respect of rights and facts. . . .

Direct confrontation and straightforwardness are the shortcuts and the most successful way to reach a clear objective. Direct confrontation concerning the Palestinian problem and tackling it in one single language with a view to achieving a durable and just peace lie in the establishment of that peace. With all the guarantees you demand, there should be no fear of a newly born state that needs the assistance of all countries of the world.

When the bells of peace ring there will be no hands to beat the drums of war. Even if they existed, they would be stilled.

Conceive with me a peace agreement in Geneva that we would herald to a world thirsting for peace. A peace agreement based on the following points.

Ending the occupation of the Arab territories occupied in 1967.

Achievement of the fundamental rights of the Palestinian people and their right to self-determination, including their right to establish their own state.

The right of all states in the area to live in peace within their boundaries, their secure boundaries, which will be secured and guaranteed through procedures to be agreed upon, which will provide appropriate security to international boundaries in addition to appropriate international guarantees.

Commitment of all states in the region to administer the relations among them in accordance with the objectives and principles of the United Nations Charter. Particularly the principles concerning the nonuse of force and a solution of differences among them by peaceful means.

Ending the state of belligerence in the region.

Ladies and gentlemen, peace is not a mere endorsement of written lines. Rather it is a rewriting of history. Peace is not a game of calling for peace to defend certain whims or hide certain admissions. Peace in its essence is a dire struggle against all and every ambition and whim.

Perhaps the example taken and experienced, taken from ancient and modern history, teaches that missiles, warships and nuclear weapons cannot establish security. Instead they destroy what peace and security build.

For the sake of our peoples and for the sake of the civilization made by man, we have to defend man everywhere against rule by the force of arms so that we may endow the rule of humanity with all the power of the values and principles that further the sublime position of mankind.

Allow me to address my call from this rostrum to the people of Israel. I pledge myself with true and sincere words to every man, woman and child in Israel. I tell them, from the Egyptian people who bless this sacred mission of peace, I convey to you the message of peace of the Egyptian people, who do not harbor fanaticism and whose sons, Moslems, Christians and Jews, live together in a state of cordiality, love and tolerance.

This is Egypt, whose people have entrusted me with their sacred message. A message of security, safety and peace to every man, woman and child in Israel. I say, encourage your leadership to struggle for peace. Let all endeavors be channeled towards building a huge stronghold for peace instead of building destructive rockets.

Introduce to the entire world the image of the new man in this area so that he might set an example to the man of our age, the man of peace everywhere. Ring the bells for your sons. Tell them that those wars were the last of wars and the end of sorrows. Tell them that we are entering upon a new beginning, a new life, a life of love, prosperity, freedom and peace.

You, sorrowing mother, you, widowed wife, you, the son who lost a brother or a father, all the victims of wars, fill the air and space with recitals of peace, fill bosoms and hearts with the aspirations of peace. Make a reality that blossoms and lives. Make hope a code of conduct and endeavor. . . .

I have chosen to set aside all precedents and traditions known by warring countries. In spite of the fact that occupation of Arab territories is still there, the declaration of my readiness to proceed to Israel came as a great surprise that stirred many feelings and confounded many minds. Some of them even doubted its intent.

Despite all that, the decision was inspired by all the clarity and purity of belief and with all the true passions of my people's will and intentions, and I have chosen this road, considered by many to be the most difficult road.

I have chosen to come to you with an open heart and an open mind. I have chosen to give this great impetus to all international efforts exerted for peace. I have chosen to present to you, in your own home, the realities, devoid of any scheme or whim. Not to maneuver, or win a round, but for us to win together, the most dangerous of rounds embattled in modern history, the battle of permanent peace based on justice.

It is not my battle alone. Nor is it the battle of the leadership in Israel alone. It is the battle of all and every citizen in all our territories, whose right it is to live in peace. It is the commitment of conscience and responsibility in the hearts of millions.

When I put forward this initiative, many asked what is it that I conceived as possible to achieve during this visit and what my expectations were. And as I answer the questions, I announce before you that I have not thought of carrying out this initiative from the precepts of what could be achieved during this visit. And I have come here to deliver a message. I have delivered the message and may God be my witness. . . .

47: Elie Weisel Pleads With Ronald Reagan

"Your Place is not There, Mr. President"

Washington, April 19, 1985

IN THE EARLY 1980'S, U.S. PRESIDENT RONALD REAGAN SOUGHT TO DEPLOY a new generation of intermediate-range nuclear missiles in Western Europe to counter a Soviet nuclear buildup in the east. The planned deployment, coming during a time of heightened Cold War tensions, inspired massive anti-nuclear demonstrations on both sides of the Atlantic Ocean. Public pressure was most intense in West Germany, where the Americans intended to install more than a hundred of the new missiles.

In the face of bitter opposition in his own country, West German Chancellor Helmut Kohl supported Reagan's plan. The missiles were installed in late 1983. The seemingly potent opposition, which rallied around the concept of a freeze on all new deployments of nuclear weapons, melted away.

Ronald Reagan warmly appreciated Kohl's support. So, when the Chancellor invited Reagan to attend ceremonies in West Germany to mark the fortieth anniversary of the end of World War II in May, 1985, the President eagerly accepted. The proposed itinerary included a visit to a German military cemetery which held the remains of soldiers who fought in defense of the Nazi regime. The cemetery was in the town of Bitburg, part of Kohl's own home constituency.

The cemetery visit was designed to symbolize reconciliation between the United States and West Germany, allies now in the battle to contain Soviet communism. But there was a political component as well: Kohl and his government faced serious challenges in local elections in 1985, and Reagan's presence at Kohl's side during the ceremonies figured to bolster the Chancellor's popularity.

The White House announced details of the Presidential visit to Bitburg in early April. The trip immediately provoked a storm of criticism from the press and from Jewish groups who objected to the notion of commemorating troops who died in defense of a genocidal regime. The criticism intensified when the press learned that among the German war dead buried in Bitburg were several dozen members of the SS, an elite corps responsible for war crimes and helping to implement Adolf Hitler's so-called "final solution"—the extermination of Europe's Jews.

A delegation of Jewish leaders met with Reagan administration officials in the White House to make the case for cancellation. Even Nancy Reagan, the President's wife and one of his most important and formidable advisors, urged her husband to change his plans. But Reagan resisted, saying that he had given his word to a friend, Chancellor Kohl. "There is no way I'll back down and run for cover," Reagan wrote in his diary. He didn't understand the controversy. "What is wrong with saying, 'Let's never be enemies again?'" The President wondered if it would be wrong for Kohl to visit the graves of U.S. soldiers in Arlington National Cemetery in Virginia.[1] Reagan's formula did not take into account that German soldiers died in defense of the Nazi regime, one of the most repugnant and murderous of any age, while U.S. soldiers died attempting to rid the world of Nazism.

Reagan refused to change his mind, but did agree to visit the Bergen-Belsen death camp, where thousands of Jews, including a Dutch teenager named Anne Frank, died. But that gesture, however welcome and important, did not still the voices of Reagan's critics.

In the midst of the controversy, in a poignant coincidence, Reagan welcomed to the White House Elie Weisel, the writer and activist who coined the word "Holocaust" to describe the mass murder of Europe's Jews during World War II. Weisel survived nearly a year of imprisonment, forced labor and inhuman deprivation in Auschwitz and other concentration camps. His mother, sister and father did not survive. Weisel bore a grim reminder of his suffering: branded onto his left arm was his camp serial number, A-7713.

Weisel, a native of Romania, came to the United States in 1955 and began a career as a witness to one of mankind's greatest crimes. He spoke and wrote about the murder of Europe's Jews long before the subject was incorporated into school curricula, academic panels, and everyday conversation. Elie Weisel forced the world to come to terms with the murder of six million Jews during the war, and he used his moral authority to condemn other genocidal regimes in the years since the fall of Nazi Germany.

In recognition of those efforts, Reagan was to present Weisel with the

Congressional Gold Medal at the White House on April 19, just three days after other Jewish leaders met with Reagan's aides to ask him to cancel the Bitburg visit. In an extraordinary bit of timing, Weisel's visit to the White House transcended the ceremony to become a moment of intense and painful confrontation between a voice for reconciliation and a witness to unspeakable horror.

As he introduced Weisel to an audience of Washington's powerful and influential gathered in the Roosevelt Room, Reagan thanked the honoree for his lifetime of labor on behalf of the voices stilled in the Nazi camps. He made no mention of his planned visit to Bitburg.

After Reagan finished his remarks, he presented Weisel with the medal and then took his seat next to his wife. The stage was Weisel's.

Reagan avoided the controversy, but Weisel would not and could not. Looking directly at the President, he delivered an impassioned argument against the Bitburg visit. Decorum and propriety might have dictated that Weisel ignore the controversy, for he was a guest of the President and was in the President's own home. He had just been presented with an award from the President.

But Weisel chose instead to confront Reagan, politely but publicly. His speech was a testament to one person's willingness to speak truth to power, directly and personally, in front of an audience more familiar with the calculated geniality of the flatterer than the moral outrage of the victim.

▼ ▼ ▼

M R. PRESIDENT, Mr. Vice President, Secretary Bennett, Mr. Agresto, Mr. Regan, very distinguished members of the Senate, my friends—and of the House:

Mr. President, speaking of reconciliation, I was very pleased that we met before so a stage of reconciliation has been set in motion between us. But then we were never on two sides; we were on the same side. We were always on the side of justice, always on the side of memory, against the SS, and against what they represent.

It was good talking to you, and I'm grateful to you for the medal. But this medal is not mine alone. It belongs to all those who remember what SS killers have done to their victims. It was given to me by the American people for my writings, teaching, and for my testimony.

When I write, I feel my invisible teachers standing over my shoulders, reading my words and judging their veracity. And while I feel responsible for the living, I feel equally responsible to the dead. Their memory dwells in my memory.

Forty years ago, a young man awoke, and he found himself an orphan in an orphaned world. What have I learned in the last forty years—small things. I learned the perils of language and those of silence. I learned that in extreme situations when human lives and dignity are at stake, neutrality is a sin. It helps the killers not the victims. I learned the meaning of solitude, Mr. President. We were alone, desperately alone. Today is April 19, and April 19, 1943, the Warsaw Ghetto rose in arms against the onslaught of the Nazis. They were so few and so young and so helpless, and nobody came to their help. And they had to fight what was then the mightiest legion in Europe. Every underground received help, except the Jewish underground. And yet, they managed to fight and resist and push back those Nazis and their accomplices for six weeks.

And yet, the leaders of the free world, Mr. President, knew everything and did so little or nothing or at least nothing specifically to save Jewish children from death.

You spoke of Jewish children, Mr. President; one million Jewish children perished. If I spent my entire life reciting their names, I would die before finishing the task. Mr. President, I have seen children—I have seen them being thrown in the flames alive. Words—they die on my lips.

So, I have learned. I have learned, I have learned the fragility of the human condition. And I'm reminded that a great moral essayist, the gentle and forceful Abe Rosenthal, having visited Auschwitz once wrote an extraordinary reportage about the persecution of Jews, and he called it, "Forgive them not Father, for they knew what they did."

I have learned that the Holocaust was a unique and uniquely Jewish event, albeit with universal implications. Not all victims were Jews, but all Jews were victims. I have learned the danger of indifference, the crime of indifference. For the opposite of love, I have learned, is not hate but indifference. Jews were killed by the enemy but betrayed by their so-called allies who found political reasons to justify their indifference or passivity.

But I've also learned that suffering confers no privileges. It all depends what one does with it. And this is why the survivors of whom you spoke, Mr. President, have tried to teach their contemporaries how to build on ruins, how to invent hope in a world that offers none, how to proclaim faith to a generation that has seen it shamed and mutilated. And I believe, we believe, that memory is the answer—perhaps the only answer.

A few days ago on the anniversary of the liberation of Buchenwald, all of us Americans watched with dismay and anger as the Soviet Union and East Germany distorted both past and present history. Mr. President, I was there; I was there when American liberators arrived, and they gave us back our lives. And what I felt for them then nourishes me to the end of my days, and will do so. If you only knew what we tried to do with them then, we who were so weak that we couldn't carry our own lives—we tried to carry them in triumph!

Mr. President, we are grateful to the American Army for liberating us. We are grateful to this country—the greatest democracy in the world, the freest nation in the world, the moral nation, the authority in the world. And we are grateful especially to this country for having offered haven and refuge and grateful to its leadership for being so friendly to Israel.

Mr. President, do you know that the Ambassador of Israel, who sits next to you, who is my friend and has been for so many years, is himself a survivor? And if you knew all the causes we fought together for the last thirty years, you could be prouder of him. And we are proud of him.

And we are grateful, of course, to Israel; we are eternally grateful to Israel for existing. We needed Israel in 1948 as we need it now. And we are grateful to Congress for its continuous philosophy of humanism and compassion for the underprivileged.

And as for yourself, Mr. President, we are so grateful to you for being a friend of the Jewish people, for trying to help the oppressed Jews in the Soviet Union and to do whatever we can to save Shcharanskiy and Abe Stolyar and Iosif Begun and Sakharov and all the dissidents who need freedom. And of course, we thank you for your support of the Jewish state of Israel.

But, Mr. President, I wouldn't be the person I am, and you wouldn't respect me for what I am, if I were not to tell you also of the sadness that is in my heart for what happened during the last week. And I am sure that you, too, are sad for the same reasons. What can I do? I belong to a traumatized generation. And to us, as to you, symbols are important. And furthermore, following our ancient tradition—and we are speaking about Jewish heritage—our tradition commands us, quote: "to speak truth to power."

So may I speak to you, Mr. President, with respect and admiration, of the events that happened. We have met four or five times, and each time I came away enriched, for I know of your commitment to humanity. And, therefore, I am convinced, as you have told us earlier when we spoke, that you were not aware of the presence of SS graves in the Bitburg cemetery. Of course, you didn't know. But now we all are aware. May I, Mr. President, if it's possible at all, implore you to do something else, to find a way, to find another way, another site. That place, Mr. President, is not your place. Your place is with the victims of the SS.

Oh, we know there are political and strategic reasons, but this issue, as all issues related to that awesome event, transcends politics and diplomacy. The issue here is not politics but good and evil. And we must never confuse them, for I have seen the SS at work, and I have seen their victims. They were my friends. They were my parents. Mr. President, there was a degree of suffering and loneliness in the concentration camps that defies imagination. Cut off from the world with no refuge anywhere; sons watched helplessly their fathers being beaten to death; mothers watched their children die of hunger. And then there was Mengele and his selections, terror, fear, isolation, torture, gas chambers, flames—flames rising to the heavens.

But, Mr. President, I know and I understand, we all do, that you seek reconciliation. So do I. So do we. And I, too, wish to attain true reconciliation with the German people. I do not believe in collective guilt, nor in collective responsibility; only the killers were guilty. Their sons and daughters are not. And I believe, Mr. President, that we can and we must work together with them and with all people. And we must work to bring peace and understanding to a tormented world that, as you know, is still awaiting redemption.

I thank you, Mr. President.

48: Ronald Reagan on the *Challenger* Disaster
"The Surly Bonds of Earth"

Washington, January 28, 1986

THE U.S. SPACE PROGRAM WAS ONE OF THE GREAT TRIUMPHS OF THE American century and a milestone in human history. From its uncertain beginnings in the late 1950's to its routine brilliance in the mid-1980's, America's space program became a symbol of mankind's quest for knowledge, love of adventure, and courage in the face of the unknown.

America, of course, was not alone in exploring the stars. Indeed, in the early 1960's, the Soviet Union's program was far more advanced. The U.S. program lagged in part because of President Dwight Eisenhower's lack of interest in space travel. Although his successor, John Kennedy, provided a vision and the necessary funds to re-launch America's entry into space, he, too, was a skeptic at first. But he also was loath to see the Soviets ahead of the U.S. in anything, never mind something so high-profile as space travel. And he came to view exploration in space as a great adventure not only for the United States but for mankind itself.

American astronauts Neil Armstrong and Buzz Aldrin landed on the moon in 1969, fulfilling Kennedy's vision of a lunar landing by the end of the 1960's. A series of additional landings followed, each carried out with remarkable precision save for one near-disaster, the flight of Apollo 13 in 1970. That mission was forced to abort plans to land on the moon when an oxygen tank exploded, crippling the spacecraft. The crew managed to return to earth safely, but not before several days of intense drama as both the crew and Mission Control in Houston, Texas, desperately improvised an emergency landing plan.

The U.S. moved away from lunar explorations in the late 1970's. In nearly two decades of exploration, the U.S. never lost an astronaut in flight, although three died in 1967 when a fire broke out in the command module of Apollo I during a routine test of equipment. While the drama of Apollo 13 demonstrated the dangers of space travel, American successes made the journeys seem routine.

In 1981, the U.S. embarked on a new phase of space exploration with the introduction of the space shuttle, a reusable spacecraft designed to transport astronauts and equipment to orbiting space stations and satellites. After several years of tests, the shuttle *Columbia* lifted off on April 12, 1981, marking the beginning of a new era in U.S. space exploration. A year later, another spacecraft, *Challenger*, joined the shuttle program.

With public interest in space travel perceived to be lagging, U.S. President Ronald Reagan announced, in 1984, the creation of a new program designed to send a teacher into space aboard the shuttle. Eleven thousand teachers applied, and after a year of consideration, the U.S. National Aeronautics and Space Administration chose a history teacher from Concord, NH, Christa McAuliffe, to be the first non-astronaut to fly into space. NASA also chose a backup for the mission, Barbara Morgan, a math and reading teacher from Idaho.

McAuliffe's presence on the mission attracted more publicity than usual. As she and her six colleagues boarded the shuttle *Challenger* on the morning of January 28 for a late-morning launch, hundreds of thousands of schoolchildren and their teachers were watching television coverage of the preparations for liftoff.

President Reagan, whose administration championed the Teacher in Space program, was scheduled to deliver his annual State of the Union address later that evening, hours after lift-off. That morning, as *Challenger's* crew prepared for takeoff, Reagan briefed Congressional leaders on his forthcoming speech. He and House Speaker Thomas ("Tip") O'Neill had a nasty exchange when the President argued that there were plenty of jobs for the nation's unemployed, but many of them simply didn't want to work. "Don't give me that crap," O'Neill, a Democrat, replied.[1] The two men glared at each other before O'Neill explained that he meant no disrespect. Later that night, in accordance with tradition, the Speaker was scheduled to introduce the President for the State of the Union message. The two men parted company under less than amiable circumstances.

After the Congressional leaders left, Reagan went back to work on his speech. Unlike so many American schoolchildren, he was not watching television when, at 11:38 a.m., the rocket carrying *Challenger* lifted off in Florida and began its journey towards the stars.

Seventy-three seconds into the flight, the spacecraft began to disintegrate. A piece of equipment called an O-ring, designed to stop hot gasses from leaking, did not work properly, in part, it was later revealed, because of cold conditions in Florida that morning. The shuttle's cabin fell back to earth, landing in the Atlantic Ocean. All seven aboard, including Christa McAuliffe, died.

Reagan learned of the catastrophe when aides burst into the Oval Office with the terrible news. After watching television replays of the awful images—the seemingly perfect launch sequence, the gentle roll of the rocket, and then the explosion of white smoke in the blue Florida sky—Reagan met with reporters, expressed his grief, and said that he would give his State of the Union message as scheduled that evening.

That plan changed, however, as the nation and the White House absorbed the magnitude of the disaster. This mission was unlike so many others in the recent past because of McAuliffe's presence on board. The nation's schoolchildren were eyewitnesses to the greatest catastrophe in the short history of space travel. By mid-afternoon, Reagan decided to scrap the State of the Union message. Instead, speechwriter Peggy Noonan was assigned the task of composing a tribute to the crew, a tribute that would include a special message of consolation to the nation's children.

The result was a poignant masterpiece that gave voice to the nation's grief while explaining to young people that great causes often entail great sacrifice. Reagan delivered the tribute at five o'clock Washington time to a national television audience. The speech's most memorable lines came at its conclusion, when Reagan incorporated phrases from a poem written by a young pilot in World War II. Although Noonan wrote the speech, Reagan would have recognized the phrases, for his actor-friend Tyrone Power carried a copy of the poem with him during his service in the U.S. Air Force during the war.

Reagan, according to biographer Richard Reeves, believed he hadn't done the speech justice. But his audience disagreed. According to Reeves, the White House was overwhelmed with messages from the public, thanking the President for his words. Tip O'Neill, the man with whom Reagan had sparred earlier in the day, later wrote that on a "trying day for all Americans . . . Ronald Reagan spoke to our highest ideals."[2]

▼ ▼ ▼

LADIES and gentlemen, I'd planned to speak to you tonight to report on the state of the union, but the events of earlier today have led me to change those plans. Today is a day for mourning and remembering. Nancy and I are pained to the core by the tragedy of the shuttle

Challenger. We know we share this pain with all of the people of our country. This is truly a national loss.

Nineteen years ago, almost to the day, we lost three astronauts in a terrible accident on the ground. But we've never lost an astronaut in flight; we've never had a tragedy like this. And perhaps we've forgotten the courage it took for the crew of the shuttle; but they, the *Challenger* Seven, were aware of the dangers, but overcame them and did their jobs brilliantly. We mourn seven heroes: Michael Smith, Dick Scobee, Judith Resnik, Ronald McNair, Ellison Onizuka, Gregory Jarvis, and Christa McAuliffe. We mourn their loss as a nation together.

For the families of the seven, we cannot bear, as you do, the full impact of this tragedy. But we feel the loss, and we're thinking about you so very much. Your loved ones were daring and brave, and they had that special grace, that special spirit that says, "Give me a challenge and I'll meet it with joy." They had a hunger to explore the universe and discover its truths. They wished to serve, and they did. They served all of us.

We've grown used to wonders in this century. It's hard to dazzle us. But for twenty-five years the United States space program has been doing just that. We've grown used to the idea of space, and perhaps we forget that we've only just begun. We're still pioneers. They, the members of the *Challenger* crew, were pioneers.

And I want to say something to the schoolchildren of America who were watching the live coverage of the shuttle's takeoff. I know it is hard to understand, but sometimes painful things like this happen. It's all part of the process of exploration and discovery. It's all part of taking a chance and expanding man's horizons. The future doesn't belong to the fainthearted; it belongs to the brave. The *Challenger* crew was pulling us into the future, and we'll continue to follow them.

I've always had great faith in and respect for our space program, and what happened today does nothing to diminish it. We don't hide our space program. We don't keep secrets and cover things up. We do it all up front and in public. That's the way freedom is, and we wouldn't change it for a minute. We'll continue our quest in space. There will be more shuttle flights and more shuttle crews and yes, more volunteers, more civilians, more teachers in space. Nothing ends here; our hopes and our journeys continue.

I want to add that I wish I could talk to every man and woman who works for NASA or who worked on this mission and tell them: "Your dedication and professionalism have moved and impressed us for decades. And we know of your anguish. We share it."

There's a coincidence today. On this day 390 years ago, the great explorer Sir Francis Drake died aboard ship off the coast of Panama. In his lifetime the great frontiers were the oceans, and a historian later said, "He lived by the sea, died on it, and was buried in it." Well, today we can say of the *Challenger* crew: Their dedication was, like Drake's, complete.

The crew of the space shuttle *Challenger* honored us by the manner in which they lived their lives. We will never forget them, nor the last time we saw them, this morning, as they prepared for their journey and waved good-bye and "slipped the surly bonds of earth" to "touch the face of God."

49: Margaret Thatcher's Sermon on the Mound
"We Must Work and Use our Talents to Create Wealth"
Edinburgh, May 21, 1988

FOR BRITONS, AS WELL AS AMERICANS, THE 1970'S WERE A DECADE OF DIS-
illusion and discontent. The ideas and policies put in place since the end of
World War II suddenly seemed inadequate, tainted, or just plain wrong.

Fears of decline were at the heart of the anxiety on both sides of the
Atlantic. The United States struggled to come to terms with defeat in
Vietnam, corruption in high places, and what commentators called a national
"malaise"—a phrase associated with a speech by President Jimmy Carter in
1979 that bemoaned the national mood but which never actually used the
phrase "malaise."

No British leader used the word, either, but a rising new political figure
certainly did not approve of the country's languid spirit and seemingly inexorable drift towards irrelevancy. Margaret Thatcher, the fifty-year-old
daughter of a shopkeeper, made history in 1975 when she was elected
leader of Britain's Conservative Party. She was the first woman to hold such
a position in one of Britain's major political parties. With the socialist Labor
Party in power, Mrs. Thatcher served as leader of the opposition in the
House of Commons and so became a familiar figure in British politics and
society.

She was quite unlike any of her recent predecessors, and not only
because of her gender and her relatively humble beginnings. While
Conservatives such as Winston Churchill, Anthony Eden, Harold
Macmillan and Edward Heath had led the country since the end of World
War II, they, like mainstream Republicans in the United States, rarely
called into question the politics of consensus that developed during the
post-war years. In Britain, all parties accepted that the age of empire was
over, that the nation's role in world affairs was in decline, and that the nation

wanted and required an expansive social welfare state.

Mrs. Thatcher declined to be a part of that consensus. While her Conservative predecessors were hardly enthusiastic socialists, she believed (as Barry Goldwater and Ronald Reagan believed) that Conservatives had not done enough to oppose the premises of the welfare state, of what she saw as the manifestations of socialism which were at the heart of Britain's anxieties in the mid-1970's.

In the three decades since the close of World War II, Britain had not only lost most of its colonies, but, not coincidentally, its economy grew at about 3 percent a year, compared to Japan's nearly 10 percent and Germany's 6 percent—Britain, of course, had helped to defeat Japan and Germany during the war. By the late 1970's, Britain was importing more manufactured goods than it was exporting, a demoralizing development for a nation proud of its role as one of the world's great industrial powers. By most measures—productivity, investment, growth rates—Britain was a power in decline.

This descent did not play out peacefully at home. Through the early 1970's, British labor unions called a flurry of strikes that furthered the country's sour mood. A coal miners' strike in 1974 led to calamitous energy shortage, shortened work weeks, and the collapse of a Conservative government headed by Prime Minister Edward Heath. The Conservative Party replaced Heath in 1975 with Thatcher, who had served in Heath's government as Secretary of State for Education and Science.

Thatcher brought to the House what author Phillip Jenkins called a "politics of conviction" that was notable for its rarity in the comfortable consensus politics of Great Britain. She believed that the Labor Party "gloried in planning, regulation, controls and subsidies," and while her Conservative Party colleagues had "opposed these doctrines" in principle, in fact, they had merely "pitched camp in the long march to the left."

The Tories, she wrote, "loosened the corset of socialism; they never removed it. It never tried seriously to reverse it."[1]

As the leader of the opposition and a Prime Minister in waiting, she preached her gospel of free enterprise and individual effort, bringing to British political debate a moralistic tone that was quite unlike the rhetoric of her predecessors. As Britain's economy continued to stagnate, as militant trade unions seized control of the Labour government, the nation's spirits sagged and voters began to question the policies and intellectual parameters that had been in place since the end of the war.

In January, 1979, a series of strikes by public employees paralyzed the nation. In a broadcast interview, Mrs. Thatcher was asked what she would do about the unions. "By God I'll confront them," she said.[2] Several weeks later, in early March, the Labor-led government of James Callaghan lost a motion of confidence by a single vote in the Commons. Callaghan was obliged to call for a new election, held on May 3. Mrs. Thatcher's Conservatives won a clear majority of forty-three seats. Margaret Thatcher received Queen Elizabeth's commission to form a new government on May 4.

The new prime minister was determined to do more than simply patch the problems she inherited. Her politics of conviction translated into policies designed to strip away the power of unions, encourage private enterprise, reduce government regulation and subsidies, and create a very different society than the one presided over by Tory and Labor ministers alike for more than three decades. Her policies, and the blunt force she applied to their implementation, became known as "Thatcherism."

The new government confronted rail workers, fought a short war with Argentina over ownership of the Falkland Islands, aligned itself with the new U.S. president, Ronald Reagan, supported a tougher line against the Soviet Union and otherwise sought to roll back Britain's social-welfare state. After winning a new term as Prime Minister in 1983, Mrs. Thatcher confronted the mine workers' union, a powerful and militant organization led by Arthur Scargill. After the government announced a plan to close redundant mines, the miners called a strike in March, 1984. A year later, the strike ended in a bitter defeat for Scargill and his colleagues as miners voted to return to work without having blocked the government closures.

The victory over Scargill symbolized Thatcher's successful overthrow of the old post-war politics. But ridding Britain of socialism was not the Prime Minister's only goal. She sought to replace faith in government with a renewed faith in markets and individual liberty.

Thatcher's power base was in England, where Thatcherism caught on from the very beginning of her tenure. But to the north, in Scotland, her party had little power to begin with, and even less in succeeding elections. The Conservatives won about 24 percent of the vote in the 1987 general election which gave Thatcher a third term as Prime Minister. It was a source of consternation—Scotland, as she was quick to note, was the birthplace of Adam Smith, the economist whose free-market beliefs formed the foundation of her policies.

On May 21, 1988, the Prime Minister traveled to Edinburgh to address the General Assembly of the Church of Scotland. Determined to place her beliefs and policies in a larger moral context, Thatcher, who addressed her remarks to the Assembly's moderator, called on her own religious beliefs and interpretation of the Bible to assert the righteousness of her reforms. Using Biblical verses and Christian imagery, she articulated a worldview that went far beyond privatization of government assets or monetary policy. She explored cultural issues as well, and sought to expand the notion of "Thatcherism" to include her views on religion, family life, and civil liberties, among other issues.

Because the hall in which she spoke was built on a hill in Scotland's capital, Thatcher's speech was labeled, mostly by her critics, as the "Sermon on the Mound." It remains a carefully crafted articulation of the core beliefs she held, and which she sought to instill in her fellow Britons. The speech's impact can be measured by the place it still holds in British society. Twenty years later, in 2008, Labor Prime Minister Gordon Brown traveled to the very same place to deliver a speech enunciating his own vision of a just society. Brown's speech was tepid compared to the crashing waves of Thatcher's speech.

▼ ▼ ▼

MODERATOR: I am greatly honoured to have been invited to attend the opening of this 1988 General Assembly of the Church of Scotland; and I am deeply grateful that you have now asked me to address you.

I am very much aware of the historical continuity extending over four centuries, during which the position of the Church of Scotland has been recognized in constitutional law and confirmed by successive Sovereigns. It sprang from the independence of mind and rigor of thought that have always been such powerful characteristics of the Scottish people, as I have occasion to know. [muted laughter] It has remained close to its roots and has inspired a commitment to service from all people.

I am therefore very sensible of the important influence which the Church of Scotland exercises in the life of the whole nation, both at the spiritual level and through the extensive caring services which are provided by your Church's department of social responsibility. And I am conscious also of the value of the continuing links which the Church of Scotland maintains with other Churches.

Perhaps it would be best, Moderator, if I began by speaking personally as a Christian, as well as a politician, about the way I see things. Reading recently, I came across the starkly simple phrase:

"Christianity is about spiritual redemption, not social reform."

Sometimes the debate on these matters has become too polarized and given the impression that the two are quite separate. But most Christians would regard it as their personal Christian duty to help their fellow men and women. They would regard the lives of children as a precious trust. These duties come not from any secular legislation passed by Parliament, but from being a Christian.

But there are a number of people who are not Christians who would also accept those responsibilities. What then are the distinctive marks of Christianity?

They stem not from the social but from the spiritual side of our lives, and personally, I would identify three beliefs in particular:

First, that from the beginning man has been endowed by God with the fundamental right to choose between good and evil. And second, that we were made in God's own image and, therefore, we are expected to use all our own power of thought and judgement in exercising that choice; and further, that if we open our hearts to God, He has promised to work within us. And third, that Our Lord Jesus Christ, the Son of God, when faced with His terrible choice and lonely vigil *chose* to lay down His life that our sins may be forgiven. I remember very well a sermon on an Armistice Sunday when our Preacher said, "No one took away the life of Jesus, He chose to lay it down."

I think back to many discussions in my early life when we all agreed that if you try to take the fruits of Christianity without its roots, the fruits will wither. And they will not come again unless you nurture the roots.

But we must not profess the Christian faith and go to Church simply because we want social reforms and benefits or a better standard of behavior; but because we accept the sanctity of life, the responsibility that comes with freedom and the supreme sacrifice of Christ expressed so well in the hymn:

"When I survey the wondrous Cross, On which the Prince of glory died, My richest gain I count but loss, And pour contempt on all my pride."

May I also say a few words about my personal belief in the relevance of Christianity to public policy—to the things that are Caesar's?

The Old Testament lays down in Exodus the Ten Commandments as given to Moses, the injunction in Leviticus to love our neighbour as ourselves and generally the importance of observing a strict code of law. The New Testament is a record of the Incarnation, the teachings of Christ and the establishment of the Kingdom of God. Again we have the emphasis on loving our neighbor as ourselves and to "Do-as-you-would-be-done-by."

I believe that by taking together these key elements from the Old and New Testaments, we gain: a view of the universe, a proper attitude to work, and principles to shape economic and social life.

We are told we must work and use our talents to create wealth. "If a man will not work he shall not eat" wrote St. Paul to the Thessalonians. Indeed, abundance rather than poverty has a legitimacy which derives from the very nature of Creation.

Nevertheless, the Tenth Commandment—Thou shalt not covet—recognises that making money and owning things could become selfish activities. But it is not the creation of wealth that is wrong but love of money for its own sake. The spiritual dimension comes in deciding what one does with the wealth. How could we respond to the many calls for help, or invest for the future, or support the wonderful artists and craftsmen whose work also glorifies God, unless we had first worked hard and used our talents to create the necessary wealth? And remember the woman with the alabaster jar of ointment.

I confess that I always had difficulty with interpreting the Biblical precept to love our neighbors "as ourselves" until I read some of the words of C.S. Lewis. He pointed out that we don't exactly love *ourselves* when we fall below the standards and beliefs we have accepted. Indeed we might even hate ourselves for some unworthy deed.

None of this, of course, tells us exactly what kind of political and social institutions we should have. On this point, Christians will very often genuinely disagree, though it is a mark of Christian manners that they will do so with courtesy and mutual respect. *[Applause]* What is certain, however, is that any set of social and economic arrangements which is not founded on the acceptance of individual responsibility will do nothing but harm.

We are all responsible for our own actions. We can't blame society if we disobey the law. We simply can't delegate the exercise of mercy and generosity to others. The politicians and other secular powers should strive by their measures to bring out the good in people and to fight down the bad: but they can't create the one or abolish the other. They can only see that the laws encourage the best instincts and convictions of the people, instincts and convictions which I'm convinced are far more deeply rooted than is often supposed.

Nowhere is this more evident than the basic ties of the family which are at the heart of our society and are the very nursery of civic virtue. And it is on the family that we in government build our own policies for welfare, education and care.

You recall that Timothy was warned by St. Paul that anyone who neglects to provide for his own house (meaning his own family) has disowned the faith and is "worse than an infidel."[fo 2]

We must recognise that modern society is infinitely more complex than that of Biblical times and of course new occasions teach new duties. In our generation, the only way we can ensure that no one is left without sustenance, help or opportunity, is to have laws to provide for health and education, pensions for the elderly, succour for the sick and disabled.

But intervention by the State must never become so great that it effectively removes personal responsibility. The same applies to taxation; for while you and I would work extremely hard whatever the circumstances, there are undoubtedly some who would not unless the incentive was there. And we need their efforts too.

Moderator, recently there have been great debates about religious education. I believe strongly that politicians must see that religious education has a proper place in the school curriculum. *[Applause]*

In Scotland, as in England, there is an historic connection expressed in our laws between Church and State. The two connections are of a somewhat different kind, but the arrangements in both countries are designed to give symbolic expression to the same crucial truth: that the Christian religion—which, of course, embodies many of the great spiritual and moral truths of Judaism—is a fundamental part of our national heritage. And I believe it is the wish of the overwhelming majority of people that this heritage should be preserved and fostered. *[Applause]* For centuries it has been our very life blood. And indeed we are a nation whose ideals are founded on the Bible.

Also, it is quite impossible to understand our history or literature without grasping this fact, and that's the strong practical case for ensuring that children at school are given adequate instruction in the part which the Judaic-Christian tradition has played in molding our laws, manners and institutions. How can you make sense of Shakespeare and Sir Walter Scott, or of the constitutional conflicts of the seventeenth century in both Scotland and England, without some such fundamental knowledge?

But I go further than this. The truths of the Judaic-Christian tradition are infinitely precious, not only, as I believe, because they are true, but also because they provide the moral impulse which alone can lead to that peace, in the true meaning of the word, for which we all long.

To assert absolute moral values is not to claim perfection for ourselves. No true Christian could do that. What is more, one of the great principles of our Judaic-Christian inheritance is tolerance. People with other faiths and cultures have always been welcomed in our land, assured of equality under the law, of proper respect and of open friendship. There's absolutely nothing incompatible between this and our desire to maintain the essence of our own identity. There is no place for racial or religious intolerance in our creed.

When Abraham Lincoln spoke in his famous Gettysburg speech of 1863 of "government of the people, by the people, and for the people," he gave the world a neat definition of democracy which has since been widely and enthusiastically adopted. But what he enunciated as a form of government was not in itself especially Christian, for nowhere in the Bible is the word democracy mentioned. Ideally, when Christians meet, as Christians, to take counsel together their purpose is not (or should not be) to ascertain what is the mind of the majority but what is the mind of the Holy Spirit— something which may be quite different. *[Applause]*

Nevertheless I am an enthusiast for democracy. And I take that position, not because I believe majority opinion is inevitably right or true— indeed no majority can take away God-given human rights—but because I believe it most effectively safeguards the value of the individual, and, more than any other system, restrains the abuse of power by the few. And that *is* a Christian concept.

But there is little hope for democracy if the hearts of men and women in democratic societies cannot be touched by a call to something greater than themselves. Political structures, state institutions, collective ideals— these are not enough.

We Parliamentarians can legislate for the rule of law. You, the Church, can teach the life of faith.

But when all is said and done, the politician's role is a humble one. I always think that the whole debate about the Church and the State has never yielded anything comparable in insight to that beautiful hymn "I Vow to Thee my Country." It begins with a triumphant assertion of what might be described as secular patriotism, a noble thing indeed in a country like ours:

"I vow to thee my country all earthly things above; entire, whole and perfect the service of my love".

It goes on to speak of "another country I heard of long ago" whose King can't be seen and whose armies can't be counted, but "soul by soul and silently her shining bounds increase". Not group by group, or party by party, or even church by church—but soul by soul—and each one counts.

That, members of the Assembly, is the country which you chiefly serve. You fight your cause under the banner of an historic Church. Your success matters greatly—as much to the temporal as to the spiritual welfare of the nation. I leave you with that earnest hope that may we all come nearer to that other country whose "ways are ways of gentleness and all her paths are peace." *[Applause]*

50: Nelson Mandela's Inaugural Address as President of South Africa

"Glory and Hope to Newborn Liberty"

Pretoria, May 10, 1994

HE WAS, FOR MORE THAN A QUARTER-CENTURY, ONE OF THE WORLD'S MOST famous political prisoners. Nelson Mandela, charismatic and fearless, was forty-six years old when he was sentenced to life in prison in 1964 for his role in attempting to overthrow white minority rule in South Africa. He had expected a worse fate, anticipating that he would be hanged for his defiance. Before he learned his fate, he told a judge in a crowded courtroom in Pretoria was he was unafraid of whatever punishment he might mete out.

"During my lifetime I have dedicated myself to [the] struggle of the African people. I have fought against white domination, and I have fought against black domination," he said. "I have cherished the ideal of a democratic and free society in which all persons live together in harmony with equal opportunities."

Then, as he reached the end of his long oration, he said in a lowered voice: "It is an ideal which I hoped to live for and achieve. But if needs be, it is an ideal for which I am prepared to die."

It did not come to that. Mandela and his fellow defendants were spared the hangman's rope. But few considered the alternative, a life sentence, a victory for justice. Mandela was, by virtue of his four-hour speech in the courtroom and his dignified and defiant presence, a symbol of righteous resistance against one of the world's most egregious outrages, South Africa's system of racial separation, called apartheid. Diplomats lobbied for a less severe sentence; demonstrators around the world gathered to express their support for the man sentenced to spend the rest of his life in a hellhole because he opposed white minority rule in the country of his birth.

Mandela was the voice of the main black opposition group in South Africa, the African National Congress, which he joined in 1943. The ANC, after a long, frustrating period of ineffectiveness, was beginning to make its voice heard as World War II ended, prompting a government crackdown in the early 1950's. Within a few years, the regime was an international pariah, excluded from global institutions ranging from the United Nations to the International Olympic Committee.

Mandela was hardly the only prominent black activist in South Africa, but he was among the most prominent. He was well-read lawyer who seemed unafraid of the government's ham-handed authority—during one of his several arrests, Mandela made a joke to a police officer, who told him he had better watch out because he was playing with fire. "Playing with fire is my game," he said, putting aside his smile and his banter.[1]

As government repression grew even more intense in the early 1960's, Mandela went underground to lead continued resistance. Opposition to the government turned violent as South Africa's majority population turned to sabotage to bring attention to injustice and to strike back against the government. Mandela was arrested in August, 1963, not long after he appeared in public in London. He was charged with leaving the country without a passport and for inciting violence against the state. He was sentenced to five years, a stiff sentence for a political crime, but when the government found new evidence linking Mandela to anti-government violence, he was brought up on new and far more serious charges. The subsequent trial and conviction, highlighted by Mandela's long speech before sentencing, seemed to put an end to Mandela's career as a revolutionary.

For the next two decades and more, Nelson Mandela was an unseen but unforgotten figure as South Africa came under increasing international pressure to end apartheid and the oppression of the nation's black majority. In the late 1980's, as the post-World War II world order began to fall apart with the crumbling of the Soviet Union and the breakup of the Eastern European bloc, white officials in South Africa began reaching out to their most famous prisoner, now in his early 70's. Like Mikhail Gorbachev in the Soviet Union, South African President F. W. de Klerk saw that the status quo was no longer acceptable, or sustainable. In early 1990, de Klerk announced that the African National Congress, banned decades earlier, would no longer be considered an illegal organization. Political prisoners found guilty of non-violent offenses would be freed. And Nelson Mandela would be allowed to return home.

He left prison on February 11, 1990, prompting joyous demonstrations around the world. The ANC transformed itself from an underground revolutionary movement to a constitutional political party. The pace of change in

South Africa, like that in Eastern Europe after the fall of the Berlin Wall, was breathtaking. Mandela and de Klerk began discussions for a new constitution and a transition to majority rule. Members of de Klerk's own cabinet were outraged over the prospect of an end to the old order, but de Klerk persisted. The two men were honored with the Nobel Peace Prize in December, 1993, just a few months before they faced each other as competing party leaders in the first truly democratic election campaign of the new South Africa.

Twenty-three million South Africans went to the polls on April 27, 1994 to choose a new government in an election that some feared would descend into chaos and violence. According to biographer Anthony Sampson, Mandela watched with delight as white farmers lined up to vote alongside the black workers they employed.[2] When the results were tabulated, the ANC won an overwhelming victory, winning nearly two-thirds of the nation's votes. Nelson Mandela, former prisoner, was elected President.

He was sworn into office on May 10, 1994 in Pretoria, in a ceremony that was televised around the world and watched by more than a billion people. The symbolism—the reality—was extraordinary: One of the world's most intractable regimes, the white minority government of South Africa, turned over power peacefully to the man it had once regarded as its most dangerous enemy. Heads of state and government, monarchs and prime ministers, turned out to witness history. The military power of South Africa, organized to defend the white regime against the likes of Mandela, turned out to salute their one-time antagonist, now their President.

Mandela's inaugural address was spare in words but rich in symbolism, reconciliation and reflection. There were no traces of bitterness from a man who spent twenty-seven years in prison, no triumphant words from a man who had beaten, at last, his jailers. The speech was a testimonial to the power of determination, patience, and forgiveness.

YOUR Majesties, Your Highnesses, Distinguished Guests, Comrades and Friends:

Today, all of us do, by our presence here, and by our celebrations in other parts of our country and the world, confer glory and hope to newborn liberty.

Out of the experience of an extraordinary human disaster that lasted too long, must be born a society of which all humanity will be proud.

Our daily deeds as ordinary South Africans must produce an actual South African reality that will reinforce humanity's belief in justice, strengthen its confidence in the nobility of the human soul and sustain all our hopes for a glorious life for all.

All this we owe both to ourselves and to the peoples of the world who are so well represented here today.

To my compatriots, I have no hesitation in saying that each one of us is as intimately attached to the soil of this beautiful country as are the famous jacaranda trees of Pretoria and the mimosa trees of the bushveld.

Each time one of us touches the soil of this land, we feel a sense of personal renewal. The national mood changes as the seasons change.

We are moved by a sense of joy and exhilaration when the grass turns green and the flowers bloom.

That spiritual and physical oneness we all share with this common homeland explains the depth of the pain we all carried in our hearts as we saw our country tear itself apart in a terrible conflict, and as we saw it spurned, outlawed and isolated by the peoples of the world, precisely because it has become the universal base of the pernicious ideology and practice of racism and racial oppression.

We, the people of South Africa, feel fulfilled that humanity has taken us back into its bosom, that we, who were outlaws not so long ago, have today been given the rare privilege to be host to the nations of the world on our own soil.

We thank all our distinguished international guests for having come to take possession with the people of our country of what is, after all, a common victory for justice, for peace, for human dignity.

We trust that you will continue to stand by us as we tackle the challenges of building peace, prosperity, non-sexism, non-racialism and democracy.

We deeply appreciate the role that the masses of our people and their political mass democratic, religious, women, youth, business, traditional and other leaders have played to bring about this conclusion. Not least among them is my Second Deputy President, the Honorable F.W. de Klerk.

We would also like to pay tribute to our security forces, in all their ranks, for the distinguished role they have played in securing our first democratic elections and the transition to democracy, from blood thirsty forces which still refuse to see the light.

The time for the healing of the wounds has come.

The moment to bridge the chasms that divide us has come.

The time to build is upon us.

We have, at last, achieved our political emancipation. We pledge our-selves to liberate all our people from the continuing bondage of poverty, deprivation, suffering, gender and other discrimination.

We succeeded to take our last steps to freedom in conditions of relative peace. We commit ourselves to the construction of a complete, just and last-ing peace.

We have triumphed in the effort to implant hope in the breasts of the millions of our people. We enter into a covenant that we shall build the soci-ety in which all South Africans, both black and white, will be able to walk tall, without any fear in their hearts, assured of their inalienable right to human dignity—a rainbow nation at peace with itself and the world.

As a token of its commitment to the renewal of our country, the new Interim Government of National Unity will, as a matter of urgency, address the issue of amnesty for various categories of our people who are currently serving terms of imprisonment.

We dedicate this day to all the heroes and heroines in this country and the rest of the world who sacrificed in many ways and surrendered their lives so that we could be free.

Their dreams have become reality. Freedom is their reward.

We are both humbled and elevated by the honor and privilege that you, the people of South Africa, have bestowed on us, as the first President of a united, democratic, non-racial and non-sexist South Africa, to lead our country out of the valley of darkness.

We understand it still that there is no easy road to freedom.

We know it well that none of us acting alone can achieve success.

We must therefore act together as a united people, for national recon-ciliation, for nation building, for the birth of a new world.

Let there be justice for all.

Let there be peace for all.

Let there be work, bread, water and salt for all.

Let each know that for each the body, the mind and the soul have been freed to fulfill themselves.

Never, never and never again shall it be that this beautiful land will again experience the oppression of one by another and suffer the indignity of being the skunk of the world.

Let freedom reign.

The sun shall never set on so glorious a human achievement!

God bless Africa!

51. Barack Obama Confronts Race and Religion
"A More Perfect Union"
March 18, 2008

DESIGNED TO INSPIRE THE FAITHFUL AT THE BEGINNING OF A NATIONAL political convention, the keynote address fell into obscurity in American politics in the late twentieth century. Like the conventions themselves, the keynote address seemed like the residue of a different age, irrelevant to the proceedings and to the concerns of viewers watching on television. In the last quarter of the twentieth century, only one keynote address—given by New York Governor Mario Cuomo at the Democratic National Convention in 1984—roused both party and public.

In 2004, however, an unknown political figure from Illinois seized the imagination of his fellow Democrats with a soaring keynote address that demonstrated the power of well-written, well-delivered words in an era that seemed to prefer sound bites and slogans. The speaker's name was Barack Obama, a state Senator in the Illinois legislature who was running for a U.S. Senate seat. Obama, a tall, rail-thin African-American with a law degree from Harvard, originally sought to challenge the incumbent junior Senator from Illinois, Peter Fitzgerald. But Fitzgerald chose to retire after a series of embarrassing revelations about his private life, virtually ensuring Obama's election in November.

The future Senator's keynote speech, which spoke of the "audacity of hope," transformed him into a national figure even before he won election. After serving in the Senate for less than half of his first term, Obama announced his candidacy for president in the 2008 election. The audacity of hope, indeed. The leading candidate of the Democratic Party's establishment was New York Senator Hillary Rodham Clinton, a political celebrity by virtue of her marriage to former President Bill Clinton and her own role as spokesperson for a generation of women who came of age in the 1960's. She was destined to become the first woman to win a major party's presidential nomination, or so it seemed in the fall of 2007, when campaigning began in earnest.

In the very first contest of a short, front-loaded primary season, however, Obama placed first in the caucuses in Iowa. Clinton finished a surprisingly weak third. The resulting media sensation over Clinton's failure and Obama's unexpected success indicated that the nomination process would be neither neat nor easy for anyone concerned.

Clinton re-established equilibrium by winning the New Hampshire primary after she took a swipe at Obama's unchallenged speaking ability. Challenging Obama on his contention that the nation needed change, Clinton insisted that change was not "about a speech you make." If nothing else, Clinton's remark was a tacit acknowledgment of her opponent's facility with words.

As the nation watched with extraordinary interest, Clinton and Obama settled into a contest that was as fierce as it was unexpected. Other candidates bowed out, leaving the field to the two candidates seeking not only the party's nomination, but a chance to make history as well.

In mid-March, with Obama enjoying a slight lead in delegates after a grueling few weeks of primaries, the news media reported that Obama's former pastor in Illinois, the Reverend Jeremiah Wright, had delivered a series of harsh condemnations of the United States from his pulpit. Wright said that blacks should not sing "God Bless America," but instead should say "God damn America." In a sermon given just days after terrorist attacks of September 11, 2001, he seemed to suggest that the strikes, which killed nearly three thousand people, were the result of U.S. foreign policies which supported "state terrorism" in the Middle East and South Africa. "America's chickens are coming home to roost," he said. Video of the clergyman's remarks, already posted on sites like YouTube, found their way into mainstream media programs.

The promising presidential campaign of Barack Obama faced a crisis. Critics seized on Wright's remarks in an effort to discredit the candidate and suggest that he shared his one-time pastor's views. The Wright controversy placed the silent but ever-present issue of race squarely before the electorate.

On March 18, Obama traveled to Philadelphia to confront the Wright controversy and the larger issues of race and religion in public life. Confident of his ability to convey thoughts and ideas through words and images, Obama delivered a memorable speech in which he spoke frankly about the progress, and the lack thereof, that America had made since the civil rights movement of the 1960's, a movement that helped lead to this historic moment when a black man would seriously contend for the presidential nomination of his party.

Obama risked his campaign with this speech, which spoke candidly about the ways in which racial hatred had scarred lives and defied the nation's highest ideals. He spoke of his own life story as the son of a black father and a white mother; his children, he said, had the blood of slaves and slaveowners. He did not hide the fact that he knew of some of Wright's views, and he condemned them. But he said he could not disown the clergyman any more than he could disown his white grandmother, a woman who sometimes made crude racial remarks.

He sought to return religion and politics to the separate spheres that were assigned them in the Constitution, signed in Philadelphia more than two centuries earlier. In taking on both race and religion, Obama tested his own skills as an orator and thinker.

Reaction to the speech was overwhelmingly positive. The editorial pages of the nation's biggest newspapers praised Obama for his courage and his eloquence. The speech revitalized the Obama campaign, helped push Wright to the background, and proved to be an important milestone on the way to the Senator's historic victory in the 2008 primaries. In August, he spoke to the Democratic National Convention for a second time, this time, as the party's candidate for president of the United States.

▼ ▼ ▼

"WE the people, in order to form a more perfect union." Two hundred and twenty-one years ago, in a hall that still stands across the street, a group of men gathered and, with these simple words, launched America's improbable experiment in democracy. Farmers and scholars; statesmen and patriots who had traveled across an ocean to escape tyranny and persecution finally made real their declaration of independence at a Philadelphia convention that lasted through the spring of 1787.

The document they produced was eventually signed but ultimately unfinished. It was stained by this nation's original sin of slavery, a question that divided the colonies and brought the convention to a stalemate until the founders chose to allow the slave trade to continue for at least twenty more years, and to leave any final resolution to future generations.

Of course, the answer to the slavery question was already embedded within our Constitution—a Constitution that had at its very core the ideal of equal citizenship under the law; a Constitution that promised its people liberty, and justice, and a union that could be and should be perfected over time.

And yet words on a parchment would not be enough to deliver slaves from bondage, or provide men and women of every color and creed their full rights and obligations as citizens of the United States. What would be needed were Americans in successive generations who were willing to do their part—through protests and struggle, on the streets and in the courts, through a civil war and civil disobedience and always at great risk—to narrow that gap between the promise of our ideals and the reality of their time.

This was one of the tasks we set forth at the beginning of this campaign—to continue the long march of those who came before us, a march for a more just, more equal, more free, more caring and more prosperous America. I chose to run for the presidency at this moment in history because I believe deeply that we cannot solve the challenges of our time unless we solve them together—unless we perfect our union by understanding that we may have different stories, but we hold common hopes; that we may not look the same and we may not have come from the same place, but we all want to move in the same direction—towards a better future for our children and our grandchildren.

This belief comes from my unyielding faith in the decency and generosity of the American people. But it also comes from my own American story.

I am the son of a black man from Kenya and a white woman from Kansas. I was raised with the help of a white grandfather who survived a Depression to serve in Patton's Army during World War II and a white grandmother who worked on a bomber assembly line at Fort Leavenworth while he was overseas. I've gone to some of the best schools in America and lived in one of the world's poorest nations. I am married to a black American who carries within her the blood of slaves and slaveowners—an inheritance we pass on to our two precious daughters. I have brothers, sisters, nieces, nephews, uncles and cousins, of every race and every hue, scattered across three continents, and for as long as I live, I will never forget that in no other country on Earth is my story even possible.

It's a story that hasn't made me the most conventional candidate. But it is a story that has seared into my genetic makeup the idea that this nation is more than the sum of its parts—that out of many, we are truly one.

Throughout the first year of this campaign, against all predictions to the contrary, we saw how hungry the American people were for this message of unity. Despite the temptation to view my candidacy through a purely racial lens, we won commanding victories in states with some of the whitest populations in the country. In South Carolina, where the Confederate Flag still flies, we built a powerful coalition of African-Americans and white Americans.

This is not to say that race has not been an issue in the campaign. At various stages in the campaign, some commentators have deemed me either "too black" or "not black enough." We saw racial tensions bubble to the surface during the week before the South Carolina primary. The press has scoured every exit poll for the latest evidence of racial polarization, not just in terms of white and black, but black and brown as well.

And yet, it has only been in the last couple of weeks that the discussion of race in this campaign has taken a particularly divisive turn.

On one end of the spectrum, we've heard the implication that my candidacy is somehow an exercise in affirmative action; that it's based solely on the desire of wide-eyed liberals to purchase racial reconciliation on the cheap. On the other end, we've heard my former pastor, Reverend Jeremiah Wright, use incendiary language to express views that have the potential not only to widen the racial divide, but views that denigrate both the greatness and the goodness of our nation; that rightly offend white and black alike.

I have already condemned, in unequivocal terms, the statements of Reverend Wright that have caused such controversy. For some, nagging questions remain. Did I know him to be an occasionally fierce critic of American domestic and foreign policy? Of course. Did I ever hear him make remarks that could be considered controversial while I sat in church? Yes. Did I strongly disagree with many of his political views? Absolutely—just as I'm sure many of you have heard remarks from your pastors, priests, or rabbis with which you strongly disagreed.

But the remarks that have caused this recent firestorm weren't simply controversial. They weren't simply a religious leader's effort to speak out against perceived injustice. Instead, they expressed a profoundly distorted view of this country—a view that sees white racism as endemic, and that elevates what is wrong with America above all that we know is right with America; a view that sees the conflicts in the Middle East as rooted primarily in the actions of stalwart allies like Israel, instead of emanating from the perverse and hateful ideologies of radical Islam.

As such, Reverend Wright's comments were not only wrong but divisive, divisive at a time when we need unity; racially charged at a time when we need to come together to solve a set of monumental problems—two wars, a terrorist threat, a falling economy, a chronic health care crisis and potentially devastating climate change; problems that are neither black or white or Latino or Asian, but rather problems that confront us all.

Given my background, my politics, and my professed values and ideals, there will no doubt be those for whom my statements of condemnation are not enough. Why associate myself with Reverend Wright in the first place, they may ask? Why not join another church? And I confess that if all that I knew of Reverend Wright were the snippets of those sermons that have run in an endless loop on the television and YouTube, or if Trinity United Church of Christ conformed to the caricatures being peddled by some commentators, there is no doubt that I would react in much the same way

But the truth is, that isn't all that I know of the man. The man I met more than twenty years ago is a man who helped introduce me to my Christian faith, a man who spoke to me about our obligations to love one another; to care for the sick and lift up the poor. He is a man who served his country as a U.S. Marine; who has studied and lectured at some of the finest universities and seminaries in the country, and who for over thirty years led a church that serves the community by doing God's work here on Earth—by housing the homeless, ministering to the needy, providing day care services and scholarships and prison ministries, and reaching out to those suffering from HIV/AIDS.

In my first book, *Dreams From My Father*, I described the experience of my first service at Trinity:

"People began to shout, to rise from their seats and clap and cry out, a forceful wind carrying the reverend's voice up into the rafters. . . . And in that single note—hope!—I heard something else; at the foot of that cross, inside the thousands of churches across the city, I imagined the stories of ordinary black people merging with the stories of David and Goliath, Moses and Pharaoh, the Christians in the lion's den, Ezekiel's field of dry bones. Those stories—of survival, and freedom, and hope—became our story, my story; the blood that had spilled was our blood, the tears our tears; until this black church, on this bright day, seemed once more a vessel carrying the story of a people into future generations and into a larger world. Our trials and triumphs became at once unique and universal, black and more than black; in chronicling our journey, the stories and songs gave us a means to reclaim memories that we didn't need to feel shame about . . . memories that all people might study and cherish—and with which we could start to rebuild."

That has been my experience at Trinity. Like other predominantly black churches across the country, Trinity embodies the black community in its entirety—the doctor and the welfare mom, the model student and the former gang-banger. Like other black churches, Trinity's services are full of raucous laughter and sometimes bawdy humor. They are full of dancing, clapping, screaming and shouting that may seem jarring to the untrained ear. The church contains in full the kindness and cruelty, the fierce intelligence and the shocking ignorance, the struggles and successes, the love and yes, the bitterness and bias that make up the black experience in America.

And this helps explain, perhaps, my relationship with Reverend Wright. As imperfect as he may be, he has been like family to me. He strengthened my faith, officiated my wedding, and baptized my children. Not once in my conversations with him have I heard him talk about any ethnic group in derogatory terms, or treat whites with whom he interacted with anything but courtesy and respect. He contains within him the contradictions—the good and the bad—of the community that he has served diligently for so many years.

I can no more disown him than I can disown the black community. I can no more disown him than I can my white grandmother—a woman who helped raise me, a woman who sacrificed again and again for me, a woman who loves me as much as she loves anything in this world, but a woman who once confessed her fear of black men who passed by her on the street, and who on more than one occasion has uttered racial or ethnic stereotypes that made me cringe.

These people are a part of me. And they are a part of America, this country that I love.

Some will see this as an attempt to justify or excuse comments that are simply inexcusable. I can assure you it is not. I suppose the politically safe thing would be to move on from this episode and just hope that it fades into the woodwork. We can dismiss Reverend Wright as a crank or a demagogue, just as some have dismissed Geraldine Ferraro, in the aftermath of her recent statements, as harboring some deep-seated racial bias.

But race is an issue that I believe this nation cannot afford to ignore right now. We would be making the same mistake that Reverend Wright made in his offending sermons about America—to simplify and stereotype and amplify the negative to the point that it distorts reality.

The fact is that the comments that have been made and the issues that have surfaced over the last few weeks reflect the complexities of race in this country that we've never really worked through—a part of our union that we have yet to perfect. And if we walk away now, if we simply retreat into our respective corners, we will never be able to come together and solve challenges like health care, or education, or the need to find good jobs for every American.

Understanding this reality requires a reminder of how we arrived at this point. As William Faulkner once wrote, "The past isn't dead and buried. In fact, it isn't even past." We do not need to recite here the history of racial injustice in this country. But we do need to remind ourselves that so many of the disparities that exist in the African-American community today can be directly traced to inequalities passed on from an earlier generation that suffered under the brutal legacy of slavery and Jim Crow.

Segregated schools were, and are, inferior schools; we still haven't fixed them, fifty years after Brown v. Board of Education, and the inferior education they provided, then and now, helps explain the pervasive achievement gap between today's black and white students.

Legalized discrimination—where blacks were prevented, often through violence, from owning property, or loans were not granted to African-American business owners, or black homeowners could not access FHA mortgages, or blacks were excluded from unions, or the police force, or fire departments—meant that black families could not amass any meaningful wealth to bequeath to future generations. That history helps explain the wealth and income gap between black and white, and the concentrated pockets of poverty that persist in so many of today's urban and rural communities.

A lack of economic opportunity among black men, and the shame and frustration that came from not being able to provide for one's family, contributed to the erosion of black families—a problem that welfare policies for many years may have worsened. And the lack of basic services in so many urban black neighborhoods—parks for kids to play in, police walking the beat, regular garbage pick-up and building code enforcement—all helped create a cycle of violence, blight and neglect that continue to haunt us.

This is the reality in which Reverend Wright and other African-Americans of his generation grew up. They came of age in the late 50's and early 60's, a time when segregation was still the law of the land and opportunity was systematically constricted. What's remarkable is not how many failed in the face of discrimination, but rather how many men and women overcame the odds; how many were able to make a way out of no way for those like me who would come after them.

But for all those who scratched and clawed their way to get a piece of the American Dream, there were many who didn't make it—those who were ultimately defeated, in one way or another, by discrimination. That legacy of defeat was passed on to future generations—those young men and increasingly young women who we see standing on street corners or languishing in our prisons, without hope or prospects for the future. Even for those blacks who did make it, questions of race, and racism, continue to define their worldview in fundamental ways. For the men and women of Reverend Wright's generation, the memories of humiliation and doubt and fear have not gone away; nor has the anger and the bitterness of those years. That anger may not get expressed in public, in front of white co-workers or white friends. But it does find voice in the barbershop or around the kitchen table. At times, that anger is exploited by politicians, to gin up votes along racial lines, or to make up for a politician's own failings.

And occasionally it finds voice in the church on Sunday morning, in the pulpit and in the pews. The fact that so many people are surprised to hear that anger in some of Reverend Wright's sermons simply reminds us of the old truism that the most segregated hour in American life occurs on Sunday morning. That anger is not always productive; indeed, all too often it distracts attention from solving real problems; it keeps us from squarely facing our own complicity in our condition, and prevents the African-American community from forging the alliances it needs to bring about real change. But the anger is real; it is powerful; and to simply wish it away, to condemn it without understanding its roots, only serves to widen the chasm of misunderstanding that exists between the races.

In fact, a similar anger exists within segments of the white community. Most working- and middle-class white Americans don't feel that they have been particularly privileged by their race. Their experience is the immigrant experience—as far as they're concerned, no one's handed them anything, they've built it from scratch. They've worked hard all their lives, many times only to see their jobs shipped overseas or their pension dumped after a lifetime of labor. They are anxious about their futures, and feel their dreams slipping away; in an era of stagnant wages and global competition, opportunity comes to be seen as a zero sum game, in which your dreams come at my expense. So when they are told to bus their children to a school across town; when they hear that an African-American is getting an advantage in landing a good job or a spot in a good college because of an injustice that they themselves never committed; when they're told that their fears about crime in urban neighborhoods are somehow prejudiced, resentment builds over time.

Like the anger within the black community, these resentments aren't always expressed in polite company. But they have helped shape the political landscape for at least a generation. Anger over welfare and affirmative action helped forge the Reagan Coalition. Politicians routinely exploited fears of crime for their own electoral ends. Talk show hosts and conservative commentators built entire careers unmasking bogus claims of racism while dismissing legitimate discussions of racial injustice and inequality as mere political correctness or reverse racism.

Just as black anger often proved counterproductive, so have these white resentments distracted attention from the real culprits of the middle-class squeeze—a corporate culture rife with inside dealing, questionable accounting practices, and short-term greed; a Washington dominated by lobbyists and special interests; economic policies that favor the few over the many. And yet, to wish away the resentments of white Americans, to label them as misguided or even racist, without recognizing they are grounded in legitimate concerns—this too widens the racial divide, and blocks the path to understanding.

This is where we are right now. It's a racial stalemate we've been stuck in for years. Contrary to the claims of some of my critics, black and white, I have never been so naïve as to believe that we can get beyond our racial divisions in a single election cycle, or with a single candidacy—particularly a candidacy as imperfect as my own.

But I have asserted a firm conviction—a conviction rooted in my faith in God and my faith in the American people—that working together we can move beyond some of our old racial wounds, and that in fact we have no choice if we are to continue on the path of a more perfect union.

For the African-American community, that path means embracing the burdens of our past without becoming victims of our past. It means continuing to insist on a full measure of justice in every aspect of American life. But it also means binding our particular grievances—for better health care, and better schools, and better jobs—to the larger aspirations of all Americans —the white woman struggling to break the glass ceiling, the white man who's been laid off, the immigrant trying to feed his family. And it means taking full responsibility for own lives—by demanding more from our fathers, and spending more time with our children, and reading to them, and teaching them that while they may face challenges and discrimination in their own lives, they must never succumb to despair or cynicism; they must always believe that they can write their own destiny.

Ironically, this quintessentially American—and yes, conservative— notion of self-help found frequent expression in Reverend Wright's sermons. But what my former pastor too often failed to understand is that embarking on a program of self-help also requires a belief that society can change.

The profound mistake of Reverend Wright's sermons is not that he spoke about racism in our society. It's that he spoke as if our society was static; as if no progress has been made; as if this country—a country that has made it possible for one of his own members to run for the highest office in the land and build a coalition of white and black, Latino and Asian, rich and poor, young and old—is still irrevocably bound to a tragic past. But what we know—what we have seen—is that America can change. That is true genius of this nation. What we have already achieved gives us hope—the audacity to hope—for what we can and must achieve tomorrow.

In the white community, the path to a more perfect union means acknowledging that what ails the African-American community does not just exist in the minds of black people; that the legacy of discrimination—and current incidents of discrimination, while less overt than in the past—are real and must be addressed. Not just with words, but with deeds—by investing in our schools and our communities; by enforcing our civil rights laws and ensuring fairness in our criminal justice system; by providing this generation with ladders of opportunity that were unavailable for previous generations. It requires all Americans to realize that your dreams do not have to come at the expense of my dreams; that investing in the health, welfare, and education of black and brown and white children will ultimately help all of America prosper.

In the end, then, what is called for is nothing more, and nothing less, than what all the world's great religions demand—that we do unto others as we would have them do unto us. Let us be our brother's keeper, Scripture tells us. Let us be our sister's keeper. Let us find that common stake we all have in one another, and let our politics reflect that spirit as well.

For we have a choice in this country. We can accept a politics that breeds division, and conflict, and cynicism. We can tackle race only as spectacle—as we did in the OJ trial—or in the wake of tragedy, as we did in the aftermath of Katrina—or as fodder for the nightly news. We can play Reverend Wright's sermons on every channel, every day and talk about them from now until the election, and make the only question in this campaign whether or not the American people think that I somehow believe or sympathize with his most offensive words. We can pounce on some gaffe by a Hillary supporter as evidence that she's playing the race card, or we can speculate on whether white men will all flock to John McCain in the general election regardless of his policies.

We can do that.

But if we do, I can tell you that in the next election, we'll be talking about some other distraction. And then another one. And then another one. And nothing will change.

That is one option. Or, at this moment, in this election, we can come together and say, "Not this time." This time we want to talk about the crumbling schools that are stealing the future of black children and white children and Asian children and Hispanic children and Native American children. This time we want to reject the cynicism that tells us that these kids can't learn; that those kids who don't look like us are somebody else's problem. The children of America are not those kids, they are our kids, and we will not let them fall behind in a twenty-first century economy. Not this time.

This time we want to talk about how the lines in the Emergency Room are filled with whites and blacks and Hispanics who do not have health care; who don't have the power on their own to overcome the special interests in Washington, but who can take them on if we do it together.

This time we want to talk about the shuttered mills that once provided a decent life for men and women of every race, and the homes for sale that once belonged to Americans from every religion, every region, every walk of life. This time we want to talk about the fact that the real problem is not that someone who doesn't look like you might take your job; it's that the corporation you work for will ship it overseas for nothing more than a profit.

This time we want to talk about the men and women of every color and creed who serve together, and fight together, and bleed together under the same proud flag. We want to talk about how to bring them home from a war that never should've been authorized and never should've been waged, and we want to talk about how we'll show our patriotism by caring for them, and their families, and giving them the benefits they have earned.

I would not be running for President if I didn't believe with all my heart that this is what the vast majority of Americans want for this country. This union may never be perfect, but generation after generation has shown that it can always be perfected. And today, whenever I find myself feeling doubtful or cynical about this possibility, what gives me the most hope is the next generation—the young people whose attitudes and beliefs and openness to change have already made history in this election.

There is one story in particularly that I'd like to leave you with today—a story I told when I had the great honor of speaking on Dr. King's birthday at his home church, Ebenezer Baptist, in Atlanta.

There is a young, twenty-three-year-old white woman named Ashley

Baia who organized for our campaign in Florence, South Carolina. She had been working to organize a mostly African-American community since the beginning of this campaign, and one day she was at a roundtable discussion where everyone went around telling their story and why they were there.

And Ashley said that when she was nine years old, her mother got cancer. And because she had to miss days of work, she was let go and lost her health care. They had to file for bankruptcy, and that's when Ashley decided that she had to do something to help her mom.

She knew that food was one of their most expensive costs, and so Ashley convinced her mother that what she really liked and really wanted to eat more than anything else was mustard and relish sandwiches. Because that was the cheapest way to eat.

She did this for a year until her mom got better, and she told everyone at the roundtable that the reason she joined our campaign was so that she could help the millions of other children in the country who want and need to help their parents too.

Now Ashley might have made a different choice. Perhaps somebody told her along the way that the source of her mother's problems were blacks who were on welfare and too lazy to work, or Hispanics who were coming into the country illegally. But she didn't. She sought out allies in her fight against injustice.

Anyway, Ashley finishes her story and then goes around the room and asks everyone else why they're supporting the campaign. They all have different stories and reasons. Many bring up a specific issue. And finally they come to this elderly black man who's been sitting there quietly the entire time. And Ashley asks him why he's there. And he does not bring up a specific issue. He does not say health care or the economy. He does not say education or the war. He not say that he was there because of Barack Obama. He simply says to everyone in the room, "I am here because of Ashley."

"I'm here because of Ashley." By itself, that single moment of recognition between that young white girl and that old black man is not enough. It is not enough to give health care to the sick, or jobs to the jobless, or education to our children.

But it is where we start. It is where our union grows stronger. And as so many generations have come to realize over the course of the two hundred and twenty-one years since a band of patriots signed that document in Philadelphia, that is where the perfection begins.

Notes & Bibliography

▼ ▼ ▼

10:
BIBLIOGRAPHY
Christopher Hill, *The Century of Revolution, 1603-1714* (New York: WW Norton & Co., 1961)

11:
1. Christopher Hill, *The Century of Revolution, 1603-1714* (New York: WW Norton & Co., 1961), pg. 64.

13:
1. Benson Bobrick, *Angels in the Whirlwind* (New York: Penguin, 1998), pg 467
2. James Flexner, *George Washington in the American Revolution* (Boston: Little, Brown, 1968), pg. 504
3. Flexner, pg. 507

21:
1. Charles Chenevix Trench, *The Great Dan* (London: Jonathan Cape, 198) pg. 264

22:
1. *www.marxists.org/archive/marx/works/1847/09/30.htm*
2. David McLellan, *Karl Marx: His Life and Thought* (New York: Harper & Row, 1973), pg. 175
3. Speech in the House of Commons, July 28, 1835. (Hansard, Vol. XXIX, London 1835, pp.1168-70)
4. Dr. Andrew Ure, *The Philosophy of Manufactures* (London 1835. Book I, Chap. I, pg. 23).

23:
1. David W. Blight, *Frederick Douglass' Civil War* (Baton Rouge: LSU Press, 1989), pg. 90
2. Frederick Douglass: *The Life and Times of Frederick Douglass* (Secaucus, N.J.: Citadel Press, 1983), pg. 249
3. Douglass, pg. 271.

24;
BIBLIOGRAPHY
Waldo W. Braden, *Abraham Lincoln, Public Speaker* (Baton Rouge: LSU, 1988)
Stephen A. Oates, *With Malice Toward None: The Life of Abraham Lincoln* (Harper & Row, 1977)

1. www.historynow.org/12_2005/historian2.html

25:
1. Denis Mack Smith, *Garibaldi* (Englewood Cliffs, NJ: Prentice-Hall, 1969), pg. 88
2. Smith, Pg. 99
3. George Martin, *The Red Shirt and the Cross of Savoy* (New York, Dodd, Mead and Company, 1969), pg. 581

26:
1. Kathleen Barry, *Susan B. Anthony: A Biography of a Singular Feminist* (New York: NYU Press, 1988), pg. 253

28:
1. Barbara Tuchman, *The Guns of August* (New York: Macmillan, 1962), pg. 101.
2. Bernadotte E. Schmitt, *The Coming of the War, 1914, Vol II* (New York: Howard Fertig, 1966) pg. 391.

29:
1. Terry Golway, *For the Cause of Liberty* (New York: Simon & Schuster, 2000), pg. 351

30:
1. John Keegan, *The First World War* (New York: Knopf, 2000) pg. 201-02

31:
1. Arthur Walworth, *Woodrow Wilson: American Prophet, volume II* (Baltimore, MD: Penguin Books, 1965), pg.144

32:
Bibliography:
Brown, Judith M., *Gandhi: Prisoner of Hope*, (New Haven, CT: Yale University Press, 1989)
Gopal, Ram, How India Struggled for Freedom, (Bombay, India: The Book Centre, 1967)

33:
1. Marie-Claire Bergere, *Sun Yat-sen* (Stanford, CA: Stanford University Press, 1998), pg. 325
2. Dr. Lothrop Stoddard: The Rising Tide of Colour against White World Supremacy (1920).

34:
1. James Dugan, *Days of Emperor and Clown: The Italo-Ethiopian War, 1935-36* (Garden City, NY: Doubleday, 1973) , pg. 163

35:
1. William E. Leuchtenburg, *Franklin Roosevelt and the New Deal* (New York: Harper Torchbooks, 1963), pg. 184
2, Alan Brinkley, *The End of Reform* (New York: Vintage, 1996), pg. 15

37:
1. George Sullivan and John Powers, *The Yankees: An Illustrated History* (Philadelphia: Temple University Press, 1997), pg. 74

38:
1. William Manchester, *The Last Lion: Alone, 1932-1940* (Boston, MA: Little Brown, 1988), pg. 634
2. Manchester, pg. 651
3. Manchester, pg. 638
4. Winston S. Churchill, *Memoirs of the Second World War* (New York: Mariner Books, 1991 reprint), pg. 221
5. Churchill, pg. 225

40:
1. Leonard Mosley, *Hirohito, Emperor of Japan* (Englewood Cliffs, NJ: Prentice-Hall, 1966), pg. 325

41:
1. William J. Duiker, *Ho Chi Minh* (New York: Hyperion, 2000), pg. 283
2. Duiker, pg. 321

42:
1. Fraser J. Harbutt, *The Iron Curtain* (New York, Oxford University Press, 1986), pg. 153
2. Harbutt, pg. 161.
3. Martin Gilbert, *Churchill: A Life* (New York: Henry Holt, 1991) pg. 865.

43:
1. William Taubman, *Khrushchev: The Man and His Era* (New York: WW Norton, 2003), pg. 240
2. *The (London) Observer*, Feb. 26, 2006
3. Taubman, pg. 270
4. *Observer*, Feb. 26, 2006

44:
1. Michael Beschloss, *The Crisis Years: Kennedy and Khrushchev, 1960-1963* (New York: HarperCollins, 1991), pg. 608

45:
1. Steven Ambrose, *Nixon: Volume III, Ruin and Recovery, 1973-1990* (New York: Simon & Schuster, 1991) pg. 394

46:
1. William B. Quandt, *Camp David: Peacemaking and Politics* (Washington: The Brookings Institution, 1986), pg.139
2. Quandt, pg. 144
3. Gertrude Hirschler and Lester S. Eckman, *Menahem Begin* (New York: Shengold Publishers, 1979), pg. 305
4. Camelia Sadat, *My Father and I* (New York: Macmillan, 1985), pg. 142
5. Hirschler and Eckman, pg. 306

47:
1. *Ronald Reagan: An American Life* (New York: Simon & Schuster, 1990), pg. 377

48:
1. Lou Cannon, *President Reagan: The Role of a Lifetime* (New York: Simon & Schuster, 1991), 499
2. Tip O'Neill, *Man of the House* (New York: Random House, 1987), pg. 363.

49:
1. Margaret Thatcher, *The Downing Street Years* (New York: HarperCollins, 1993), pg. 11
2. Peter Jenkins, *Mrs. Thatcher's Revolution: The Ending of the Socialist Era* (Cambridge, Mass.: Harvard University Press, 1989), pg. 23

50:
BIBLIOGRAPHY:
Mandela: a Critical Life, by Tom Lodge, (New York: Oxford University Press), 2006

1. Anthony Sampson, *Mandela* (New York: Knopf, 1999), pg. 73
2. Sampson, pg. 483